A Hard Local War:
The British Army and the Guerrilla
War in Cork, 1919–1921

A Hard Local War
The British Army and the Guerrilla War in Cork, 1919–1921

William Sheehan

SPELLMOUNT

To all those who fought and died in Cork, 1919–1921

To children ardent for some desperate glory,
The old lie, *Dulce et decorum est*
Pro patria mori.

Wilfred Owen

Front jacket image: four soldiers found blindfolded and dead on the morning of the Truce. See page 160. (Courtesy Imperial War Museum, Q107756)

First published 2011
The History Press
The Mill, Brimscombe Port
Stroud, Gloucestershire, GL5 2QG
www.thehistorypress.co.uk

British Library Cataloguing in Publication Data.
A catalogue record for this book is available from the British Library.

ISBN 978 0 7524 5882 3

Typesetting and origination by The History Press
Printed in Great Britain

Contents

Abbreviations

AAG	Assistant Adjutant General
AA & QMG	Assistant Adjutant & Quartermaster General
ADC	Aide De Camp
ADRIC	Auxiliary Division, Royal Irish Constabulary
AIR	Air Ministry
ASC	Army Service Corps
ASU	Active Service Unit
ATO	An t-Óglach
ANZAC	Australian & New Zealand Army Corps
Batt	Battalion
BIM	British in Ireland Microfilms
BMH	Bureau of Military History
Bn	Battalion
BWM	British War Medal
Capt	Captain
CB	Companion of the Bath
CBE	Commander of the Order of the British Empire
CC	Cork Constitution
CCA	Cork City and County Archives
CE	Cork Examiner
CMG	Companion of the Order of St Michael and St George
CMO	Courts Martial Officer
CO	Colonial Office
Col	Colonel
Cpl	Corporal
CQMS	Company Quartermaster Sergeant
CSM	Company Sergeant Major
CWN	*Cork Weekly News*
DAAG	Deputy Assistant Adjutant General
DAQMG	Deputy Assistant Quartermaster General

DMP	Dublin Metropolitan Police
DORA	Defence of the Realm Act
DSM	Distinguished Service Medal
DSO	Distinguished Service Order
ERG	*Essex Regimental Gazette*
GHQ	General Headquarters
GOC	General Officer Commanding
GSM	General Service Medal
GSO	General Staff Officer
HRJ	*Hampshire Regimental Journal*
II	*Irish Independent*
IMA	Irish Military Archives
IRA	Irish Republican Army
IRB	Irish Republican Brotherhood
IT	*Irish Times*
IWM	Imperial War Museum
JP	Justice of the Peace
KM	Kings Medal
KOSB	King's Own Scottish Borderers
KSLI	King's Shropshire Light Infantry
LG	*Lilywhites Gazette*
LHCMA	Liddell Hart Centre for Military Archives
Lt	Lieutenant
MBE	Member of the Order of the British Empire
MC	Military Cross
MM	Military Medal
MP	Member of Parliament
MRG	*Manchester Regimental Gazette*
NAM	National Army Museum
NAUK	National Archives United Kingdom
NCO	Non-Commissioned Officer
NLI	National Library of Ireland
OBE	Officer of the Order of the British Empire
OTC	Officer Training Corps
Ox & Bucks	The Oxfordshire and Buckinghamshire Light Infantry
Pte	Private
QM	Queens Medal
UCDA	University College Dublin Archives
UDC	Urban District Council
RA	Royal Artillery
RAF	Royal Air Force
RAM	Royal Artillery Museum
RAMC	Royal Army Medical Corps

RAMR	Royal Artillery Mounted Rifles
RASC	Royal Army Service Corps
RDC	Rural District Council
RE	Royal Engineers
RFA	Royal Field Artillery
RFC	Royal Flying Corps
RGA	Royal Garrison Artillery
RIC	Royal Irish Constabulary
RM	Resident Magistrate
RM	Royal Marines
RMLI	Royal Marine Light Infantry
RN	Royal Navy
RSM	Regimental Sergeant Major
SAA	Small Arms Ammunition
Sgt	Sergeant
SOGM	Soldiers of Gloucestershire Museum
TS	*The Times*
VM	Victory Medal
WO	War Office
WS	Witness Statement

Acknowledgements

'No man is an island, entire of itself, every man is a piece of the continent, a part of the main.'

John Donne

This book would and could not have happened without the help of many people all throughout my life, in fact too many to mention. My interest in history comes from my grandfather, William Sheehan, my namesake and a member of the IRA in Cork during the War of Independence, and my father, Peter Sheehan, both now sadly deceased. Their gift to me was a love of learning and truth, and I dedicate this book primarily to them.

I must also acknowledge the great support of my remaining family: my partner Dr Rachel MagShamhrain; my mother Noreen Sheehan; my sisters Eileen O'Donoghue and Bernadette McAuliffe; their husbands, Patrick and Michael; and my nephews and niece Peter, Joseph, Eve, Matthew and Faye.

I was extremely fortunate in my PhD supervisor, Dr Maura Cronin, who has been a great guide and friend over the last few years. This book could not have been written without her invaluable assistance and support. It was refreshing to work in the professional and yet informal environment of the history department, Mary Immaculate College, and to have had the support of academics of the calibre of Liam Irwin, Dr Deirdre MacMahon, Dr Una Ni Bromill and Dr Liam Chambers. I could not have pursued my PhD without the financial support of the teaching assistantship, which Liam Irwin so generously provided. In addition, I would also like to thank Dr Stephen Thornton, head of the philosophy department and director of postgraduate studies for nearly all my time in the college. The companionship of an excellent group of fellow postgraduate students also made my years there a pleasure.

One of the most important resources for my research at Mary Immaculate College has been the library, or more correctly the fine staff therein. I would like in particular to thank Phyllis, Elizabeth and Maureen. I would also like to thank the following Irish archives and libraries for their support in allowing me to access material: the National Archives; the National Photographic Archive; the National Library; the UCD Archives; the UCC Library; the Cork City and County Libraries; and the Cork County Archives. I would also like to thank the Military Archives and in particular Commandant Victor Laing and Commandant Pat Brennan for their invaluable assistance on this and other projects.

This book has greatly relied on the assistance and support of many British archives. I would like to thank the Imperial War Museum, the Liddell Hart Centre for Military Archives, Kings College, London, the National Army Museum, the Royal Artillery Museum, and the Leeds University Library. I would especially like to thank Anthony Richard, Stephanie Clarke and Lucy Farrow of the Imperial War Museum and Kate O'Brien of the Liddell Hart Centre for Military Archives. Further, I would also like to thank all the copyright holders for allowing me to quote from an array of private papers. Appendix 4 is courtesy of UCD Archives.

Finally, I would like to thank my agents, Paul and Susan Feldstein, and also Shaun Barrington and Miranda Jewess at The History Press, whose editing and guidance made this a far stronger book.

Any and all failings in this book are my own.

Introduction:
Historical Revisionism

A famous cartoon by David Low (see picture section, page 8) neatly sums up the abiding public memory of the British campaign in Ireland. It was printed in the *Star* following the imposition of martial law in Ireland, and the instigation of a policy of official reprisal; the 'punishment by fire' in the cartoon's background reflects the then recent 'Burning of Cork'. It is a straightforward presentation of British policy in Ireland as brutal and inept, two words which have come to define the conduct of the British Army in Ireland during the War of Independence, a testament, per-haps, to the work of Frank Gallagher and the *Irish Bulletin*, which did so much to shape the view of the war at the time and since. The campaign has left no enduring memory in the popular imagination of the British public, for these events took place during a period of history which for the British will always be dominated by the experiences of the First World War.

Irish Historical Revisionism

Nothing in Irish historiography has generated as much bitterness and hostility as the work of academic historians revisiting the history of the War of Independence. This criticism has often come from those outside the discipline, such as Seamus Deane, a distinguished scholar of Irish literature, who has argued that 'revisionism' is 'not a genuine attempt to write value-free history, but a politically loaded project, an anti-nationalist project, in fact a Unionist project.'[1] One local historian dismisses the work of 'revisionist' historians who, in the light of much new evidence, including that provided by the Bureau of Military History, are re-examining this conflict. He has gone even further by claiming that revisionist historians are agents of the British state, and that 'by virtue of its power of patronage, which is very much greater than that of the Irish state, Britain has secured the services of many academics in the Irish

Universities, paid for by the Irish tax-payer, in doing this work.'[2] Many respected public commentators retain the most naïve view of the events of 1919–1921 and of the IRA. John Waters, a columnist for the *Irish Times*, has talked about how 'passionate thoughts and deeds had inspired their generation to expel the conqueror for good.'[3]

Nor are government ministers immune to such historical commandeering, as was demonstrated by the speech given by Éamon Ó'Cuív, then Minster for Community, Rural and Gaeltacht Affairs, at the Aubane Community Centre near Millstreet, on 30 January 2004, in which he presented the war as 'a story of ordinary people rising up against tyranny and overwhelming odds, arming themselves with guns dispossessed from their enemies and at all times willing to make the ultimate sacrifice.'[4] Ó'Cuív justified the IRA's burning of Protestant houses with the explanation that, 'War is no fun. But if you have no implement left to defend the poor of the society from having their houses burned down one after the other except to meet fire with fire and knowing that the sympathisers of the British would quickly put a stop to the burning because they were under threat for the first time.'[5] The IRA's crushing of various nascent Irish workers' soviets which developed during this period perhaps should be taken as more indicative of their views on the working class revolution. This trenchant protection of the story of the War of Independence – as devised by what Tom Garvin described as the Fianna Fáil School of Revisionism – highlights a deep insecurity amongst many about the founding of the Irish State and the historical path that led to its creation. As Mike Cronin and John M. Regan have said '[r]epublican teleology had no use for Irish parliamentarians, Redmondite politics, Irish Volunteers in France, Flanders, and Gallipoli, or the first ten years of independence.'[6] And as Charles Townshend has pointed out, 'a republican-dominated perspective has obscured the majority view in late nineteenth and early twentieth century Ireland' and indeed many of our previous histories have simply been the 'presentation of the victory of revolutionary politics as inevitable.'[7]

A key role in the creation of the mythology of the war in the popular Irish imagination has been played by the numerous memoirs of IRA veterans such as Tom Barry, Liam Deasy, Ernie O'Malley and Dan Breen, all of whom have been bestsellers for years in Ireland, accepted and largely unquestioned. These works have been reinforced by a multitude of local historians who have been instrumental in shaping and influencing the public view of the conflict. They have often treated local myths as facts, and made accusations of the most serious of crimes on the basis of local stories rather than actual evidence. *Execute Hostage Compton-Smith*, for example talks about 'the unethical war-like butchery of British troops in Ireland, at the behest of the British Government,'[8] and also claims that the position of the British government, 'long admired and respected, was shattered in the screams of women and young girls being raped by the Hampshires.'[9] The work also presents a fanciful if not uncommon version of the Crossbarry Ambush of 1921 in which:

> 2,000 personnel converged at Crossbarry five miles from Bandon, under Major Percival where they were attacked by Tom Barry and his West Cork Brigade unit numbering

104 men. It was extremely humiliating for Major Percival of the Essex Regiment to be forced to flee and on looking back to see the abandoned lorries in flames having been set on fire by the victorious IRA.[10]

Similarly, Liam Deasy's *Towards Ireland Free* presents Crossbarry as a triumph and the Truce as a victory, claiming that '[t]he efficiency of the movement as a guerrilla army, and its mounting achievements in the face of the ruthless British murder machine ... succeeded in making it impossible for the British Government to rule in what was practically seven-eighths of Ireland's territory,' and claiming that for the grateful people of West Cork, 'nothing was good enough for the brave soldiers who had forced the enemy to call a halt.'[11] Brian Murphy, although not a local historian, writes in a similar vein in a recent work. In *The Origins and Organisation of British Propaganda in Ireland 1920*, he makes sweeping claims including that 'the British engaged in deception and dissimulation; the Irish did not,'[12] and 'the British Army was inspired by racist sentiments, and that the IRA, while attacking loyalists did not engage in sectarian activities.'[13] This type of broad statement is particularly unfortunate, since the main body of the work – a detailed examination of the work of Basil Clarke and the propaganda department based at Dublin Castle – is suitably detailed and takes care to validate both the provenance and intent of the historic material used. But there are two difficulties with Murphy's work. One is the uncritical way he treats all the assertions made by the IRA, assertions which should surely also be treated with the same rigorous scrutiny as Clarke's material. The second problem is Murphy's obvious outrage at untruths in British propaganda, a fact that would be unsurprising to most observers given that the very nature of wartime propaganda is to misdirect and undermine the opponent.

This failure to preserve an emotional distance from the material is also evident in the work of Meda Ryan, in particular *Tom Barry: IRA Freedom Fighter*. While here again much of the writing is excellent and obviously based on considerable research, Ryan remains overly reliant on Tom Barry's own account for the section on the War of Independence. Crossbarry is the subject of a more in-depth analysis in this work, where there is an examination of the considerable dangers of using Barry's *Guerrilla Days in Ireland* as a source. In short, in 'popular history' we all too often encounter the tendency unquestioningly to cast the Irish protagonists as good and the English as evil. The debate surrounding the work of Peter Hart illustrates one of the key problems concerning the historiographical treatment of this period.[14] Hart has been criticised by some for his sources on the Kilmichael Ambush, allowing his better work on the killing of members of the Protestant community to be largely dismissed and ignored. The German historical term, *Vergangenheitsbewältigung*, which means coping with history, particularly with the terrible and uncomfortable areas of the national past, might well provide a useful model for Irish historians. This German model actively foregrounds the darkest hours of German history as a necessary corrective to any mythologising of the past in the service of ideology, a discursive practice that is also, it is hoped, a principle informing this analysis.

Revisionism is of course as old as the Treaty itself, not least the revisionism which presented dominion status and partition as the fruits of some form of military victory on the part of the IRA. The national attitude to the memory of the campaign was nuanced from the very beginning, as O'Casey's *The Plough and the Stars* demonstrates. Over the years, the work of Tom Garvin, J.J. Lee, Roy Foster and others has changed the academic understanding of late-nineteenth and early twentieth-century Ireland, and of the achievements of Irish constitutional nationalism. As Lee noted, it was 'Irish constitutional nationalism [that] had destroyed landlordism.'[15] Tom Garvin has also demonstrated in his work the precarious nature of support for independence in Ireland, noting that 'the Irish revolutionary movement derived its energies from a series of grievances that were slowly being rectified.'[16] It is on this tradition of critical and scholarly historical analysis that 'revisionism' is based. What makes revisionism such a contentious form is that it possesses 'a preparedness to correct the distortions involved in the creation of national foundation myths.'[17] Perhaps what disturbs the opponents of revisionism most is the thesis offered by Charles Townshend, that 'the most challenging "revisionist" proposition [is] the argument that all the most important objectives of national liberation – including some such as unity, that were lost as a result of 1916 – could have been achieved without bloodshed or violence.'[18]

The last ten years have seen considerable evidence being unearthed in support of this proposition. A significant corpus of new research, such as Peter Hart's work on Cork, Michael Farry's on Sligo, Marie Coleman's on Longford and Joost Augusteijn's work on Tipperary and Mayo, have all contributed to a far more nuanced understanding of the complex nature of the Irish revolution.[19] As Townshend has pointed out, 'the most constructive development has been seen in local and community studies.'[20] These studies have examined the IRA at the local level, looking at its formation and membership, and exploring how the experiences of both the war itself and the violence of the campaign had an impact on the Volunteers, their communities and opponents. Farry, for instance, considers the reasons for Sligo's relative inactivity in the War of Independence and its prominent role in the Civil War, examining the competition between parliamentarianism and revolutionary nationalism, the social background of the activists and the regional differences in military activity within the county. Coleman again examines the social background of the republican activists and teases out the complex reasons for their involvement in the campaign, as well as the paying off of old local scores in the setting of the revolution. Hart and Augusteijn have paid particular attention to the subliminal sectarianism within the conflict, and considered how retrospective accounts have confused the historical realities.

These works have greatly increased our understanding of the revolution at regional level and have drawn from the new material contained in the Bureau of

Military History, and though they have broken considerable new ground in our understanding of the Irish Revolution, they remain focused firmly on the Irish experience of the campaign. This book, too, adopts a local framework for analysis, but focuses particularly on the British Army's experience of 1919–1921. All the modern scholarship on the Irish revolution has shown the IRA's rural guerrilla campaign tailing off by the summer of 1921. Marie Coleman attributes this cessation in Longford directly to British pressure, as does Peter Hart in the Cork context.[21] But the precise degree of this increased British pressure has been left largely unexplored; it is that gap in the historiography of the war that this book seeks to fill.

The British Army's role has been under-researched and under-analysed, with some historians still portraying it as a lumbering giant around whom the pimpernels of the IRA ran rings. Back in the 1970s, some academics such as Tom Bowden criticised the British Army for the absence of tactical reflection, and believed 'it was heavy handed when there was need for finesse,'[22] although he failed to define 'finesse' in this context. From this he has produced a standard argument about the history of the period, namely that British forces lacked initiative. 'The policies and actions of the British forces were limited to reaction against the moves of their opponents.'[23] This concept of a British lack of initiative also informs what is one of his article's most contentious claims regarding the British officers killed during Bloody Sunday: 'Then, on 20 November 1920, he [Collins] assassinated the core of this group in one operation. There was little chance from that point on that the British would win.'[24] As a corrective to such views, it is important to situate the Irish conflict in the context of the wider war in which the British were simultaneously engaged at the time. Equally important to note here is that one could argue with at least as much conviction that after the capture of almost the complete active portion of the Dublin IRA at the Custom House, there was little chance the IRA could win.

In a similar vein another American historian William H. Kautt has argued that 'the operations that the Crown forces did conduct were rarely timely [and] usually failed to reach their tactical objectives (when they had any),'[25] so that, 'this war proved that a "small nation" could defeat a global power bent on winning.'[26] Even some recent works, like Paul McMahon's *British Spies and Irish Rebels*, still stubbornly hold the view that 'the notion that the British crown forces had brought the IRA to the point of collapse, only to be betrayed by cowardly politicians, would gain more and more ground as the campaign receded into the past – it helped explain away Britain's defeat at the hands of the rag-tag army.'[27] However, McMahon like many others seems to have a contradictory view of the military realities of the campaign. While in the above quote he talks about an IRA victory, in an earlier part of his work discussing the war in 1921, he states that 'the initiative may be said to have passed to the Crown Forces for the first time since May 1920.'[28]

In recent years, some historians like Michael Hopkinson have begun to deviate from the traditional position and acknowledge some improvement in British tactics, conceding that 'for all the limitations of the British methods, the IRA had been placed on the defensive by the end of June.'[29] Ferriter's *Transformation of Ireland, 1900–2000* also demonstrates a modified attitude to the British Army's performance, describing its impact on the IRA in the following terms: 'any possible negotiation gave much room for manoeuvre and a possible rest to a war-weary and stretched IRA, though the extent to which they were on the verge of military bankruptcy has been disputed.'[30] Both these studies are perhaps limited by the lack of research on British military performance at a local level. Despite this recent revisionism, other prominent historians still maintain that there was a military stalemate in 1921. Richard English states in his recent work *Irish Freedom* that 'in the summer of 1921 stalemate had been reached and a truce was declared,' echoing David Fitzpatrick's work of almost thirty years previously when he felt confident in stating that 'both sides accepted defeat with the truce.'[31]

A further key difficulty in assessing British performance has been something of a lack of familiarity with British military history on the part of Irish historians. Many historians, both local and academic, fail to distinguish sufficiently between British soldiers and 'Black and Tans' or Auxiliaries. A similar lack of distinction is found with regard to commissioned officers and non-commissioned officers, with anyone seen giving orders to troops invariably reported as an officer. More dangerously, there has been a failure on the part of historians to place British tactics and operational methods within their appropriate context. For example, tactics like 'drives' are seen as wasteful and a sign of tactical weakness and a lack of innovation on the part of the British Army, but 'drives' were in fact a standard tactic used by all armies of the period in this type of warfare and indeed are still used today. They allow soldiers to familiarise themselves with the terrain, show the army's control of the area, disrupt potential guerrilla operations and most importantly allow an army to maintain a tempo of active operations, keeping soldiers sharp. In this and other areas, such as martial law, communications and intelligence work, the British Army in Ireland drew from its considerable experience in imperial policing, and from then recent operations such as the occupation of the Rhineland, where both Generals Strickland and Jeudwine had already held divisional command.

The only detailed examination of British performance during the War of Independence remains Townshend's *British Campaign in Ireland, 1919 to 1921: the Development of Political and Military Policies*, published in 1975. This is, however, more an examination of British strategy than an analysis of the experience of the ordinary soldier on the ground, or of the development of tactics at unit and regimental level. Townshend also repeats the idea that the majority of the officers and men in Ireland had little experience, or if they had, it was only the experience of trench warfare during the First World War.[32] This fosters the idea that the British Army in Ireland was completely inexperienced with regard to guerrilla warfare and at a disadvantage from the beginning. Townshend reinforces this point later in his work, when he argues that these shortcomings meant that the British soldiers did not have the necessary skill to deal with the IRA in combat, arguing that 'every soldier needed to be an expert skirmisher and sniper.'[33] An examination of the background of the various British officers and the conduct of British military operations reveals that this was not the case. Again, in his conclusions, Townshend talks about the failure of the use of military force by the British, arguing that this was because the 'Republican guerrilla campaign proved too determined, too resilient and too resourceful,' and that the British lacked similar energy and drive.[34] But it must always be remembered that regardless of the state of government policy, regiments and men on the ground still had to deal with and master the situation as they faced it. Paralysis at cabinet level if it existed did not, therefore, necessarily translate into inactivity or inertia on the ground.

So as yet, despite the considerable advances in research into the Irish revolution, there has been no detailed analysis of British tactics and operations at a local level – vital to a more balanced interpretation of the events of 1918–22. This book aims to begin to fill this gap. It suggests that no military stalemate existed in Ireland. On the contrary, both sides were continuing to learn and evolve, and were beginning to find innovative solutions to the military problems that they faced.

The British Perspective

When one examines the descriptions and assessments by the British officers cited in the official histories and in their private correspondence, a key question arises. Why were so many so convinced that it was they, not the IRA, who were close to victory? Even if we accept that there is an obvious and natural bias in such accounts, this conviction is remarkable. Brigadier-General Frederick Clarke, then a lieutenant in the Essex Regiment, reflected on the truce thus: 'We did not see the rabble waiting somewhere nearby to take over the fort, which they never would have captured, but which our politicians had given to them.'[35] Captain Jeune, one of the intelligence officers to escape on Bloody Sunday, recalled a conversation on New Year's Day 1921 with Major-General Boyd, the commander of the Dublin District, who said 'Well, Jeune, I think we have broken the back of the movement now, don't you?' Jeune continued 'Yes, Sir and I think six months should see it out' to which Boyd answered 'Yes I think you are right.'[36] Jeune goes on to say in his memoirs that 'by the early summer the IRA were driven into the southwest corner of Ireland, and would have been quickly finished.'[37] This view was shared by Brigadier-General Viden, then a lieutenant in the Suffolks, who believed that by the time of the truce, 'the Royal Irish Constabulary and the Army obtained the upper hand.'[38] The official history, the *Record of the Rebellion in Ireland*, offers the following view on the position of the IRA in the summer of 1921:

> The rebel organisation throughout the country was in a precarious condition, and the future from the Sinn Fein point of view may be said to have been almost desperate. The flying columns and active service units into which the rebels had been forced, by

the search for prominent individuals, to form themselves were being harried and chased from pillar to post, and were constantly being defeated and broken up by Crown forces; individuals were being hunted down and arrested; the internment camps were filling up; the headquarters of the I.R.A. was functioning under the greatest difficulty.[39]

The official history of the 6th Division in the Strickland papers put it very differently but no less forcibly: 'There is no doubt that the truce of July 11th, 1921, was just as unwelcome to the British Army in Ireland as the Armistice of 11th November, 1918, was welcome to the British Army in France.'[40]

One could dismiss this as sheer bravura by the British forces. But the British officer corps found an unlikely supporter of this belief in Richard Mulcahy, the IRA Chief of Staff. In his treaty speech to the Dáil, Mulcahy stated:

[W]e are not in a position of force, either military or otherwise, to drive the enemy from our ports. We have not – those to whom the responsibility has been for doing such things – we have not been able to drive the enemy from anything but a fairly good-sized police barracks. We have not that power.[41]

Even more importantly, Mulcahy rejected the die-hard option of a terrorist campaign, because it would remove any possible future of friendship with the English people themselves. As he put it 'how can we do it by choosing a weapon which will put the responsibility upon us of killing, in self-defence, the Crompton-Smiths of England?'[42] At the end of his speech, Mulcahy gave his honest view about how the war had gone: 'I do feel we have suffered a defeat at the present moment – but I do feel that the hour of defeat in any way is not the hour for quarrelling as to how it might have been avoided. We have suffered a defeat.'[43]

British Historical Revisionism

'The First World War was about infantrymen and machine guns and massacres of British Soldiers. The Generals had been unbelievably incompetent, I learned, and millions had died as a consequence.'[44] This is how Gary Sheffield, the noted military historian, explains his first exposure to the history of the First World War, adding in another section that 'it is believed that the war was conducted by bone-headed British generals who, faced with trench deadlock, could think of nothing more imaginative than to hurl long lines of troops against German trenches and barbed wire.'[45] This view has been promoted by individuals as diverse as A.J.P. Taylor, Winston Churchill, David Lloyd George and perhaps most famously, Alan Clark in his book, *The Donkeys*. Gradually, with the release of the official documents from the mid 1960s on, British historians have been forced to re-examine their understanding of the First World War, from the conduct of the war by Field Marshal Haig and other generals, through the development of infantry tactics, to the integration of new technologies such as the tank, the aeroplane and the wireless. As David Stevenson puts it in his *1914–1918, The History of the First World War*:

> The 1960s saw the beginnings of divergence not only between Taylorite interpretations and new research into the politics and diplomacy of the conflict, but also popular understandings of the military history of the war and new investigations into its strategy. This dichotomy was already evident in the BBC series,[46] which owed its memorable artistic impact to its combination of disturbing images, plangent music, and sombre narration, but whose script, much of it written by John Terraine and Correlli Barnett, tried to convey that the struggle had been necessary, and that the Western Front concentration had been unavoidable, and that British generalship had risen to the challenge of intimidating circumstances. Similar themes appeared in Terraine's *Douglas Haig: the Educated Soldier* (1963), and in a succession of later works by the same author, which at the time went against the grain of much writing on the war, but grew in influence in the 1980s and 1990s when a later generation of researchers drew on the newly opened War Office and cabinet archives and private papers. Some of their work still criticised the British high command, on occasion severely, but it depicted the BEF and the Dominion forces as learning from their mistakes, increasing their effectiveness, and playing a major role, perhaps the major role, in breaking the German army.[47]

At the core of this work is a parallel reassessment of British military performance in Ireland from 1919 to 1921, through a detailed analysis of the most contested region, Cork city and county. The shortcomings of past histories of the War of Independence, and the fact that the British Army's experience at the 'sharp end' has been largely unexamined and ignored, and no real analysis has taken place at a local level, has left a vacuum. British historians' revisionism with regard to the army's experience in the First World War has not yet filtered through to an examination of the British tactics in Ireland. This book, in an attempt to redress this, will detail and analyse the experience of the British soldiers in Cork during this period, and the effectiveness of the British tactics against the IRA, and test these against the myths that surround the events of the period. The goal is, as far as possible, to separate the past from the propaganda.

This book focuses on the experiences of the British Army in Cork at the smallest echelon, that of the units, the men. It studies the degree of success of British counter-insurgency operations, and examines the factors that helped and hindered performance. How did the officers and soldiers feel about the Irish and the campaign? How did British tactics at a local level develop? How effective was military intelligence and what was its contribution to the British campaign? What were relations with the local communities like, and in what unofficial reprisals did the British soldiers engage and why? To answer these questions, new sources are explored. These include previously unused personal accounts, war diaries from the Royal Artillery, British local newspapers, RAF records held at Kew and new elements of the *Record of the Rebellion*, such as the section on law also held at Kew.

This study focuses on several key themes including the British memory of the campaign, the evolution of British tactics, the development of British intelligence and the use of martial law and law in general during counter-insurgency. It will also examine the nature of 'unofficial' reprisals, and suggest that they may be better understood by locating them in the widespread street violence of the period. The former focus on British strategic difficulties has, it can be argued, led to an underestimation of British performance at a local level.

Section One

The Informal War

I don't want to be a soldier,
I don't want to go to war.
I'd rather stay at home,
Around the streets to roam,
And live on the earnings of a well-paid whore,
I don't want a bayonet up my arsehole,
I don't want my bollocks shot away.
I'd rather stay in England,
In merry, merry England,
And fuck my bleeding life away.

First World War British Soldiers' Song

I wore a tunic,
A dirty khaki tunic,
And you wore civilian clothes.
We fought and bled at Loos
While you were on the booze,
The booze that no one here knows
Oh, you were with the wenches
While we were in the trenches,
Facing the German Foe.
Oh, you were a-slacking
While we were attacking
Down the Menin Road.

First World War British Soldiers' Song

This section explores the experience of British soldiers in Cork through the examination of two areas, firstly the issue of unofficial reprisals, and secondly the soldiers' own experience and understanding of the conflict itself.

'Unofficial reprisals' have long been problematic in the history of the campaign. Were reprisals, as many have alleged, orchestrated by senior army officers, or were they a phenomenon that originated within the rank and file as a response to the circumstances in which they found themselves in Ireland? It will be argued that 'unofficial reprisals' can be better understood within the culture of enlisted men in the army and within the context of local street violence in Cork, that there was no political or senior military authorship of the events in question and they were more part of what Private Cordner of the Argyll and Sutherland Highlanders remembered about the time and location, recalling that in 1918 paydays in Kinsale were extremely rough, and fistfights were a common occurrence.[48] It is significant that much of the violence in Cork that was linked to the 'unofficial reprisals' occurred on weekends and late in the evening, presumably after the considerable consumption of alcohol.

A local newspaper from Shropshire, the *Wellington Journal and Shrewsbury News* reported the feelings of the men of the King's Shropshire Light Infantry as they left Fermoy in East Cork: 'They were not sorry to leave a town in which not a man had the courage to express sympathy with the murdered man's relatives.'[49] The murder in question was the killing of Private Jones during the Wesleyan Raid in September 1919, when a church parade of the Shropshires was ambushed and the men had their weapons seized. The paper also informed its readers that Shropshire had given more during the First World War than the whole of Ireland, a remark which reveals much about the attitude of the English public towards the campaign in Ireland. 'We fought and bled at Loos, while you were on the booze,' the lines of the First World War song quoted, sum up the feelings of many in the Kings Shropshire Light Infantry who were awaiting demobilisation in Fermoy.

Remembrance and commemoration play an important role in British military life, and the British Army's collective memory of the conflict in Ireland will be examined through the published histories of the various regiments involved in the campaign. The regimental histories rarely discussed any of the unofficial reprisals engaged in by the troops, and, if they did, offered opinions such as: 'It never easy for men to remain steady when true stories were widespread of officers and men, who had survived the worst of the Western Front, being shot in the back by plough boys using weapons bought with American money.'[50] But most of the histories remained entirely silent on the campaign in Ireland, lost as it was between two world wars.

Chapter One

Reprisals

Arguably the most emotive word used in the historiography of the War of Independence is 'reprisal'. From 1919 to 1921, these 'outrages' formed a staple of Sinn Féin propaganda, as evidenced in the *Irish Bulletin,* and played a key part in their campaigns to garner sympathy through overseas press coverage. The reports of homes destroyed, women attacked and children terrorised were all carefully designed, packaged and presented to support the Republican cause. And while this discourse was designed with the specific political goals of the time in mind, it remains the most powerful and enduring understanding of these events in Ireland today.

There can be no doubt that quite apart from any conflict with the IRA, significant street fighting did take place between civilians and soldiers in Cork city and county, and that British soldiers did engage in unofficial reprisals. Nevertheless, these events do not speak for themselves, and therefore need to be located and understood both within and in relation to the particulars of the period. This allows a more nuanced analysis of perhaps the most lasting view of these incidents, which is that unofficial reprisals were deliberately engineered and encouraged by both the British government and senior British officers, or, in a more damning interpretation led by the senior officers themselves.

One can read the street fights which occurred all through this period as something of an unofficial war. They were fought outside the war *per se*, as they were not fought for the Crown or the Republic, but can be considered an almost primitive struggle for the possession of public space, and on occasion for the control of local women.

The Origins of Reprisals

From the surviving papers of Lieutenant-Colonel Hughes-Hallett, then a junior officer in the King's Shropshire Light Infantry, comes a description of how the news broke of the attack on the Wesleyan Church party in September 1919.

Then – one Sunday – while the main body of the Battalion was falling-in in front of the Church, after Church parade, a hatless soldier rushed up calling out that he had a message for the C.O. After been [sic] jumped on (!) by the R.S.M., he was fortunately seen by the C.O., who called him up. His story was that he was one of the Wesleyan Party, going to their chapel in Patrick Street, some 'baker's dozen' strong. As they filed into the chapel door-way (he was last man in the file and a cross-country runner) a gang of locals, sitting lounging around – in ambush – on various walls, suddenly produced revolvers and 'loaded' staves from their sleeves, and opened-up on the backs of the troops at point blank range. The troops were carrying their rifles (for safety, just as was the custom in India), but no ammunition. One soldier (Pte Lloyd) was killed on the spot and the rest knocked down. Their assailants seized their rifles (13, I think) and drove off towards Cork.[51]

The private killed was in fact William Jones, a young Welshman from Carmarthenshire. Jones, only 20, was to have been discharged that week and was due to get married to his fiancée Gladys Thorpe the following week when he returned home.[52] Such an IRA attack resulting in an army casualty was rare at this stage of the conflict, but the *Wellington Journal and Shrewsbury News* offered an insight into why the IRA may have opened fire on the church parade rather than simply taking their rifles. It noted that the soldiers were attempting to fix bayonets just before they were fired on, thus implying a defensive element to the IRA's shooting of these British troops.[53] Whatever the reason, both Jones' death and the failure of the Fermoy jury to deliver a murder verdict directly contributed to the reprisal carried out by the British troops.

The loss of a comrade was the key link amongst many of the reprisals carried out in the Cork region, as the cases of Bandon and Cobh show. Bandon, a prosperous market town in West Cork was subjected to a reprisal by the Essex Regiment in July 1920, the catalyst being the killing of Lance Corporal Maddox while on intelligence duty. The anger of the soldiers was fuelled by their frustration at the fact that it was uncertain whether or not an inquest would be held into the killing.[54] Cobh, on Cork Harbour, was soon to join Bandon and Fermoy in experiencing the anger of British troops, in this case the Cameron Highlanders. Following the death of Private Hall in an ambush, the Camerons decided to vent their frustration on the town, and on 27 August 1920, at about 10pm, some 20–30 Highlanders 'entered the town armed with rifles and heavy pieces' to exact retribution[55]. In nearly every case of serious violence, the reprisal was the direct consequence of the killing of a British serviceman in the immediate area.

An exception to this was the reaction of British troops to the kidnapping of Brigadier-General Lucas. Lucas and two other officers, Colonel Tyrrell and Lieutenant-Colonel Danford, were staying in a fishing hut near Kilbarray, about seven miles from Fermoy. The officers were abducted on 26 June 1920 by IRA volunteers. While they were being driven away by their captors, the British officers planned their escape in the rear of the car by conversing in Urdu. However, the escape attempt failed, resulting in the serious wounding of Lieutenant-Colonel Danford. The IRA left Colonel Tyrrell behind with Danford, and the two officers made their way back to Fermoy, and word of the kidnap began to filter down to the troops in the various barracks in Fermoy.

On the following night, soldiers were out socialising in Fermoy, some in the local cinema and others in the public houses, while some were boating on the river. However, between 11 and 11.30pm, as some of these men were on their way back to barracks, other troops left the barracks and entered the town. Soon hundreds of British troops from the Buffs, the Royal Field Artillery and the Royal Air Force had taken to the streets. They 'made their way to the town, singing, shouting and exclaiming, "We want our General", "Give us our General" and proceeded to run amok along Pearse Square!'[56] According to newspaper reports,

> The outbreak was on a much more extensive scale than those of September and November last, when considerable damage was done to property, and there can be no doubt that the present scene of destruction must have been carefully planned by a large number of soldiers, who were the principal participants in it.[57]

The *Cork Examiner* went on to state that it considered these events to be a military reprisal for the kidnapping of the General and that 'it was a cruel and terrifying experience to which to subject inhabitants, who could have no participation in the kidnapping of Brigadier Lucas.'[58] While the kidnapping of Lucas did not involve a fatality, it is possible that many of the soldiers involved in the reprisal may have believed that the General was dead or that he was about to be killed.

When we examine the days on which the reprisal took place, one could suggest that the connection between soldiers drinking and unofficial reprisals was not confined to the case of Lucas. The Cameron Highlanders' reprisal on Cobh was on a Friday night, the Essex sacked Bandon on a Thursday, both nights when as the weekend drew near drinking could be expected. The King's Shropshire Light Infantry were moved to Victoria Barracks in Cork on 14 September in an effort to defuse local tensions in Fermoy and rebuild relations with the local community there. However, this was not an end to the problems; the tension transferred to Cork, and on the nights of 9 and 10 November, a weekend, soldiers from the regiment conducted running street battles with local civilians in Cork city. Hughes-Hallet recalled:

> Cork was not a happy station. There was soon trouble, started by Sinn Fein gangs cutting off the hair of girls seen to be chatting with soldiers, who naturally resented it. Entrenching-tool handles soon found their real use, up the sleeve, and heads were being cracked and opponents being pushed into the River.[59]

As this quote suggests, other issues besides fatalities had the potential to cause or exacerbate trouble. It was a confrontation over local women that provided the spark that ignited the street fighting on that November weekend. In the words of the *Cork Examiner*,

On the night of 9 November 1919, a group of soldiers proceeding down from the barrack to King Street, behaving in an aggressive fashion, were booed and jeered by civilians. The soldiers broke through the police lines and the soldiers and members of the crowd were soon in handigrips [sic] and fighting took place at different points along the thoroughfare.[60]

However, that was not the end of the confrontation, and violence again erupted on the following night, when various groups of soldiers – mainly composed of the Kings Shropshire Light Infantry – who were apparently in a festive mood as they marched through MacCurtian Street, engaged in 'some cheering and sing loyal songs'.[61]. Like fraternising with local women, this raucousness provided locals with an excuse to restart the fighting, and indeed it was probably the intention of the servicemen to provoke the locals to violence against which they could then defend themselves with impunity. No doubt this trouble would have continued the following night and, indeed, young local men gathered in MacCurtian Street in anticipation of another clash.[62] The soldiers, whose provocative behaviour had been partially responsible for the clashes, were confined to barracks.

Whatever the catalysts at local level, the actions of British soldiers in Ireland must be understood in the context of Britain as a whole. Ex-servicemen had been at the forefront of many riots in Britain in 1919,[63] often a reaction to the perceived unjust treatment of soldiers or ex-servicemen. A police station in Wolverhampton, for instance, was attacked in July 1919 in order to release two soldiers who had been out drinking and had been arrested by local police. The violence of the assault on the local police station can be gauged from the newspaper report that, '[s]tones began to fly, a long wall 6 ft. high was torn down, brick being used freely as missiles, while battering rams were improvised in attempts to break in the doors of the police station.'[64] The police remained under siege until reinforcements arrived from other towns. Likewise, participants in Peace Day celebrations in Swindon – predominantly ex-servicemen – also attacked a police station the same weekend.[65] In another incident, in June 'after two Canadian soldiers were arrested and locked in the cells of Epson Police Station, about 400 of their comrades besieged the station, demanding their release.'[66] A police sergeant, Thomas Green, was killed in the resulting disturbance. There was also serious rioting in Luton that July, because of 'the town council's refusal to the ex-soldiers of Wardown Park for a memorial service.'[67] *The Times* reported that 'the town hall has been practically destroyed, together with most of its contents,' while other premises were targeted but saved by local firemen, of whom fourteen were injured in the riot.[68] While the police were reinforced from surrounding areas, they found themselves face to face in street battles with a combined force of soldiers and ex-servicemen. *The Times* noted: 'there is a military camp at Biscot, within two miles of Luton, in which are numbers of soldiers on furlough and awaiting discharge, and it is certain that amongst the mob which took part in the firing of the Town Hall were several men in uniform.'[69] As Keith Jeffery has noted, there were also riots by soldiers in Folkestone over the extension of their service in January 1919.[70] Charles Carrington, an officer in the First World War and later a publisher with Cambridge University Press remembered, 'there were many soldiers' riots during the war ... though they were not published in the newspapers, most of them ebullitions of hot temper by men exasperated by some abuse.'[71] He also noted that 'several times Whitehall was invaded by mobs of servicemen who had seized army lorries and had driven to London to demonstrate outside the War Office.'[72] Such disturbances were then not confined to Ireland, and grew from the frustration of both soldiers awaiting demobilisation and ex-servicemen who faced bleak employment prospects on return from the front. These outbreaks were every bit as violent in England as they were in Ireland and underline the fact that no political direction or encouragement was required for soldiers to violently redress any perceived slight or attack.

Irish ex-servicemen were not immune to this kind of irregular assertion of their rights, and they were behind the single largest street confrontation with the British Army in Cork. *The Record of the Rebellion,* which called these events in a somewhat overblown fashion 'The Battle for Cork', provides the following account of the incidents which ignited the violence:

> One party of troops operating in the Shandon area was attacked by a party of civilians, who endeavoured to disarm two soldiers, one of whom was wounded. The troops opened fire on these rebels, killing one. On the following night, as a reprisal for the shooting of their comrade, a large number of rebels concentrated in the main thoroughfares of the city and attacked a number of unarmed soldiers who were out on pass and some indiscriminate shooting on the part of these rebels resulted in the wounding of two young ladies in the King Street area. The civil authorities called on the troops for assistance, and a party of troops was sent out at once. As the party entered King Street, fire was opened on them by a number of rebels, who had taken up position in houses and laneways. The troops returned fire, and a number of rebels were killed.[73]

The *Record of the Rebellion* went on to describe the 'battle' proper as follows:

> Disturbances took place in Cork City during the night, and one man was shot by troops during a fracas in which he and others attacked a patrol. On the following evening about 500 civilians man-handled unarmed soldiers in the town, and indulged in a good deal of indiscriminate firing. An armed part of about 50 men was at once sent out from the barracks. This party was fired at on reaching the principal street. The fire was returned at once and a considerable number of casualties inflicted, and after two or three hours patrolling, during which fire was opened on them from side streets and a few bombs thrown, they restored order completely in

the city. The troops suffered no causalities, but inflicted severe loss on their attackers. The exact number was never discovered, but was believed to be about 25. The press was almost silent on the subject, so it is probable that they included no women or children or persons about whom Sinn Fein propaganda could have protested.[74]

This 'battle' is noticeably absent from IRA records and memoirs, and with very good reason. As we shall see, they had little involvement in this event. The absence of IRA accounts begs the question as to who these rebels were and what actually happened.

The *Record of the Rebellion* is correct in identifying the incident that sparked the 'battle'. Early in the morning of 18 July, James Bourke, a local man, was killed by a British military patrol. He was a labourer in a local chemical works and an ex-gunner in the Royal Field Artillery, having seen service in the Boer War and the First World War. Bourke and other ex-servicemen had attended a boxing tournament in the Cork Opera House on the night of 17 July. He and his friends, three other ex-servicemen, encountered two soldiers of the Hampshire Regiment, an NCO and a private, at a fish and chip shop near the Opera House and there were some verbal exchanges. The groups parted, but met again on the North Gate Bridge several minutes later, where a fight broke out between them. An RIC patrol led by a Sergeant Sullivan arrived on the scene and succeeded in separating the groups. However a military patrol from the Hampshires passed by and opened fire, wounding James Bourke, who was then finished off by bayonet. The remaining ex-servicemen were actually protected and led away by a group of Republican police. At any rate, this was the account of events accepted by the inquest and supported by the RIC.[75]

The official British Army version was quite different and it is interesting to note the points on which the RIC, army and even newspaper accounts differ from one another. According to the British Army,

Two soldiers on pass were twice accosted and attacked by the same three armed civilians. On the second occasion, the N.C.O. blew his whistle to alert a military patrol, which arrived (twelve strong) and was also attacked by these three men. In the ensuing struggle, James Bourke was shot.[76]

The second account was that of the RIC county inspector who stated in his monthly report that the matter began as a drunken squabble between soldiers and ex-soldiers, and was being broken up by the police when an approaching military patrol fired three to four shots, killing James Bourke. Interestingly, the soldiers from the Hampshire Regiment involved in the altercation with Bourke were reported in *The Times* as being drunk,[77] yet although the RIC labelled the case as a homicide, there was no further investigation.[78] Unlike the *Record of the Rebellion*, which was written later, the army press release made no mention of any soldiers being wounded in this incident, and while the *Record* stated that the two soldiers were on operations and armed, the press release claimed they were unarmed and on pass. Tellingly and perhaps in an attempt to address local rumour, the press release specifically stated that no bayonets were used. However it also failed to mention that the RIC were present at the scene. Neither the RIC nor British Army mentioned finding any weapons on Bourke. All the inconsistencies in this case can perhaps be linked to the army's embarrassment that this incident involved the death of an ex-serviceman, and a desire to manage the reporting of the event to minimise that embarrassment.

When Gunner Bourke was buried on the afternoon of 20 July, over 5,000 ex-servicemen from all over the city and county attended the funeral and accompanied the hearse through the streets; the procession was led by three bands, while thousands lined the route to witness its passage. This was larger than most Sinn Féin or IRA displays and indicates the number and significance of Irish ex-servicemen as a group within Irish society at the time. It is significant that contrary to tradition, no Union flag was placed on the coffin. However Bourke's honour guard consisted exclusively of ex-soldiers,[79] hardly the men one might expect to be provide the guard of honour for a dead Irish 'rebel'. Another rather famous ex-member of the Royal Field Artillery was present at the funeral to pay his respects and march in the funeral procession: Tom Barry of West Cork. Remember this was just four months before the Kilmichael Ambush, and Barry was an important IRA commander at this point. But old British Army loyalties still had the power to bind.[80] David Fitzpatrick has surmised that 'the Irish experience suggests that many ex-servicemen easily lowered one flag for another.'[81] But this requires some qualification; ex-servicemen did join the IRA and played a role beyond their numerical representation, but even given the provocation of killings like that of Bourke, never in substantial numbers.

An inquest into Bourke's death began on 19 July under the supervision of the city coroner, solicitor William Murphy. A jury was sworn in, the foreman of which was Cornelius O'Connor, another ex-soldier. The medical evidence provided was clear and graphic. 'There was a gaping wound three inches below the right nipple, the liver was lacerated, the diaphragm was torn, as was the right lung, and the seventh and eighth ribs on the right were broken.'[82]

The RIC provided full cooperation with the inquest and this is important to note as the military authorities in Cork refused to cooperate with the coroner's court. They sent a solicitor called Mr Woulfe to inform the court of this, and to announce that it was remarkable that a jury could not be found to examine the case of Lieutenant-Colonel Smyth who had been killed on the same day. The verdict of the court was damning:

> We find that the deceased, James Bourke, died on the morning of the 18th inst, from shock and haemorrhage, caused by a bayonet wound, wilfully inflicted at close quarters by one of the military patrol. We also find that there was no justification for it, in accordance with the evidence of Sergeant Sullivan, R.I.C.

The *Cork Examiner* called in an editorial for a full public inquiry into the killing, but this was never granted.

Despite the presentation of the riot by ex-servicemen after the killing of Bourke in *The Record of the Rebellion* as a battle between the army and rebels, the fact that the battle had been fought between ex-servicemen and serving soldiers was well known in Cork and indeed throughout Ireland. Even the *Irish Independent* reported that 'isolated but concerted attacks on army men [had occurred]. The men demobilised were apparently incensed against the active service men in connection with the shooting and bayoneting of James Bourke.'[83] Even Terence MacSwiney wrote to the ex-servicemen to warn against a confrontation with the army: 'I am given to understand on very good information that the military will be turned out to-night in force and early. As some of your members of your organisation, naturally labouring under great anger at the murder of your comrade, Burke, [sic] may be on the streets, I think it well to let you know of the danger threatening.'[84] He urged the ex-servicemen to cooperate with the IRA in forming patrols to remove people from the streets. However the night after Bourke's death, the ex-servicemen in Cork city were determined to mete out the punishment they felt the serving soldiers merited.

As already noted, fatalities were not the only reason for reprisal or street fights; there had been clashes between locals and soldiers long before the clashes with the Shropshires in November 1919. Soldiers were targeted on Peace Night in July 1919.[85] The fights occurred again on Peace Day, 20 July 1920, when 'anti-British rowdies, male and female, commenced a course of misconduct in Patrick Street.'[86] Soldiers were a key target, but also 'young women wearing red, white, and blue rosettes were mobbed, hustled, and forced to leave the streets.'[87] Again it comes as no surprise that these incidents also took place on nights when large quantities of drink would have been consumed.

However, conflict on the streets between Sinn Féiners, Loyalists, soldiers and others particularly over local women had begun much earlier. There were several street fights in Cork during the summer of 1917 between Sinn Féiners and other locals and some counter demonstrations by a number of young women who had relatives at the front.[88] One of the most serious incidents occurred on 22 June 1917, when individuals identified with Sinn Féin attacked a recruiting office and some local women who were walking in Patrick Street and MacCurtian Street. This riot was so violent that it could only be suppressed by an RIC bayonet charge with military support. Later in September 1917, four young men were convicted of assaulting female munitions workers.[89] They had beaten the women for singing 'patriotic songs'.[90]

The principal reason the IRA gave for assaulting women during the War of Independence was to prevent British access to potential intelligence. However, when one considers the response to the arrival of American sailors in Cork in 1917, this explanation of the campaign against women by the IRA can be seen as providing only an incomplete explanation. The arrival of the Americans prompted a strong response from the Catholic Church, which appealed 'to parents in the present dangerous conditions to exercise the closest vigilance over their young daughters, that we again call on the public authorities to safeguard public morality in the outskirts of the City.'[91] The presence in the streets of American sailors accompanying local girls inevitably got a hostile reaction,

> [y]oung boys displayed much activity, hissed and jeered American sailors … the hurly burly started in King's Street. American sailors accompanied by young girls attracted the attention of a number of young fellows, who immediately vented their resentment.[92]

These clashes were to continue for months. Again, as noted above, the fighting took place in MacCurtian Street, a street with many public houses and on the route to Victoria Barracks and the train station. The sailors eventually stayed away from the city and drank in Cobh, and girls would take the train from the city and meet them there. An organised attempt was made to stop this: dozens of these young women were the subject of a carefully planned attack in Glanmire Railway Station, where they 'were roughly handled, assaulted, and their garments torn.'[93] In September 1917 a man named Dowd was arrested and successfully prosecuted by the RIC for 'slapping' women who were dating American sailors. The RIC believed that the Roman Catholic clergy were actively encouraging these attacks on local women through the mechanism of a vigilance committee, which they had established in 1917 in conjunction with Sinn Féin.[94]

While at an individual level, sexual jealousy was a possible motive, these attacks also fed into a larger political game during the War of Independence. Two key aims of the IRA were to destroy any sense of normality for soldiers and to stop the passage of information to the British. Leo Buckley, a member of the 1st Cork Brigade, gave this as the reason why they stole bicycles from the soldiers: 'our motive in taking the bicycles was that of discouraging the military from entering Cork city, as it was known that on occasions they picked up useful information from girls with whom they had become friendly.'[95] Buckley went on to point out that more direct measures were taken to prevent liaisons that might either normalise relations with the British Army or to allow information to be leaked. One such direct measure was to 'bob the hair of persistent offenders. Short hair was completely out of fashion at the period and the appearance of a girl with 'bobbed' hair clearly defined her way of life.'[96] The expression 'way of life' suggests prostitution, and, indeed, girls who dated British soldiers were regarded as akin to prostitutes in republican circles. These attacks did not go unnoticed by the British forces, with Tudor, the General in charge of the RIC warning his men, that 'women must invariably be respected; because the cowardly blackguards of the IRA cut women's hair it is no reason why the R.I.C. should retaliate by similar action.'[97] General Neville Macready, however, noted in his memoirs that 'this particular form of outrage was checked by shaving the heads of prominent male rebel sympathisers in localities where women had been victimised in this way.'[98] The attacks on British soldiers dating women in Cork were even raised in the House of Commons by Major Glynn, the MP for Stirling. He told the Commons in March 1920 that it 'may surprise the House to know that decent British soldiers can hardly walk out with a girl or anyone else without being insulted by the whole population of Cork.'[99] Cork was not alone in these attacks, with women in Limerick being attacked as early as 1918, 'apparently through jealousy of the success of the soldiers with local girls'.[100]

However, not all attacks were as mild as an unwanted haircut or a beating. And it is here that the Irish fight for independence starts to look considerably less noble than it is often presented. In March 1921, a Fermoy woman called Nellie Carey was walking along a country lane near the town when she and her British soldier fiancé were surprised by two men. After he had been shot and wounded, 'the murderers then turned their attention to the girl who was kneeling, and praying by the side of her fiancé.'[101] Several shots were then fired, but the fatal shot came from a soft-nosed bullet, a fact indicated by the nature of her wounds. Nellie 'crawled into a house close by to get help, but was deserted by the occupants who turned out the light.' She had been warned and threatened by several women in the town for seeing the soldier, but she had continued to see him. While dying she identified her attackers as local men.[102] Another of these fatal attacks on women took place in Youghal, East Cork, when on 7 May 1921 three ex-soldiers and two local girls returning at 5am from a dance in the military barracks were attacked. They were shot opposite Green's Quay as they walked down Main Street. Though two died, the main target seems to have been one of the girls, Essie Sheehan, who was shot four times in the back, the other fatality being Thomas Collins, an ex-serviceman who died of his wounds. Their attackers fled in a motor car. The *Cork Examiner* reports concentrated on the fear of reprisals which past experience had taught the populace to expect, and it also suggested that there was an attempt to keep these events out of the newspapers because of the less than noble light they cast on the perpetrators.

> Much tension prevails locally, fearing possible reprisals, and residents of Green's Quay are leaving their homes. Miss Sheehan, one of the victims of the shooting was brought into hospital in a precarious condition. Collins leaves a widow and three young children. It is stated that some disguised and unknown man threatened pressmen who were making enquires.[103]

Nor were the killings of Nellie Carey and Essie Sheehan the only two incidents of their kind; Isabella Scales was killed in Limerick because of her romantic involvement with an Auxiliary.[104] Any attempt to establish the actual scale of violence against women by either side is rendered practically impossible by the fact that these events were rarely recorded or reported. Likewise, little remains in the British material to suggest what impact this violence against Irish women had on the British soldiers who were romantically involved with them.

The Conduct of Reprisals

Reprisals for the most part focused on the destruction of property, as was the case in Fermoy during the riot that followed the jury verdict on the Wesleyan Raid in September 1919. According to the *Cork Examiner*:

> About nine o'clock, an organized window smashing party appeared in the streets, led by soldiers from the Shropshires and the Royal Field Artillery. Their campaign continued for about one hour without any interference whatsoever. They wrecked premises wholesale in Bank Street, Patrick Street and The Square. The party of soldiers was led by one soldier, who gave signals with a whistle and directed all movements. They were followed in their reckless work by a mob, the members of which looted everything they could lay their hands on.[105]

In this account we have all the key elements of the unofficial reprisal: the high degree of organisation by the soldiers in question; the destruction of property; and the assistance of locals. The report of one of the officers who witnessed the sacking of Fermoy, a Lieutenant Hughes-Hallett, supports the idea that it was the rank and file who had organised the punishment of Fermoy. He noted that all the officers were at their mess preparing for dinner when news came to them that the troops were in the town. They heard the sound of breaking glass and hurriedly changed into service dress and headed in the direction of the noise. In Hughes-Hallett's words:

> The troops had worked out a splendid plan. First, they send a screen ahead of the main body to clear the streets, ordering everybody who was on foot into their house to stay there. Then a demolition party proceeded to every shop and place of business of the members of the jury who had brought in their infamous verdict.[106]

Hughes-Hallett's account reinforces the *Cork Examiner*'s report, which also identified both a high level of organisation and the focus on the destruction of property. Importantly, the destruction of property was not random, focusing mainly on the commercial premises and the houses of members of the jury that had heard the Private Jones case. Patrick Ahern, the intelligence officer of the Fermoy battalion, IRA, and a participant in the Wesleyan Raid, claimed in his record of events that 'the British forces stationed in the town ran riot. They smashed up the windows and looted everything worthwhile in the shops.'[107] Ahern, of course, completely neglected to mention that the greater part of the looting was done by local residents of Fermoy itself, while the report in the more disinterested *Cork Examiner* clearly distinguished between the soldiers and the looters.[108]

The picture emerges of a controlled and focused punishment by the enlisted soldiers rather than a riot, as the specific targeting of the jury members showed. This was clearly designed to punish those whom the soldiers held accountable for the verdict. It was commonly believed by locals, however that the reprisal was organised by officers, 'large bodies of English troops acting under the orders from their officers who went amongst them in mufti, issued from their barracks and wrecked the town of Fermoy smashing the principal shops and spreading the contents throughout the streets.'[109] *An t-Óglach's* reaction to the reprisal at Fermoy was revealingly that 'abuse from the enemy is always welcome.'[110] While it is to be doubted that the majority of residents of Fermoy felt this way, it was clearly in the republican interest to cast the actions of the British soldiers in the worst possible light.

The same tendency can be seen in the *Irish Independent's* description of the scene following the kidnapping of Brigadier-General Lucas in June 1920. It reported that, 'for an hour and a half pandemonium reigned, and women and children were terrified at the crash of glass and the cheers of the soldiers.'[111] But again as with the Wesleyan Reprisal, many local civilians followed the soldiers and took advantage of the situation to loot the shops. The aftermath was there for all to see the following day: 'throughout each street nothing but devastation of valuable property was apparent.'[112] It is also important to note as a corrective to the image of marauding British soldiers that here too it was the commercial premises of the town that were targeted. Moreover, a great portion of the goods taken from the shops by the troops was simply thrown into the Blackwater. The *Cork Examiner* suggested that items from Coles, the jewellery store, were taken by the soldiers, and this is supported by British records as fifteen soldiers from the Buffs were found with stolen goods in their barracks.[113] Likewise five men from the 21st Battery RFA, and five from the 53rd Battery RFA were also caught in possession of stolen goods.[114] However the commander of the 2nd Brigade RFA attempted in his letter to defuse the charges against his men and place the blame on locals: 'the evidence produced has convinced me that in practically every case – this loot was picked up off the ground or given to them on the way up Barrack Hill – quite half of these men were on pass, and walked into this riot on their way in from the country.'[115]

From the British side we have further reports of local looting, with Colonel Bartlett of the RAMC noting that,

> as soon as the soldiers had left O'Brien's shop I saw a man run down the side street opposite and take an armful of white garments from the shop window and run back up the street. Other people, men, women, and girls began to collect. Some time after the soldiers returned and I saw them throwing parcels to girls who were following them.[116]

This account was supported by Major Stewart, RAMC in his statement to the army inquiry.[117]

Following the death at Bandon of Lance Corporal Maddox on the night of Tuesday 27 July 1920, more than twenty soldiers from the regiment entered the town and 'carrying trench tools marched through the streets, and jostled and assaulted civilians.'[118] Again commercial premises were targeted, but, unlike the actions at Fermoy, an attempt was made in this case to set fire to two premises in Watergate Street. Strangely the houses in the poorer areas were also targeted.[119] Several of those assaulted by the soldiers were ex-servicemen, and a local JP, Mr Burke was also attacked. The *Cork Examiner* reported that 'Rev. John McSwiney, CC, was chased by the soldiers while crossing the bridge, and he ran across Bridge Street and escaped into [a] house.'[120] The Essex attack on Bandon appears to have been more indiscriminate than the reprisals on Fermoy, with houses in the poorer areas and ex-servicemen being victims, suggesting an unfamiliarity with the geography of the town.

A month later, the reprisal against Cobh seems to have involved an escalation in the level of violence. But while the *Irish Independent* described the Highlanders as being armed with service rifles, this is unlikely as the *Cork Examiner* only recorded the use of entrenching tool handles, a similar tactic to that in Fermoy and Bandon.[121] The Highlanders left the Belmont Hutments, entered the town via East Hill and headed for the promenade and the beach, smashing and looting shops on the way. The official report from Dublin Castle calculated the destruction as six shops wrecked, 64 partially wrecked, and three shops looted.[122] A local IRA captain, Michael Burke, gave the following description: '[T]he military came out that night, broke in doors and windows and fired shots indiscriminately all over the town to terrify people.'[123] Walter Callan, a local resident magistrate, was out and about in the town and met the Cameron reprisal party which he described as sober, and according to him, 'a party of sixty Camerons had wrecked a large portion of the town'.[124] Callen continued: '[N]early 100 houses, mostly shops on a frontage of half a mile were attacked. The damage consisted mainly of broken windows. Three shops were looted, a jeweller, a bookshop, and a hotel (Rob Roy).'[125] Callen went to the Admiralty to seek assistance from naval or marine personnel, but on leaving the Admiralty, he discovered 'the Cameron patrols had arrived and were clearing the streets.'[126] Again, all the elements of the previous reprisals are present: the organisation and the attacks on mainly commercial property. However, given Callan's testimony, the troops on this occasion may not have been under the influence of alcohol.

Following a raid on the military barracks in Mallow in September 1920 and the death of Sergeant Gibbs, Mallow feared that it too would suffer the fate of towns such as Fermoy, Bandon and Cobh. It did not have long to wait, for that very night Mallow was set on fire. The impact of the reprisal on Mallow was vividly rendered in the *Cork Examiner*:

> A great many of the residents, fearing reprisals, left the town during the day and spent the night with friends in the countryside. They were fortunate, for those who remained behind had a terrible ordeal. With blazing buildings all around, and with the prospect of venturing on the street only a little less dangerous, their position was a trying one. But they did not waste time in weighing the alternatives; their houses were threatened, and they were powerless to save them, so taking what belongings they could put together they sought refuge in the open fields.[127]

The incident was sufficiently serious to be covered in the British press. *The Times* left its readers in England in no doubt as to what had happened at Mallow: 'business in the town of Mallow was almost completely suspended during the day and in most instances the shops were shuttered with corrugated iron. Large crowds of people, mostly women and children left the town in view of any possible further disturbance.'[128] Many of the local residents found protection in the local police barracks, while the RIC fought the blazes.[129] The *Cork Examiner*'s description of the townspeople leaving Mallow is an image familiar from many modern wars: 'a big exodus from the town on every train, particularly of women and children. On the roads, carts and cars bearing refugees and their belongings made a sorry spectacle.'[130] The element of arson at Mallow separates it from the other reprisals, owing to the extreme danger to which the local population of the town were exposed as a result.

Reprisals were uncontested by the local populations of Fermoy, Mallow, Bandon and Cobh, the residents merely seeking shelter from the storm. But not all encounters were without contest as the Shropshires found in Cork city in November 1919. The conflict of 9 November began on St Patrick's Bridge around 8pm, when 'a wrangle over some ladies caused a large crowd to gather.'[131] And then, to quote the *Cork Examiner*, 'words were bandied, and eventually a few blows were exchanged.'[132] Before it could escalate, both the Military Police and the RIC arrived, and the soldiers involved were ordered back to barracks. The soldiers complied, perhaps reluctantly, and left under police protection. However the soldiers were followed through MacCurtian Street by a crowd who taunted them by 'shouting and singing'.[133] The police formed a barrier at Summerhill to allow the remainder of the march back to the barracks to proceed undisturbed, and to contain the local crowd. The evening's entertainment over, the civilians began to disperse, but, perhaps encouraged by this retreat or in reaction to the taunting, the soldiers suddenly turned and charged the crowd. They removed their belts and used these to assault people and smash windows on MacCurtian Street. The RIC baton charged the soldiers and drove them off MacCurtian Street and back to the barracks, then ordering the crowd to disperse. When the crowd failed to comply, they too were baton charged, and in the stampede to escape the police batons, several women and children were injured.[134] The potential gravity of the situation can perhaps be gauged by the *Cork Examiner*'s report that, 'were it not for the tactful manner in which the constabulary handled the situation, serious consequences might have ensued.'[135]

On the following night, 10 November, fighting broke out again in MacCurtian Street but this time the locals had prepared for the encounter. Sinn Féin followers began to throw stones and other missiles at the servicemen, and also responded to the soldier's songs with their own repertoire. 'The mob sang their Sinn Féin songs, and many of them with revolvers in their hands were out for reprisals for the severe treatment which they had received from the constabulary on the previous night.'[136] The RIC faced the difficulty of policing both the soldiers and civilians in Cork, and were often at the receiving end from both communities. The soldiers under revolver fire retreated back through MacCurtian Street in the direction of St Lukes, still being pelted with a hail of stones and other objects. The *Cork Constitution* described the scene as having a 'most terrifying character'[137] with the soldiers out-numbered twenty to one. A military police patrol was sent out under the command of Captain Harris, the Assistant Provost Marshal for Victoria Barracks. This patrol began to cordon off the area around MacCurtian Street, in an effort to protect the soldiers who were falling back towards the barracks. The retreating soldiers began to reassemble in the area around St Lukes Cross. The military police patrol now came under the same revolver fire as the soldiers on pass, and Captain Harris, the patrol's commander was shot near York Hill. In the rather dramatic words of the *Cork Constitution*, 'Captain Harris fell to the ground with a bullet through his thigh. He regained his feet and crawled more than walked to the Palace Theatre.'[138] Harris was evacuated from the scene by military ambulance, and in an incident that suggests that this riotous attack on the soldiers had been organised, a voice was clearly heard to issue instructions for a halt to firing to allow the ambulance to leave.[139]

Word of the shooting of Captain Harris spread amongst the soldiers, and a collective decision seems to have been made there and then to retaliate on behalf of the wounded officer. The soldiers returned to MacCurtian Street and began to throw stones at the locals loitering in the street. Nor were the soldiers alone; many civilians fought alongside them.[140] Neither the *Cork Weekly News* nor other papers could identify these civilians; they may have been ex-servicemen or merely friends of the soldiers. As in Fermoy, the soldiers once again targeted commercial premises, beginning in the residential areas of St Lukes, Summerhill and the Lower Glamire Road, and working their way back to MacCurtian Street. A tram and a car were also seized and destroyed.[141] The *Cork Examiner* estimated the destruction at over twenty shops.[142]

The RIC and the military picquets clashed with the troops and eventually the soldiers were rounded up and forced to return to barracks. The whole series of clashes lasted two hours, with the military patrol finally returning to barracks at 11pm, leaving the RIC in possession of MacCurtain Street. The seriousness of the violence can be judged by the seniority and numbers of police present at the incident. County Inspector Clayton and District Inspectors McDonagh and Swanzy were in attendance and there were approximately 200 police patrolling MacCurtain Street by the end of the night to prevent any further outbreak of violence.

The attack on serving troops by Irish ex-servicemen in July 1920 also tellingly began in the interface area of MacCurtain Street. When the story of the killing of James Bourke spread to ex-servicemen throughout the city, they began to assemble there. It was a street where parties of soldiers on leave from Victoria Barracks often went drinking. The British Army's official press release described the riot as follows:

About 9.30pm, on July 18, a large body of civilians began to manhandle and ill-treat soldiers who were walking out on the town and policemen who were returning off-duty in the neighbourhood of Shandon. In the vicinity of King's Street, shots were fired by civilians at soldiers who were unarmed. A military patrol, preceded by an armoured car, were sent down into the town and patrolled King St, Patrick Street, Grand Parade and South Mall, they also went to Blackpool and Bridewell. They were fired at on several occasions by civilians'[143]

Though the word 'civilians' is used in *Record of the Rebellion*, the presence and role of ex-servicemen in the riot was clearly well known to the military. General Strickland summoned John Flynn – the secretary of the Demobilised Soldiers and Sailors Federation – to Victoria Barracks to ask if the attack on the troops was officially authorised by the body. The secretary's evasive response was that 'as far as he was aware it was not, the federation had organised no attack on the military; but they could not be responsible for what individual members might do.'[144] In one of the more unique situations of the entire War of Independence, British soldiers were protected from the rioting ex-servicemen by Republican police.

An armed military party was sent out from the barracks, screened by an armoured car to the front, and it moved through MacCurtain Street firing on people as it passed. But this was not a unit that was out of control, or as reported in the papers firing indiscriminately. This is evident from the injuries included in the lists of the wounded provided to the papers by the city hospitals, with most shot in the arms or legs.[145] These injuries were not the result of random or frenzied shooting and fit with the military protocols, later written down by Field Marshal Montgomery, then a Brigade Major in Victoria Barracks. Troops using these protocols were instructed to aim for the legs and arms when dealing with rioting crowds. When compared with other clashes or reprisals, the greater scale of this street fight can easily be seen with over 40 people wounded. One of the most seriously wounded, William McGrath, an ex-soldier of the Leinster Regiment, later died from his wounds. In all, three people died in the course of these events, notwithstanding the rather hysterical reports in the *Cork Constitution* and the *Star* that 70 soldiers were seriously wounded in the fighting. The army claimed that it had suffered no wounded.

An IRA volunteer serving as a republican policeman in the city was amongst the three killed by British forces. He was John O'Brien, an eighteen-year-old orphan, who was killed by two shots to the stomach while assisting an elderly woman to escape gunfire close to the Metropole Hotel.[146] The figures of three killed and over 40 wounded give this incident the largest casualty list in Cork during the War of Independence. But as it was a street fight between the army and ex-servicemen, it has often been forgotten; it fails to fit neatly into the narrative of the independence struggle.

Despite the eulogising of the republican effort in Cork, the greatest single confrontation and challenge the British Army experienced on the streets did not come from the Republican movement but from disaffected ex-servicemen.

The Control of Reprisals

Michael Hopkinson has noted that suspicions existed in London, voiced by *The Times* and the *Westminster Gazette* that unofficial reprisals were being ordered by higher authorities.[147] Another historian of the campaign is more direct in his accusations; J Bowyer Bell claims that 'without formal recognition, the British choose to permit unofficial counter-terror.'[148] He is supported by later commentators such as John Borgonovo, who also claims that 'the reprisal mentality espoused by the Anti-Sinn Féin Society was shared at the highest levels of the British Government.'[149] These statements tend to distort what was actually happening in Cork and form a stumbling block to any proper understanding of the nature of unofficial reprisals as committed by British soldiers. While there may have been some sympathy amongst senior officers for the reprisals, the actions themselves were seen as a direct threat to military discipline and on those grounds alone were considered intolerable. As Macready put it, 'no-one with the interests of the Army at heart can for a moment approve of reprisal.'[150] It is important to note that this statement is taken from private correspondence between Macready and Wilson, two British generals both unsympathetic to Irish demands, and was not intended for public release.

Allegations of the involvement of officers were made by several people at the public meeting that followed the first reprisal in Fermoy in September 1919, but these were dismissed as hearsay by Colonel Dobbs at a public meeting in Fermoy. However, one officer, a Lieutenant-Colonel Fitzgerald, then a second lieutenant with the Shropshires, gives the only indication of any involvement of officers in the reprisal: 'Godfrey led the battalion into Fermoy armed with entrenching tool handles and broke up the town.'[151] Godfrey was identified by Fitzgerald as an officer in the regiment. This is the only evidence for the involvement of British officers in any reprisal in Cork, and there is no supporting evidence for this particular claim.

Strickland took the riot seriously enough to visit the Shropshires on 10 September and to take them to task for their conduct. Nevertheless his speech still contained some trace of sympathy for their actions:

> Next morning the Divisional Commander [Strickland] from Cork addressed the Battalion. He said we had had a damned dirty trick played on us and had had an adequate revenge. But enough was enough. It was his job to see that discipline was observed and that there would be no more.[152]

The lance corporal who led the reprisal was arrested, charged and punished, showing that Strickland was true to his word when he said that he would ensure that discipline would be enforced[153]

During the reprisal in June 1920, after the Lucas kidnap, Company Sergeant Major Dennis, 'B' Coy, the Buffs,[154] who was living out in Fermoy described how a young artillery officer took charge of ending the riot and stopping the looting of the town. Dennis noted that most of the looting was by local women: 'I saw civilians, mostly women, laden with all kinds of loot. There were about 50 women.'[155] He stressed to the army inquiry that an artillery officer confiscated the loot from these women. This officer was undoubtedly Captain Dallas-Edge of the 87th Battery, RFA who was active in bringing the soldiers under control. Dallas-Edge having ensured that the 87th Battery were secure in barracks, went into the town some time after midnight with a Lieutenant Green of the RFA, and a Mr Bamber from Fermoy. He and Green removed the goods carried by any looters and had these items secured firstly in the YMCA, and later in the Imperial Hotel, where they were placed under the supervision of the Vice-Chairman of Fermoy UDC. Dallas-Edge described his experiences as follows, 'I then went round the whole town with the Vice Chairman of the UDC Fermoy who asked permission to accompany me. I did my best to reassure everyone that all would be quiet.'[156] Dallas-Edge also added that he received the universal thanks of the owners of the shops. He certainly impressed Strickland, who cited his conduct in his letter to Macready: 'Captain Dallas-Edge deserves much credit for the action he took, and he undoubtedly saved considerable loss of property and checked the disturbance.'[157] He also addressed the issue of looting during the reprisal. 'It is to be noticed that much of the looting was done by the rabble of Fermoy, for which I can take no responsibility.'[158] Much of the correspondence between the various officers deals with the issue of responsibility for the outbreak, with all blaming each other's units for instigating it. Unfortunately, however, the full inquiry report is absent from the file in the National Archives at Kew.[159]

Officers also ended the reprisal in Cobh, but it was not until midnight that they appeared in the town to control the Highlanders. Whether this was because the officers had given the action their tacit approval or they were unaware of the events is not clear. Douglas Wimberley, a young officer at the time, described what he saw upon running into town to catch up with the troops: 'I soon ran into a party of some fifty NCOs and men, under the RSM himself.[160] They arrived only with tools, wooden handles, and they were systematically breaking every shop window they passed.'[161] Wimberley attributed the outbreak to a general feeling amongst the Highlanders that they were not being allowed to properly deal with the enemy. As he marched them back to the barracks in Cobh, his view of their general demeanour was that they 'were rather pleased with themselves, and they rather reminded me of a pack of naughty dogs caught out in forbidden rabbit hunting.'[162]

This rather indulgent view was not shared by General Strickland, who threatened the Camerons' commanding officer with dismissal. However, Wimberley was of the view that it had been good for the soldiers to let off steam, and it showed the politicians that the soldiers were prepared to take matters into their own hands.[163] But this action by the Highlanders had been anticipated by both the UDC and local volunteers for several days. A warning from these bodies to remain off the streets at night had been 'well observed for the last few nights'.[164] But still some civilians on the streets were assaulted and both unionist-owned shops and private houses were targeted, even the Royal Soldiers' Home falling victim. This random selection suggests that the Camerons were not yet familiar with the political geography of Cobh. After the Highlanders returned to barracks, the surreal nature of the night persisted for local residents as 'later searchlights from destroyers were played on the town, and marines with military patrols paraded the streets.'[165]

Mallow was to prove an embarrassment to Wilson, who only a week earlier had written to the Secretary of State for War, promising that 'everything will be done to prevent violent, harsh, or inhumane action by troops.'[166] Several soldiers were punished for the Mallow reprisal, as shown in a memorandum from Macready to Wilson in October 1920. Macready reported: 'At an interview I had with the Officers Commanding units to which certain men engaged in the burning of houses at Mallow were traced. I elicited from them that a feeling of soreness existed amongst the men that they should have been picked out for punishment, while others equally, and perhaps more, guilty escaped.'[167] A government reply to Sir A. Williamson in the House of Commons indicted that six NCOs involved in the reprisal in Mallow were reduced in rank from periods of five months up to one year for the offence of taking a vehicle without leave and that the driver of the vehicle, an NCO in the RASC, had been given 168 hours detention and reduced to the ranks.[168]

The Shropshires' conduct in November 1919 in Cork city was widely reported in the press and also condemned by the local Comrades of the Great War. Strickland was well aware of the conduct of the Shropshires and their responsibility for it, when he wrote in his diary: 'Bad trouble last night, started by our own men.'[169] The army had in the end, however, controlled the Shropshires on the night, establishing an army piquet at the Coliseum, where shouting matches between the off-duty soldiers and the picquets were observed.[170] As the *Cork Weekly News* reported, 'there was a lively scene between the armed pickets and some of the indignant soldiers, but eventually the men were forced away.'[171] Strickland, sensitive to the public position of the army in Cork, wrote to the Lord Mayor, W.F. O'Connor, to assure him, 'I am taking steps to bring to justice any offenders who are guilty of taking a leading part in any disorder or inciting others to do so.'[172] The letter was printed in the local newspapers, along with an expression of appreciation by the Lord Mayor. The idea that the soldiers were the main instigators of the trouble was supported by an RIC report: '[O]n the following night a party of soldiers belonging to the KSLI and Oxford and Bucks Regiment turned out in a disorderly manner armed with trench tools and their weapons.'[173] The RIC county inspector noted that the soldiers had received no provocation that night. The following day, Strickland ordered the confinement of all troops stationed at Victoria Barracks, and according to newspaper reports several soldiers were arrested and were to face court martial.[174] The damage to the various premises was estimated at £500.[175] As the above letter to the Lord Mayor showed, Strickland was concerned about public support, and in it he requested from the Lord Mayor his 'cooperation as Chief Magistrate of the City of

Cork with a view to bringing about better feeling between the civil and military elements so as to avoid any further friction.'[176]

However, some British officers did not share Strickland's view about the responsibility of the Shropshires on 9 November 1919. Brigadier-General Willis, the 6th Division's artillery commander believed that the first night 'was not a vulgar brawl on the part of some soldiers as the Sinn Féin Press have made out, but a serious outbreak by local rebels.'[177] Many on both sides seemed to believe that brawls were being orchestrated by higher powers.

Strickland's letter was not the first attempt at public reassurance. A public meeting held in Fermoy the day after the Wesleyan reprisal was attended by all prominent locals and by a Colonel Dobbs representing the British Army. He was the Assistant Provost Marshal for the Southern District and his desire to forge some link with the locals was evident when he identified himself as an Irishman during the course of the meeting. The Fermoy locals led by Father O'Donoghue assured the military that they deplored the Wesleyan Raid. However, Dobbs seemed to lack the required public relations skills to win over the burghers of Fermoy. He stated that the jury's verdict was absurd and continued:

> Do you think that the soldiers are going to sit down and take no notice of it? You seem to think that you can do what you like, and the soldiers should take no reprisals. The troops are to be confined to barracks tonight. I don't see myself how you can expect men whose comrade has been murdered, I call it murdered, not to get excited about it and try to get a bit of their own back.[178]

Dobbs openly condemned the town for failing to assist the fallen soldier. On being told that no-one came to assist them when their windows were being broken, he made the following reply: 'Damn your windows, you have got no industry, you are simply living on the Army, and but for them you would be taking in each other's washing.'[179]

The Cobh Urban District Council called an emergency meeting the day after the Cameron reprisal. It was attended by the business community and by the local branch of the Comrades of the Great War. The destruction of the town was of course unanimously deplored and condemned. The protection of the Royal Navy was requested, and was granted by Vice-Admiral Sir Reginald Tucker. Tucker brokered an agreement with the Camerons to ensure that the town would be jointly patrolled by both marines and Highlanders.[180] However, matters remained tense in the town and the uncertainty regarding the attitude of the Camerons towards locals was raised again when a local resident, George Walker, was shot and killed by a patrol of Highlanders.[181] It was claimed that another local resident, John O'Connell, was also killed that night by the Camerons. In Michael Burke's account, 'they came on John O'Connell, blacksmith and owner of the forge at the quarry.'[182] The officer in charge of the military party recognised O'Connell, a man of some sixty years, walked over to him, drew his revolver and shot poor O'Connell dead.'[183] Other reports differ; in an unsigned letter to Lord Bentinck dated 30 May 1921, contained in the O'Donoghue papers in the National Library of Ireland, the author attributes this death to three drunken Cameron officers, who on leaving a club, indulged in a peculiar sport on the way back to Belmont, forcing civilians to salute them at gunpoint. When O'Connell refused he was shot. This account is supported by the report from the Court of Inquiry, which stated that 'the deceased was killed by the accidental discharge of a pistol by a military officer in the execution of his duties; the officer was "covering" the deceased at the time. He has been found to have been guilty of negligence and has been censured by his brigade commander.'[184] However another witness, Malcolm Moloney, of Wilmount Avenue, believed that the killing of John O'Connell took place on the night of 15 May 1921, stating that three Camerons were involved in the killing.[185]

It is clear that the main concern of senior British officers concerning reprisals was a belief that the failure to deal with the rebels was having an adverse affect on the morale of the army. The failure to arrest senior rebels was particularly galling. This they felt was a situation which was beyond the power of comprehension of the junior officers and men, both of the army and the police force, who, having borne the brunt of the outrages with great patience for a long time, began to take the law into their own hands. Several cases of retaliation had occurred amongst the RIC, and although the army had been practically free from this taint, there had been two or three cases amongst the troops.[186]

In an attempt to control troops and ensure that officers restrained their men, Macready issued a special general routine order on 17 August 1920.

> It has further been inferred that soldiers indulge in acts of retaliation on the civilian population as a whole, for acts committed against them, as distinct from defending themselves when threatened or attacked. Such action would reflect the utmost discredit on the Army and would indicate a lapse of discipline, which if committed on active service, renders the offenders liable for the death sentence. To uphold the discipline of the Army and prevent any discredit falling on the good name of the regiment must be the determination of all ranks. I therefore look to officers to ensure that there will not be the least grounds for allegations of looting or retaliation, and though confident that these orders will be rigidly adhered to, must point out that any dereliction would be met by the severest disciplinary measures.[187]

The *Record of the Rebellion* understated the level of reprisals by soldiers and of conflict in general between soldiers and civilians in Cork, listing only 'outbreaks' by the troops at Fermoy, Cobh and Mallow. Neither are of all Macready's comments completely accurate:

> On only four occasions did the troops indulge in retaliation: at Fermoy after the kidnapping of their Brigade Commander; at Cobh, as a result of a rebel attack on unarmed soldiers; at Mallow, after the barracks, during the absence of the greater part of the

garrison, had been seized by rebels with the connivance of civilians employed on engineering work inside, when a Sergeant was murdered.[188]

The threat of reprisal did remain, linked specifically to the soldiers' loyalty to their commanding officers. As the *Record of the Rebellion* notes, the attack on General Strickland, if successful, would have undoubtedly led to action by the troops against Cork: 'General Strickland's immediate action in ordering the arrest of 12 prominent Sinn Féiners in the City of Cork probably saved an outbreak on the part of the troops.'[189] This is a view supported by General Macready in his book, *Annals of an Active Life*. When discussing the aftermath of the attempt to assassinate General Strickland, he complimented Strickland on ordering the arrest of several leading republicans, because the raids kept the troops busy and ensured they felt that matters were being adequately dealt with. According to Macready, 'had Strickland been killed, no power on earth would have restrained the troops from taking their toll of vengeance on the town.'[190] He made the same comment with regard to General Boyd and General Tudor:

> If General Boyd, the very popular officer commanding the Dublin District, came to his death, no power on earth would have prevented the troops from taking their revenge on the city, and the same could be said in regard to the action of the R.I.C. if their chief, General Tudor, to whom they were devoted, was killed.[191]

The attack on Mallow on 28 September was the last serious unofficial reprisal in Cork by British troops. Later reprisals such as the burning of Cork were carried out by members of the Auxiliaries. This move was partly due to improved discipline within the army and can also be traced to the increase in the tempo of military operations. After September 1920, the British Army had assumed a more active role and was allowed by the government to conduct independent operations against the IRA. One has only to contrast the cases of Brigadier-General Lucas and Brigadier-General Cummings. In 1920, Lucas was merely kidnapped; later in 1921, Cummings was killed in action at Clonbannin. Yet there were no unofficial reprisals after the death of Cummings. Again, after the bombing of the Hampshire regimental band on 31 May 1921, Youghal suffered no reprisal. In fact matters had altered to the degree that an attempt by the Royal Marines to cause trouble in Cobh in May 1921 was stopped by the Cameron Highlanders, the *Cork Examiner* noting that 'but for the picquets of fully equipped Cameron Highlanders on duty in the streets, the damage would have certainly been far greater.'[192]

The attacks by British troops on various Irish towns were a significant embarrassment to the IRA, particularly as they seemed to expose their powerlessness in the face of aggression from the rank and file of the British Army. An operations memorandum was issued by the 2nd Cork Brigade, containing the following order: 'The moment demands that reprisal parties and parties who destroy and ill-treat the people in raids and otherwise, shall not be allowed to do so with impunity. It must be secured even at the cost of life that such parties are attacked and punished.'[193] However no record exists of any such confrontation. The memorandum was dated October 1920, and by that time unofficial reprisals by soldiers had ended.

An examination of the evidence concerning reprisals sheds light on the complexity of civil-military relationships in Cork city and county. After the 'Battle for Cork' the *Cork Examiner* reported that volunteers and ex-soldiers were officially operating joint 'peace patrols' in the city, while the soldiers were being confined to barracks.[194] It should be noted that there was no RIC presence in these patrols. The events on MacCurtain Street in July 1920 showed some extraordinary interactions between the various groups in Cork, as Republican police protected ex-servicemen, serving soldiers and civilians, and the RIC testified against the army. The British Army allowed 'peace patrols' made up of ex-servicemen and the IRA and Tom Barry attended the funeral of his old army comrade. Members of the Auxiliaries helped to tackle the fires in Mallow and protect locals from the military reprisal while local civilians fought alongside British soldiers against republican street gangs, and even engaged in looting in the aftermath of reprisals. However, despite such extraordinary alliances, there was never any cooperation between the RIC and the IRA; that divide was simply too deep. In Cork, the lines of loyalty and conflict were often blurred, with various groups clashing and cooperating depending on the circumstances and fluid alliances, and at times it is difficult to determine where authority actually lay.

Shifting Alliances

What the closer examination of unofficial reprisals in Cork shows is that they are better understood within the culture of the servicemen themselves who took to the streets in England as well as in Ireland during this period. Moreover, reprisals are revealed to be not uniquely British. Irish ex-servicemen, as shown in the 'Battle for Cork,' were capable of the same tactics when provoked. What is important is that the unofficial reprisals were, it would appear, carried out without sanction from above, being led by NCOs rather than officers. Though often referred to as riots, the reprisals were planned and were largely directed at the commercial premises of the town, rather than being a wholesale punishment of the entire population. The evidence also shows that the soldiers were assisted by opportunistic local civilians, locals who were in fact responsible for most of the looting. One factor which must not be discounted was the role of alcohol on all these occasions. It certainly played a major role in the street fights within Cork city, as the locations, days of the week and time of day reveal. For all the apparent simplicity of these street fights and reprisals, when examined closely these present a more complex picture of relationships in the city and county. Civilians joined with soldiers to attack Sinn Féin, ex-servicemen were killed by the army, Republican police protected British infantry and the RIC baton-charged rioting soldiers. Driven by events, parties chose their ally of the moment, revealing an unexpected fluidity of loyalty and identity in Cork. Past theories, indeed one might say conspiracy theories, that reprisals and street fights were planned at the highest level of British government are simply not tenable. Though many senior officers expressed sympathy for the emotions of the soldiers who carried out the reprisals, it would be entirely wrong to see this understanding as necessarily translating into collusion or approval. Army discipline in the end was far more important, and Strickland and other British officers in Cork took steps time and time again to deter reprisals and punish offenders, until 'unofficial' reprisals were eliminated by the end of 1920, at least as far as the army was concerned.

Chapter Two

The Soldiers' Experience

There is a large resource of memoirs documenting the experiences of the IRA veterans of the Anglo-Irish conflict but can we restore the forgotten British experience of the war to the public memory? Can the perspective of British servicemen be reconstructed from official and unofficial records? Individuals like General Sir Neville Macready and Brigadier-General Francis Crozier have left behind their accounts of service in Ireland, but what of the junior officers and the rank and file?

Much material remains that can be used to reconstruct the British experience and is housed in the National Archives at Kew, at the Imperial War Museum, the National Army Museum, the British Library and in various local and regimental archives throughout the United Kingdom. This material includes official documents as well as more personal items such as letters, diaries and unpublished autobiographies. Correspondence, articles and cartoons from the regimental journals also provide valuable insights, helping us to reconstruct how British officers and men saw the IRA, the Irish people, their own politicians and the conflict itself. And while valuable inasmuch as they reveal the opinions of individual soldiers, they also constitute an important counterpoint and corrective to the standard repertoire of autobiographies of the IRA volunteers and witness statements.

One of the most interesting aspects of studying the experience of the British Army in Cork is a comparison of the official and unofficial literature produced during the period of the campaign, and the written and oral reminiscences collected at a later date. The material taken together allows a picture to emerge of how British soldiers perceived the Irish, Ireland, the IRA and the war. For many who had fought in the First World War or seen colonial service, the war in Cork often seemed no more than a nuisance, albeit a tedious and sometimes deadly one. In the ranks, the prevailing attitude was that the Irish should be left to themselves, a feeling that the country was simply not worth the effort, and amongst officers, the belief was prevalent that the conflict required either a political solution or else a more substantial military effort under the full cover of martial law.

An Unwanted Posting

When considering the British experience of the war in Cork, one also has to consider the background of the officers and men who took part in the campaign. W.J.P. Aggett in his history *The Bloody Eleventh*, quotes Major Reginald Graham on the men in the Devonshire Regiment.

> If I described the medals worn in the Bn one can visualize what a mixed yet experienced bunch we were. Two or three Tirah Campaign of '97, almost 20–30 South African medals, Pip, Squeak, and Wilfred of the 14–18 war were in abundance. Several wore the special medal issued to pre-war Territorial Army who had served overseas. There were several medals for gallantry. About 50 per cent of the Bn had served in such diverse areas as France and Flanders, Italy, Palestine, Mesopotamia, Salonika. One in China, for he had been with the Somersets in the capture of the German Treaty Ports. Also a large number had served with Murmansk relief force.[195]

The quality and experience of some of the British soldiers was noted also by the IRA. Commanders like Joseph Ahern, the commandant of the 4th Battalion, 1st Cork Brigade, commented on the Cameron Highlanders: '[W]atching them at close quarters, I noticed that with few exceptions they were veterans of the Great War, 1914–1918, and therefore, seasoned soldiers.'[196] However Lowe, an officer in the Essex Regiment, remarked of the British troops at the beginning of the conflict that 'many of them were boys; many of them owing to insufficient education during the war, were ignorant and undisciplined,' but they 'became strong men, and, moreover by degrees they became disciplined.'[197] This view of recruits is supported by historians, such as T.R. Moreman, who notes that 'the majority of those battalions posted overseas … were filled with young, poorly trained and inexperienced soldiers.'[198] However by May 1921, Macready, the British commander in Ireland felt comfortable enough to state that 'the rank and file are in excellent health, keen on their work, and thoroughly under discipline.'[199] Most of the units operating in Cork were made up of a mixture of veterans and new recruits seeking relief from the post-war dole queues in Britain.

Life for British soldiers in the various barracks and detachments in Ireland was not without hardship. In a letter to Macready, Jeudwine, the commander of the 5th Division, wrote 'one of the present hardships of the service in Ireland is the severance of a large number of officers and men from their families. It is a hardship that is keenly felt.'[200] Macready communicated these concerns to Wilson in May 1921:

> Married men have been separated from their wives and families for a considerable time, and see no prospect of either returning to them or having them out to live with them, and the unmarried men, except in the larger cities (and there only with increased danger) are denied the usual amusements which normally exist when serving in the British Isles.[201]

This clearly refers to issues like the street fights in Cork, and the tension between soldiers and local men concerning the involvement of soldiers and local women.

Many officers simply did not wish to serve in Ireland, and refused appointments to positions. In a letter and attached memorandum from Henry Wilson to Winston Churchill on 23 October 1920, Wilson listed over twelve colonels and 21 majors and captains who did not want to serve in Ireland. The reasons given were summarised as 'not desirous of appointment' and 'not agreeable to accept appointment' but many gave no reason at all. One officer who refused was Colonel H.J.G. Cameron, who in the end was ordered to go to Cork and take command of the 16th Brigade.[202] Wilson wrote:

> I get more and more troubled in my mind about Ireland. The number of officers who have refused to go there, the number of officers who are there and who either have to be withdrawn or ask for permission to come away steadily increase.[203]

A handwritten note shows that this letter was seen even by David Lloyd George. Field Marshal Montgomery later noted that 'officers were loath to serve in the campaign.'[204] Even Strickland offered his resignation to Macready.[205] Many of the officers were, of course, Irish Protestants and feared for their extended families and properties in Ireland. However, some were not; the war in Ireland was clearly unpalatable to many in the army. Similar sentiments must have existed in the rank and file; however in their case refusal to serve was not an option.

Added to these problems was a pervasive paranoia engendered in the soldiers due to the nature of the campaign, which began almost on landing in Ireland. H.L. Adams, a member of the Machine Gun Corps, noted how 'great caution was needed in unpacking the boat owing to the probability of an undesirable encounter with the Sinn Féiners.'[206] Even train travel was problematic, as Lieutenant Cadoux-Hudson of the Hampshire Regiment noted, expressing his relief in a letter to his mother that he had been in a train carriage which contained only British officers: 'We certainly felt more comfortable than if we had been mixed up with Irishmen.'[207] Even letters home were a source of concern, as 'one never knows nowadays as the mails are always liable to be looked over by our friends.'[208]

British Soldiers and the IRA

The army's view of its enemy was, generally speaking, quite jaundiced. Macready's opinion of the IRA was unflattering, at least partially inaccurate and fairly typical: 'Many were of a degenerate type and their methods of waging war were in the most cases barbarous, influenced by hatred and devoid of courage.'[209] A further indication of Macready's view of the IRA can be found in his special order of the day issued on 25 February 1920, following the death of unarmed members of the Essex Regiment and the Oxfordshire and Buckinghamshire Light Infantry. He instructed his soldiers that, 'the Commander in Chief looks to the troops, even in the face of provocation such as would not be indulged in by the wildest savages of Central Africa, to maintain the discipline for which the British Army is, and has always been, so justly renowned.'[210]

The army in general held the IRA in contempt, principally because of the nature and methods of the urban and rural guerrilla war being waged by them. As Major-General Gwynn noted in *Imperial Policing*, there is 'natural proneness in regular troops to despise their guerrilla enemies'.[211] The following comments added as an afterthought to the account of the Mourneabbey Ambush of 1921 in the *Record of the Rebellion* are indicative of this attitude to the IRA.

> As long as they were in a safe position, from which they could pour a murderous fire into unsuspecting troops passing along the main road, their morale was good, but they could not fight in the open, and, as has been shown on numerous occasions, they would never risk an engagement with Crown Forces advancing in extended order.[212]

When one examines the attitude of certain officers – such as Lowe from the Essex Regiment – one finds a more complex and nuanced view of the IRA. Lowe wrote that the command of IRA flying columns 'was usually in the hands of some cut-throat called a "commandant"' yet was also able to remark that 'to give them their due, the rebel columns were clever and extraordinarily well commanded.'[213]

The opinion of the East Lancashire Regiment as expressed in their regimental gazette in late 1921 was perhaps more typical, and certainly less ambivalent.

> [W]hen we hear the Shinner outdoing the Kaiser in his references to heavenly support, and then discover him shooting our neighbours, the police, when leaving church, we real-ise the cowardly hypocrisy of these men who pollute the honourable name of 'soldier'.[214]

The strength of the sentiment is apparent. This was, however, written in the direct aftermath of the killing of an unarmed member of the regiment, Private Fielding in Liscarroll, North Cork. Given that the British Army was a conventional army that had just fought its way to victory in the First World War, this contemptuous attitude is perhaps understandable, born of their own perception of what soldiering should be.

One of the many ways that British soldiers expressed their contempt for the IRA was to circulate mock versions of the IRA newspaper *An t'Óglach* containing accounts of fictional IRA operations, as in the following:

> At Macroom, while the difficult and dangerous operation of robbing an orchard was being carried out, an enemy agent betrayed the presence of our troops. After the operation was carried to a successful conclusion, the agent was court-martialled and sentenced to suffer the extreme penalty. As after the expenditure of all ammuni-tion, the donkey was still alive, the stormtroops advanced and finished it off with an axe.[215]

Robbing an orchard is of course an activity usually associated with children, while their identification of a braying donkey as the enemy agent portrays the IRA as buffoons. An example of this mock newspaper reached and was kept by Strickland:

> The Carrignavar company reports that in accordance with Napoleon's famous maxim to the effect that an army goes on its stomach, they have been assiduously practising this method of progression. Although considerable improvement has been shown, the O.C. Coy states that if IRA HQ insists on upholding all Napoleon's maxims, he will be forced to resign his commission.[216]

The IRA's lack of formal military education was made fun of to a militarily literate readership. A poem, 'A National Communiqué' was kept by Lieutenant-General Percival, then a captain with the Essex Regiment. It has similar themes to the mock version of *An t'Óglach*, but in this case poking fun at what the British officers saw as an obsession with rank in the IRA:

> Me and Casey and O'Dea,
> With Keating, Connell and O'Shea,
> In Sam Brown belts and Bedford pants,
> We were the Colonel-Commandants.
> Behind us marched in rows of four,
> Sixty Vice-commandants or more,
> Colonels and Majors, one hundred odd,
> With Captain Hynes and Pte. Todd.
> We had three carts full up with bombs,
> Thompsons and obsolete pom-poms,
> A Crossley Tender in the rear,
> Was full of Generals-Brigadier.

This perceived fascination with rank is further reinforced by the final line of the poem which notes the death of the only private in the IRA unit.

> And Pte. Todd,
> I should have said
> Was sniped on Thursday,
> and is dead.
> It leaves us short
> our Private gone,
> Pray send us up another one.[217]

The Hampshire Regiment had its own perspective on the IRA and the war: 'Active service and martial law combined have made this country a very busy place both for the troops and for the "poor-young-boys-of-thirty-five-who-have-no-interest-in-

politics-and-would-not-kill-a-fly-or-even-a-policeman-except-in-self-defence-
no-they-would-not".[218] The IRA were not without their own version of muscular
Christianity, and were equally contemptuous of British soldiers, who were 'slave
soldiers', 'cowardly conscripts', while the IRA were 'no pale, puny, anaemic prod-
ucts of the English factory towns, but the pick of Irish manhood, the product of
our Irish soil, clean-limbed, strong, and wholesome.'[219]

Despite the opinions outlined above, a certain mutual respect and understanding can be seen in some accounts of the encounters between soldiers and
volunteers. One IRA man, Thomas Barry, took part in an ambush in Glanworth,
East Cork on 26 November 1920. In the aftermath he gave some medical assistance to a young British officer who had been wounded. Later, when Barry was
captured, the lieutenant whom he had helped was asked to identify him as one
of the IRA volunteers at the ambush. The lieutenant 'remarked that he had never
seen me before.'[220]

Denis Collins, a member of the Ballinspittle Company, had rather different
memories than most of being held prisoner by the Essex Regiment remarking that
'a sergeant and some tommies, all belonging to the Essex Regiment could not do
enough for us. They got us cigarettes, plenty of food, liquor for any who wanted a
drink and cards for us to play with.'[221] The Essex sergeant gave a simple reason for
this treatment: he had been a prisoner of war in Germany for four years.
Collins was transferred to Victoria Barracks in Cork. About this time, six British
soldiers were killed in Cork in retaliation for the executions of the IRA volunteers captured at Dripsey. The soldiers went to the cages where the IRA prisoners
were held to exact some revenge. The provost corporal in charge of the cages, a
man named Coleman, turned out the guard to protect the IRA prisoners and 'he
told the mob of tommies who were thirsting for our blood that he would not
hesitate to use his revolver if they persisted in their attempt to get us.'[222]. Collins
also remembered that Bob Fitzgerald, the IRA captain of Ballinspittle, was only
saved from being killed by an auxiliary when a British sergeant intervened.[223]

When asked toward the end of the campaign to reflect on the future treatment
and status of IRA prisoners taken in active combat, British military commanders felt that those who fought in uniform and cleanly should be given status of
prisoners of war:

> A precedent for this line of action existed in the case of the 1861–64 campaign[224]
> when the North treated the Southern rebels according to the laws and customs of
> war without definitely recognising them as belligerents, and dealt with all breaches of
> international law as war crimes, though they reserved the right to deal with leaders for
> high treason.[225]

As a result, confidential orders were issued that rebels wearing a uniform clearly
identifiable at a distance, were to be interned rather than dealt with by drumhead
court-martial.

British Soldiers and the War

The Buffs held what was a common view amongst the British troops, namely that 'we are at war – a pretty "cushy" war as wars go.'[226] It was a view that was certainly held by many of the soldiers in Cork, particularly those who had been through the First World War. Moreover it was an opinion re-enforced by the reports and the casualty lists coming from Iraq and Afghanistan. In fact, one of the difficulties commonly expressed by the British officers in their surviving papers involved persuading British troops at the beginning of the campaign that they were in actual danger. Certainly this was the experience of Douglas Wimberley, a lieutenant in the Cameron Highlanders, and later a Major-General, who wrote: 'It was very difficult for some weeks to teach the jocks that we were now in what was largely a hostile country.'[227]. The Camerons had, unfortunately for them, to learn this lesson the hard way, through ambush and fatality in the summer of 1920. In a document captured by the IRA, Montgomery, later a Field Marshal, took a rather positive view of the campaign, reducing it to an invaluable training exercise rather than seeing it as a war at all, and claiming that 'the state of guerrilla warfare that at present exists is, in itself, magnificent training for the men, and the very real risk which any lack of alertness and readiness actually entails a most stimulating effect on any instruction that is given.'[228]

The campaign's effect on certain soldiers went beyond the previously mentioned sympathy for IRA prisoners. Some went so far as to provide material assistance to the IRA, probably due to entrepreneurial rather ideological motives. Michael Coleman, a captain in the Barryroe Company, recalled how they managed to arm themselves with the help of British servicemen; another IRA man called Michael Murphy was 'in touch with some soldiers stationed at Ballincollig Military Barracks and it was possible to buy arms at a reasonable price.'[229] After the company raised some money, they 'procured two rifles, two revolvers, six Mills bombs, eleven hundred and fifty rounds of rifle ammunition and a considerable quantity of revolver ammunition'.[230] Michael Murphy was even able to purchase a Lewis gun from a soldier at Ballincollig for £50.[231] Coleman's testimony is also supported by an IRA captain from the 2nd Battalion based in Cork city, Patrick Collins, who purchased revolvers from the soldiers at Ballincollig.[232] As Collins stated,

> So far as G Company was concerned our main source of supply was from British soldiers stationed at Ballincollig, about three miles south of our district. We secured quite a large quantity of rifle and revolver ammunition which we bought from these soldiers, who were quite willing to do business at a price.[233]

In fact, much of the ammunition used by the IRA at Crossbarry came from these soldiers. And soldiers far further afield than Ballincollig sold their weapons too. Michael Murphy also bought two Lewis guns in London for £20 each and some revolvers, describing the motives of one soldier in Woolwich who sold the arms thus:'All he wanted was money and to upset the British government.'[234]

In 1977, David Fitzpatrick felt able to assert that no soldiers deserted to the IRA.[235] But some soldiers did go further than just selling weapons. Peter Monahan, who became critical to the IRA because of his expertise in mining, had deserted from the British Army to join the IRA in Cork. Denis Collins, an IRA man from Kinsale believed that Monahan, who was eventually killed at Crossbarry, had been a sergeant with the Camerons; he had in fact been a private in the Camerons, deserting from Cobh.[236] Marie Coleman also found evidence of this phenomenon in Longford, noting one IRA raid 'would not have been possible without the assistance of a soldier, known only as "Jordy", who had deserted from the Army when he came under suspicion for selling arms and ammunition.'[237]

The business activities of some of these British soldiers were publicly known. For example, the court-martial of a Private James Robertson of the Royal Army Ordnance Corps, based at Ballincollig, who had attempted to purchase ammunition on behalf of the IRA, was reported in the *Cork Examiner* on 8 July 1920. This case was of course known to Strickland who issued the following warning in routine orders to his troops:'the Major-General commanding wishes to point out that we have a number of very undesirable characters in the ranks who are in touch with the SINN FEIN movement and do not even refrain from selling arms.'[238] Even a recipient of the Victoria Cross, Sergeant Martin Doyle, provided intelligence to the IRA.[239]

The suggestion of military failure and betrayal was obviously a sensitive issue for the British Army. *The Record of the Rebellion* defended the army as follows:

In view of the fact that an impression was allowed to gain publicity, and is likely to be handed down in history as fact, to the effect that the Crown forces had failed in their task, and had been worsted by the I.R.A., it is well to consider what the task before the Crown forces had been, and what had been the aim of the I.R.A.

The aim of the I.R.A. was to drive the Crown forces out of the country and to set up a Republic. Neither of these objects was accomplished, and never really within reasonable chance of accomplishment until a final settlement was reached. In a speech in the Dail during the discussions of the terms of settlement in December, 1921, Richard Mulcahy,'Chief of Staff' of the I.R.A. stated that the I.R.A. had not been able to drive out the Crown forces, and that the greatest success of which it had been capable was the taking of a moderate-sized police barracks.

The solution of the Irish problem and pacification of Irishmen was not, and never could be, the task of soldiers. This was a political problem, and no military operations could bring it about. All the military ever claimed that the troops could do was to reduce the armed rebels to a state of sufficient impotence, to create a situation in which a political solution would have a reasonable chance of acceptance.[240]

The bitterness of the officers and men towards the Truce was clearly evident in a document called *The Land of the Free,* which General Strickland retained in his personal papers. No author was identified.

> Ireland, through the Truce, is winning her freedom, freedom of course in the best sense of the word: freedom to wear uniforms, a parodied music-hall edition of the English 'service dress'; freedom to enforce the Belfast boycott, which continues unabated, freedom to drill and manoeuvre, even to carry out practice schemes and operations.[241]

This clearly illustrates the belief amongst the military that the Truce was a virtual surrender by British politicians. Strickland expressed his own feelings at the end of the conflict quite clearly in his diary:

> And so this is the end of two and half years toil, a year ago we had a perfect organisation and had them beat, a short time more would have completed it thoroughly. They knew this and the politicians to negotiate with the present results, never has a country been in such a state.[242]
>
> ... All our labours and energy have been thrown in the gutter, to say nothing of the expense and deprivation. It almost makes one wish one had never been concerned with the show.[243]

Strickland's bleak view of the outcome was not shared by some of his subordinates. Lieutenant Douglas Wimberley felt that the government's decision to negotiate was the only sensible course and that a more severe policy would force discontent underground, only for it to emerge at a later date.[244] But many other officers like Lindsay-Young were more forthright and tended to share Strickland's perspective, as the following demonstrates:

> So the troops left still carrying out the will of the politician! They had raided to his order, burned to his order, killed to his order, they had let the enemy escape to his order; and now with victory in their hands, they had been called off the kill and handed the fruits of the victory to the vanquished.[245]

Frederick Clarke, then a lieutenant in the Essex Regiment recalling their departure from Kinsale wrote: 'every Officer and other rank felt angry and ashamed as we marched out in the darkness from the fort which had been held by British troops for about 350 years.'[246]

A journalist from the *Southend Standard*, who was with the Essex Regiment as they left Kinsale, recorded the prevailing attitude of the Essex men as follows:

> The men, foregathering on the station platform, cast no "longing, lingering look behind." It is usually pleasant to turn the page, and I have yet to learn that life at Kinsale and its district had been congenial.[247]

The *Lilywhites Gazette* took the opportunity on their departure from Buttevant to point out the perfidy of the locals, saying, 'We had no "send off." There was no demonstration of good will from the inhabitants, who have lived for generations on the British Army.'[248]

The theme of the IRA as rank-obsessed was also continued in the accounts of the handover of the various barracks:

> [Handing] Mallow Barracks to our one-time enemy. These were the first barracks to be so handed over, and we feel that we should make our apologies to the distinguished officers sent to carry out the transfer. We were represented by two subalterns, whereas the other army sent a number of senior officers, one of whom was the Divisional Commander. In plain clothes he was not distinguishable from the smaller fry.

And in the handover of Buttevant, 'the Divisional General had earlier in the week inspected the barracks and noted certain deficiencies and dilapidations. The taking over party consisted of thirteen commandants and two privates. Some of them when passing the "cage" had pleasant memories of their period of occupation.'

While the officers of the 6th Division nursed grievances against British politicians for prematurely ending the campaign, the *Lilywhites Gazette* summed up the feeling of the rank and file of the East Lancashire Regiment: 'We were not particularly interested in the discussion in the Dáil, but we were interested in our move to Dover.'[249] The East Lancashire Regiment described their departure from Buttevant and their deliberate destruction of the barracks thus:

> The holy carpet [the main lawn] was desecrated. It made an excellent exercise ground for the transport horses, and the troops took an unholy satisfaction in walking over it. In fact they lived on it and even the three ton lorries made use of it as a short cut to the barrack gate.[250]

The view of the rank and file can also be reconstructed from some of the material left behind, songs being especially enlightening. One from the Essex Regiment went as follows: 'We are the boys of the Essex, So Brave, So True, So Bold, we fight for the flag of Old England, and bugger the Green, White and Gold.'[251] Another chant went: 'Old yer raw, What did yer say, We kills all the Shinners what comes our way.'[252] The celebration of the killing of IRA volunteers was a key theme of the military songs. One was composed to celebrate the hoped for death of Séan Hales, a key target of the Essex Regiment in West Cork. It was an adaptation of the children's song 'Who Killed Cock Robin', the chorus of which was 'And the Siens [sic] in the land rent the air with wails, when they heard of the death of their friend John Hales.' The following is a revealing selection of some of the verses:

Who killed John Hales,
I said, the Sgt Major,
I did it for a wager,
I killed John Hales.

Who caught his blood,
I said, the Quarter,
I mixed it with water,
And served it up hot in the cookhouse pot,
I caught his blood.[253]

These songs were meant, much as modern football chants, for public performance. One of the ways to flavour the public performance of these songs, and to ensure a greater and more provocative impact on the population of West Cork, was to co-opt songs associated with Ireland and alter the lyrics. The Essex Regiment, for example, put their lyrics to the famous tune, 'When Irish Eyes Are Smiling'. One of the verses celebrated both the potential death of IRA volunteers and the work of the Essex Regiment latest innovation, the 'active-service platoon'.

There's a tear in your eye and I'm wondering why,
For, it ought not to be there at all,
There's some Shins in the woods, who've just understood,
They've been seen by the A.S. platoon,
You've a smile on your face when you think of the chase,
That is shortly about to begin,
But you'll laugh all the more when you think what's in store,
At the end of the run for the Shin.[254]

An example of the use of songs in a public confrontation comes from an account of the execution of those captured at the Dripsey Ambush, in which the conduct of soldiers at the execution is recorded as follows:

While we were praying, the soldiers were shouting and singing, and telling us not to be wasting our time. We had blessed candles in our hands. At five minutes past eight, we heard the first volley and we all started the Rosary for the dying, Mrs. MacCurtain leading. After the volley had been fired we were inclined to think that the six men had been shot together, and we outed the candles but still continued praying but one of the soldiers shouted from the tank. 'Oh light up again, there are more to come.' After the second volley was fired, they cheered and continued singing, hissing and used language which I cannot repeat.[255]

Two other accounts of this incident are contained in the O'Donoghue Papers. In one the song sung by the British soldiers was recorded as an adaptation of 'Old Fashioned

Mother of Mine'. The Essex Regiment was not the only British unit given to verse. This poem from the National Archives (CO 904/168) was written by an unknown Black and Tan, someone drawn from the same military culture as the British Army.

> In the B and T mission of which we sing
> We serve and acknowledge our Empire's King
> In loyalty ever all goodness grows
> And disloyal men are the country's foes
> If the flame of rebellion, the Sinn Feiner fans
> He will meet short shift from the bold Black and Tans.

British Soldiers and the Irish Population

Strickland recorded in his diary receiving letters asking him if he liked torturing children, commenting sarcastically that these came from 'delightful people'.[256] Peter Hart has expressed a rather simplistic view of the feelings of the British officers and men towards the Irish, stating that 'this hatred [is] deeply etched in nearly every regimental journal, letter, or memoir from this period of service.'[257] Statements from Cockerill, a British officer, would seem to support Hart. Cockerill wrote that while 'in November, 1919, both officers and men, felt no animosity towards the people … the troops gradually learned to hate the Irish and have been inclined to brand them a nation of murderers.'[258] There is certainly a trace of racism or, at the very least condescension, in the attitude of certain officers, with the authors of the *Record of the Rebellion* describing the Irish as 'a difficult and unsatisfactory people. Their civilization is different and in many ways lower that that of the English.'[259] This prejudice was also expressed in a tongue-in-cheek fashion, as when the *Hampshire Regiment Journal* noted after the burning of Cork that, 'the Irish are a very difficult race. A little time ago they were complaining about the Black and Tans; now these have gone they are grousing about the Black and Ruins.'[260]

Other officers such as Cadoux-Hudson were even more extreme in their view of the Irish, describing them as 'an extremely backward race', and expressing the belief, meant here in a derogatory sense, that the Irish skull was similar to that of the African negro.[261] He was confident that independent Ireland would fail, and that 'Ireland [would] be in an awful mess under a government of its own.'[262] On occasion, Dublin Castle issued in its press releases copies of letters that soldiers had sent home; these were forwarded to them by officers within regiments assigned to the task of providing newsworthy items to the Propaganda Department. One letter dated 11 May 1921 contained the following paragraph.

> The latest comic opera command of Dail Eireann is an order issued by Earnan de Blaghd, which translated means Minister of Trade, prohibiting the importation of British makes of the following articles:- Biscuits, boot polishes and soap. If this sort of

thing continues the British empire will collapse – with laughing. You mustn't laugh. It's a serious matter. For what is going to happen to our export trade if the Irish refuse to clean their boots? What is the use of having command of the seven seas and the finest mercantile fleet in the world if the Irish refuse to use soap?[263]

Officers such as Lieutenant-Colonel French of the Hampshire Regiment, also tried to ensure that his regiment treated all Irish people with suspicion and issued an order on 30 June 1921 that 'men must be at all times prepared to defend themselves and must realize that under present conditions in Ireland, every person other than members of Crown Forces is a potential enemy.'[264] This point was reinforced by the document *Sinn Fein and the Irish Volunteers* issued to the troops in Ireland, which warned the soldier that '[h]e must always be vigilant and never allow himself to be lulled into a sense of security by the apparently peaceful appearance of his surroundings.'

> Every soldier in Ireland must realise that the most harmless looking civilians may be armed or hostile – that he has cunning and desperate men to deal with who will stop at nothing, and are capable of committing any outrage – providing the risk to themselves is not great, but who, if stood up to, generally consider that discretion is the better part of valour.[265]

The view of Ireland as backward was perhaps linked to the poverty that many soldiers witnessed. As Aggett noted in his regimental history of the Devonshires, '[T]hose who had never been to the south of Ireland before were struck by the general air of poverty; those who had contrasted it with the comparative affluence of the north.'[266] Lieutenant Grazebrook of the Gloucestershire Regiment wrote about his arrival at the workhouse in Kanturk:

> To one who doesn't know Ireland and the squalor and filth of the cottages of that country it would be impossible to describe the condition of the building and its inhabitents [sic] … [the wards were] absolutely stinking and could scarely [sic] be entered, the rest probably had'nt [sic] been touched in years, and was full of all sorts of rubbish.[267]

Private Cordner, a member of the Argyll and Sunderland Highlanders stationed in Cork in 1918, reflected on his experience in Ireland saying 'I did observe the lowliness of the Irish farmer at that time, where a farmer slept in bunks with a family of two teenage girls in their sleeping quarters, one room, and the poultry and piglets wandering in and out below.'[268] The view that rural (particularly southern) Ireland was an impoverished and primitive place is also evident in a cartoon by the Manchester Regiment (see picture section, page 8). The stone walls, poor clothing, weathered features, the colloquialism in the caption and the little barefoot child were all symbolic of poverty and backwardness.

But that is not the full extent of the British perspective; some soldiers held more nuanced views, showing sympathy particularly towards the local loyalist population. 'None take any action and nearly all hide their sentiments because they live in terror of their lives or fear that their homes may be destroyed.'[269] The Manchesters paid a particular tribute to Mrs Lindsay, who provided the information which led to the capture of so many IRA volunteers at Dripsey:

> Never it is to be hoped, will the Manchester Regiment forget Mrs. Lindsay's heroic action. A lady living alone in a rebel district, knowing well the danger she ran in giving information to the troops, did not hesitate to do her duty. It was a great example of courage and devotion to the Empire.[270]

Indeed some of the letters homes held by the Propaganda Department at Dublin Castle were openly sympathetic to the non-Unionist population, as the following excerpt reveals:

> [T]o brand the whole of Ireland for the misdeeds of 2000 men is to say the least of it unfair. The majority of the Irish people are as disgusted with the doings of the IRA as everybody else but they are in the unfortunate predicament of being too frightened to say so. The extremists who are at the bottom of the whole wretched business make murder a hobby and for an Irishman or an Irish woman to openly disagree with them is simply a novel way of committing suicide.[271]

After the shooting of a Patrick Nunan near Liscarroll in North Cork during an arms raid in late 1920, one soldier of the Hampshire Regiment was prompted to send the following letter to the *Cork Examiner*.

> Dear Sir – I hope you will find space to insert this in your paper in regard to the most cowardly act that has happened since my regiment has been in Ireland. We all send our sympathy to the family of poor Patrick Nunan, and we all hope you will do all in your power to bring the people who are responsible for this act to justice for their crime. We fought the Germans in the last war and beat them fairly with our gallant Irish beside us, but we did not make war on women and children.
>
> At present my regiment is serving in Cork, where we have always been respected, and hope to remain so, as we are poor soldiers not cowards. May God bless poor Patrick Nunan and keep him safe.[272]

The letter was signed, 'A Soldier of the 2nd Hampshire Regiment, 15 months in Ireland.'[273]

Further evidence of British military sympathy for the Irish can be found in a report on curfew patrol in Cork, where the un-credited author wrote the following about the RIC sergeant who worked alongside them: 'He is the Irishman of story and song, courteous, polite, humorous, demonstrative, and as loyal a subject as the King could wish for.'[274] The Hampshires expressed particular sympathy for the many civilians injured in IRA bomb attacks, and noted that amongst the vast majority of the Irish population, 'amongst the humble folk' as they phrased it, the only wish they had was 'a fervent wish to see the end of the present troubles'.[275] Even Sir John French cautioned Bonar-Law against a rush to judgement concerning the Irish with regard to failing to support the British effort in Ireland: 'Whilst we call such a population cowardly and pusillanimous we must remember that they have a certain amount of reason on their side.'[276]

Still there was a sense that the Irish position was as absurd as it was extreme, with an anonymous author pointing out in a deliberately Biblical style:

Now, this town was named Corkira because Cork was the name of the original town in prehistoric days; the name of the town has been lengthened to Corkira, because 'Ira' means wrath, and in Cork there are people amongst the 'οἱ πολλοί' who conceive much anger and hatred in their hearts, and are naughty; yea, their naughtiness is as prevalent as the sand that is by the sea-shore.

Now, in this town there is a large building, girt round with high walls; yea very high walls, and the only entrance to this 'Mecca' is through a gate which is strong, being mainly composed of much weighty material, and being, moreover, strengthened by many bars; moreover this building is so strong that no-one within can proceed without, and no-one without can enter the precincts, unless authorised to do so.

In this haven of refuge all the naughty are confined; yea, they are placed in small rooms, where the light of day is little noticed.[277]

The key word in the above text is 'naughty', reflecting the attitude found in some of the material (including the description of the fictional IRA orchard raid above) that the Irish were almost child-like. Macready also regarded some of the opinions expressed by the Irish as absurd, as in this account of a discussion about Cork taken from his autobiography, *Annals of an Active Life*:

As I was discussing the state of the county one day with a gentlemen who held a high civic position in County Cork, he suddenly broke out in a strong Irish brogue with: 'D'ye know what it is, General, d'ye know what it is?' I told him I wished to heaven I did, for then I might see better how to check the outrages. Drawing his chair close to mine, he slowly and emphatically said: 'It's the Phoenician blood.' I happened to know that the Phoenicians were supposed in faraway times to have traded in the South, but it had not occurred to me that they could be responsible for the atrocities of the modern gunman. I told my friend that no doubt that accounted for the Irish of to-day accepting a half-breed Spaniard for their leader, a thing I could not understand in a people who were never tired of talking about their ancestry.[278]

Even Macready changed his mind over time, noting in a letter to Field Marshal Henry Wilson that:

At one time it was thought that the trouble in Ireland was caused by a band of extremists who were generally tarred with the name of murderer. I am bound to say that I myself held that view when I first took over this command, but for many months past, owing to a deep study of the conditions prevalent throughout the country, I have been satisfied that the Government is not up against a small band of extremists, but is faced with a considerable proportion of the manhood of Ireland.[279]

Army Life in Ireland

If the Irish position was regarded by many as absurd, the absurdity of the British Army's role and life in Ireland was not lost on the soldiers either. In every regimental journal self-derision is evident, particularly in a section found in many of the publications called 'Things we would like to know?' The *Lilywhites Gazette* wanted to know 'the name of the officer who, when chasing imaginary "Shins" over hedges and ditches, shouted to his men to keep in step.' It also asked 'who is the officer who frequents Mallow, and for what purpose. Be sure his 'S(h)ins' will find him out.'[280] The *Hampshire Regimental Journal* meanwhile, wanted the IRA to know 'that the people who described us as "The Army of Occupation" know we are certainly fully occupied.'[281] Many regiments regarded their problematic relationship with the local population with a certain degree of humour, the Hampshires noting that 'in Cork, however, many quite agreeable people are called "black-baskets". It is apparently a term of endearment and is often applied to soldiers. That shows how popular the Regiment is in Ireland.'[282]

So, if the IRA was held up to ridicule, fellow soldiers were not spared either, particularly when it came to relationships with local women. The regimental journal of the Cameron Highlanders wondered 'if the hot weather is responsible for the drawing of birds to the roofs of Belmont Hutments recently, and whether this applies to all species of "birds" seen in the vicinity of the Mess of late.'[283] The Hampshires were inclined to question publicly some of their fellow soldiers:

> We are all wondering who the Sergeant is who gives advice to his bed chum about the ladies that dwell in Cork. Does he come from 'Pompey,' by any chance? (But, 'he that is not with us is a Guinness,' which is a favourite drink.)[284] ... Who was the Sergeant who gave the description of a young lady to a chum over a well-known telephone? No wonder we can't get an Irish Colleen to enter for the matrimonial stakes.[285]

Local rivalries within the regiment also made it across the Irish Sea, as Hampshire mainlanders made fun of those from the Isle of Wight, wondering if they too wished to secede from the Union.

> Has the Isle of Wight declared for a republic? And is it official that a C-Q-M-S, and a Staff-Sergeant of that nation in this Battalion have been appointed a Divisional Commander and a Quartermaster-General, respectively, in the I.W.R.A?[286]

Some of the soldiers penned hymns or poems to their Irish homes, such as 'The Ballad of Ballincollig', to be sung to the tune of 'The Mountains of Mourne'.

> Ballincollig it is a most beautiful spot,
> It is killing me fast and will soon kill the lot;
> There's nothing but raindrops for far and for near.
> And they get in the milk and they get in the beer.

This was perhaps a none too subtle allegation that the locals were watering down the soldiers' beverages. Another verse described the elusive nature of the soldiers' real local quarry: '[w]e have ferrets for rabbitting and we're out every day / But so far the rabbits have kept right away.'[287]

Some British soldier humour took the form of jokes, as in the following offering from the *Manchester Regiment Gazette*.

> An Irish soldier on sentry duty had orders to allow no-one to smoke near his post. An officer with a lighted cigar approached, whereupon Pat boldly challenged him, ordering him to put it out at once. The officer, with a gesture of disgust, threw away his cigar; but no sooner was his back turned than Pat picked it up and quietly retired to the sentry-box. The officer, happening to look round, observed a beautiful cloud of smoke issuing from the box. He at once challenged Pat for smoking on duty. "Smoking, is it, sur? Bedad, and I'm only keeping it lit to show to the corporal when he comes as evidence agin you.[288]

It must be remembered that many of the British Army's officers and rank and file in Ireland were Irish.

The description of the improvements to the Sergeants' Mess in Victoria Barracks also provided an occasion for sarcastic humour: '[M]odern improvements such as electric light over the billiard table, linoleum on the floor, and a big bar; we are indeed fortunate.'[289] However some of the physical improvements were far less welcome:

> With a view to testing the effects of different colours on the human temperament, extensive experiments are being carried out. In our barrack rooms the homely Government jaundice yellow is fast disappearing from the walls, and delicate tints of blue and pink and even flaming red have been substituted. The occupants of the room with the last named colour are being closely watched.[290]

The various regimental journals also provided members of the army with an outlet for their artistic impulses. The following extracts are taken from an article in the *79th News*, the journal of the Cameron Highlanders, with regard to fresh instructions issued to officers in the 17th Infantry Brigade about the playing of the game of golf:

Parties will invariably send out advance and rear guards, the actual players being regarded as the main body. Before the players drive off a pair of fore-caddies will be sent on to make good the first line of bunkers, and as soon as the players have left the tee, their caddies will push on by bounds to the green and will exploit as far as the next tee, where they will take up a suitable defensive position …[291]

… In the event of attack the action of all must be characterised by a determination to close with the enemy with the niblick. It is only by such tactics that a decisive result can be obtained, and the object can only be achieved by the application of fire and move-ment and mutual support. Personnel armed with pistols will immediately take up a suitable position in a bunker or ditch, and will endeavour, by the provision of covering fire, to enable the niblick-men to counter-attack the enemy.[292]

It is a testament to the robustness of the soldiers' morale that the war in Ireland could be parodied through golf. Morale was not only sustained by humour but by numerous sporting competitions at regimental, brigade, divisional and army level. Even sporting failure did not dampen morale; rather it became an opportunity, as in the case of the East Lancashire Regiment, to poke fun at fellow soldiers: 'We hear that the sergeants, in no way downhearted at their defeat by the officers at cricket, are contemplating an offensive on the tennis courts. That's the spirit.'[293] This resilience in the ranks can also be seen in the First World War, as J.G. Fuller showed in his examination of popular culture in the British and Dominion armies during that conflict: 'British humour was to many the war-winning quality, the key to understanding how the troops had endured so long.'[294] Or as one soldier put it, the British soldiers endured, 'Not because our Empire's peerless, Not because we have got more "tin", But when things look worse than cheerless, We can set our teeth and grin.'[295]

The War in British Regimental Memory

Another body of material that provides us with an insight into the army's views and experience in Ireland are the regimental histories. These histories were often written by those who had served in the regiment or were commissioned from professional historians by the regiments themselves. They are of interest in the sense that they demonstrate the degree of importance attached to the campaign in Ireland and how it is positioned in the memory and history of various regiments.

Strikingly, from an Irish perspective, most of the histories make no mention whatsoever of the campaign in Ireland: books such as Alan Wykes' *The Royal Hampshire Regiment*,[296] John Downham's *The East Lancashire Regiment*,[297] or Blaxland's *The Queen's Own Buffs: The Royal Kent Regiment*.[298] Many provide only the most basic details, a mere acknowledgement of regimental service in Ireland. In the chapter 'Between the Wars' in Michael Barthop's *The Northamptonshire*

Regiment, the author simply states that 'For eighteen months the 48th were involved against the Sinn Féiners in internal security operations of a type now all too familiar, but which in 1920 were a novelty to most British soldiers.'[299] Michael Langley notes in his book, *The Loyal Regiment*, that both battalions, the 47th and 81st, served in Ireland explaining that '"The Troubles" as they were rather euphemistically called were particularly near home for the Loyal Regiment, which coming from Lancashire, inevitably had several Irishmen in it.'[300] Michael Glover's history of the Royal Welch Fusiliers again provides little information concerning the regiment's experience in Ireland, noting only that the 2nd Battalion was rebuilt for service in Ireland in May 1919, and that there were only 5 officers and 75 other ranks in the battalion and of these only 10 had landed in France in August 1914.[301] Apart from stating that the 2nd Battalion arrived in Limerick in August 1919, Glover provided no further details on the regiment's operations. He did note, however, that the regiment's tour was 'marred by a great tragedy', the death of Major Compton-Smith,[302] reprinting the following note from Compton-Smith in full:

> I am to be shot in an hour's time. I should like you fellows to know that this sentence has been passed on me and that I intend to die like a Welch Fusilier with a laugh and forgiveness for those who are carrying out the deed. I should like my death to lessen rather than increase the bitterness which exists between England and Ireland. I have been treated with great kindness and, during my short captivity, have learned to regard Sinn Feiners [sic] rather as mistaken idealists than as a 'murder gang'.[303]

The words, 'disorder', 'murderous' and 'brutal' are often applied to Ireland in the regimental histories. A history of the Manchester Regiment gives the following reason for its deployment in Ireland: 'During the preceding months the state of Ireland had been wholly deplorable and caused far more anxiety than had ever before been known in the history of the country' … There were many murderous attacks upon the police; and a reign of terror gradually became established in Ireland.'[304] Powell's *The History of the Green Howards* described the introduction of the army into Ireland as a measure designed to restore order after the collapse of the RIC meant 'that many rural areas were virtually abandoned to rebel control.'[305] Powell attributed the failure of the RIC to a campaign of assassination and terror. J.M. Cowper saw Bloody Sunday as the reason for the army's active involvement in Ireland, writing that

> British troops were still not actively engaged in the troubles in Ireland and officers and their families were living out of barracks in Dublin … [when] on November 20, the Sinn Féiners turned against the British Army and murdered fourteen defenceless British officers in their beds. The whole army was profoundly shocked, yet there were no reprisals, to the great credit of all ranks.[306]

Before this according to Cowper's *The King's Own*, the war was one primarily fought between the police and the IRA.[307] David Scott Daniell's *Regimental History of the Royal Hampshire Regiment* states that the regiment was 'keeping the King's peace in the midst of a bitter civil war'.[308]

Another recurring theme in the histories is the alienation of the troops. Describing the positioning of detachments in Millstreet, Ballyvourney and Inchigeela, a Manchester history notes that 'almost at once in some of these new garrisons the troops were made to feel as though they were some foreign invaders, for at Millstreet the people showed some reluctance to sell articles of food to the soldiers, at Ballincollig the railway authorities refused to carry two truck-loads of military stores.'[309]

This was a view echoed by the South Wales Borderers: 'Duties were hard, accommodation indifferent, and chances for recreation scanty, while the troops were surrounded by a population most of which were sullenly hostile and only deterred by fear from a more active and violent opposition.'[310]

Powell, on the other hand, claims in his history that the Green Howards were able 'to establish friendly relations with some of the local people'[311] but that this was hard to maintain due the actions of the Black and Tans and the Auxiliaries. As the campaign wore on, Powell notes that 'the Green Howards were further embittered by the news that a popular and brilliant young regular officer, who had been promoted into another regiment during the war, had been kidnapped and then shot after a farce of a "court-martial".'[312]

The Green Howards' history also includes a quote from their regimental gazette during this period: 'We hate our job here, but none of us would like to leave Ireland without first seeing an end to Sinn Féin and its despicable tale of murder, robbery, intimidation and anarchy.'[313] Many of the regimental journals and private papers make reference to this sense of duty and the feeling that the army was in fact, making a positive contribution to Ireland's peace and security. However as Cockerill noted concerning the service of his battalion in Ireland:

> Generally, however, the picture that emerges is of a humdrum, manifestly boring yet tense period in the Battalion's history. Only one man died 'on active service' although a number were wounded on patrol. If they were failures, there were also a number of successes, which seem to have been only briefly remarked and have long since been forgotten so that when in late January 1922, the warning order came for the move to the UK there seems to have been fairly widespread relief.[314]

Similar sentiments are recorded in a Hampshire history which noted, 'it was dull duty and dangerous, but every opportunity for training, sport, and social function was taken, and morale remained good.'[315]

Diverse Perspectives

All the evidence left behind by the servicemen points to a diversity of views, attitudes and experiences in Ireland. Even in an area as small as Cork, it is impossible to standardise their experiences. Their remaining written accounts show deep conflicts of opinion. Some materials can be seen as 'racist', others as showing a considerable degree of sympathy with the Irish position, and others again lampooning both the Irish and British positions. The reactions of the British servicemen are complex and show that neither the army collectively nor the servicemen individually can be easily stereotyped or viewed as a whole. Much of the material in Cork shows, moreover, that they were not lacking a sense of humour. In much of the archival material, perhaps the most dominant thread was distaste for the operations which the army was asked to perform in Ireland and a desire to return home, but counter-pointed by a belief in the benefits of such an operation, and a conviction that the reputation of the service demanded the most professional response. The conflict is largely ignored by the British regimental histories, indicating that it is seen as relatively unimportant, lost amongst what were considered vastly more important campaigns from the army's perspective. And while this is understandable in terms of the overall history of the campaign, it has left a distorted historiography in need of balance.

Section Two

The British Army and the People

In order to achieve their goals in Ireland, the British Army required the support of the local population. This section will explore how the British Army sought to achieve this in Cork and will detail the evolution of British strategy and tactics in its attempt to garner the public's assistance. This examination of military-public interaction focuses on three intersecting areas: intelligence, propaganda and law. Archival records relating to the intelligence war are patchy at best, but there exists sufficient material to allow an assessment of the effectiveness of British intelligence-gathering and British success in such operations, indicating the level of active support from at least certain sections of the population. British attempts at public persuasion – the content and target audience of its propaganda – sheds light on how the army and public perceived one other and interacted in the pursuit of divergent or common goals. The important questions are who did the British Army believe they could win over to their side? How did they seek to do this? How did they target members of the IRA, and with what message? Can the elements of a rudimentary 'hearts and minds' strategy be discerned in Cork? How did Crown forces use the law in Cork to secure public support? Or was the campaign, the opposite of 'hearts and minds,' – did the Crown forces rely on law as a coercive force? Was law a means of forcing compliance? An examination of these areas also reveals the gradual evolution of British strategy in Ireland and how the British Army came to terms with a sophisticated and highly politicised insurgency, which they had to fight under international and local media scrutiny.

Chapter Three

The British Army's Intelligence War

In 1977, David Fitzpatrick's comment that 'the army's inability to obtain reliable intelligence was only one symptom of a more general military failure' is and remains a fairly typical conclusion regarding the success of military intelligence in Ireland.[316] This traditional and prevalent view has, however, been challenged by other historians such as Peter Hart who maintains that the army was 'generally successful in improving quality and quantity of information by early 1921' and that 'by the time of the truce, most battalions and Auxiliary companies had a very accurate picture of the organisation and men they were fighting.'[317] These are mutually exclusive perspectives, and speak directly to the extent of the British Army's ability to win over the population, because if the army was unable to recruit supporters to its cause then its intelligence gathering could not be successful. If Hart is correct, then we may assume that the army did begin to win a proportion of the locals over, convincing them to provide information critical to its operational success. Naturally, incentives such as bribes and coercion must be considered in any examination of intelligence gathering improvement.

The Foundations

Information is of course critical to the success of any military campaign, and in Cork a determined and often violent intelligence war was waged by both parties, the success of which was a critical factor in the final outcome of the campaign. No comprehensive military intelligence structure existed in Cork in 1918, and indeed there seems to have been a consensus amongst the military that there was little requirement for one, 'as the sole duty of the troops was to support the civil authorities.'[318] The RIC supplied all the information required for court martials held under the Defence of the Realm Act so it was 'unnecessary to organize or establish any military intelligence system of importance'.[319] Of course, the reality was also that the army did not have the personnel to create an extensive military intelligence system in the area. The Intelligence Branch at HQ Southern District, consisted of one officer based in Victoria Barracks who was 'chiefly concerned with matters connected with enemy aliens and other subject appertaining to the Great War.'[320] Intelligence officers were also responsible for legal matters; in fact they 'combined the duties of prosecutors, Intelligence Officers, and legal advisers to the various military commanders'.[321] Liaison with the RIC was also one of the duties of the intelligence officers, and they were often requested by the police to examine applications to purchase arms, ammunition or explosives.

A key factor in the army's neglect of its intelligence capability was the perception that the IRA was essentially a criminal organisation, a murder gang, and therefore a matter almost exclusively for the RIC. The British Army would later adopt a similar view at the beginning of the outbreak of the Mau Mau Revolt in Kenya in 1952.[322] This meant that 'intelligence regarding the enemy's organisation plans, or equipment was not collected to any great extent.'[323] The army made no attempt to identify the IRA order of battle in Cork or Munster, and personnel information on individual members was only collected when linked to a court martial prosecution.

Outside of the Intelligence Branch based in Victoria Barracks, in the various military sub-districts, intelligence reporting was assigned as an additional duty to young second lieutenants, who often served as orderly officers for the brigade majors or signals officers. As an extract from a report from the Limerick sub-district in September 1918 showed, there was often little to report:

> At about 11pm on the 2nd inst. two stacks of hay, each containing 15 cwt., the property of _____, were maliciously burnt down. £12 compensation has been claimed. _____'s son is alleged to have seduced the daughter of a neighbouring farmer; this is supposed to be the motive for the outrage.[324]

No doubt due to the perception that there was little intelligence of a military value to be gathered, battalion intelligence officers rarely existed prior to 1919. As the *Record of the Rebellion* puts it: 'The first occasion on which an intelligence officer was appointed to a formation lower than a brigade was on 28 October, 1918, when one was appointed to the West Cork Special Military area.'[325] This officer had little experience of intelligence work and no training. His only roles were to identify communities or institutions on which restrictions should be imposed and to control entry into the special military area through the use of a permit system. So before 1919, officers assigned to intelligence duties in Ireland had primarily an institutional and administrative role.

It was the deployment of army officers to these special military areas that laid the foundations of the military intelligence system in Cork. But within army circles two obstacles to the expansion of any intelligence system still remained. Firstly, as outlined above, the belief was still prevalent that dealing with the IRA was a police matter, and secondly, when officers of ability were sent to England to undertake specialist training, they were often subsequently send abroad and lost to their units in Ireland, a situation which discouraged senior officers from sending their officers at all. As the *Record of the Rebellion* saw it, 'it is only natural, therefore, that those responsible for selecting the officers in the first instance were disappointed at the result of their efforts.'[326]

Nevertheless, as experience with the special military areas demonstrated, the presence of specialist intelligence officers improved communication with the RIC, and these officers began to build up a rapport with the police rank and file. The officers were often given on-the-job training in their roles by the local 'Crime Special' sergeant or constables, who had long been responsible for the collection of political intelligence, including the recruitment of local agents. Contrary to Paul McMahon's assertions in *British Spies and Irish Rebels* that RIC sergeants were reluctant to share information with the army, it was these men that provided the initial training and introduction to Ireland for young army officers; this early cooperation is also ignored by Hart in his introduction to *British Intelligence in Ireland*.[327] The importance of RIC sergeants to the British Army is clear from the diary of a British military intelligence officer, Lieutenant Grazebrook, who noted 'of all the sergeants, Donovan was one of the real old type of the R.I.C., absolutely invaluable, "the rat" he was called by many of the country folk and he certainly could rat out information impossible to other people in a most wonderful way.'[328] Grazebrook also praised other RIC sergeants in his diary, namely Connelly in Kanturk and Garvey in Newmarket.

> By degrees, a certain number of civilians were selected for intelligence purposes, and, as a result of visiting these occasionally, especially after an outrage had been perpetrated, it was found that a good deal of information regarding the individuals concerned could be obtained, although, owing to their fear of the rebels, actual evidence was never forthcoming.[329]

The final line of the above statement shows the difference between military and police intelligence requirements.[330] Police needed information that would be admissible in a legal prosecution, while the military simply needed information to facilitate the conduct of an operation. In 1919, when the British Army decided to work independently from the RIC to get the information required for its purposes, the first and central goal of military intelligence collection was the identification of the IRA order of battle in Cork.[331]

It should be remembered that British intelligence gathering did not take place in a socio-political vacuum or in the face of absolute local resistance. Many in Cork, and not just those from the Unionist community, were quite prepared to assist the British campaign. Indeed, the IRA actually felt that the local population in Cork was hostile to them. Tom Barry in a report to the OC 3rd Cork Brigade in February 1921, describing the area around Rosscarbery, noted that 'the country surrounding is populated by people who are not sympathetic to our cause.'[332] Nor was Rosscarbery exceptional in this. Another IRA man, Jack Buttimer, noted that the population of Dunmanway was also 'very strongly opposed to us in the town.'[333] This was, in part, more for practical than ideological reasons, as Daniel Canty, an IRA officer, noted that IRA seizures of cattle for the arms fund were unlikely to win hearts and minds. What was seen as the public opposition of local newspapers was also a concern for the IRA, who considered the *Cork Examiner* 'the most dangerous rag in Ireland'.[334] The IRA believed that the paper's pretence of a moderate stance veiled a not-too-hidden hostility towards the republican movement, and that its influence and large circulation made it particularly damaging to the IRA cause. On the other hand, the *Cork Constitution*, while openly hostile, was regarded as ineffectual, owing to its confinement to a largely Unionist readership.[335]

The arrests made in the aftermath of the Wesleyan Raid in September 1919 are evidence of the quality of early RIC intelligence. Within three days of the incident, the RIC arrested James Fanning, John Swanye, Lawrence Condon, Thomas Griffin, Michael Fitzgerald, Patrick Leahy and John Mulvey.[336] All were known to the RIC as being involved in the Republican movement and, indeed, the involvement of Fitzgerald, Condon and Fanning in the raid is confirmed in Patrick Ahern's witness statement in the Bureau of Military History.[337] Another member of the raiding party, Leo O'Callaghan, the driver of the getaway car, was arrested two weeks after the raid.[338] The quality of early RIC intelligence was recognised by IRA members like John Barrett, a battalion quartermaster, who noted in August 1920:

> At this time the RIC, and Black and Tans, supported by Military (the Cameron Highlanders) were raiding and searching by day and night the homes of known IRA men. The RIC had done their work well and most of the earlier active volunteers were known to them.[339]

Another example of this accurate pinpointing of individuals can be found as early as April 1919 when the RIC identified Walter Leo Murphy as a key IRA officer.[340] A further example of the degree of detail achieved is provided by an early intelligence raid on a carpenter's shop in Cork city by the RIC; information had been given that a Patrick Driscoll would be there and in possession of a firearm.[341] The army, after suffering a fatality during the Wesleyan Raid and given the prompt arrests made by the RIC, reassessed its relationship and 'steadily improved their liaison with the R.I.C.'[342] The RIC remained a key source of intelligence to the army throughout the campaign, but most especially in 1919 and 1920, and as Hart has commented on RIC intelligence gathering, they 'were also more successful than they are generally given credit for' and that prior to mid 1920, it was not 'all that hard to identify or arrest most rebels'.[343]

Despite the fact that the army had relied on the RIC in the Special Military Areas and for early intelligence successes, a feeling still existed that the RIC was failing the army. Sir John French writing to Winston Churchill complained 'We are suffering terribly in Ireland for the want of a proper Criminal Investigation Department. There used to be quite an effective one, but Mr. Birrell for reasons best known to himself broke it up entirely.'[344] This was a view endorsed by Strickland when he wrote to Macready complaining that 'at present there is an enormous waste of valuable information which cannot be rectified until the RIC possess an intelligence organisation in some form,'[345] an opinion also recorded in the *Record of the Rebellion*.[346] Strickland's private thoughts were even less flattering; his diary recorded that he felt the local RIC officers were 'of the poorest type'.[347] In spite of this criticism of the RIC, it was to them that the army turned after the Wesleyan Raid for IRA intelligence, and it was the RIC that provided initial training in the collection of front-line political intelligence to young military officers.

The Dangers and Difficulties of Intelligence

One attempt to improve the collection of intelligence in late 1920 and 1921 was the deployment of undercover military officers in Cork. This proved a hazardous mission for many; Charles Browne of the Macroom Company recorded the capture of two British officers, Lieutenants Rutherford and Browne, who were 'dressed in civilian clothes, were armed, and were travelling in a motor-cycle with side-car attachment'[348] and that they were later executed as enemy spies. Brown and Rutherford were kidnapped while travelling from Fermoy to Killarney on leave. They were never seen again, nor were their bodies recovered. The army acknowledged that 'Brown and Rutherford had been employed from time to time on intelligence work, and … this may have been the reason for their murder.'[349] Another British officer, Lieutenant Vincent, was captured near Watergrasshill and was shot while trying to escape.[350] Around the same time, Captain Thompson, the intelligence officer of the 1st Battalion, Manchester Regiment, was found dead in a field between Cork and Ballincollig. The failure of Captain Thompson to return to barracks did not raise any suspicion amongst his fellow officers in the Manchesters, since, as Lieutenant-Colonel Dorling pointed out in a report to Churchill, it was not unusual for intelligence officers to be absent for days.[351] Thompson was found blind-folded and shot seven times.[352] He had left on his own, travelling into Cork on a motorcycle. A further three British officers were killed on the same day. Captains Green and Chambers of the Royal Army Educational Corps and Lieutenant Watts of the Royal Engineers were taken from the Cork–Kinsale train. The IRA believed that they were intelligence officers; however this was not the case. As teachers, Green and Chambers were non-combatants, and Watts was not connected to intelligence work. One motive suggested for their abduction has been that Green and Chambers were witnesses in a murder case. As with Brown and Rutherford, the bodies of these men were never found. However, the authors of the *Record of the Rebellion* noted that: 'It is gratifying to be in a position to record that the rebel commandant responsible for the murder and assassination of the four last named officers – Walther [sic] Leo Murphy of Ballincollig – was subsequently killed in an encounter with British officers.'[353]

In 1921 British officers did attempt to work undercover in Ireland, but as Siobhan Lankford noted, they were identifiable by their walk and general demeanour.[354] Failure to disguise identifying traits sufficiently was not the only mistake made by undercover officers, as IRA man Martin Corry recalled in relation to the capture of an unnamed officer in March 1921, who had been dressed like a tramp, but when stripped was found to be wearing monogrammed silk underwear, and in possession of a monogrammed cigarette case. He refused to talk and was shot as a spy.[355] The naivety of some British officers in Ireland is also evident in Sir Kenneth Strong's reflections in his autobiography, *Intelligence at the Top*, where he recalled: 'I'd no previous intelligence training and I was often worried by the fear that my inexperience may have led to some tragedies.'[356] Strong recalled examples of his own amateurism, and remembered wandering around his assigned area with a donkey cart and an English accent.

One of the more well-known abductions was that of Major Compton-Smith, believed by the IRA to be a key British intelligence officer in Munster. They had hoped to exchange him for a member of the IRA who had been sentenced to death, but when this failed Compton-Smith was killed. Maurice Brew of the Donoughmore Company described his execution as follows:

> When removed to the place of execution he placed his cigarette case in his breast pocket of his tunic and asked that after his death, it should be sent to his regiment. He then lighted a cigarette and said that when he dropped the cigarette it could be taken as a signal by the execution squad to open fire.[357]

Smith was determined to behave like a gentleman to the end, and indeed control the moment of his own execution.

The killing of intelligence operatives continued to the end of the campaign. A Lance Corporal A.W. Hill was killed in Tivoli in May 1921, as was an RIC constable named Sterland, who was shot outside the Rob Roy Pub.[358] Sterland's death was reported on 9 May 1921 in the *Cork Examiner*: 'A tall man, dressed in a grey suit was shot dead in Cook Street. He had only emerged from a public house when shots were fired into him from both sides of the street.'[359] The killing of Sterland had in fact been an abduction gone wrong.

One of the covers adopted by British agents was that of a commercial traveller. A memorandum from the headquarters of 1st Cork Brigade to the Intelligence Officer of 1st Southern Division IRA, noted the arrival of a new drapery salesman in their area during the Truce, a man called Buckley, who worked for Welch Margertson of London and Londonderry. The man was an ex-captain in the Royal Flying Corps and a former intelligence officer. The memorandum added that 'it may be coincidence, but at the same time as he was appointed a traveller, two other former intelligence officers were appointed too.'[360] That this new British intelligence service was created after the truce to monitor Irish affairs is confirmed by an officer, Captain Jeune:

> I learned later from a friend of mine, Jeffries, who had been in our show in Dublin. When this broke up [the War of Independence] he, with a staff officer, Cameron, was instructed to set up from London a proper secret service in Ireland, which was very successfully accomplished.[361]

Not all intelligence agents were unsuccessful. One undercover agent, Shiels, is believed to have obtained information which led to the interruption of the IRA ambush at Mourneabbey, and the successful British drive during March in Nad. Sheils was an ex-serviceman who had joined the Kanturk IRA battalion in 1920, and was working locally as a farm labourer. On the morning of the drive in Nad, he was seen in an auxiliary uniform.[362] Lieutenant Grazebrook claimed in his diary that the IRA had conscripted Shiels, and that the uniform he wore in Nad was that of the Machine Gun Corps, into which he had been enlisted.[363] His information almost led to the capture of Liam Lynch, and certainly led to the deaths of several IRA volunteers.[364] Paul McMahon does not seem to have come across Shiel's activities, which directly contradict his assertion that 'the intelligence agencies failed to recruit or place agents within the enemy's ranks.'[365] Indeed, Major Percival and Lieutenant Grazebrook were both able to recruit IRA officers as agents in Cork.

The IRA targeted anyone providing intelligence, with the RIC Inspector General reporting that a family who had identified an arms raider required constant police protection.[366] As one RIC report in 1920 noted, 'Loyal people feel that they would be digging their own grave coming forward.'[367] The danger of giving information is demonstrated by the murder of William Mohally by members of the IRA; Mohally was pulled from a hospital bed, having been wounded in a previous attack, and dragged through the North Infirmary. As a Liverpool newspaper reported 'Mohally, having been taken to the roadway outside the gate, one of the men bent down over him, placed a revolver in his mouth and fired.'[368] These killings were widely reported in the newspapers in vivid detail. The general public was left in no doubt as to what the IRA did to people whom they believed to be informers.

In some cases suspicion rather than hard evidence was considered enough to merit a death sentence, as in the case of the execution of Dan Walsh, a homeless man. He was murdered for providing the information that led to the destruction of the IRA column at Clonmult, but it is extremely unlikely that he possessed the information or had any contact with British forces.[369] When seeking IRA pensions or other assistance, some IRA men claimed to have killed spies in order to look like good volunteers. Thomas Cotter, a lieutenant in the Carrigtwohill Company, swore in a letter that he had killed two spies in April and June 1921, an M. O'Keeffe and a Dan Callaghan.[370]

In spite of the threat of dire punishment, evidence indicates that the recruitment of local informers continued, Sir Kenneth Strong noted 'I had to be careful and selective in my recruiting, if I were to get any worthwhile information for my money.'[371] He recruited mainly from shopkeepers, bartenders and railwaymen, whose various positions at the centre of local life might make them more privy to local news. These groups were also identified in the *Record of the Rebellion* as key information providers, as indeed were the Roman Catholic clergy.[372] Indeed it was a local priest who ensured that the army received the information it needed to thwart the ambush at Dripsey. Even Tom Barry was able to attest to the strength of British intelligence in West Cork in April 1921, noting with regard to the attack on Rosscarbery Barracks that it was 'difficult to obtain information necessary or approach the position from which I could conveniently attack without the enemy being informed of our movement,' adding that this was largely because 'most of the people were hostile to a great extent.'[373]

While spying was punished wherever it was found or imagined, a degree of mutual respect existed. Florence O'Donoghue paid tribute to the British intelligence officers in Cork: 'Whether they had official encouragement, or were acting out of a strong sense of duty, I do not know for certain, the latter, I think, for they were fine characters, looking at the job as soldiers.'[374] This compliment was returned within the *Record of the Rebellion,* which said of the IRA in Cork that 'their officer class was probably the best in Ireland.'[375] This regard for the ability of the IRA continued after the campaign, with Major-General Gwynn in *Imperial Policing* recommending that 'those who desire to study irregular operations of a guerrilla character will ... do well to read books which have appeared giving the personal experiences of some of our opponents.'[376] Gwynn directed his readers to the material being produced by the IRA veterans, his favourite being *With the Dublin Brigade.*

Alongside this mutual admiration was mutual danger. British intelligence operatives were not the only ones exposed to peril. Florence O'Donoghue recalled sending a young boy to follow Captain Kelly, the principal British intelligence officer in Cork, but 'the enemy I.O. came to the gate in plain clothes, walked across to him, whipped a gun out of his pocket and said, "[C]ome inside lad, I'll give you something else to do besides watching me".'[377]

The Development of Military Intelligence

Despite the difficulties outlined above and no doubt because of the great risks undertaken by some officers and men, British intelligence steadily evolved in Cork, and by the time of the Truce it was quite formidable. As counter-insurgency theorists such as Sir Robert Thompson have pointed out, the single most important goal for intelligence is acquiring information which allows the targeting of the infrastructure of insurgency.[378] In his words, 'concentrating intelligence on the enemy's infrastructure, then, must always be a major strategic concern for any regular force.'[379] Accordingly from 1919 onwards, the human and physical infrastructure of the IRA became the key target for British intelligence in Cork.

In late 1919, elements of the army began to react to the rise in IRA violence. The Essex Regiment appointed an intelligence officer to collect and coordinate intelligence in the battalion's area around Bandon and Kinsale in West Cork. This was successful, and even the police 'took more interest in his doings, and were prepared to ask for his assistance.'[380] The other units such as the Buffs, the Lincolns, the Royal Welch Fusiliers and the Manchesters in the 6th Division quickly copied this innovation. These officers were volunteers, and selected from amongst junior officers in each regiment, because 'although their knowledge of Intelligence organisation was nil, they were men of action who rapidly made their presence felt.'[381] Following the example of intelligence operations in the Special Military Areas, these intelligence officers gained the support of the RIC at a local level and through the recruitment and use of civilian agents were able to gather a great deal of information about the IRA. As Hart points out, the achievements of these officers were 'all the more impressive when the youth and inexperience of most of the battalion intelligence officers – who did most of the actual information gathering – is taken into account.'[382] But it is again important to note that Hart is incorrect in claiming that they were left to their own devices in Cork. Cooperation with the RIC was critical throughout the campaign.

The general feeling in the army was that 'this was the first step made in the development of intelligence amongst lower formations and units in the Division, and it proved an excellent foundation on which a fairly efficient system was subsequently built.'[383] In addition, by early 1920 many units also appointed battalion scout officers to assist in intelligence gathering.[384] These officers commanded the active service platoons, which undertook long-range patrolling in hostile areas. Other structural improvements to British military intelligence soon followed. By May 1920, an additional intelligence officer was given to each division, the divisional commanders got funds for secret service work, staffs were increased at brigade headquarters, documents officers were appointed at divisional and brigade level and a photographic bureau was established in the 6th Division.[385] By December 1920, a decision was made to provide the divisional commissioners of the RIC with intelligence officers to improve cooperation between the army and the RIC. It was believed that a lack of collaboration was damaging intelligence operations, apart from Cork and Limerick 'where the liaison between the military and the police was very good.'[386] However it was not until April 1921 that these so-called Local Centres were established, and were able to centralise all intelligence gathering from captured IRA documents. Nevertheless, problems persisted until the end of the campaign and a 'double system of police and military intelligence continued to involve loss of efficiency, duplication of work, and complications.'[387]

The declaration of martial law also increased the resources assigned to the intelligence staff at divisional headquarters, which now consisted of three officers and three clerks. Brigade intelligence staffs were increased in each case to two officers, a clerk and photographer also added.[388] Intelligence collection became more systematised as the campaign progressed. One of the key difficulties was identification of suspects and to address this problem, the so-called 'Black Lists' were created. The 'Black Lists' at the 6th Divisional Headquarters contained the details of 2,000 rebel leaders, 'all of whom were fit cases for deportation.'[389] These lists were designed to provide basic biographical and descriptive details of IRA operatives. The following selection gives an idea of the material they contained, including data which was highly descriptive and sought to redress the absence of photographic material in some cases. The degree of detail also demonstrates that British military intelligence was able to gather considerable information about IRA volunteers, from the particulars of their physical appearance to their positions within the IRA hierarchy.

John Driscoll, Main Street, Ballydehob
Carpenter's Son, Age 24, Ht. 5′ 6″. Round Face. Dark Hair. Dk eyebrows. Short nose. Pale complexion. Clean shaven. Stout. Lieut. 4th or 7th Battalion, 3rd Cork Bde. Local Organiser. Seen in command of 100 rebels engaged in destruction of a bridge.[390]

James Fitzgerald, 4 East Hill, Cobh
Is now in Cork City. Chairman Q'town Urban Council. Member, Cork Harbour Commissioners. An active Sinn Fein Leader was Vice Comdt 4th Bn, 1st Cork Bde and also a S. F. Judge. Has taken part in several outrages on Crown Forces. A clever and dangerous rebel. Electrician and Book shop keeper. Has been on the run for about two years. Age 27. Ht. 5′ 11″ Blue grey eyes. Dark brown hair. Pale complexion. Regular face and nose. Medium build. Rather large lips. Clean shaven. Wears glasses. Respectable appearance. Usually wears dark clothes and soft hat.[391]

Daniel Forbes, Ballinaboy, Ballinhassig
Farmer. Age 24. Adjutant I.R.A. On the run, took part in murder of Police in Ballinhassig.[392]

Miss Kitty Leahy, Wolfe Tone Park, Fermoy
A very dangerous young woman. Member of Cumann na mBan. Implicated in, if not responsible for the murder of Nellie Carey on 18.3.21. Known to have threatened soldiers' wives on two occasions.[393]

Women are frequently mentioned in British material as being critical in terms of the provision of intelligence. One of the few detailed accounts of the use of a female agent in the 6th Division History relates to the capture of eleven IRA volunteers on 8 February 1921. The entire Active Service Unit of the No. 1 Battalion of the No. 1 Cork Brigade was captured at Rahanisky House at Killeendaniel, north of the city. It was a female agent who had worked with the army for over two years who supplied the information to Captain Kelly, the intelligence officer for the 6th Division. Regrettably no details survive of the woman's name, age or background, so she must have been good at her job. The eleven men captured were tried by court martial and given prison sentences. The writer of the 6th Division History left no doubt as to his views on how they should have been treated:

> The failure to execute these desperados, who were all liable to the death penalty under Martial Law, had the worst effect possible. It encouraged the rebels to think that the full penalties prescribed in the proclamations would not be carried out, and correspondingly discouraged Crown Forces.[394]

The use of women raised some moral issues for the army:'Women were particularly useful ... but their employment sometimes required relations which were more than friendly.'[395] This may be one reason for the particular acknowledgement of the value of NCOs and privates in intelligence work, people who could and were willing to '[tap] sources which it was not always easy for the intelligence officer to reach.'[396]

Captured IRA documents proved to be an excellent source of intelligence from the very beginning of the campaign. Indeed, Hart believes that these captures were critical to British success in 1920 and 1921.[397] Their proliferation and the frequency with which they were captured by the British Army reflected a tendency towards bureaucracy in the Sinn Féin movement that was not in evidence in earlier Irish separatist movements. In fact, the *Record of the Rebellion* describes captured documents as 'the most important source of information ... the foundation on which the IRA List and the Order of Battle were built.'[398] An example of the vulnerability of the IRA in this regard is provided by a raid on the Shandon Street Sinn Féin Club, when the RIC and British Army seized all the membership cards.[399] In fact many of the army raids in Cork were attempts to capture documents that could be used for intelligence purposes.[400] The loss of some documents was worse than others, and the British forces were able to deal a particularly severe blow to the IRA when, 'captured cheque books led to the confiscation of about £30,000 of Sinn Fein money.'[401] An idea of the administration behind all the intelligence work can be glimpsed from the Grazebrook diary describing his work:

> The collection of further information as to the composition, organisation, strength and movements of rebel units, the history, habits, and moves of their leaders; their training; their weapons; their past and future tactics and operations; the general feeling of the people of the country; the views and fears of loyalists, etc. etc. was now my daily task. Information received had to be sifted, checked as far as possible, compiled, filed away for the future and forwarded to Brigade and to other battalions as necessary.[402]

Captured documents were not the only source of information available to Crown forces. Prisoners were also regarded as potentially valuable resources. However, it was acknowledged that interrogation was a rather complex process and different opinions existed within the British Army as to how to conduct it. Lindsay-Young noted that for some officers 'the only rule was to get the information.'[403] A Captain Boddington, in a lecture on 'Ruse and Interrogation' at the post-war intelligence conference in Chester in October 1921, asserted that 'ill-treatment, blows, &c, should not be resorted to, [as] they are neither justifiable nor useful.'[404] He suggested the following alternative:

> A friendly talk on two or three occasions is the best method. Very few notes should be made. These can be filled in from memory later. During the final 'conversation' the prisoner can be made to realise the extent of his interrogator's knowledge. Often he is so amazed that with very little more persuasion he will turn King's evidence.[405]

But difficulties persisted, as did the division over the approach to interrogation. Lindsay-Young attributed much of the failure of intelligence to the inability of officers to interrogate captured prisoners appropriately, and to distinguish between different types of prisoner.

> Local Intelligence in some cases became a failure because intelligence officers often adopted the same method of adducing information from a captured farm hand as that employed to interrogate a man of even better education than the interrogator himself ...[406]
> ... It was ludicrous to watch an interrogator trying to badger information out of a doctor, or other professional man by the means of a two foot ruler and a gun; or hanging on to the throat of a crofter, whose only tongue was Gaelic, and trying to make him give information in English.[407]

However, not all espoused this soft approach; Denis Collins, an IRA volunteer, remembered Majors Percival and Spooner subject a fellow IRA member, David Manning, to a mock execution in order to make him provide information.[408]

No matter how they were carried out, interrogations provided the critical intelligence the British needed, and it was noted that: 'the best information, i.e., that on which the most successful operations, where the heaviest loss of life was inflicted on the IRA, were based, was that given by IRA deserters and prisoners under interrogation.'[409]

Aside from the direct interrogation of prisoners, a more covert tactic was sometimes employed by the British intelligence officers: that of planting an agent masquerading as an IRA prisoner amongst the prison population, a role that undoubtedly required some nerve. Captain Kelly wrote to another officer to tell him he was sending him an agent who had been successful in this role, stating that 'he will play the Shinner and pump the bird.' Michael Collins acknowledged the problems presented by this technique in a letter to Florence O'Donoghue, conceding that there was 'no doubt that much harm is being done,' but that talking in jails was inevitable.[410]

On the other hand, there were some spectacular early intelligence failures. The raid on Cork City Hall on 9 August 1920 had led to the capture of nearly all the senior IRA men in the city, yet without a proper system of identification (which

British intelligence could not yet provide), only MacSwiney remained in custody.[411] Nevertheless, Borgonovo is correct to point out that 'this raid underlined the IRA's vulnerability when the British possessed accurate information of the Brigade's movements.'[412]

There was a strong sense in the spring of 1921 that an intelligence corner had been turned and that information was starting to flow in from members of the public. The RIC county inspector's reports for the city and East Riding confirm this. In February he wrote 'many reports of ambushes in preparation for Crown Forces have been received,' and later in March that 'information is coming in especially as to preparing ambushes and some of the information has been transmitted with good results' noting by April 'the I.R.A. have been less active than in previous months and the fact that information has been obtained freely as to men "on the run" gives hope for the future.'[413] Reports like these filled with descriptions of RIC intelligence successes could be seen as attempts to justify their efforts, but taken in context with incidents like Dripsey, Mourneabbey and Clonmult, these claims of increased effectiveness cannot be discounted.

This improvement took place despite the IRA's killing of suspected informers. It is interesting to note the RIC county inspector's conclusion that information was easier to get precisely because the IRA flying columns now contained large numbers, amongst whom were therefore inevitably some who were inclined to give information either voluntarily or under duress.[414] When Sean Moylan was captured by Lieutenant Grazebrook, Moylan was stunned at the quality of the information he had on the local IRA, and Grazebrook's informers were of course local members.[415] By the time of the Truce, a total of 45 undercover agents were working for British military intelligence in the 6th Division area, and of these, 23 were considered reliable.[416] The British Army's assessment of the effect of the IRA's shooting of informers on their intelligence network was that it had little or none, noting that 'in every case but one, the person murdered had given no information [and] in that one case the murdered man was an agent known to be untrustworthy.'[417] So from the army's perspective, the widespread killing of ex-servicemen and local loyalists had no impact on their intelligence gathering.

The Development and Protection of Signals Intelligence

One critical factor in any military campaign is the creation of secure lines of communications, and so securing the communications infrastructure was a critical priority for the British Army in Cork. The precise nature of the situation it faced in Cork is outlined in the 6th Division History:

> The problem of intercommunication between the various units and detachments scattered over the South of Ireland during 1920 and 1921 was a difficult and interesting one. All methods of communication, except wireless telegraph, were more or less at

the mercy of a population who were actively or passively hostile, and 99 per cent of the staff who dealt with telegrams and telephone calls were themselves ardent rebels. Theoretically, therefore, communication by these means ought to have been far more difficult than it actually was; the only reason why it operated as successfully as it did being that the rebels had to use the same channels themselves.[418]

Despite the fact that communications were not as adversely affected as might have been the case, the army experimented with various different methods to ensure no interruption to communications, from the use of couriers and aeroplanes to deliver dispatches, to the introduction of a wireless telegraph system, and even the use of carrier pigeons.

In an early attempt to ensure the safety of dispatches, the army established its own postal system. Dispatch riders were used until the summer of 1920, when several were attacked in Cork and the dispatches seized.[419] Finally, understanding the vulnerability of these motorcycle couriers, the army introduced a system of mail cars in May 1920. This consisted of specialised Crossley tenders, which had been armoured on the driver's side and equipped with Lewis guns. However:

It was obvious that this service would not be allowed to run unmolested for very long. At the end of July, the mail car was attacked on two successive days. Although the mails were kept intact, heavy casualties were inflicted on the escorts, and it became apparent that unless a convoy of several cars was used, mail cars were no longer a practicable method of forwarded secret correspondence.[420]

Faced with this dilemma, the army decided to take advantage of the increasing number of aeroplanes in Ireland to secure its dispatches by creating an aerial mail service. Linking the various divisional headquarters to their brigades and battalions, this became a daily service from the early summer of 1921. In August 1920 there were 38 mail flights daily, rising by December of that year to 69, and 108 by May 1921.[421] Apart from official military correspondence, soldiers knew that even private mail could be read and used as a source of information by the enemy, as when Cadoux-Hudson wrote to his mother, 'I am afraid there is very little to write about as our letters are liable to be opened by S.F.'[422]

Bizarrely, perhaps to modern eyes, pigeons were also pressed into service.

Pigeons were useful for intelligence work and in the case of emergency for convoys, all of which were provided with them wherever possible. Birds were issued in pairs, the S.O.S. message being inserted in the message carrier on the bird's leg before it left the loft. In one case the arrival of a bird at Cork without any message was the first intimation received of the ambushing of a mail car, and enabled a relief party to take to the road immediately.[423]

However, these pigeons also became targets in the campaign. The capture of some birds during the ambush of an army patrol is recorded: 'A certain number of pigeons fell into rebel hands, and one bird on arrival in the loft was found to be carrying a greeting to the G.O.C., 6th Division from a rebel humorist.'[424] The nature of the greeting is not recorded.

In addition to the difficulties involved in moving sensitive military documents, the army had another problem. One of the more intriguing aspects of the intelligence campaign was the use of telephone tapping on both sides; the IRA even created specialist units to gather intelligence in this manner. The army responded by running telephone taps on the phone calls of known IRA suspects.

> A very satisfactory method of tapping the main lines was instituted, which was never discovered by the rebels, but no valuable results were achieved. The use of Post Office telephones appears to have been confined to the passing of general information, arranging for the rendezvous of individuals, and the passing on of letters by hand. Exchange operators either passed the information themselves, or arranged illicit calls for others. These calls were put through after heavy traffic hours in the absence of supervisors. Christian, 'Pet', or bogus names were used, but were not altered from time to time, and with a little practice it was possible to recognize the voice of the person speaking.[425]

In addition to various IRA sympathisers in telephone exchanges as mentioned above, the IRA in Cork also had a specialist phone-tapping unit. A detailed circular was issued by IRA GHQ in April 1921 on the requirement for and methods involved in successful phone taps (see picture section). [426] IRA robberies, which had seen telephone linesmen robbed of their mobile phone equipment in December 1920, had flagged this development.[427] Even prior to the interception of the circular by the British Army, senior British officers had been aware of this problem. As Florence O'Donoghue explained in a lecture in the Curragh in the 1950s, the IRA tapping service worked on a 24-hour basis, and was able to cover communications not being routed through the telephone exchanges.[428] British military telephones continued to be tapped even during the Truce, with 1st Cork Brigade reporting to IRA GHQ that 'a permanent station is maintained and the results have shown that it is worthwhile. The working of this station and the communication system in connection with it are all that can be desired.'[429] During the Truce, British signals security seems to have been lax. One of the phone calls that the IRA recorded and transcribed, dated 25 August 1921, took place between Macready and Strickland. Macready was recorded as saying, 'If it is not too much inconvenience to you, come up tomorrow morning. I want you on a very important matter for criticism. I want a good fighting General should trouble arise again.'[430] Another transcript recorded vital information on army strengths and intentions from a tapped conversation between the duty officers at GHQ and Victoria Barracks, during which they discussed the possible use of British troops to protect local loyalists in Cork.

> G.H.Q: Can you let me know the strength of the forces in the Mallow area at present for protection purposes for the loyalists?

Cork: They've got the wind up, have they?

G.H.Q: Yes.

Cork: Strength of the forces in Mallow at present is 3 officers and 49 other ranks. Buttevant, 21 officers, 287 other ranks.

G.H.Q.   You cannot take any man from Buttevant, you'll see to that.

Cork: Yes.[431]

Even without the aid of phone tapping, much information could be collected. A great deal of the telephone traffic between British Army posts in Munster was routed through the telephone exchange at Mallow. This came to the attention of Anne Barrett, a supervising telephonist at the telephone exchange, and an intelligence agent for the IRA's 2nd Cork Brigade. She would arrange meetings with her two IRA contacts, Dan Hegarty and Owen Harold, and 'relay all military and police messages passing through Mallow during my spell of duty to the Mallow Intelligence section of the Irish Volunteers.'[432]

In an attempt to counter this, the British Army developed a wireless telegraphy network in Cork to secure their communications. The scheme was set up as follows:

The British Army Wireless Network in Munster, 1921

6th Division Main Scheme	Cork x 2
	Bantry
	Limerick x 3
	Ennis
	Templemore
	Buttevant
	Kanturk
	Killarney
	Tralee
	Fermoy
	Kilkenny
	Tipperary
	Waterford
Cork Brigade Scheme	Cork
	Ballincollig
	Macroom
	Kinsale
	Bandon
	Clonakilty

Other wireless sets were located at the Admiralty in Cobh, at Bere Island, at Bantry RIC and at the RAF base near Fermoy.[433] In addition to this, a radio-telephone system was located in Victoria Barracks, with a five-mile operational radius for troops on duty in Cork city.[434] This development promised that all the key British military centres would be able to communicate directly and securely with one another and without the danger of IRA tapping. By December 1921, after the Treaty the IRA were able to intercept wireless transmissions from British GHQ which were broadcast in clear, but many were also in code limiting their overall usefulness as intelligence.[435] This communications war shows the resilience, inventiveness and tenacity of both sides.

Another method of ensuring communications security was to make sure that access to the Playfair ciphers needed to decode sensitive military transmissions was controlled as tightly as possible. An extract from a memorandum by Major Dickenson – the Brigade Major of the 16th Infantry Brigade – testified to the precautions taken: 'These keywords will be delivered by hand and will never be sent by post. If this letter cannot be kept locked up in a safe the key words must be committed to memory and the paper burnt.'[436] The military's various efforts at securing their communications were noted by Florence O'Donoghue, who knew that the IRA was powerless to penetrate the system of aerial mail and lacked the expertise or equipment to fully intercept wireless communications. As wireless communications became the norm in Cork, the effectiveness of IRA intelligence gathering from army communications was rendered utterly negligible.

The 6th Division History recorded that it was not only the army that was compromised by poor communications security. It recorded lapses in operational security by individual IRA volunteers using the telephone system.

> Calls were made from exchanges, hotels, or private houses, but there was little variation in each individual case. The same person usually called up from the same place and at about the same time, provided that the 'right' operator was on duty to work the connection.[437]

In an effort to disrupt this form of IRA communications, all telephone and telegraph offices which were not controllable from a military perspective were closed, and the equipment confiscated.[438]

Intelligence Success

The raid on Rahanisky House in Whitechurch in early 1921 demonstrates how useful certain agents were to the British Army. Captain Kelly was approached by a female agent on the night of 7 February 1921 with information that the Active Service Unit of No. 1 Battalion of the 1st Cork Brigade was billeted in

Rahanisky House, the home of Patrick McAuliffe, an ex-Justice of the Peace[439] and 'amongst them were some prominent members of the Cork Murder Gang.'[440] According to the *Record of the Rebellion*, these members included the brother of Terence MacSwiney, Mary Bowles and an ex-clerk in the office of the garrison Adjutant of Victoria Barracks. However, though the woman had reported to him for two years, Kelly still did not trust her, suspecting she was selling information to both sides, and that 'the agent appeared very anxious to ascertain the exact hour at which the operation would take place.'[441] So when she asked when the raid would happen, Kelly told her that operations would begin at 10am the following morning. Four Crossley tenders carrying Captain Kelly and the selected troops from the Hampshire Regiment left Victoria Barracks at 4.45am. They debussed before reaching the house and covered the remaining ground on foot so as to retain the element of surprise. The house was quickly surrounded before the sentry had time to raise the alarm; the latter made good his escape but was wounded, leaving part of his hand behind.

The army then called on the volunteers to surrender, and despite initial reports that 'a desperate conflict had taken place, and that the battle extended over a wide area, resulting in a big casualty list'[442] the ASU surrendered without firing a single shot. They left the house one by one and were taken into military custody.[443] The *Hampshire Regimental Journal* recorded the moment as 'eleven of the most daring members of the IRA appeared unarmed at doors and windows and proceeded to surrender with remarkable speed. Their extraordinary efficiency in the "arms upwards stretch" movement suggested many weeks of tireless practice.'[444] In all the army took fourteen prisoners, thirteen men and one woman. As noted in the *Cork Weekly News*, 'the round-up was accomplished by the military without any resistance being offered.'[445] Once the prisoners were in custody, the army began mopping up operations, and 'before leaving, in order to make certain that none of the rebels were overlooked, three bombs were thrown into the outhouses, and, as a result of this, another rebel appeared,' and was taken into custody.[446] The capture of this ASU shows how effective the army was at mounting small-unit operations when given the intelligence to work with. Information from local agents was to lead to the death of Walther Leo Murphy, the capture of Sean Moylan and the seizing of many arms dumps, and shows that the careful management of local agents was very productive for the army in Cork.

Another critical area for intelligence was the identification of the location of IRA arms dumps. Given the limited resources of the republican movement, the capture of arms was in many ways almost more important than the capture of men. After the introduction of martial law, British forces had their most successful period in this regard, success that was a 'direct result of information furnished by civilians'.[447] For example, gunners from the 2nd Brigade, RFA, acting on information provided locally in the Clondulane area near Fermoy, discovered a large quantity of arms and ammunition and official IRA documents. In the middle of January, searches were made in the Clogheen area after a soldier of the Hampshire

Regiment received information from a girlfriend that the IRA were active there, information he promptly passed on to the intelligence officer. This officer had two further sources that confirmed the soldier's information, and provided the additional details that dugouts were being created in the area and that an empty house was being used as an arms store. A raid on the area led to the capture of a young sixteen-year-old girl, Mary Bowles, who was found wearing trench armour, carrying a Lewis gun and with two revolvers stuffed in her pockets. On the same day, 12 January 1921, a patrol from the Buffs 'obtained information as to the location of a rebel arms dump in the Glanworth [area] – this information was also interestingly obtained through a woman.'[448] Yet again this led to the capture of a large amount of ammunition, and also the spare parts for a Lewis gun.

On 19 January 1921, an RIC constable and his girlfriend discovered a large cache of arms and ammunition near Cork city, a note in the *Record of the Rebellion* stated that 'the exact manner in which he made this discovery may not be published.'[449] Further searches of the area led to the discovery of another major arms dump. The following day, the army was given information by the naval intelligence officer in Cobh, who had 'obtained information through a civilian agent as to the location of a large quantity of arms in an empty house near Barrymore, Cobh.'[450] Not all arms discoveries were unqualified successes, however. The discovery by the RIC of a significant arms dump in High Street led the IRA to execute John Sheehan, an ex-serviceman who they thought was the informer.[451]

Improved intelligence allowed the RIC and the army to reduce the IRA's capacity during the spring and summer of 1921. In February 1921 the Essex Regiment found the arms dump for the Kilbrittan Company.[452] In a discovery the following month, in a farm near the city, the RIC found two touring cars, one motorcycle, 108 bombs, 16 land mines, 8 revolvers, 4 rifles and various items of bomb making equipment.[453] Townshend correctly described these combined events as 'a staggering blow to IRA supplies'.[454] He calculates the total war material lost by the IRA as 300 rifles, 731 pistols, 554 pistols and over 45,000 rounds of ammunition nationally.[455]

British military intelligence was also given considerable assistance in Cork by RAF reconnaissance flights and aerial photography. One of the RAF's principal missions was to locate and identify IRA facilities, in particular dug-outs where military supplies were stored. In an operations report for May 1921, the RAF reported finding no less than four IRA dug-outs from Glenville in mid-Cork to the Paps Mountains near Rathmore on the Cork-Kerry border.[456] As *an t-Ólgach* noted, the 'best means the English have at their disposal for locating our standing positions, strong points, and dumps in the country is the aeroplane photographer.'[457] The importance of this new challenge was known to IRA officers such as Florence O'Donoghue, who possessed a captured letter dated 17 June 1921, from Colonel Cameron of the 16th Infantry Brigade addressed to his various battalion commanders informing them that he hoped 'to get air photos soon of suspected areas'.[458] Photographic aerial reconnaissance became a key part of British intelligence gathering in Cork, and remained a threat up to and indeed after the Truce, and one against which the IRA could do very little.

Alongside arms stores, key individual IRA officers were also targeted. British military intelligence received information that Walter Murphy, commandant of No. 3 Battalion of the 1st Mid-Cork Brigade held meetings in a public house in Killumney as a matter of routine.[459] Murphy, the IRA officer responsible for the killing of Captain Thompson, was a key target for the army. The raid was led by Captain Vining, Thompson's successor as the Manchester Regiment's intelligence officer. On the night of 28 June 1921, four officers led by Vining were sent in plain clothes in two Ford cars to surprise Murphy and the others at this public house. However, Murphy was not there and after a quick discussion, a decision was made by the officers to try a public house in Waterfall often used by the target.

> The party arrived at Waterfall, and surrounded the building without being observed by the enemy. At first sight the place appeared to be deserted. However, on the party closing in, a number of men attempted to escape through the back. This attempt was frustrated by the officers detailed to the rear of the building. Walter Leo Murphy then dashed out of the front door in the hopes of escaping. He was at once shot dead.[460]

Over 45 prisoners were taken, including 23 of the key personnel of No. 3 Battalion. The majority had not been armed and only two rifles and three pistols with some ammunition were found at the scene. The approving commentary in the 6th Division History was:

> This most successful operation is an example of what can be achieved by skill, enterprise, and carefully prepared arrangements. It shows that the rebels had not the spirit to engage with a determined body of troops, no matter how inferior as regards numbers the latter may be.[461]

'Operationally Useful'

In one sense, the intelligence war in Cork was similar to the overall conduct of the First World War, in that it too was almost a war of attrition. As pointed out by the *Hampshire Regimental Journal*, 'minor successes have also been gained; many rebels of varying degrees of activity have been arrested, and in certain cases, arms, ammunition and equipment have been captured. The steady pegging away at the elusive Sinn [Féin] is undoubtedly telling on their morale.'[462] The view offered by Florence O'Donoghue's lecture at the Curragh, that the British Army's 'military intelligence organisation was neither designed nor fitted to deal with the kind of situation then confronting it in Ireland'[463] is not sustainable in light of the evidence in Cork. Indeed it is flatly contradicted by an IRA assessment of the period which states that 'captured enemy documents indicate that quite often they are informed beforehand of intended ambushes – and even of the actual position.'[464] Not only did British intelligence gathering continually evolve, but the army made every effort to ensure that its communications became more secure as the campaign progressed. As Hart has noted, 'British operational intelligence improved sufficiently to reveal the serious weaknesses in the IRA's own system.'[465] They failed to establish any effective counter-intelligence system and stem the flow of information from within their own ranks to the army. As Thomas Mockaitis has pointed out with regard to the development of British military intelligence in Ireland, it 'proved that in guerrilla war the foundation of military intelligence is the battalion and detachment system and that the best information is obtained from front-line troops.'[466]

British intelligence did evolve in Cork and become more successful and focused as the campaign continued, through the use of undercover officers, local agents, and the application of new techniques developed during the First World War, such as aerial photography, which were used to erode the infrastructure of the IRA. The success of this effort is reflected in the high number of fruitful arms raids in 1921, in the prevention of ambushes at places like Dripsey and Mourneabbey, and in the capture or elimination of entire IRA units at Clonmult and at Rahanisky House. These successes contradict the view held by some historians that 'the Crown Forces received little operationally useful information from their array of agents and touts.'[467] The British Army also sought to reduce its vulnerability to IRA intelligence gathering, through the creation of an aerial mail system, and the development of an internal wireless army network. They also restricted access to operational material to officers, in order to prevent either civilian employees or soldiers from leaking information either willingly or unwittingly to the IRA. The structure of intelligence at battalion, brigade and divisional level improved as the war progressed, and specialist units such as document and photographic bureaux were developed. All the evidence shows a strong military commitment to the continual improvement of intelligence gathering, and, as in the tactical arena, the application of the new technologies developed in the First World War was widespread.

Chapter Four

Law and Propaganda

The Use of Special Military Areas

Following an attack on two policemen in Eyeries, West Cork, a Special Military Area was declared on 30 September 1918 by Lieutenant-General Shaw. The authority to declare special areas was granted under DORA regulation 29B.[468] By 7 October 1918 the *Cork Examiner* reported that the West Cork Special Military Area covered nearly all of West Cork, and that it had taken the British military only two days to take full control of the locale.[469]

The greatest punishment visited on a population confined within a Special Military Area was the restriction of business, in that all fairs and markets were prohibited; the *Cork Examiner* estimated the losses to Macroom by February 1919 at over £20,000.[470] The impact on local trade was criticised by a Mr Fitzgerald of the Macroom Urban District Council, who saw the sanctions as 'severe and hard', claiming that the army had only ever been 'treated decently and hospitably' in that town.[471] In addition to economic restrictions, the social life of a community was also hit by the application of a Special Military Area, as meetings, public assemblies and processions were often banned.[472]

The use of Special Military Areas had quite a clear aim, the 'object of the Government [being] partly, to isolate the district as a punitive measure, and partly, by restricting and controlling the movement of the civil population within it, to facilitate the restoration of order.'[473] Special Military Areas were used four times in Munster by the British Army: in Clare from February to April 1918; in Tralee from June to August 1918; in West Cork from September 1918 to February 1919; and in Limerick in April and June 1919. After the Limerick imposition, however, the British Army abandoned the measure as an unsuitable response, particularly in larger urban environments.[474] Though having some utility for the period of application, ultimately Special Military Areas were an ineffective tactic. They were too crude, and were almost sure to alienate moderates, especially members of the agricultural and business communities. There had been attempts to control single individuals under DORA, notably in Antrim, but these too had proved unsuccessful, owing to the difficulty of maintaining a continual watch on a single person.[475]

That is not to say that the Special Military Area did not have its supporters; Sir John French noted the 'salutary effect' the measure had in West Cork, where 'the unruly elements have been brought to realise that the Government are determined that law-abiding citizens shall not be interfered with.'[476] This was clearly a premature assessment of the impact of the Special Military Areas, as in the end they achieved none of the results French outlined in his State of Ireland report.

Others were equally in favour of the technique, and French's initial optimism was shared by senior members of the RIC. Its Inspector General noted in June 1918 that 'the punitive action by the Commander in Chief in placing certain disturbed areas under military control, and the generally increased rigour in dealing with the seditious movement have had a satisfactory and deterrent effect.'[477] This view was echoed by the county inspector responsible for West Cork who considered that 'the effect of this activity is very noticeable in the improved demeanour of the people.'[478] As Townshend pointed out however, the employment of Special Military Areas rested on a flawed analysis of the situation and any 'success [was] dependent on the fact the moderate majority could still control the men who were taking to the gun.'[479] The view of the RIC had radically altered by 1919 when the county inspector noted the continuation of 'the state of unrest which exists and which is only kept in check by presence of troops throughout the Riding.'[480] The Inspector General also noted that 'there was no improvement in the attitude of people towards the RIC, who, in the most disaffected counties are treated with bitter hostility.'[481] The military view had also changed, as is shown by a memorandum drafted by Colonel Brind and submitted to Field Marshal French by Lieutenant-General Shaw: 'The present system of declaring military areas, besides having many other disadvantages, tends to throw the moderates into the arms of the extremists. It is purely a punitive, almost a defensive measure and fails to 'set at' [sic] the organization which we know is primarily responsible.'[482] The failure of the Special Military Area as a measure has been outlined by Michael Laffan in *The Resurrection of Ireland*, where he notes that even before any conscription crisis the police in West Cork faced a state of anarchy and had had to fortify their barracks.[483]

During the application of these Special Military Areas, the Irish Government began to come under public pressure and received petitions from towns in the Special Military Areas requesting an end to the measures, specifically those restricting local trade. Castletownbere suffered under the restrictions imposed and on 5 May 1919 local business interests petitioned the local military for an easing of the sanctions.

> We feel it incumbent on us to enter a strong protest against the fact that this Town should be victimised for a wanton attack on police in another parish, and with which the people of this district have no sympathy whatever. We maintain that if police and

people in other areas cannot agree, and as a result outrageous acts are committed, it is extremely hard, if not entirely unfair, that this Town should be penalised for such conduct. Moreover the people feel that they may be placed under military restrictions all their lives, if the acts of irresponsible parties in neighbouring parishes are to be continually served up as excuse to prevent them from following their everyday avocations.[484]

A petition from the Bantry branch of the Cork County and City Traders Association was sent to Edward Shortt, Chief Secretary, Colonel Owens, Military Commander of the Special Military Area, Colonel Frazer, OC of the Bantry District and District Inspector Cruise of the RIC, demanding an end to the economic restrictions imposed. The effects of the ban were detailed as follows:

We now wish to point out that the prohibition of Fairs presses with great severity, as times goes on. Fairs are being established in surrounding villages, to the detriment of the trade of this town. Farmers are unable to dispose of their surplus stock, hence they cannot pay their half-yearly accounts to the traders, or their half-yearly instalments to the Irish Land Commission, which falls due this month. The consequence is that trade in the town is at a standstill, artisans and all others are suffering from the same cause. One class, in particular, the industrious poor, who endeavour to keep a pig or two, cannot cart their pigs to outside Fairs, so have to sell at a loss to some local buyer and cannot replace them.[485]

This appeal was also supported by the local magistrates from the district in a letter sent to Ian McPherson.[486] Colonel Owens sent his views on the success of the Special Military Area to the Intelligence Officer at GHQ in Dublin in a letter dated 28 December 1918.

The inhabitants [are] now behaving themselves because the disloyal element are fully aware that if they don't, further restrictions will be imposed which will mean pecuniary loss, and touching their pockets is the most effective form of punishment for the many lawless acts committed in this West Riding. I have very carefully gone into the question of restrictions with the County Inspector, Royal Irish Constabulary, and while admitting that there is a most marked improvement in the state of the County Cork [West Riding], I consider the time has not yet arrived when I can with any degree of confidence recommend any modification of those now in force.[487]

The request by the Bantry traders for an ease in the restrictions was turned down by the office of the Chief Secretary on 31 December 1918.[488] This was no doubt seen by both the military and civilians as a punitive measure and as a reprisal for past deeds. Towards the end of January 1920, District Inspector Cruise wrote to Colonel Owens supporting the appeal of the magistrates for an easing of the restrictions on the town of Bantry:

I beg to state, I am of the opinion that the time has arrived when the restrictions may be relaxed and I recommend that the petition of the Magistrates be granted. The restrictions have had an excellent effect. There has been no serious occurrence in this district attributable to Sinn Fein since the military area was established. There is a marked difference in the attitude of the people to the police. Everybody – including the police – has learned the valuable lesson that wanton and brutal assaults on loyal men brings a widespread punishment.[489]

The restrictions were lifted on 17 February 1920. The Special Military Areas achieved little and only strengthened local resentments, and clearly demonstrated, as Townshend had said, that all these SMAs did was show that local leadership and authority rested with the gunmen rather than the traditional local leaders. However, the military were not the only authority capable of imposing economic restrictions on local communities; the IRA stopped a fair in Charleville in August 1920 because the locals had applied for a military permit.[490]

The Legal Foundations of Military Operations

The concept of population control and his past experiences were never very from Sir John French's mind, as his assessment of the difficulties in Ireland suggests: 'I can best describe the situation here as it presents itself to my mind as something in the nature of an incipient Boer War.'[491] In the same letter to the Chief Secretary, he pointed out that it was only the controls placed on Boer civilians that in the end turned the tide in South Africa, 'They remained unconquered until we wired them all up inside concentration camps. That is really how we won the Boer War and it is the only way we will settle the business over here.'[492] Many of these arguments had been rehearsed during the Boer War between the British generals and Cape Colony politicians, for example with Sir Richard Solomon the Attorney General for the colony resisting the authority of military courts, and even Lord Milner clashed with Lord Roberts over his insistence on use of civilian judges in military courts.[493] So when faced with Sinn Féin, French replayed the Boer context, ordering the organisation's suppression and that of other nationalist organisations in Cork, Limerick, Clare, Tipperary and Dublin in September 1919, under the Criminal Law Procedure (Ireland) Act, 1887.[494]

The legal foundation for the regulations enforced in Ireland was the Defence of the Realm Consolidation Act, 1915. DORA had been in force in Ireland since 24 April 1916 and was to last until 9 August 1920, when it was replaced by the Restoration of Order in Ireland Act. DORA gave the military considerable powers to deal with 'persons suspected of acting in a manner prejudicial to the public safety.'[495] It gave wide powers of search, interrogation and arrest, and allowed the military to control the civilian population. These measures were resented by the

Irish government, and led to conflict in that 'the Irish government claimed that every case was to be referred to them before determination.'[496] Demands for civilian control over military courts continued and even in the War of Independence, the British Army still faced cases in the civilian courts. Still, over time, the army tried more and more cases under DORA.

Trials under DORA in Ireland, 1916–1920

Year	Tried	Convicted	Percentage Convicted
1916	16	8	50%
1917	125	118	94%
1918	170	149	88%
1919	168	140	83%
1920	526	390	74%
Total	1005	805	80%

The above figures exclude 740 cases tried under ROIR in 1920. These figures show a significant rate of acquittal and in general a concern by military courts to secure a fair outcome.[497] This was in part due to the fact that the military were not exempt from public scrutiny. One of the key points to remember is that military courts were open to the public and the proceedings were extensively covered in the local media. Access by members of the general public to the courts made many British officers uncomfortable, as is evidenced by Lindsay-Young's statement on one such occasion. 'The court carried on with a fine audience filled with spies, and a general creepy feeling throughout the proceedings, that the court itself might become the subject of another inquiry into shooting.'[498] After the Wesleyan Raid, during the reporting of the trial of the men accused of killing Private Jones, all the military witnesses were identified, indeed a Lieutenant Thomas Lanyon was named as the KSLI's intelligence officer in court.[499] Even Major A.E. Percival's evidence in a case was reported in the *Cork Examiner* in July 1920.[500] One of the key problems for the British at the beginning of the campaign was this public identification of personnel, which, although part of the judicial process, certainly jeopardised their safety by making them clear targets for the IRA.

Tensions remained between the army and Dublin Castle over the prospect and later implementation of martial law, a fact acknowledged by the army in the *Record of the Rebellion*, which noted that one of the key factors 'operating against this [the adoption of martial law] was the reluctance of the Civil Government in Ireland to allow their function to devolve upon the Military authorities.'[501] So as Townshend pointed out, in the absence of the option of martial law the army decided to push DORA to the limits of its possible application.[502]

One of the problems in implementing a legal element to overall British strategy with regard to controlling the insurgency was how to deal with the IRA's use of hunger strikes to force the release of volunteers from prison. The military view of the government treatment of the hunger strikers in April 1920 can be seen in a correction to the *Record of the Rebellion in Ireland*, where the original sentence, 'The Government gave in' was replaced with 'and the Government decided to release them.'[503] Government attitudes towards the use of the hunger strike hardened in late 1920, with the *Cork Examiner* reporting David Lloyd George's comment that 'these men, all of whom are awaiting trial, were arrested either in the act of making murderous attacks upon police or soldiers, or upon direct and clear evidence or for other such serious offences.'[504] The IRA in Cork would have read Lloyd George's message that the government would not concede to hunger strikes in their local newspapers.

In an effort to avoid the declaration of martial law, the government introduced the Restoration of Order in Ireland Act. This act was designed to replace DORA and give the army greater legal powers to suppress the rebellion. The pressures this brought to the army were clearly detailed in the *Record of the Rebellion*, which notes that 'the effect of this measure was to transfer to the military authorities practically the whole administration of justice in Ireland.'[505] ROIA required the British Army to recruit extra officers to enforce it. Officers from the RFA and RGA were attached to infantry regiments to free officers from regimental duties. However, officers with both legal and military training were required to staff the court martial system. ROIA required the army to select officers for the military courts from 'a panel of commissioned officers who had been certified by the Lord Chief Justice of England or Lord Chancellor of Ireland as persons of legal knowledge and experience in accordance with Section 1 (2) (b) of the R.O.I.A.'[506] The difficulty lay in attracting qualified individuals, for while many solicitors and barristers had served in the First World War, there was little to encourage them to serve in Ireland.

Two new categories of post were created. The first post was that of legal officer; six were appointed by August 1920 and charged with 'generally supervis[ing] the work of formations.'[507] Secondly, specialist assistant legal officers and court martial officers were recruited. By the time of the Truce, over 57 officers had been recruited, of whom 6 were legal officers, 11 assistant legal officers, and 40 court-martial officers. The following table shows the deployment of these officers in the 6th Division area.

Distribution of Legal Officers in the 6th Division[508]

Formation	Legal Officers	Assistant Legal Officers	Court Martial Officers
6th Division HQ	1	1	3
16th Brigade	0	1	1
18th Brigade	0	1	2
Buttevant	0	0	2
Waterford	0	1	2

The model of the Boer War and the occupation of the Rhineland was clearly acknowledged in the *Record of the Rebellion,* which states that 'the proclamations issued were based on those issued in South Africa ... and those issued when the Army took over the British sector of the Rhine.'[509] The similarities to martial law in the Rhineland are obvious when one compares some of the declarations there in 1919 and those in Ireland in 1920.

One example is the fixing of occupant lists on the doors of buildings. In Germany these were 'fixed on the inside of the outer door of each inhabited building, a list stating the name, nationality, sex, age, and occupation of every person residing in the building.'[510] In Ireland, similarly, 'the owner, lessee or responsible occupier of every building shall have on the inside of the outer door of each inhabited building a list stating the name, sex, age, and occupation of every person residing in the building.'[511]

A further similarity between the codes was the ban on wireless telegraphy. In both cases it was almost identically worded, stating in Ireland that 'the use of Wireless Telegraphy is forbidden. Any person possessing apparatus for wireless telegraphy must inform the nearest Military or Police Officer, and hand it over at such time and place as may be appointed' and in Germany: 'the use of Wireless Telegraphy is forbidden. Any persons possessing apparatus for wireless telegraphy must inform the British Military Authorities and hand it over at such time and place as may be appointed.'[512] While some of the Rhineland regulations were directly transferred to the Irish context, it seems it was considered inadvisable to transfer others such as the requirement to respect all British officers by raising one's hat to them, and that all civilians remove their hats during the British anthem.[513] The British Army surely considered these last two a step too far.

As punitive as the regulations in Ireland may have seemed, the martial law regulations which the British imposed in Constantinople were far harsher. There, General Harington's application of martial law not only permitted the death penalty for warlike acts or possession of arms, but the execution of the occupants in a house from which an ambush was conducted for failing to provide information on the ambushers, or for damaging telephone equipment. Even Marshal Foch warned the civilian population on the entry of the Allied Army into Germany in 1918 that there would be no acceptance of any disobedience and that 'all breaches of Regulations which have been brought to the knowledge of the inhabitants, and all refusals to obey orders, will be severely punished.'[514]

Sheila Lawlor has noted that one of the key elements of general British policy in Ireland was to drive a wedge between moderates and extremists. This certainly informed the type of sanction imposed and the severity with which it was imposed. As we have seen in the Cork context, the various mechanisms used to influence the local population, from the implementation of various restrictions to the development of British propaganda, support this assessment.[515]

The Use of Curfews

Curfews, which the British Army deployed as a punitive measure throughout the twentieth century, were an attempt to control the streets at night and prevent any large scale public disorder, and were aimed primarily at the control of the general population, and only in a secondary sense as an attempt to disrupt IRA activities. As Thomas Mockaitis explains, curfews were 'designed to make the inhabitants of an area uncomfortable.'[516]

Curfews were often imposed in retaliation for some specific event; Strickland imposed a complete curfew in response to the so-called 'Battle for Cork' detailed above, conducted between the British Army and ex-servicemen. The order for this curfew was given under the Defence of the Realm regulations; it began on 21 July, running from 10pm to 3am.[517] The measure was universally unwelcome in Cork, with the *Irish Independent* commenting: 'It is no exaggeration to say that the new order will paralyse the life of the city.'[518] The *Cork Examiner* noted a month later that the 'usual "frightful" display of armed military ... entered the city at 10 o'clock in several motor lorries.'[519] The curfew patrols did not go unchallenged in Cork, and were regularly subject to attack, as least in the early days of its imposition.[520] In a published report on the curfew, Major Eastwood, the Brigade Major of the 17th Brigade, recorded that 'two bombs were thrown and several shots fired at a patrol in Patrick Street, at 23.20 hours. Fire was returned.'[521] These curfew reports by the British military became a regular feature in the local newspapers, designed to impress upon the local population the military's commitment to enforcing the curfew.

Offenders were brought to the Cork police court, where prior to and during the early stages of martial law, they were tried by the local magistrates, and mostly given fines ranging from one shilling to twenty shillings for breach of the curfew. A report in the *Cork Examiner* showed that many of those arrested had been out drinking. The paper noted that most were fined a shilling, but one man who made jokes about his appearance before the court, a Joseph MacCarthy, was fined five shillings.[522] Military evidence was required but this was often impossible to provide because through the pressure of duties many of the military witnesses were absent.[523]

Military dissatisfaction with the civilian magistrates led to the military assuming the judicial function with regard to the punishment of curfew offences. Commencing on 18 March 1921, officers in charge of curfew patrols were given authority to act as summary court officers. They could levy fines of up to £5 or sentence individuals to one month in prison, a far more serious level of punishment than had been meted out by the civil magistrates. In all, 55 officers acted as summary court officers in the 6th Division and dealt with over 2,296 cases, imposing 549 custodial sentences and accumulating fines of over £3,277.[524] These officers included the Cork curfew patrol officer, but were based throughout the Division area and handled a variety of cases besides curfew offences.

Failing to obey the curfew patrols in the streets carried far more serious consequences. In November 1920, a man named as Mulcahy was shot dead on Bachelors Quay near the North Gate Bridge in the city centre for failing to stop when ordered. On the night of this shooting however, matters had been tense in the city, with over twenty arrests on Shandon Street in the course of just a few hours.[525] The patrols were often a testing experience for the soldiers involved, as this account from the *Hampshire Regimental Journal* called 'Curfew in Cork' shows:

> As the cars thread their way through the streets each man glances sharply with his rifle always ready, at the hurrying pedestrians, most of whom, poor souls are making home as fast as their legs can carry them. Still it is necessary to be on the alert always and everywhere and the men have learnt to leave nothing to chance.[526]

The article also details how the patrols operated: 'The patrol moves in open formation, the men working in pairs, closely examining noisome alley-ways, dark entrances, and such like hiding places.'[527] All places an IRA man could be waiting with a revolver or a grenade.

One of the major problems that had to be dealt with in Cork during curfew was local civilian theft and looting. As the *Cork Examiner* put it, 'the burning of the business houses roused a desire to loot, and the worst sections of the population congregated in Patrick Street.'[528] Another problem was an increase in the burglary of commercial premises. Most of these crimes, such as the looting of several clothing and jewellery stores on 28 November 1920, were committed by locals.[529] The looting reached such a serious level that Strickland received a civic deputation asking for action, resulting in his promise to the commercial interests that looters would be shot on sight.[530] No objection was raised by the grandees of the city to this solution. Indeed matters reached such a state that the Bishop of Cork, Daniel Colohan, had to issue a public statement condemning civilian looting.[531]

The Employment of Martial Law

Proclamation No. 1 under martial law was that all weapons were to be handed over to government forces, and while the *Record of the Rebellion* notes that the response to this order was poor, still 'the first orders issued against the carrying of arms were considered to have demoralized the rebels, and for a month or two before the truce, it was seldom that anyone was found in possession of arms, unless captured during operations with a large force.'[532] The simple reason for this was it allowed anyone found with weapons to be treated as a rebel, on the assumption that any loyal person would have handed in his arms.

Another practice introduced under martial law in Ireland was the use of civilian hostages as protection against ambush. A public notice was displayed in Fermoy by

Brigadier-General Steele, the then acting commander of the 16th Infantry Brigade, to the effect that 'all motor lorries and vehicles in this area carrying His Majesty's troops will also carry one or more officers or leaders of the so-called "Irish Republican Army."'[533] The removal of these military notices by locals in Fermoy led to a £100 fine being levied on the Urban District Council.[534] The practice of hostage carrying spread nationwide, and the hostages used were not confined to the ranks of IRA supporters. In Dublin, a Colonel Moore, a former home ruler and former commanding officer of the 1st Battalion, Connaught Rangers, found himself on a truck.[535] The impact of this on transport security will be discussed in more detail in the following chapter, but this approach can be linked to another form of hostage use, that of the 'civic guards'.

One of the more damaging choices made by the British Army in Cork in terms of winning public support for the military campaign was the creation of these guards, a move which was largely seen by the public at large as nothing more than a crude form of hostage-taking. The principle was that local men, irrespective of any republican, nationalist or unionist connections, were selected and held accountable for any action by the IRA. *The Times* described the basic operation as follows: 'All the male population between the age of 17 and 50 in the towns of West Cork martial-law area are being required to form platoons of 18 members each, to act as civil guards in their respective area.'[536] These unfortunates were caught in an unenviable dilemma. They faced imprisonment by the British authorities for failing to provide information, or execution by the IRA if believed to be guilty of doing so. This dilemma was highlighted in the *Manchester Guardian*, which under the headline 'Forced Service under Martial Law' informed its readership that 'the Irish gunmen ... will wreak their vengeance upon the members of the guard, who will be suspected of informing on their movements.'[537] It even became the subject of a critical cartoon by David Low (see picture section, page 9).

This was a practice employed by several regiments. On 27 January 1921 men in Waterfall were told by Captain Vining of the Manchester Regiment that they would be held accountable for all future IRA actions in the area.[538] The problem with this approach was not publicly acknowledged by the army, but these guards were eventually allowed to disperse quietly, owing both to the hostility of public opinion in Ireland and England, and the lack of any real military utility in the continuation of the scheme.

One of the most significant pressures exerted on the IRA by DORA and martial law was internment, a direct targeting of the human infrastructure of the IRA. Hart has described this as 'the first hint of a British counter-insurgency strategy', in that 'a plan was drawn up to systematically deport and intern dangerous persons.'[539] There was some confusion at the start as to who could be arrested under this scheme, as Strickland noted in his diary. He was given the broadest terms from GHQ: 'We can now arrest after an outrage anyone near the place who is associated with the I.V. [Irish Volunteers] even those not suspected of complicity in the outrage.'[540] Strickland duly ordered the arrests. Laffan has shown that by the time of the Truce, the British had interned 19 brigade commanders, 90 battalion commanders and over 1,600 company officers.[541] Hopkinson notes that by July 1921 there were only 2,500 active members of the IRA as opposed to over 4,500 interned members.[542] Macready summed up the situation: 'In the Martial Law area, the arrest and internment of officers of the Irish Republican Army has dislocated the organisation of the rebels and Sinn Fein Courts have become inoperative.'[543]

Legal difficulties persisted throughout the whole period of martial law, both within the military and externally in relation to the civilian courts. Despite the fact that 'all writs of habeas corpus, certeriorari, mandamus, prohibition, quo warranto, and other writs directed against the Military Authorities' were to be suspended for the duration of martial law, Strickland was served with a writ for damages after one official reprisal.[544] Incidents like this led to frustration on Macready's part, and he complained to Henry Wilson, saying 'I must point out that the actual enforcement of Martial Law in Munster is by no means the Martial Law that is understood by military men.'[545] He meant that the army did not control the police or have full administrative control of Munster, in that they were never fully free from civilian oversight.

Other martial law regulations aimed to limit the mobility of the IRA, such as removing bicycles, which may seem strange to modern readers but was very effective. Targeting insurgent mobility is the foundation upon which the ultimate goal of disrupting supplies and communication is built, as in Vietnam in the 1960s when Sir Robert Thompson described an encounter with an American officer in Vietnam: 'One of them even proudly proclaimed to me on one visit that he had captured three hundred bicycles yesterday! This time he had the strategy correct. Those three hundred bicycles were a very important supply element to the other side.'[546] (A tactical triumph perhaps, though we know what happened in the end.)

Some officers who served in Ireland seemed to have forgotten this important restriction on bicycles in their memoirs; Major Dening notes that 'In Ireland, a restriction was placed upon the movement of all motor vehicles and an extension of these restrictions to bicycles would certainly have affected the mobility of the rebels.'[547] Despite the gap in Dening's memory, the prohibition on the use of bicycles was enforced and the penalties could be severe. Eleven men arrested by the Manchester Regiment in May for cycling near Ballincollig were all sentenced to six weeks hard labour.[548] In recognition of the particular difficulties posed by the urban element of the war, and in an attempt to prevent ambushes, loitering on the street was also declared a criminal offence under martial law. This was a source of some public resentment and was 'looked upon as another injustice aimed at a time-honoured recreation of the Irish people.'[549] Still, as the authors of the *Record of the Rebellion* noted, it reduced the number of ambushes and saved soldiers' lives.

The requirement for householders to display a list of occupants was also regarded as a successful measure in the Irish context, as it hugely increased the difficulties for IRA men on the run, by 'prevent[ing] many of them from sleeping in houses and [driving] them to unhealthy and vermin infested dug-outs,' dug-outs which were meanwhile being identified by British aerial reconnaissance, and the numbers of which were thus being steadily reduced.[550]

Official and Unofficial Reprisals

The term 'official reprisal' is often used in the histories of the Irish War of Independence. This form of reprisal has been mistakenly linked in Irish popular memories of the war, and in much of the historiography since to the unofficial acts of soldiers who punished towns and villages after the deaths of their companions. Official reprisals, which dated from January 1921 were different and are actually a constant thread in British military policy of the period – the concept of collective punishment.[551]

Given the statements of many of the senior British figures at the time the link made between unofficial and official reprisals is unsurprising. For example, during an interview with a representative of the Associate Press of America in 1920, General Macready denied that the government endorsed any policy of reprisal, but did acknowledge that such a policy might be required if the IRA campaign continued. However, with regard to his position on unofficial reprisals, he concluded that when men felt 'there was no certain means of punishment ... it is only human that they should act on their own initiative.'[552] Macready went on to explain and even excuse RIC reprisals:

> Formerly, in Ireland, if a police officer were murdered there was no thought of direct reprisals in the minds of the RIC. They thought only of justice, confident that they would be dealt with quickly and adequately by the courts. But now the machinery of the law having been broken down, they feel there is no certain means of redress and punishment, and it is only human that they should act on their own initiative.[553]

In this, Macready seems to have had the support of David Lloyd George, whose toleration of the army and RIC reprisals was clearly spelled out in a speech in Carnarvon on 10 October 1920 in which he listed the extent of attacks on the police, and complimented their restraint over the past two years. He then stated: 'There was no great doubt that at last their patience had given way, and that there had been some severe hitting back.'[554] He noted that while IRA murders had been ongoing, Sinn Féin had remained silent, and used the excuse that a war was being waged. Then to the approval of the Welsh crowd who were listening to him, he asked: 'Were the police to be shot down like dogs in the streets without any attempt to defend themselves?'[555] These views were also supported in London by the foreign secretary, Lord Curzon, who believed methods used in India could be applied in Ireland with positive results and that 'troublesome towns and villages could be punished with progressive fines and even whole districts blockaded by British Forces.'[556] This perspective, however, did not take into account the failure of the special military areas, the enormous manpower required to blockade areas or the international and British public reaction likely to result from this approach.

Taking all this into account, when Wilson applied in November 1920 for permission to conduct official reprisals, the 'substitution of regular, authorised and legalised reprisals for the unauthorised reprisals by the police and soldiers,' he was likely preaching to the converted.[557] Strangely, despite the government's eventual acceptance of official reprisals, the *Irish Times* reported that the official reprisals in Midleton on 1 January 1921 had come as a surprise to the government as Strickland had not consulted them. But, the paper noted, despite his failure to inform the government, Strickland would still receive Cabinet support.[558] This seems a rather feeble washing of the hands after the act. Equally feeble was the claim that this policy of official reprisals was designed to prevent unofficial reprisals, since the last serious outbreak by soldiers had been close to three months prior to Wilson's application. Soldiers had been punished for the Mallow outbreak in late 1920 and the example made of them had resonated in the 6th Division. Reprisals continued by members of the RIC and Auxiliaries, notably the burning of Cork in November 1920, yet attempts to correct the problem within the police were never as effective as within the army. As Michael Hopkinson has pointed out, 'blame for the reprisals should be applied less to the Black and Tans and Auxiliaries than to the politicians who set them up without a disciplinary code and clear definition of purpose.'[559] However, as the generals had ended unofficial reprisals by the soldiers in Cork, the responsibility of continuing police reprisals must fall on Tudor and Crozier.

So from January 1921, this policy of official reprisal really seems to have been pursued in an attempt to place pressure on the local population to cooperate with the British Army, but perhaps even more as an attempt to punish senior republican supporters. In Midleton on 1 January 1921, seven houses were burnt down.[560] *The Times* reported that the 'burnings have caused consternation in the district and have brought home to civilians that they will not be allowed to observe an attitude of neutrality.'[561] This view echoed that of the British Army, who, in a public notice printed in the *Irish Independent* warned that 'persons must remember that an attitude of neutrality is inconsistent with loyalty and will render them punishable.'[562] While the public line of these official reprisals at the time was that it was a punishment imposed on general members of the public for the failure to cooperate, a closer examination reveals something quite different. The official reason given for the Midleton reprisal was the failure to provide advance intelligence of an ambush.[563] Most of the buildings demolished were occupied or owned by members of the IRA or Sinn Féin; Edmund Carey was a Sinn Féin magistrate, as was Paul MacCarthy, while John O'Shea was an IRA officer.[564] Carey was also the chairman of Midleton UDC, and O'Shea was chairman of the Poor Law Guardians.[565]

Another official reprisal conducted on 1 April 1921 in the Macroom area destroyed the houses of Daniel Corkery and C. Kelleher, both IRA officers. Evidence of this deliberate policy of targeting members of Sinn Féin and the IRA can be found in some of the British source material, such as the *Hampshire Regimental Journal* which, when commenting on a reprisal in May, noted that 'as a further punishment three houses of disaffected persons were blown up on the 24th.'[566] The journal joked: 'It is a good thing that only a few of the disaffected are treated in this way, for otherwise there would soon be a most serious housing shortage in this country.'[567] It also described the earlier events as 'a punitive expedition to Middleton to discourage the indiscriminate shooting of policemen in that neighbourhood.'[568] Further evidence concerning the real nature of official reprisals in May 1921 was provided by the army itself in the *Cork Examiner*, when they acknowledged that the houses of Patrick Hegarty and William Connell of Castlemartyr were destroyed 'on the grounds that their owners are supporters of armed rebels.'[569]

The claim that official reprisals specifically targeted members of the republican movement was also made by an IRA member, Sean O'Donoghue, who witnessed the destruction of houses at Dillon's Cross on the north side of Cork city: 'Finally, British war tanks recently transported from the battlefields of Flanders were brought into action, and, in the name of "official reprisals", the houses of prominent IRA men and sympathisers were demolished.'[570] The tanks were not as robust as they appeared to be, with the *Hampshire Regimental Journal* noting that while 'the tanks efforts were successful … they both suffered somewhat in the battle and one had to stay out for three days.'[571] The idea that official reprisals targeted republican politicians and volunteers is supported by Marie Coleman's work on Longford, when she notes that 'the majority of the damage done in this way was to the property of those associated in some way with the Independence movement'[572] The psychological pressure this caused to IRA members was considerable, with Hart noting that even years later, the loss of their homes and the suffering of their families remained by far the worst memories for most IRA veterans.[573]

In the end, the policy of official reprisals was dropped, primarily as pointed out by Thomas Mockaitis, because these actions were far more damaging to British prestige than any unofficial reprisal.[574] The tactic was dropped despite the pressure the policy was obviously putting on senior members of the IRA, exposing them as individuals who despite their claims that they too were members of an army could not even protect their own homes. The end of the policy could have been yet another source of conflict between the army and British politicians, but no trace of resentment regarding the stopping of official reprisals can really be found in British documents. Perhaps this is because many officers took the view of Colonel Cameron of the 16th Brigade who was able to reconcile himself to the termination of reprisal: 'I do think that this decision by the Cabinet has been arrived at because of the vapouring of some insignificant member of the House of Commons. I believe it to have been largely due to His Majesty's influence, so in that case we can all be perfectly happy about the decision.'[575] While the destruction of property entailed in official reprisals was very understandably a source of popular grievance, things could have been much worse; Sir Henry Wilson had argued for more extreme reprisals in October 1920, arguing that 'the obvious course of action would be to at once arrest the principal members of the IRA in a town or village, and give them twenty-four hours to produce the murderer on pain of being shot themselves.'[576] However, this was largely venting and he did acknowledge in the same correspondence with Winston Churchill that such a course of action would not be possible because of the outrage such a measure would provoke in Britain and internationally.

Executions

The severest sanction under martial law was the death penalty. The first such execution in Cork took place on 1 February 1921. The volunteer Con Murphy had been captured on 4 January and convicted for possession of arms.[577] The policy of executions led to a severe reaction from the IRA. After the capture of IRA volunteers at Dripsey, the IRA were determined to prevent further deaths, and kidnapped a Mrs Lindsey, who had carried the information about the ambush to the army, intelligence which had incidentally been given to her by the local priest. The seizure of Mrs Lindsay, a close personal friend of Strickland, placed him under what one can only imagine was extraordinary emotional pressure. He had visited her house many times, and she his. In a note directly addressed to him, Mrs Lindsay wrote:

> I have just heard that some of the prisoners taken at Dripsey are to be executed. I write to beg that you will use your influence to prevent this taking place. I have just been told that it will be a very serious matter for me if they are executed. My life will be forfeited for theirs. As they believe I am the direct cause of their capture. I implore you to spare these men for <u>my sake.</u>[578]

Her last note to Strickland contained a final plea which, if granted, would mean that, 'I shall be allowed to go home and if not I cannot say what shall be my fate.'[579] The men were not released and Mrs Lindsay was killed.

This was not the only major consequence of the Dripsey captures. One of the most interesting internal British conflicts of the campaign was conducted over the application of the death penalty in the case of these captured IRA men.

The central actors in this drama were Macready and the Judge Advocate General of the British Army, Sir Felix Cassel. In January 1921 Cassel requested that all death penalty cases in Ireland be supervised by his office, as 'death sentences stand upon a wholly different footing from all others as in the case of these sentences if carried out no injustice can be remedied upon review.'[580] Cassel pointed out that review by the Judge Advocate General had been standard practice during the First World War. This minute to Sir George Macdonagh, the Adjutant General, was prompted by a communication from Macready dated 9 January, which rejected any role for Cassel in Ireland, stating that he was 'not required to submit' to the Judge Advocate General's advice or interference.[581] Macready demanded that the IRA men captured at Drispey be executed immediately. A minute from Macdonogh's own staff advising him on the matter noted that the 'decision in this case really is out of the hands of the Army Council, as the J.A.G. holds his Letters Patent direct from the King,' phrasing which suggests that Cassel's dismissal may have been contemplated.[582] Macdonogh's staff noted 'we are impotent to override him [Cassel] if we so desired.'[583] They offered another option; if the Prime Minister was not consulted on the death penalties, then Macready could do as he wished, however if the matter reached Lloyd George, then he would be obliged to accept Cassel's position, a position which could be said to follow the letter but not the spirit of the law. Cassel had written directly to Macready on 15 January and outlined his key concern that the legality of the death sentences depended wholly on the judgment that would be given in the Allen case, and advised Macready to wait for this judgment.[584] Cassel seems to have attempted to placate Macready's hostility by saying 'the findings of the [military] Court and the sentences were according to law.'[585] However, Cassel may have written this because he had not been given the full details of the court martial, and in further correspondence, namely in a letter to Sir Laming Worthington Evans, Churchill's replacement at the War Office, he clearly stated that the sentences imposed

> ...cannot be justified as sentences of a court-martial under the Restoration of Order in Ireland Act 1920 on the following grounds: (a) There was no member of the court nominated by the Lord Lieutenant as required by Section 1 (2) (b) of the Restoration of Order in Ireland Act, 1920. (b) There was no investigation or determination by a competent military authority as required by the Regulation 68 of the Restoration of Order in Ireland Regulations. (c) The accused were treated as competent witnesses contrary to Section 1(5) of the Restoration of Order in Ireland Act 1920.[586]

This strong rebuttal of Macready's position was prompted by the latter's continuing insistence that he did not have to wait for any judgement in the Allen case, that the Allen case could continue indefinitely and make martial law a farce, that the IRA men had been 'levying war against the King', and that he was 'at a loss to understand on what legal grounds I should not put the sentences into execution.'[587] This argument rumbled on, all related correspondence now being directed through Sir George Macdonogh's office, with Cassel now insisting that the judgment of the Allen case had been made critical to the legality of the executions by Macready's own actions:

> The Commander in Chief had in effect submitted himself to the jurisdiction of the High Courts by filing an affidavit … if the Commander in Chief wished to carry out the sentences regardless of law and of the court to whose jurisdiction he had submitted he should not have asked for my legal opinion.[588]

Despite all the arguments, Macready waited until the Allen judgement, in which the High Court found in his favour, and indeed cited his affidavit as fundamental to their decision. The High Court found that it had 'no power to interfere with a finding of a military court while war was being waged.'[589] As the *Record of the Rebellion* put it, 'the civil courts could not control the Military Authorities "durante bello".'[590] Despite Cassell's concerns regarding the validity of their conviction, the men were executed on 28 February.[591] Four more IRA volunteers captured at Clonmult were executed on 28 April, their trial in March having lasted only eight days.[592] By May 1921, with the introduction of drum-head court martials, the process was even faster. Patrick Casey, an IRA volunteer captured in the ambush at Kildorrey, was tried on 2 May 1921 and executed the following day.[593] A second IRA volunteer, Daniel O'Brien of Liscarroll, was captured on 11 May, tried on 15 May and executed on 16 May.[594] With the institution of these drum-head court martials, Henry Wilson seems to have got what he wanted the preceding December. In the case of individuals involved in the carrying of arms and the killing of soldiers and civilians he had said: 'Both these offences, in my judgment should be dealt with by putting the men up against a wall and shooting them.'[595]

The Development of a Propaganda Machine

Examining many of the traditional histories of the war, one might imagine that any British propaganda campaign was doomed to failure from the start. However, many members of the IRA were all too aware of the fragile nature of their support from the general Irish population. To Patrick Ahern, an attack on a Sinn Féin parade in Fermoy in May 1917 was indicative of 'the outlook and mentality of the people of Fermoy at this time'.[596] Many IRA men like Dick Cotter believed that most of the Irish population supported the British Army, noting that it was 'a very difficult job collecting the arms levy around Ballincollig as the majority were on the enemy side.'[597] This lack of support has been noted by historians such as Richard English, when he points out 'that many nationalists did not support the killing and maiming which the republican army practised', and Marie Coleman who points out that in Longford many areas were hostile to the republican movement.[598] Michael Laffan's view that the British officers had an overly simplistic view of the republican movement, seeing it as encompassing almost all the indigenous population, is to some extent true but it requires qualification. The army had divided up the republican support base into various groups based on their support for violence, and most if not many officers would have concurred with Laffan's own view that 'only a small minority of the population was active in its hostility to British rule.'[599] The army accepted that the most of the population was indifferent or waiting on the outcome of the conflict.

The volume of the *Record of the Rebellion* dealing specifically with the use of legal measures during the insurgency states that under DORA, certain newspapers had been suppressed, namely the *Westmeath Independent, Mayo News, Weekly Observer, Cork Free Press* and the *Freemans Journal*. However no application was made under ROIR for any action against newspapers during the War of Independence.[600] Despite repeated calls from army officers to establish some form of control and system of censorship over the Irish press, these were effectively resisted by British administration in Dublin and by British politicians, who feared the negative consequences of any such action, namely the reaction of the British and international media.

This protection of the press was not unwelcome in British military circles. Foulkes, the director of British propaganda, strongly argued against censoring newspapers: '[W]e might even go so far as to forego censorship: we only want the truth to be known, and are not afraid of its publication.'[601] He continued in his note on the production of a weekly intelligence summary that 'we would gain greater advantage by the forced publication of our own communiqués in papers which are read by all the hostile elements in Ireland than by suppressing these papers.'[602] Even Macready courted the Irish press, inviting members of the media to meet him in August 1920, and 'explain[ing] to them that in future they would be given the facts about any events in which the troops were concerned.'[603] A press section of the General Staff was set up, the primary functions of which were to liaise with the press, issue press releases and contradict inaccurate reports. The goal was to build a working relationship with the press and ensure, from the army's perspective, more balanced media coverage. The army believed that this approach worked and that 'the Press welcomed this section and made considerable use of it.'[604]

Foulkes was aware of the delicate nature of propaganda and the focus and scrutiny to which any army statement would be subjected, and stated that the '1st axiom [was that] only truthful statements must be made' because 'misrepresentation in time brings its own refutation and causes harm.'[605] Foulkes was clear from the outset that if the *Irish Bulletin* was to be counteracted, the highest standard of work would have to apply since 'it should be noted that the truth is not generally regarded as propaganda, whereas it is the real propaganda.'[606] Like good news coverage, 'the rapid receipt of information is a matter of very great importance to a department which must compete successfully against private journalistic enterprise.'[607] In one of his notes dealing with the production of a weekly intelligence summary, he advocated the employment of professional journalists in the Propaganda Department. These individuals were to work on the creation of a new journal, *Irish Intelligence*, the distribution of which in the United Kingdom and further afield would target public figures such as politicians and ambassadors. Despite the sophistication of his views on the goal, creation and distribution of propaganda, his views on the IRA volunteers were crude and misinformed. He saw 'their chief characteristics [as] ignorance, emotionalism, credulity, and unquestioning obedience to the Roman Catholic Church.'[608] Given the continuation of the war by the IRA in the face of excommunication, this view hardly reflected the complexity of the situation in Ireland.

Critical to success, according to Foulkes, was the alteration of existing beliefs which were 'not good from the view of public,' by which he meant of course the British public.[609] The army must work to 'remove the impression that Ireland has been harshly governed, but show that England has done a great deal for her' and 'emphasise that the country is being ruined by the disorder.'[610] Foulkes again addressed the goal of any propaganda campaign in Ireland in 'Some Special points as regards Propaganda in Ireland' where he held that the Government must 'propaganda [sic] the population so as to show them what THEY should do to help us put matters to rights.'[611]

In Foulkes' view, the public perception of the IRA had also to be destroyed, and the army must 'show that they are a gang of terrorists, that they are a murder gang; compare them to Lenin and Trotsky.'[612] This was a perspective that had some currency in Ireland, as one senior home ruler, Stephen Gwynn had previously noted, saying 'Sinn Féin is becoming increasing Bolshevist.'[613] It was also important in Foulkes' view to emphasise that 'the IRA gallant deeds are done miles away from any offensive fighting body in almost every case. Their actions are not honourable, they are treacherous and mean, murders of old men and women, theft, arson, etc.'[614] One of the key elements of British propaganda was, therefore, to undermine the IRA as a military force in the eyes of both the Irish population and amongst its own rank and file, sowing the seeds of distrust. Foulkes believed that the key way to influence the IRA foot soldiers was to point out that their actions were contrary to church teaching, that no help was coming from America and that the goal of the IRA, an Irish republic, was impossible to attain.[615] The principal means of doing this would be the distribution of pamphlets by air-drop and by British Army patrols who would hand out leaflets in the street. He would target the IRA rank and file who were 'to be found amongst the farm hands all over the country, and the shop assistants in the villages and towns.'[616]

Foulkes had already conducted a limited propaganda operation in Fermoy during 1920, where he had organised several others to assist him in countering local news stories, his greatest success being an article in the *Morning Post* concerning the 'Sinn Fein War on Women'.[617] Now, in Dublin, he was frustrated at the level of cooperation from the various brigades and divisions, noting that 'only two suitable newspaper articles have been sent in (from the 16th Brigade) and I have had only one voluntary contradiction of *An t-Óglach* (from the 6th Division).'[618] It is interesting to note it was only officers from the 6th Division who forwarded material to Foulkes, but the goal of British propaganda in Ireland was clear: 'to destroy the morale of the so-called IRA.'[619]

Religion, Economics and the Rules of Engagement

The idea that propaganda should play on the religious convictions of volunteers is evident in the pamphlet *To the Irish Republican Army* in which Foulkes quoted Cardinal Logue, who 'has said "it is an act of murder – no-one need tell me to the contrary – to lie behind a wall, and if a policeman goes for an ounce of tobacco to shoot him."' The pamphlet repeated the decree of ex-communication by the Bishop of Cork, and quoted the bishop as saying 'the resolution of DAIL EIREANN is not sufficient to constitute Ireland a Republic according to the teaching of the Church.' The final ploy of the pamphlet was to couch the choice facing the IRA volunteer in the following terms: 'You must choose between those you have always revered and the extremists who care nothing for the church.'[620] This represents a rather naïve view of the importance of religion in the lives of the IRA, most of them evidently caring little about their excommunication, but it may have struck a chord with a few. The issue of possible (or, as the propaganda would have it, impossible) American support was addressed in the pamphlet *U.S. and Ireland*, which quoted US Secretary of State Hayes as saying 'Great Britain is a friendly power, and we have no right to meddle in her internal affairs.' The warning that followed was clear 'Washington will not meddle, Berlin cannot. Will you trust in Moscow?'[621]

As this mention of Moscow suggests, one of the goals of British propaganda was to establish in the minds of IRA volunteers and of the general population a correlation between republicanism and communism, as in the comparison of IRA leaders with Lenin and Trotsky above. This was followed through in the pamphlets *Irishmen* and *The Farmer's Peril*, both directed at the farming community. In *Irishmen*, farmers were warned that 'the extremist leaders are negotiating with the Bolsheviks who have abolished all rights to private property,' and ended with the warning that it was the Irish farmer who would suffer under any future government.[622] *The Farmer's Peril* contained an even starker warning: 'The forces of assassination, allied with the Bolshevists, are destroying your prosperity, and they will nationalise your land.'[623] The conduct of the IRA campaign also provided the British Army with opportunities to exploit the division and discontent growing in the farming community. As the RIC county inspector based in Mallow wrote, 'The cutting of roads, and the blowing up of bridges has seriously damaged the wellbeing of the farmer who is beginning to speak, and the closing of the creameries by the Military Governor is having an excellent effect.'[624] J.J. Lee noted, 'farmer support for separatism was very conditional,' and Stephen Gwynn, a member of the Home Rule Party wrote that 'there is a "middle public", including vast numbers of businessmen perfectly prepared to accept the status of self-governing dominion.'[625] The economic consequences of these closures must have had an impact on all members of the rural economy, from substantial farmers to farm labourers.

The pamphlets also played on rural class conflicts between volunteers and members of the farming community. As one IRA report noted, 'the volunteer movement was ridiculed by farmer's sons in this area. The movement was good enough for the labouring class but beneath them.'[626] This sophisticated targeting of the pamphlets – which were carefully tailored to speak to the fears of specific audience groups – suggests that the British were far more nuanced in their analysis of the Irish population than has previously been believed. This resulted in differentiated propaganda, but which still retained some stereotypical notions of the Irish in general.

Another theme which ran through many of the pamphlets was the idea of abandonment, the suggestion that once the war failed the senior members of Sinn Féin would run and leave the rank and file behind to face a British victory: 'If you support them, and they should succeed in escaping from Ireland and from Justice, BE SURE THAT THEY WILL LEAVE YOU TO YOUR FATE.'[627] The implicit threat was that continued loyalty to the IRA would not be forgiven after the inevitable British victory. Another attempt to undermine IRA leadership can be found in the pamphlet *To the Members of the IRA*. Its purpose was clear, 'Read this and if you still decide to be led astray by your leaders in the belief that you are a "soldier" and entitled to be treated as soldiers, you have only yourself to blame.' The pamphlet then gave a brief lesson on the rules of war, and particularly the Hague Conventions with regard to the obligation to wear a uniform and carry arms openly. In one of the very few references in British military documents acknowledging the presence of significant numbers of ex-servicemen in the IRA, it asked volunteers to seek confirmation of this from the ex-servicemen in their ranks. Another pamphlet advised the IRA that these rules were not drafted just by the British, but by all civilised nations, 'in order that war between white men should be carried out in a sportsmanlike manner.'[628]

Another pamphlet, *The An T'Olgac* [sic] *Lie System*, again sought to erode the confidence of the rank and file in the leadership of the IRA. It quoted a copy of *An t'Ólgach* dated 20 May 1921, which said that 'the enemy had 7 killed (including an officer, a sergeant-major, and 2 R.I.C sergeants, and 22 wounded, 18 soldiers, 3 R.I.C., and a marine.' The pamphlet refuted these figures stating that only one RIC sergeant had been killed, and one sergeant and one private of the Royal Scots wounded.[629] Again it is important to remember that these pamphlets were dropped from the air and read by the general public.

No opportunity was missed to place the responsibility for the continuation of the conflict squarely on the shoulders of the IRA. Even the declaration of martial law was indirectly blamed on the insurgents, the propaganda claiming 'Great Britain has no quarrel with Irishmen; her sole quarrel is with crime, outrage, and disorder; her sole object in declaring MARTIAL LAW is to restore peace to a distracted and unhappy country.'[630]

The Impact and Importance of Propaganda

Not all British propaganda emanated from official sources. Soldiers were encouraged to write and ask friends and family in the United Kingdom to explain to others the difficulties and hardships that they faced in Ireland, as in the *Lilywhites Gazette*, in which soldiers were reminded that 'our old friends of the regiment can do much in spreading the truth so skilfully turned aside by our lying enemy.'[631] The *Hampshire Regimental Journal* printed an article called 'The War in Ireland', which was written 'to give readers of the Journal an idea of the enemy who opposes the troops,' describing the IRA as 'a past master in the more cowardly form of assassination' and comparing the members of the IRA flying columns to 'savage wild beasts.'[632]

It is difficult to assess the overall impact of the work of Foulkes and others on the Irish population and the IRA, as little material remains that would allow an accurate assessment of how or whether it altered their views. One can probably safely assume that some of the considerable and not unsubtle material produced must have had an effect on some. Whatever its effect, the propaganda should be seen as part of the overall attempt by the British government to impose and maintain pressure on the republican movement to force an agreed settlement.

An examination of British military propaganda contradicts the opinion of some historians such as Paul McMahon when he asserts that 'rather than adopt a surgical approach that might separate extremist from moderate, they use the bluntest of instruments based on nothing more sophisticated than possession of superior force.'[633] The evidence above indicates that this is not the case. The campaign ended before the full effects or promise of British propaganda could be realised, nevertheless 'it was the sort of machinery employed during the Malayan Emergency 30 years later.'[634]

'Rigorous Law is often Rigorous Injustice'

The accurate assessment of the use of law in Cork during the war remains problematic – and Terence's observation has some relevance. It was used as a substitute for a crumbling civilian system, but also as a means of imposing strict controls on the local population, with the ultimate intention of forcing them to align themselves with the British Army. However, aspects of this approach were manifestly unsuccessful, such as special military areas and the use of civic guards. But the pressure of martial law, including restrictions such as curfews, permits for motor vehicles, lists on house doors and the prohibition of bicycles, must have created a psychological burden on the local population that made them want to see an end to the campaign. It is likely that some of these restrictions led the commercial and agricultural classes to provide greater information to the British Forces in the hope that, in exchange, what they saw as draconian economic sanctions would be lifted.

There was a complex relationship between official and unofficial reprisals by the British Army and others, and unofficial reprisals by members of the army had stopped long before the introduction of official reprisals. Although it was claimed that the official reprisals were designed to placate troops and punish members of the public for failure to cooperate with the army, they were clearly aimed at senior Sinn Féin politicians and IRA officers, since the greater part of the property destroyed belonged to these two groups. In short, this policy was a focused punishment of senior republicans and can be seen as a sustained attempt to undermine republican morale. The same can be argued of the executions. Despite early difficulties in the implementation of this strategy, by May drum-head court-martials were being widely used, and anyone reading the various newspapers in Cork at the time would have been aware that any captured IRA member could be tried and executed within two days, which put huge pressure on the IRA. Nevertheless, problems remained, and the legal elements of the campaign in particular needed refinement. The British Army recognised 'that the legal procedure was too slow and cumbrous to be really effective against a whole population in rebellion.'[635]

With regard to propaganda, the British began late, but managed to create a formidable machine, albeit one which was only a few months old by the time of the Truce. It had analysed its audience carefully although not always correctly, and identified specific social groups to target. It developed themes which directly addressed the fears of these elements of Irish society in order to undermine support for the republican cause. This military and legal pressure was supported by an increasingly effective propaganda campaign from the Crown forces, reaching all corners of Cork through the RAF leaflet drops. The propaganda campaign had been carefully thought out, and targeted two key groups, in particular the IRA rank and file and local commercial and agricultural interests. These leaflets sought to undermine the volunteers' faith in the republican leadership and highlighted the opposition of the Church to the IRA campaign. They also sought also to undermine the information being provided by *An t-Óglach* by contrasting its accounts of ambushes with official reports. British propaganda also tried to link Sinn Féin and the newly emerging Communist regime in Russia, and thereby create fears in the business community regarding their property and profits. As Thomas Mockaitis points out, there is an alternative government strategy to 'hearts and minds'; a government can 'make the cost of continuing a struggle too high.'[636]

No document remains which reveals a grand strategy combining the elements of intelligence, law, propaganda and active military operations. However, all the disparate operations directed against the IRA and its support base saw British intelligence targeting both the individual and the infrastructure of the IRA, reducing over time its ability to conduct a meaningful guerrilla campaign, and slowly reducing the effectiveness of the insurgency. The use of law as a means to break the will of the IRA and the local population to continue the campaign was critical. Internment and execution reduced the numbers of IRA volunteers the army faced on the ground, while ROIA gave it control over the general population, allowing it to use military courts to punish civilians for breaches of both civil and martial law. It also served to emphasise the army's very real authority, contrary to the claims of national sovereignty by the republican movement. Propaganda targeted different IRA resources by questioning their legitimacy and morale. All of these efforts show a coordinated approach.

Section Three

The Guerrilla War

'History was forged in sudden death on a Tipperary by-road as surely as it ever was in meetings at Downing Street.'
Nicholas Mansergh

'In Ireland, there was no defined objective, no front line; from the moment a soldier left his barrack gate, he was in what may be described as a mist of murder.'
General Sir Neville Macready

The War in Cork will perhaps forever be associated with the romantic image of the IRA flying columns, moving across the countryside, hotly pursued and hopelessly outnumbered. However, the campaign in Cork was more complex than that image suggests. This chapter focuses on hitherto neglected elements, and will show for instance that the British response to the military problems posed by the campaign was more sophisticated than has previously been considered. It will examine the impact of the improvements in logistics, the development of British active-service platoons and the deployment of air power in support of ground operations. It will also show how escalating British military pressure forced a reshaping of IRA strategy in Cork. The Crossbarry Ambush is a good case study to explore how the post-war mythologies have distorted both popular and academic understanding of the campaign.

Mansergh's statement concerning where history is made is certainly supported by the evidence from the Cork area during the War of Independence. History was indeed made in the county by-roads and hedgerows of Cork, and on the streets of Cork city, where many met sudden deaths or suffered wounds. This was a bitter war by any standards, fought without quarter, in which British soldiers, Irish volunteers and innocent bystanders all paid dearly.

Chapter Five

The Military Challenge
of the IRA

Violence against British soldiers began in Cork even before the Soloheadbeg Ambush of January 1919. In September 1918 alone, three separate incidents took place in Cork in which three soldiers were attacked and disarmed in Cobh on 8 September, a soldier's rifle was stolen in Cork on 11 September and two soldiers were attacked in Eyeries in West Cork on 18 September.[637]

In January 1919, two British soldiers, Privates Hardman and Perry of the 454th Protection Company of the Royal Defence Corps were attacked and shot at Monard Bridge near Blarney railway station, with the *Cork Weekly News* reporting that: 'The soldiers who were taken by surprise had not time to recover themselves, when a volley was fired which brought them to the ground.'[638] The IRA men used shotguns and the soldiers were severely wounded in the head and thigh. The 454th Protection Company had been camped in Blarney for some time and the attack was deeply unpopular in the area. The violence associated with this attack was atypical of these early clashes between the army and the IRA, but nevertheless the object of the assault remained the seizure of the soldiers' weapons.

The first fatal attack was on the Kings Shropshire Light Infantry in Fermoy in September 1919, and was consistent in tactical terms with the other early attacks: the soldiers were overwhelmed by surprise and superior numbers. Here again the prime intent of the IRA appears to have been the securing of rifles, more lethal attacks during this period being reserved for the RIC. This reality was not lost on the police, with the county inspector noting with regard to an attack on the police in West Cork that, while the earlier attack on soldiers near Blarney had met with popular disapproval, 'the entire sympathy of the community [now] seems to be with the criminal, their chief regret being that the police were not fatally injured.'[639] Attacks on police barracks were also 'by far the most popular form of rebel outrage' as the *Record of the Rebellion* put it, because of 'the small danger incurred by the attackers.'[640] However, the army still remained largely aloof from the conflict, feeling itself under-resourced and therefore reluctant to become engaged. As Townshend has pointed out, General Shaw felt in late 1919 that he had insufficient troops to be able to assist the police.[641]

Throughout 1919, individual or small groups of unarmed soldiers remained a focus of attacks by the IRA, though these encounters were no more than a nuisance to the army. They went no further than simple assaults in most cases, as in the attack on a member of the East Riding Regiment in September 1919, in the course of which the soldier's bicycle was destroyed.[642] An assault like this, resulting in the destruction of personal property, was still something of a rarity in 1919. Most of the attacks on British servicemen were attempts to seize their rifles, while the soldiers themselves were rarely harmed. Several incidents of this kind took place in 1919: five soldiers were disarmed in Macroom in West Cork on 26 January; another party in Macroom on 15 March; three more at Carrigaloe Railway Station in Cork Harbour on 12 October and another soldier in Macroom on 24 November. Private Jones, who had been killed during the Wesleyan Raid, remained the only military fatality in Cork in 1919.[643]

In a raid, similar to the Wesleyan Raid – which had taken place the previous September in Fermoy – a Private William Newman[644] of the Nottingham and Derbyshire Regiment was killed in Cobh on 27 February 1920.[645] Newman, who like Jones was a week from discharge, was only the second military death in Cork in the first fourteen months of the conflict, a fact which shows how small a military threat the IRA posed at this time to the army. The goal in the assault that killed Newman was the same as in Fermoy; the attackers were attempting to seize the men's weapons. In Private Henry Abrahams' testimony to the inquest:

> [When the picket got] level with the gas works lane, twenty armed men rushed out at them with revolvers. They told them to drop their rifles and put their hands up. The attackers formed a semi-circle around them, and presented their revolvers at them and grabbed their rifles.[646]

As with the Wesleyan Raid, there was considerable confusion over the purpose and nature of the IRA attack. The *Cork Constitution* initially reported that the raid had been an attempt to steal blasting explosives, which were commonly used in Rushbrooke Docks.[647] This was contradicted by Corporal Leslie Gooder, the commander of the patrol, who in his statement to the inquest testified that the patrol had no explosives. Gooder, however, did state clearly that Newman had been shot after they had all disarmed. Contradictions like this in the surviving evidence can make reconstructing the events difficult, although Gooder as the patrol commander is perhaps more reliable than the reports of a local newspaper. Newman's fatal mistake was that he attempted to escape, running in the direction of the docks.[648] Patrick Griffin, a local boilermaker working there, found Newman, 'sitting on the roadway near Rushbrooke Bridge, waving his right hand.'

All he could tell Griffin was that he had been shot.[649] Griffin, along with two RIC men, got him to the local Royal Army Medical Corps hospital. Anthony Carroll, the crown solicitor at the inquest, demanded that the jury, composed largely of prominent local businessmen, return a verdict of murder, reminding them that 'it could not be said that he was shot because he might shoot back as the rifle had been taken from him, and he had been simply trying to escape.'[650] As in the case of Fermoy, the jury did not return a verdict of murder, finding instead 'that Private William Newman of the 51st Sherwood Foresters, met his death as a result of a gunshot wound inflicted on him by some person or persons unknown at Rushbrooke.'[651] However, they did express their personal sympathy to Private Newman's brother who was at the inquest, perhaps seeking to distance themselves from a verdict that they felt obliged to render because of the fear of IRA reprisal, and also perhaps by British soldiers on Cobh.

The events surrounding Newman's death notwithstanding, these arms seizures were infrequent, localised and relatively unaggressive, and as such were largely treated little more than a nuisance by the army. However they continued to be the main problem that the Crown forces would experience from the IRA until the summer of 1920.

In short, the period up to the summer of 1920 can almost be regarded as a 'phoney war', declared but not prosecuted by either side, at least in terms of the IRA and the army. General Douglas Wimberley, then a captain in the Cameron Highlanders, described one of the last of these non-lethal attacks, which took place in Carrigtwohill on 5 June 1920.

> An unsuspecting rifle patrol, with their rifles stupidly clipped on to the side of their bicycles, were surrounded in a village street by a number of young men supposedly playing a game of hurly on the village green, a game akin to our shinty. They apparently made friendly remarks and gestures, and gradually closed in on the cyclists. A few seconds later, they had knocked the jocks of their bicycles with their hurlysticks and held up the men with revolvers.[652]

A report on this attack was printed in the *Cork Examiner*, which, although its description of what the attackers had been doing before the Highlanders' arrival deviates from that provided above, gave an excellent picture of IRA tactics during this period. The patrol of eleven Highlanders and one RIC constable

> …overtook a party of men bowl-playing on the road. The civilians, who numbered from fifty to sixty, ceased playing, when they saw the soldiers approaching, and stood aside, as if to make way for them to pass. The soldiers, suspecting nothing, rode on, but when they were well within the two files of the 'bowl-players' – one on either side of the road – they were suddenly pounced upon, pulled off their bicycles and disarmed. Five men took charge of each member of the patrol, so that resistance was out of the question.[653]

The attack on the Camerons took place at 9pm on a summer's night, and as reported in the *Irish Times*, 'the soldiers and policemen cycled leisurely and when they were in the middle of the crowd, the entire lot suddenly whipped out revolvers.'[654] Joseph Ahern, an IRA officer, provided a different account of the ambush, claiming that contrary to the accounts of Wimberley and the *Cork Examiner*, the Camerons were not pounced on but rather 'after a little parley, they agreed [to surrender], and came towards us with their hands up.'[655] Strickland was particularly unhappy with the performance of the Highlanders and noted in his diary that 'a crusade is required to impress on everyone how to act.'[656] Again the elements of deception, surprise and overwhelming numbers, so critical to IRA success in previous encounters, were present in this attack. Taking the rifles from a British military patrol this large demonstrated that the IRA were capable and organised, and started to make clear to the army that the insurgents were becoming a real problem, a group self-confident enough to challenge significant bodies of armed troops. The raid on the barracks in Mallow is another case in point; primarily a raid for arms rather than an attempt to seriously engage British forces, it resulted in the death of Sergeant Gibbs and the volunteers secured a valuable Hotchkiss machine gun, a weapon which proved to be of considerable value in later IRA operations.[657]

The summer of 1920 marked something of a transition from phoney to real war. The Camerons were to experience more ambushes in the following weeks, and it was in these that they began to suffer their first fatalities in Ireland. In August 1920 Private Young was killed at the Hutments in Cobh, and another three soldiers were wounded on 25 August 1920.[658] Two days later, a lorry patrol of Camerons was attacked near Cahirmore, an ambush which resulted in the death of Lieutenant Begg, the severe wounding of Private Winterton and minor injuries to two other privates.[659] In the course of these attacks the more carefree attitude of the Highlanders rapidly disappeared, and the troops learnt that 'we must be ever vigilant of all local Irish, and all were our enemy unless we knew otherwise.'[660]

The summer of 1920 saw an escalation in the intensity of encounters between the British Army and the IRA, as the latter began actively to target British motor transport in the city and county. On 20 July a Manchester patrol was ambushed in Ballyvourney, west of Macroom, and on 18 August another patrol of the Manchester Regiment was ambushed in the same area, while the Cameron Highlanders were ambushed near the East Cork town of Midleton on 27 August. The writers of *Record of the Rebellion* felt that the lack of sufficient resources significantly increased the vulnerability of troops to such attacks as the army 'had to rely largely on moving to the scene of action in one or two lorries.'[661] This reduced the number of soldiers that could be sent out at any one time, and so exposed them to attacks by larger numbers of IRA volunteers. Nevertheless, in the opinion of the British official history, the IRA did not maximise the tactical opportunities made available to it by these circumstances. The *Record of the*

Rebellion felt that transport weakness 'gave a great opening to the rebels, of which they took considerable advantage, and the only wonder is that the number of ambushes which were brought off by them was not even larger.'[662] Whether or not the IRA made the most of British transport weaknesses from mid 1920, when ambushes and army casualties began to increase dramatically, their attacks could no longer be considered simply a nuisance.

The vulnerability of small patrols was amply demonstrated when two lorries containing three officers and twenty men from the Essex Regiment were ambushed at Newcestown, about eight miles from Bandon, between 11pm and 12am on a Saturday night in October 1920, as recorded in the *Record of the Rebellion* (NAUK, WO 141/94).

> The first lorry was allowed to pass. It passed on 200 yards in advance of the second, which when the attack opened, pulled up only to find itself virtually surrounded. The soldiers, about 20 in it, got out and taking up positions on both sides of the road, opened fire. The occupants of the second lorry then apparently tried a flanking movement and this brought all combatants into very close range. The attack and counter attack was desperate. The ambushing party seemed to have been numerous, and the soldiers totalled about thirty.

The Newcestown Ambush was an opportunistic attack by the IRA on a British patrol which had entered the district. The fact that they were prepared to mount such an *ad hoc* attack so quickly and effectively reflected the growing confidence of the IRA in dealing with British military forces. The new level of violence involved can be judged from the report that appeared in the *Cork Examiner*:

> Rapid rifle fire and counter fire, the sharp crack of revolvers, and the louder reports of gunshot and rifle [swept] over a particularly desolate and lonely stretch of countryside. It was a terrifying ordeal for the residents in the widely scattered farmhouses or labourers' dwellings.[663]

The British suffered several casualties. Captain Richardson, RAF, on attachment to the Essex Regiment, was killed by a headshot while a Lieutenant Robertson was badly wounded in the stomach and a Corporal Hoare had his jaw shot off.[664]

The Essex Regiment was again attacked on 22 October 1920 when a Crossley carrying military despatches to Cork was ambushed at Annaghbeg near Innishannon. Over 40 volunteers were reported to have been involved in the ambush, and an 'attempt was made by the rebels to explode a mine under the leading tender.'[665] This failed, and the first Crossley sped off to Ballinhassig RIC barracks. However, the engine of the second Crossley was hit and the vehicle was forced to stop. At this point, Lieutenant Dickenson ordered his men out of the truck and into a defensive position facing the IRA fire. But the cover provided by the ditch was poor, and in the space of twenty minutes Dickenson and three of his men were killed and the rest seriously wounded. At this point the IRA left their positions and launched an attack to secure the British position. The *Record* stated that the IRA then 'regardless of the agonies which the troops were suffering ... dragged off their equipment, and one, more savage than the rest, recognising Lieut. Dickenson, kicked his dead body.'[666] In a military press release that would foreshadow the allegations made after Kilmichael, the army publicly accused the IRA of mistreating the wounded men: 'They gave no assistance to the wounded, but, on the contrary, searched the pockets of both the dead and wounded for loot.'[667]In what was perhaps a further effort to encourage public sympathy, a rumour that the dead were mutilated by bayonets was also circulated.[668]

Cork city could not fail to be aware of the ambush and the degree of violence involved as the lorries drove through en route to the military hospital. In the words of the *Cork Examiner*, 'the vehicle [that] passed through the city with the dead and wounded, besplashed with blood ... was seen by thousands, and caused a painful sensation.'[669] The *Irish Independent* was even more lurid in its description, and noted that this attack was a departure from previous less violent attacks:

> The man sitting next to the driver had his tunic opened and was leaning back, apparently dazed. Three soldiers were lying down near the rear of the lorry, the head of one being supported by a comrade's arm. Some of the soldiers appeared to be bleeding profusely, and indeed there was plenty evidence of an ambush of a nature far more serious than recent attacks on lorries.[670]

It is also important to note that the events at Ballinhassig were identified in the *Record of the Rebellion* as one of the first attacks on the army by an IRA flying column.

By early 1921 the British Army believed that the pressure they were then exerting on the IRA was provoking a backlash and that 'the result of this was that during February and March there occurred some of the bitterest encounters between the troops and the rebels.'[671] One of these encounters took place at Dripsey, when, acting on information provided by Mrs Lindsay, the Manchester Regiment sent out a party of 70 officers and men to surprise and stop an IRA ambush. The *Irish Times* estimated that they were over 60 IRA volunteers in the ambush party.[672] The British Army considered that the aim of the Dripsey Ambush had been the assassination of Major Holmes, the RIC divisional commissioner.[673] The 6th Division History describes the British attack as follows:

> The majority of this party debussed at Dripsey, and advanced along the Coachford Road, while another party proceeded by lorry to Peake Station, which was in the left rear of the rebel position. The approach of the main body was reported by the rebel scouts, and the rebels fired a spasmodic volley at them. Some fifty rebels then fled and were pursued and fired on by the troops. There were no casualties to

the Manchesters. Two rebels were shot dead; five wounded; and five unwounded prisoners, ten shot-guns, three rifles, four revolvers, a quantity of ammunition and documents were captured by troops.[674]

Another similarly violent encounter took place on 15 February 1921 when the army received intelligence that an IRA ambush had been prepared in the Mourneabbey area.

> A party of police, and a party of the East Lancashire Regiment, were ordered to move out in lorries to the vicinity of Ballinvuskig, and at 10 a.m. to move in small parties across country towards Jordan's Bridge. At the same time, parties from the same Regiment from Buttevant were to move across country from the direction of Pendy's Cross Roads. It so happened that a patrol of twenty-seven men of the Manchester Regiment were also approaching at this time along the Cork–Mallow road, and at about 11 a.m. reached Jordan's Bridge. Here they noticed the carts drawn across the road. Their cars stopped and they debussed and advanced in extended order on either side of the road. Several armed civilians were seen running both east and south-west. They were fired upon. Those that went east were intercepted by the parties from Mallow, and all were killed or captured. The majority went south west and escaped.[675]

In this case four IRA volunteers were killed during the fire fights and five were taken prisoner. The army, however, felt that the operation had been a failure on one level: poor cooperation meant that not all elements of Crown forces were in place before attempting the counter ambush.[676] Local problems of co-ordination were also again felt to be the principal reason for the escape of many of the IRA men present, and 'but for the delayed arrival of one of these parties a big capture of rebels must inevitably have followed.'[677] This opinion is supported by the local IRA who felt that they only escaped due to an army map-reading error.[678] Again, the public could not fail to be aware of the new levels of violence in army/IRA encounters. The death of the IRA men at Mourneabbey was brought home in a brutal way to the population of Mallow as the RIC drove through the town. As Siobhan Lankford noted 'cheering himself hoarse was Sergeant McGill of the RIC. At his feet were the bodies of three young volunteers, Paddy Flynn, Paddy Dorgan, and my brother Eamonn.'[679] The remaining dead and wounded at Mourneabbey were taken to Cork by train.[680] As with many of the ambushes in Cork, the British Army felt that Strickland was the target.[681] It is important to note that the Mourneabbey engagement was not accidental. The army was acting on local intelligence, for as an article in the *Liverpool Daily Post and Mercury* noted, the ground troops were supported by an aeroplane in the hunt for the IRA, which suggests that Mourneabbey was planned by the army.[682]

Intelligence and better tactical organisation in 1920 had led to a fall in the number of attacks on British transport, decreasing from 69 in July 1920, to 40 in September 1920 and 13 in December 1920, with the majority of those taking place in December being directed against the RIC.[683] The army felt it was not only the pressure that they were applying during drives and searches for IRA personnel, but also improvements in transport security that was forcing the IRA to rethink their strategy in Cork and organise into larger units. In other words, the flying columns now had to mount a more effective military response: 'The rebels leaders fully realised that their organisation, so far as brigades, battalions, etc., were concerned was inadequate as a means of waging war, and that it was necessary to re-organise.'[684]

Although IRA organisation was evolving in response to British developments, local intelligence was being received which allowed the British Army to conduct successful counter ambushes. The Essex Regiment, acting on information provided, sent a lorry as a decoy to an ambush at Brinny Bridge near Bandon, while 'another small party of troops, under an officer, set out across country, and whilst the rebels were still staring open-mouthed at the lorry and waiting for it to come near, they were attacked in the rear.'[685] Local intelligence again played a key part in saving the lives of soldiers on 3 October 1920, when a local farmer warned the RIC that an ambush was being prepared near the Viaduct on the Cork to Bandon road. A detachment of the Hampshires was sent to surprise the IRA. However the soldiers, 'owing to the nature of the country, could not get close to the rebels' position without being seen.'[686] This led to a running fire fight in which at least one IRA volunteer was killed. Searches of the ground and a nearby outhouse led to the discovery of a large amount of ammunition. The troops, unsure if they had retrieved all the munitions from the building, destroyed it by fire.

Not all ambushes could be forestalled as successfully. The *Record of the Rebellion* records that '5th March [1921] was a successful day for the rebels in North Cork,'[687] by which it meant the killing of Brigadier-General Cummings, the commander of the Kerry Brigade, 6th Division, in an ambush at Clonbannin in Northwest Cork. Cummings had left Killarney that morning at 7am for Buttevant in his touring car, his escort including a Rolls Royce armoured car and three Crossley tenders carrying soldiers from the Royal Fusiliers. Information had been received that an attempt would be made to ambush the Colonel, but the suspected site was between Barraduff and Rathmore.[688] Details of his route and time had been given to the IRA by an intelligence agent at the Mallow exchange.[689] The Royal Fusiliers debussed and searched possible sites around Barraduff, while a party from the East Lancashire Regiment was searching around Rathmore. Cummings had been in the wrong place at the wrong time, as the real target of the Clonbannin Ambush had in fact been Major-General Strickland,[690] the hope presumably being that his death would grab headlines. Yet, despite the death of Cummings, the army demonstrated its ability to evolve in response to enemy tactical innovations, and that it had learnt the lessons of past ambushes; one of the factors which considerably reduced the number of British casualties at Clonbannin was the armour-plating of the lorries to resist this type of ambush, and the support provided by the Rolls Royce armoured car.[691] These lessons were also being applied by the RIC and the Auxiliaries, as the IRA noted in the last major ambush in Cork at Rathcoole on 16 June 1921, when all four lorries were armoured and spread out over two miles. The lorries protected the Auxiliaries and gave them a platform from which to counterattack.[692] The *Lilywhites Gazette* paid Colonel Cummings a final tribute, 'fearless and just, he died as he lived – *miles inter milites*.'[693] The army felt that the newfound ability of its troops to counterattack unexpected ambushes successfully had been proved by the Green Howards at Lackelly, and that after such events the IRA 'showed little keenness to undertake other operations of a similar nature.'[694]

British troops also became more proficient at hunting down and ambushing IRA columns. One of the most disastrous days for the IRA in Cork was the destruction of an entire flying column at Clonmult in an action described in the 6th Division History as follows:

> Shots were then exchanged between the rebels in the house and the troops outside. The latter took precautions to ensure that no rebels escaped, and also sent three men to the Police Barracks at Midleton for reinforcements, as the rebel position was a strong one. Firing continued for some time, and, owing to the inferior numbers of troops engaged, it was feared that the result might be a stalemate, but at 5.20pm, twenty four police under the County Inspector arrived on the scene. The situation was still unchanged. At 5.50pm, to bring matters to a head, the Brigade Intelligence Officer, at great personal risk, climbed on to the house and set a light to the roof, and directly afterwards, bombs were thrown into the house through the hole thus made.[695]

An attempt was made to surrender by some of the IRA, but others remained defiant and continued firing and, as a result, the encounter was fought to its bitter end. Daniel Cashman, a member of the East Cork flying column, squarely attributed the blame for the column's demise to its own failures in terms of operational security, saying: 'I would like to stress this point as undoubtedly the lengthy stay of the column for five or six weeks in the one place was in great measure responsible for the tragic events of Sunday, 20 February, 1921.'[696] Coinciding with this lapse in vigilance by the IRA, we have seen that the British Army was taking far greater precautions, such as increasing convoy size and armouring lorries.

Higginson, the brigade commander, was full of praise for the operation at Clonmult, describing it as 'the first occasion on which the operations undertaken have resulted in the complete destruction or capture of the whole party.'[697] This was a view enthusiastically endorsed by Lieutenant-Colonel French, the CO of the Hampshires, who felt that the 'operation was well conceived and the troops skilfully led.'[698] Lieutenants Koe, Hammond and Hook were all praised for their efforts. Koe, who had planned and commanded the operation, was recommended for an MC, and Hammond, who had fired the roof, was recommended for a bar to his MC.

An t-Óglach – probably to reinforce the myth of IRA bravado – estimated the attacking force at 50, with the IRA killing twelve.[699] But in reality, the British Army personnel committed to the operation were just four officers and 21 other ranks. One NCO and six other ranks were left behind to guard the vehicles. En route to the cottage, the party split in two. The first party consisted of Lieutenants Koe, Hammond and seven soldiers, the second of Lieutenants Hook and Dove and six soldiers. When the fire fight broke out, three men were sent back to secure reinforcements from Midleton. At this point the IRA were facing only fourteen British soldiers, but suffered from being in a much weaker tactical position.[700] The surrounded IRA began to defiantly sing 'Amhrán na bhFiann', and as the *Hampshire Regimental Journal* recorded, this served to increase the soldiers' commitment to the destruction of the IRA column: 'as this song stated that "their lives were pledged to Ireland," the Hampshires took active steps to get possession of the pawn tickets.'[701] But later account in a regimental history recorded the following sentiment, Clonmult, 'like all the Irish operations, it was hateful to the British troops.'[702] RIC reinforcements arrived later in the form of the local county inspector and 24 policemen, bringing the final figures involved on the British side closer to those suggested by *An t-Óglach*.[703]

The army drew vital tactical lessons from this encounter, Lieutenant-Colonel French recommending in his report that all officers should be armed in future with rifles, and that rifle grenades should now be issued to all units to assist in any future actions of a similar nature.[704] Rifle grenades would have increased the firepower of small British units significantly, making it easier to defend convoys and attack standing IRA positions. Rifle grenades had proved their value in Iraq in 1920, Lieutenant-General Sir Alymer Haldane noting that: 'Rifle bombs are of great value. The Arabs hate them, and the infantry acts much more boldly when it can fire a bomb or two.'[705] One of most puzzling features of the campaign in Cork is that rifle grenades appear to have been used only once to counter attack at an ambush near Charleville in January 1921, and they were used not by the army but by the RIC.[706] No explanation appears in any military document to account for the fact that these weapons were not more widely issued and used.

On Sunday 1 May 1921 an IRA unit attempted to ambush a patrol of British troops, four miles northeast of Kildorrery in north-east Cork. The equipment seized from the IRA in this attack is very significant. According to an official report:

The Crown Forces vigorously engaged the attackers for one and half hours. The latter retreated, leaving behind two dead and two wounded. These two were taken prisoner along with four unwounded men. Near the scene three rifles, a large quantity of ammunition, some bombs and equipment, were seized by the Crown Forces, who suffered no causalities.[707]

While ambushes got the headlines of the day and the attention of historians since, the greatest and most formidable operational challenge the IRA posed for the

British Army during the entire campaign was in their use of explosives, hand grenades and roadside mines. That the IRA intended to use explosives was signalled in 1918 when large quantities of gelignite were stolen in Cork and Kerry, over 350lbs alone in April of that year.[708] This indicated that the IRA was going to invest resources in the development and refinement of explosive devices. The bomb had been the device of choice for the IRB for many years; according to the county inspector's comments on the unplanned explosion at Grattan Street in the city centre, it was evident 'that the young men … were engaged in experiments on the manufacture of bombs.'[709] A slightly later report from May chronicles an early attempt to use these explosives to attack local loyalists. In this case a bomb similar to those constructed in Grattan Street was left on the windowsill of the Cork County Club on the Grand Parade.[710]

By 1920 IRA explosives manufacturing had become quite sophisticated, and in the opinion of the RIC, IRA grenades were as effective as Mills bombs.[711] One member of the IRA was not so complimentary about the engineering prowess of his compatriots, referring to their efforts as 'tin-can bombs'.[712]

Bomb manufacture, particularly clandestinely, was naturally not without risk, and bombs sometimes posed as much of a danger to the IRA volunteers as the intended targets. 'The deafening crash of the blowing up of the seemingly large quantity of explosive material came with startlingly suddenness,'[713] was how the *Cork Weekly News* reported the explosion at 33 Grattan Street. Several people were seriously injured including an IRA volunteer called Michael Tobin who later died of his injuries.[714] The scene was a picture of devastation, with the front of the shop knocked out at the rear, an annex with it walls backing the yard knocked down while the kitchen itself had been blown to bits.[715] The extent of the damage revealed the quantity and destructive power of IRA explosives. Both the Fire Brigade and RIC were immediately on the scene, and an officer from the Royal Army Ordnance Corps had to be called to make the area safe. It quickly became apparent that the house was being used as a major bomb factory and the explosives found constituted an accidental but very significant coup for the RIC and the British Army. Over 500 finished and unfinished bombs were discovered, and other material such as gelignite, powder, cartridges and cartridge caps were also found at the scene. The report in the *Cork Weekly News* reveals why they were referred to as 'tin-can bombs':

> The pattern of the bombs, which weighed from 1lb to 3lb each, was rather unique. The outer shell consisted of a tin or canister, and in this was packed cement, with a hole ready to receive a charge of gelignite or other explosive. With the application of a 'cap', the most of these destructive preparations were ready for use.[716]

The nature and size of these bombs would indicate that they were intended for urban ambushes in Cork city. The accidental explosion in Grattan Street led directly to further unrest. The RIC launched a series of raids throughout the city and its suburbs, in Grattan Street, Greenmount, Pouladuff, Douglas Street and Blackpool. The searches turned up very little but led to the arrest of two IRA volunteers, Jeremiah and Cornelius Hurley, of 52 St Mary's Terrace, Greenmount who were charged with the possession of a German automatic pistol. In a later incident on 23 November 1920, two IRA volunteers, Edward O'Donoghue and Patrick Murphy, were carrying an explosive device through Patrick Street when it accidentally detonated, causing a huge panic as 'hundreds of people fled in all directions.'[717] At least sixteen civilians were wounded. Later in November, two other volunteers, William Mulcahy and Christopher Morrissey, were killed in an explosion at a bomb factory on an undertaker's premises in Watercourse Road on 26 November.

An example of one of these 'tin-can bomb' attacks was the Barrack Street Ambush of 9 October 1920, when the IRA ambushed an army lorry in that street. The IRA had received intelligence from a woman working in Captain Kelly's office that a lorry would leave Elizabeth Fort in the morning. They were incorrectly informed however, that it would be an Auxiliary patrol, when in fact it carried soldiers from the Hampshire Regiment. Sean Hegarty ordered the ambush regardless of the possibility of civilian casualties from the homemade explosive devices, and Mick Murphy, who was assigned to organise and lead the attack, mobilised over 30 volunteers to carry it out.[718] According to the next day's *Cork Examiner* (which interestingly referred to the IRA combatants as civilians):

> At 8.40 yesterday morning a lorry full of soldiers proceeding along Barrack Street was ambushed at the corner of Cove Street by a party of civilians, who first threw bombs, and then opened revolver fire on the military. The first bomb struck the side of the lorry, but the second was more carefully aimed, and exploded amongst the soldiers, two of whom were seen to fall.[719]

The IRA attacked the lorry with bombs and revolvers, despite the presence of hundreds of 'real' civilians on the streets.[720] As the *Cork Examiner* went on to point out with regard to the timing of the attack, 'the confusion was made all the greater by the fact it was school hour, and there were scores of little boys and girls in the streets. Fathers and mothers rushed out into the streets in search of their children, and there was a din of shouting and crying along the streets and laneways.'[721] Seventeen-year-old Private John Gordan Squibbs of the Hampshire Regiment was seriously wounded by the bomb thrown into the lorry, and subsequently died from a combination of wounds caused by both the bombs and revolver fire. An unidentified eyewitness told the *Cork Examiner* that they were 'horrified to see a soldier [Squibbs] in the lorry with a portion of his hand blown away and blood flowing profusely from what remained.'[722] After the initial attack the street erupted in gunfire, as both the IRA and the Hampshires engaged each other at close quarters. The Lance Corporal in charge of the lorry described the attack to a military court of inquiry held in Victoria Barracks in the following terms; they leave no doubt as to its severity:

> I heard three bombs explode in the attack on the lorry. One went off just as I saw Private Squibbs bend down. I personally fired fifteen rounds, and the escort also returned fire. I had six men with me, but only four of them were firing. After the firing died down, I heard that Squibbs was in the lorry. I found he was badly wounded in the left hand, and I assisted in carrying him to the fort. Three other members of the company were hit during the attack.[723]

Other eyewitnesses saw a wounded soldier limping in shock down the street, while others described finding Private Squibb's hand on the footpath and seeing pieces of flesh on the walls. A military doctor giving evidence on the extent of the wounds suffered by Private Squibbs stated:

> There was a gun shot wound in the chest, a gun shot wound in the middle of the back, a gun shot wound in the left hand, a portion of which was completely blown off; multiple wounds on both thighs and legs, and a small gunshot wound to the left shoulder. All the wounds with the exception of the one in the left shoulder, could have been caused by the bombs.[724]

The doctor's view was that death occurred due to shock and haemorrhage. The residents of Barrack Street were fearful of British reprisals and many left the street with lorries and vans full of furniture, while women left their homes carrying clothes in baskets.[725] Two members of the IRA were also injured in the attack; IRA captain Tadgh O'Sullivan was wounded in the back by shrapnel and Mick Murphy was injured by bomb splinters.[726]

A witness to the ambush, Robert Walsh, a carpenter with Cork Corporation, ran into a house to hide with many others and described the fear of a young mother he found there, 'a girl in the house with a baby in her arms. She was as white as a board, and she was crying because the other children had just left for school.'[727] Three civilians, Thomas Madden, Denis Buckley and Katie Fitzpatrick were seriously injured by the explosions.[728] They were all treated in the South Infirmary while another man, Jeremiah Linehan, was treated for facial injuries at the Mercy Hospital.

This disregard for civilian casualties became a hallmark of IRA bomb attacks in Cork, as shown by the example of the King Street RIC barracks. The barracks was bombed at 6.45pm, and as the *Cork Examiner* reported, 'the street is one of the busiest in Cork, and at that hour crowded.'[729] Even Strickland heard the explosion during a tennis game in Victoria Barracks.[730] In another incident, a grenade attack on some British lorries on Washington Street at 10am one morning in November 1920 led to the wounding of more than five civilians by shrapnel, the youngest being a two-year-old girl.[731] Another bomb attack on Washington Street took place

British soldiers under attack in the their trench on the Western Front during the First World War. For many veterans of France, service in Ireland was not an attractive prospect. (Library of Congress)

'Second line coming up amid shell fire to win the trench.' British soldiers in action during the First World War. The IRA had a grudging respect for their opponents, although many of the British soldiers thought little of the rebels. (Library of Congress)

Mr. JOHN DILLON, M.P.

ON

RECRUITING IN IRELAND

"It was a lie to say that any Nationalist who went into the Army betrayed Ireland; on the contrary, the men who joined the Army and took their stand beside the Irish Guards, the Dublin Fusiliers, and other gallant Irish Regiments, who had nobly maintained the traditions of our race, were doing a patriotic act. Any man who sought to intimidate anyone from recruiting was doing a wrong act, and acting falsely to Ireland."

JOIN AN IRISH REGIMENT TO-DAY

WHY NOT JOIN
THE
ARMY
FOR THE
PERIOD OF THE WAR?
YOU WILL LIKE IT.
YOUR PALS WILL LIKE IT.
THE KAISER
WILL HATE IT.

Apply for particulars of Allowances, &c., or send a post card to Director of Recruiting in your District.

Some of the many posters released in Ireland to encourage recruitment during the First World War. (Library of Congress)

Somebody's Son.

Above: A cartoon remembering the dead of the First World War, the *Star*, 11 November 1920.

'Surrendered' by John Scott. A dead man lies in the ruins of a cottage, which represents the attempt to create an Irish Republic. His hat, labelled 'Sinn Fein Revolt', lies upended on the ground next to him, as does his rifle marked 'Made in Germany'. (Library of Congress)

Special Military Area poster, Cork, 1918.

Below: A cartoon critical of the new 'Civic Guards' by David Low.

Recruiting — for the Enemy.

The Chapel Royal of Dublin Castle, 1919. Basil Clarke and the British propaganda department were based at the Castle during the war. (Library of Congress)

A typical street in Cork in the 1920s. (Library of Congress)

Women March for Free Erin. American women urge the cancellation of all treaties with England until the recognition of the Irish Republic, 1 April 1920. (Library of Congress)

A group of American women carrying signs against America's support of the English against the Irish, and burning a Union flag, 3 June 1920. (Library of Congress)

A cartoon by David Low, the *Star*, 8 October 1920, 'The persistent suitor.' Lloyd George visits Miss Ireland carrying jewelled blarney in one hand and martial law in the other.

A cartoon by David Low, the *Star*, 4 January 1921, 'A Market Place in an Irish Village'. Old Irishwoman holding forth to her crony: 'Sure, and what with the soldiers and the Black-and-Tans and all the other young fellows trying to kill each other, we never know the minute we may be hurled into *maternity*.'

A cartoon from the *Manchester Regimental Gazette*, October 1921.

British tanks conducting the reprisal at Dillon's Cross. (Imperial War Museum)

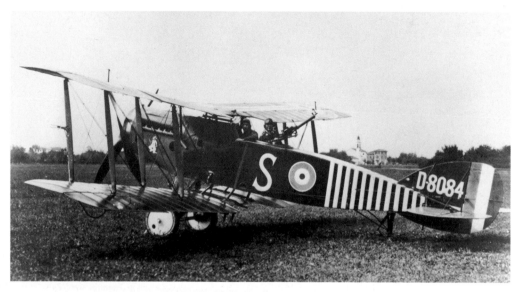

A Bristol Fighter of the type based at Fermoy during the summer of 1921 (Imperial War Museum)

Two views of Ireland from the Carpenter Collection. It was in this environment that the soldiers of the British Army patrolled as part of active-service platoons. (Library of Congress)

The 'active-service' platoon of the Essex Regiment at rest during the summer of 1921. (Imperial War Museum)

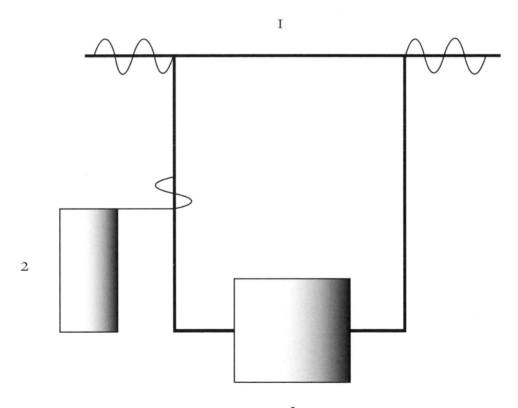

IRA phone taps in Cork. 1. Line 2. Receive 3. Condenser (2 microfarads).

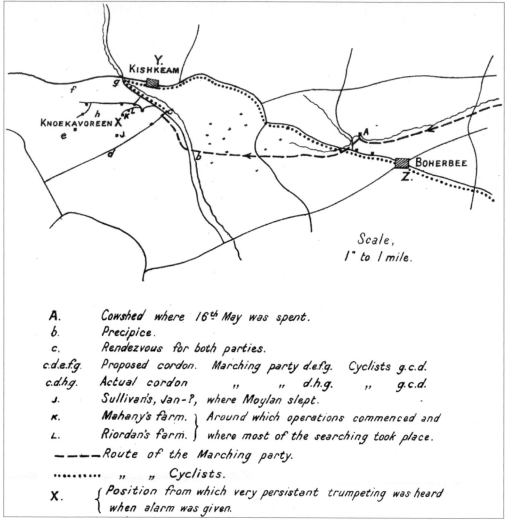

A.   Cowshed where 16th May was spent.
b.   Precipice.
c.   Rendezvous for both parties.
c.d.e.f.g. Proposed cordon. Marching party d.e.f.g. Cyclists g.c.d.
c.d.h.g. Actual cordon   ,,   ,,   d.h.g.   ,,   g.c.d.
J.   Sullivan's, Jan-?, where Moylan slept.
K.   Mahany's farm. ⎫ Around which operations commenced and
L.   Riordan's farm. ⎭ where most of the searching took place.
————Route of the Marching party.
············ ,, ,, Cyclists.
X.   ⎰ Position from which very persistant trumpeting was heard
        ⎱ when alarm was given.

British map of the Kiskeam Operation which resulted in the capture of Sean Moylan.

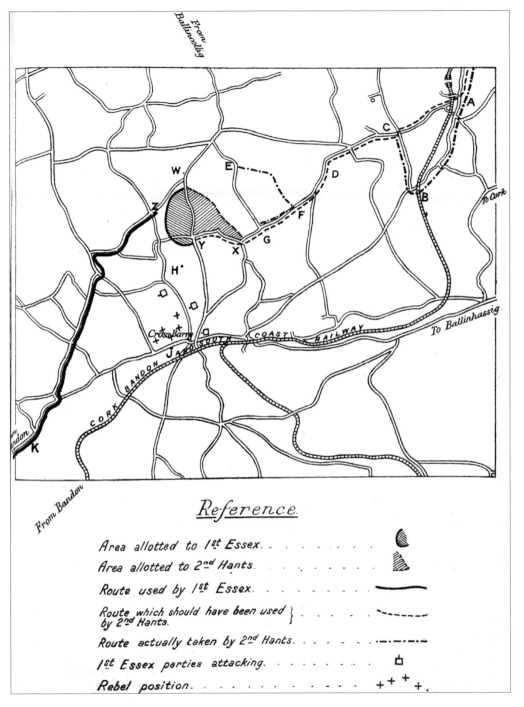

British map of the Crossbarry Operation.

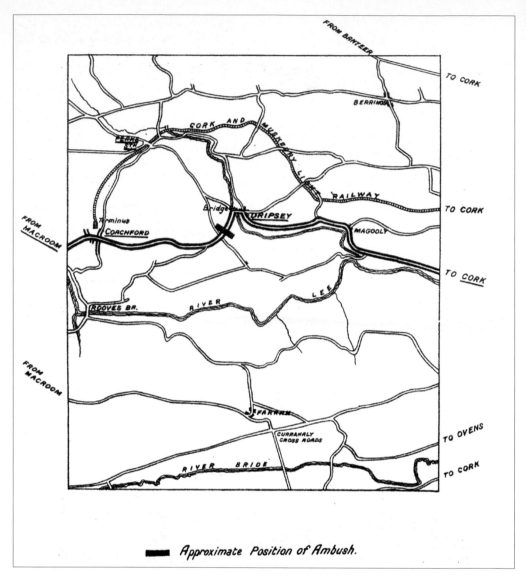

Approximate Position of Ambush.

British map of the Nad Operations.

Brigadier Higginson interviews prisoners during the Clydagh Operations. (Imperial War Museum)

Éamon de Valera, who opposed the British practice of taking hostages, in a photograph taken between 1918 and 1921. (Library of Congress)

Below: The four British soldiers killed in Cork after the Truce. (Imperial War Museum)

at 1pm on 21 May 1921, when a car of officers in civilian clothes was attacked with an improvised grenade. Two civilians wounded in the attack were admitted to Mercy Hospital.[732] In fact, Washington Street was a favourite location for such grenade attacks, as the *Cork Examiner*'s description of the ambush of two RIC lorries which took place in April 1921 reveals:

> A bomb was hurled from the southern side of the street. It missed the first lorry at which it was apparently directed, and striking off the kerbstone on the opposite side there was a terrific explosion. This was followed by two further big explosions, and immediately there was an intensive rattle of gunfire.[733]

Again, this attack took place at 10am in the morning, in a street which would then inevitably be crowded with pedestrians. Unsurprisingly five civilians were seriously wounded in the course of this attack.

Rural civilians were also the victims of IRA explosives. In Rosscarbery, West Cork, on 31 March 1921, there was a significant number of civilian casualities during an attack on the RIC barracks. The explosive device was used in an attempt to breach the walls of the police barracks which was under heavy attack at the time. In addition to the civilian deaths, there were also two police fatalities; Sergeant Shea and Constable Bowles were killed during the attack, while three constables were seriously wounded and a further six suffered minor injuries.[734] The power of the IRA explosives used meant that

> The streets of the town were littered by debris of all kinds, broken glass, dislodged slates, etc, whilst scarcely a house but bears palpable traces of the terrible force of the explosion. Roofs were stripped and windows shattered, even in the most distant parts of the village, whilst the interior of the houses opposite the barrack were one mass of wreckage.[735]

Two locals were killed: John Collins, a 60-year-old farmer from the townland of Derry and George Wilson, a 24-year-old farmer from the locality of Derryduff. At least seven civilians were seriously injured, three of whom had to be sent to Cork for further treatment. In short, disregard for civilian losses was not confined to the urban war in Cork, where it could be argued this collateral damage was the inevitable result of warfare in an area where large numbers of people occupied a confined space. Moreover, no mention of these civilian casualties was made in *An t-Ólgach* reports, although the civilian causalities of British operations regularly featured in both *An t-Ólgach* and the *Irish Bulletin*.[736]

The drive to improve IRA explosives capabilities was one of the reasons behind the theft of portable telephone equipment in Cork throughout 1920.[737] This technology allowed the IRA to detonate road mines remotely. The make-up of these roadside mines differed depending on the material available locally. The bombs used at Crossbarry, for instance, 'were made by filling a wooden box 2″ x 9″ x 6″, with earth and shrapnel. They were charged with gun cotton and fixed for detonation by means of electric exploders. The canister bombs were made by filling cocoa tins with shrapnel and charging them with a stick of gelignite.'[738] In East Cork, on the other hand, naval shells dredged up by local fishermen were the containers of choice.[739]

The pinnacle of IRA explosives development was the roadside mine, often incorporated into the ambushes of IRA flying columns. And after the demise of the flying columns by the summer of 1921, roadside bombs became the key offensive weapon of the IRA. The intention was noted in a letter from Cork No. 2 Brigade to IRA GHQ, which stated that for future operations, 'we intend to work largely on mines.'[740] The single most devastating deployment of roadside mines was the attack on the band of the Hampshire Regiment at Youghal as they made their way to annual practice at a local firing range. Many of the injured were teenagers. In the *Cork Examiner's* description:

> Marching around Frogmore, they reached the new line. Here a road mine was exploded under the band, and three bandsmen were killed outright and three others were wounded, dying later. Several other were badly injured. Apparently those who fired the mine ran away at once.[741]

The newspapers further noted that the landmine used in the attack was detonated electrically from over 60 yards away. The *Hampshire Telegraph and Post* reported that 'the mine would appear to have been a 5.9″ shell, exploded by electric detonation.'[742] The use of a shell was supported by a British officer, Cockerill, who noted that 'the mine apparently was a large calibre shell filled with high explosive.'[743]

It was the distance of the attackers and the use of remote detonation, combined with the age of the bandsmen that led to the vilification of this attack. A naval officer, Lieutenant-Commander Baille-Grohman, came across the ambush an hour after the explosion, and described it as a 'sad and bloody spectacle'.[744] A press release from Dublin Castle condemned the bombing in similar terms: 'Such a cold-blooded atrocity is almost unbelievable in the present century. The facts speak for themselves and even those most deeply in favour of Sinn Féin must detest the unutterable cowardice and depravity of such deeds.'[745]

The *Cork Examiner* was in no doubt that what it significantly described as an 'unarmed' regimental band was the target of the mine, reporting that 'the attack appeared to have been aimed at the band, the members of which were all unarmed, as the mine was not fired until the musicians reached the spot.' The same reporter also speculated that this was perhaps a reprisal for Clonmult.[746] The fact that a military band was targeted, as opposed to a fighting force, and that the IRA were engaged in a kind of cowardly *actio in distans* with their remotely detonated devices, also featured largely in English newspaper reports, with the *Hampshire Telegraph and Post* reporting that 'a tremendous explosion occurred in the middle of the band, which was playing at the time ... Arrangements were conducted by the IRA in such a way that it would be most unlikely that any of their number could be touched.'[747] Cockerill also supported the idea that the band was specifically targeted, pointing out that 'the band could not only be heard, but the whole column, could be seen from the point where the mine was electrically exploded.'[748]

Cockerill's description of the aftermath of the attack highlights what became a significant point: 'For one sickening moment it was not possible to realise what had happened or even who was hurt, but as the clouds of dust settled some twenty men and boys of the band were seen stretched on the ground.'[749] The killing of the band-boys was something that disgusted many in the British forces and led to a hardening in their attitude to the IRA. Cadoux-Hudson, encapsulating reaction to the attack, described it as 'pure cold blooded murder, I think it is the worst thing they have ever done.'[750] A Hampshire regimental history felt the band had been targeted because 'it had been very popular; it had accordingly been marked down for destruction by the IRA.'[751]

One of the most interesting features of this ambush was the restraint of the British soldiers afterwards. Youghal suffered no reprisal, either official or unofficial. 'All ranks, from the Colonel down, expressed their warm appreciation of the kindness of the local people who helped their wounded at the terminus. They also gratefully acknowledge[d] the skill and care exercised in the local hospital by the doctors and nurses'.[752] The sympathy of the residents of Youghal was surely due to the young age of many of the victims. At any rate, the aftermath of the bombing demonstrates that army discipline had considerably improved since 1919.

The nationwide commitment of the IRA to this new tactic can be seen in the mining of the railway tracks which led to the derailment of a troop train at Ardvoyle, Co. Armagh on 24 June 1921, leading to the death of three soldiers and 51 horses.[753] The last three major attacks or attempted attacks on British troops in Cork were by mines alone. Additional support for this new approach is found in the various engineering circulars issued by IRA GHQ in the final months of the campaign, which focus almost exclusively on land mines, road mining and incendiary devices.[754]

Little information remains in British military archives about how the army felt about the new threat to their operations posed by landmines. In any case, because of the low numbers of personnel required and IRA stockpiles of explosives, by July 1921 the roadside bomb had replaced the flying column as the principal military threat faced by the army.

IRA Ambushes and Mine Attacks on British Forces in Cork, 1921

Month	Ambushes	Mines
January	3	0
February	6	0

March	3	0
April	4	0
May	2	1
June	0	3
July	0	0

The Securing of British Transportation

Transport shortages, the lack of armoured vehicles and the resulting inability to create effective motor convoys were regarded by the army as the principal difficulties faced in defending against attacks on their logistics, because as has been mentioned above, they 'had to rely largely on moving to the scene of action in one or two lorries.'[755] The vulnerability of British logistics during this early period is demonstrated by an ambush near the North Cork town of Kanturk in October 1920, when a ration truck carrying food supplies from Buttevant to Newmarket was ambushed by 80 men, resulting in the deaths of two soldiers.[756]

The British Army was painfully aware of the transport issue and made efforts to address these difficulties. A cabinet memorandum of 7 December 1920 recorded that over the previous nine months mechanical transport in Ireland had been more than doubled,[757] a claim supported by government figures.

A memorandum provides the following information on transportation in Ireland: on 31 March 1920, the British Army had available for service in Ireland 156 lorries, 46 cars, 290 vans, 62 ambulances and 332 motorcycles. By 31 October 1920 the numbers were 319 lorries, 64 cars, 379 vans, 42 ambulances and 331 motorcycles. By 15 January, 447 lorries, 93 cars, 604 vans, 71 ambulances and 498 motorcycles. This represented, in a ten-month period, a 186 per cent increase in lorries alone.[758] Supporting this logistical commitment were an additional 1,097 drivers from the Army Service Corps who were sent to Ireland along with the vehicles. The increase in vehicle numbers allowed greater tactical protection on the ground, a fact attested to by IRA volunteer Joseph Ahern, who recalled that 'our difficulties increased considerably as the British authorities considered nothing less than half a dozen lorries safe.'[759] This assessment was supported by Tom Barry who noted in a report that the army 'never travel the same route more than once a week. Also they travel always in convoys of more than seven lorries generally accompanied by an armoured car.'[760] Yet as late as November 1920 the army was still forced to commandeer local lorries to support a drive in West Cork.[761] The RIC also still had issues with its own transport in March 1921, claiming to be handicapped by 'inadequate transport and almost impassable roads'.[762]

A shortfall in armoured cars was also addressed. On 31 March 1920 only 25 serviceable armoured cars were available for use, while by the end of December there were over 70. Peerless armoured cars had been dispatched to Ireland, along with eight new Rolls-Royce armoured cars, and an additional 26 Rolls-Royce cars were earmarked for Ireland, to be sent as soon as they had been produced. In tandem with this increase was a drive to armour-plate as many lorries as possible as a protection against ambushes. The army requested 160 armour plate sets, of which 40 were sent in August 1920, with a further 30 to arrive weekly thereafter. Revolver-proof armour was requested specifically for urban areas, and 181 sets were duly sent, along with a further 20 sets for cars. The armoured cars were critical to convoy protection, and the ambush at Clonbannin would have been far more serious without the firepower of the Rolls-Royce and the armour plating on the lorries. Grazebrook, the Gloucestershire Regiment's intelligence officer claimed that the Rolls-Royce car was 'intensely disliked by the Shins and their moral effect was large.'[763]

Although the motorisation of forces was designed to maximise the potential of troops in Ireland, this policy was disliked by many soldiers. Clarke, then a lieutenant in the Essex, opined that 'movement in trucks was unsatisfactory, [because] not only did it give the game away, but one soon heard that the most successful ambushes of the troops and police were when riding in vehicles.'[764]

Another ploy developed to protect these very visible motor convoys from ambush, was the carrying of hostages. As Ian F.W. Beckett has pointed out, this tactic had been previously used during the Boer War when South African civilians were forced to ride trains as a protection against attack by Boer commandos.[765] In the Irish context, this tactic became widespread, concurrent with martial law. In January 1921 a public notice was issued by the 16th Infantry Brigade in Fermoy announcing this new policy of carrying hostages.[766] However, the usefulness of this approach was questioned in the 6th Division History:

> How far such action prevented ambushes it is difficult to say – as a matter of fact, there were hardly any cases of convoys accompanied by a 'mascot' being attacked – but it probably served its purpose, as it produced a great outcry in the pro-rebel press.[767]

The carrying of hostages did indeed have an impact on the thinking of the IRA. James Cashman, an IRA lieutenant from Kiskeam, acknowledged in his statement to the Bureau of Military History that his column did not ambush any convoy that was accompanied by hostages.[768] This was also acknowledged by Sean Moylan, an IRA commandant in North Cork, when he described an abortive ambush near Newmarket in 1921, perhaps the same ambush as mentioned by Cashman which was called off owing to the presence of hostages.

> We soon heard the sound of approaching lorries, immediately they were in sight. They were crowded with men in civilian dress and these seemed to outnumber the soldiers they carried. My anticipation was sound. When the British sighted the car they slowed, their rifles were pointed outward. Two lorries moved past it. One pulled up in line with it. The last lorry twenty yards to the rear of this. Had there been no hostages

there would have been slaughter. Each lorry was in a perfect position for our purpose. An officer and some men dismounted to examine the car. The other remained in the lorries with the hostages, all of whom were handcuffed. Where I lay half a dozen British Tommies were five yards away, no member of the group more than fifty yards from an I.R.A. rifle. Yet I could not blow the whistle. I could not condemn those unarmed, handcuffed men to the death that would surely be theirs if the fight started. The British remounted their lorries and drove away, never suspecting how close they came to death.[769]

The deterrent effect of hostages upon the IRA has also been noted in Longford by Marie Colman.[770] Hostage carrying also exercised the minds of the most senior members of the republican movement, and de Valera issued a public criticism of the practice, which was reported in British newspapers.[771] From a modern perspective, this tactic may also seem both cruel and illegal. Nevertheless, as the testimony of the IRA officers above shows, it was highly effective in countering potential attacks.

Not all the British responses to IRA threats on logistics drew on the experiences of the Boer War; one took its lesson from German naval tactics of the First World War. This new approach, the Q lorry, was one of the more ingenious army responses to IRA attacks on British lines of communications, named after the disguised German naval raiders. It was pioneered by Lieutenant Frederick Hook of the Hampshire Regiment.[772] The goal was to ensure that the IRA did not attempt to interfere with broken-down lorries or cars, and so a fake lorry was left in a seemingly broken-down state, with soldiers hidden inside. *The Record of the Rebellion* describes the first such mission as taking place on 28 September 1920, near Ballymackeera.

> Several of them approached the lorry with petrol cans and even mounted it before Lieut. Hook took any action. He then declared his identity and a fight ensued in which the rebels were driven off, with the loss of one officer, IRA, and one man killed.[773]

However, the *Cork Examiner* described an incident involving a Q lorry as early as 6 September. Three lorries were driving along the road near Ballyvourney village when one of the vehicles appeared to break down. The driver was collected by another vehicle, which then drove on.

> There it lay on the side of the road, apparently deserted, and with no signs of life within. Little children from the village begin to congregate around it and there was the greatest curiosity to know what was inside. Soon the crowd became somewhat larger, and was composed largely of children and young boys. One little lad had the temerity to lift the canvas and gaze inside. Immediately a volley of rifle fire was opened, and the frightened crowd fled in all directions.[774]

Two people were killed, William Hegarty, an IRA volunteer from Ballymakeera and a local boy called Michael Lynch, two of whose older brothers were serving in the RIC. The troops are reported to have fired a machine gun from the lorry, and refused to give any information to the local priest when he arrived on the scene to tend to the wounded. The 6th Division History records the death of two rebels in this ambush, but in reality only one member of the IRA died. While the two descriptions are undoubtedly of the same ambush, the *Cork Examiner's* date is probably more accurate, meaning that the first operation was conducted on 6 September.

Another operation using this lorry was subsequently carried out in Co. Limerick, and after several of these incidents, the IRA finally ended the practice of approaching and burning abandoned lorries.[775] The development of the Q lorry and its operations was widely reported in the local press, and its use by the British forces was no doubt well known to all IRA volunteers in Cork, knowledge which played an important part in the tactic's effectiveness.

Yet another means of improving road security was the constant patrolling of all roads and train tracks. These types of operations are recorded in some detail in the Grazebrook diary and seem to have constituted a large proportion of Gloucestershire Regiment activities. These details not only deterred IRA operations, they did on occasion lead to captures. The Gloucestershire Regiment captured two IRA officers near Banteer railway station in April 1921, Denis Mulchinock and James Hayes, the latter having given his name as O'Connell.[776] However the day was not entirely successful:

> A man on horseback who gave the name of Sheehan was on the road near the point where the two men were first found but as he didn't appear to be implicated was unfortunately allowed to go. In all probability this man was Tim Sheehan, one of the family of brothers all of whom were believed active members of the local I.R.A. company.[777]

Grazebrook was determined to capture more of the Banteer IRA company and in a search three days later, Tim Sheehan's brothers William and Larry and other local men were captured.[778]

The IRA also adapted its tactics and targets to the changed situation. One of its responses to improved convoy protection was a series of attacks on trains in early 1921. Trains had, it is important to note, previously been spared attack due a prolonged rail strike.[779] Members of the 1st Battalion Royal Fusiliers were ambushed at Rathcoole Station, near Banteer, en route from Cork to Killarney. One sergeant was killed and an officer and several men were wounded. The British Army promptly adapted their own strategy, issuing instructions to all troops travelling in trains that effectively made the civilian passengers a shield for the military personnel aboard, in a variation on the use of hostages in road transport. The *Record of the Rebellion* notes, in a manner that downplays the increased risk to civilians, that it was 'difficult to ambush troops travel-ling in ordinary trains without endangering the lives of civilian passengers ... thereby making the practice too unpopular to be tolerated, even in the south of Ireland.'[780] Indeed, another train ambush, at Upton in West Cork on 15 February 1921, proved disastrous for the local passengers, when 'fire was opened indiscriminately on all carriages.'[781] The troops had scattered them-selves through the carriages, and while only a few soldiers were wounded, six civilians were killed. The risk to civilians made such attacks too unpopular, something the IRA could not politically sustain, as indicated by an IRA memo to its chief of staff Richard Mulcahy; 'It is impossible to do anything on trains since the Millstreet Ambush, as they travel with passengers.'[782] It is also possible that the new aerial escorts of trains also deterred any further attacks of this nature; in any case, only one more train ambush in Munster was attempted, at Headford Junction on 21 March 1921. However by July of 1921, trains began to fall victim to improvised mines.

The Evolution of British Tactics

Charles Townshend has noted that 'it was not until the spring of 1921 that some of the front-line troops began to realise that the motor transport was too clumsy to achieve surprise.'[783] The British had begun to adjust their tactics and created active-service platoons. These platoons consisted of handpicked men who were to operate in small groups and stay out in the countryside, hunting the IRA col-umns. Lieutenant Grazebrook described their creation in the Gloucestershire Regiment: 'The men were all specially selected by the company commanders, and were all volunteers.'[784]

According to Tom Barry, '[by] the middle of March, 1921, the British invari-ably operated in West Cork in units of not less than three hundred.'[785] His view was supported by IRA volunteer Jack Buttimer, who felt 'the only difficulty with the British was to get them out in the country to fight.'[786] This must be seen as retrospective bravado as these opinions fail to take into account the active-service platoon innovation of 1921. The development of the British Army's own active-service platoons or 'flying columns' was even reported in the contemporary press. Many units adopted these small-unit tactics, and they spread throughout the 6th Division area, as a newspaper report from the spring of 1921 shows: 'A detachment of military have been encamped on Knockenada Hill, a high eminence midway between Freemount and Liscarroll. They have been patrolling the surrounding dis-trict for the past few days.'[787] Historians of British counter-insurgency such as Tim Jones, argue that prior to 1944 the British Army had 'not embraced the concept central to accepted modern counter-guerrilla practice, namely prolonged small unit area patrolling.'[788] As can be seen in Cork, the army was already engaged in what is termed small unit patrolling in 1921.

The following account demonstrates the tactics employed by these new units On 16 and 17 February 1921 the Essex Regiment conducted operations in West Cork, primarily aimed at the Hales Flying Column. Percival had 'obtained information from civilian sources which indicated the location of certain rebel gangs,'[789] deemed to be responsible for recent attacks and for trenching the local roads. Grazebrook in North Cork was also given the names of local IRA men by farmers and businessmen who blamed the IRA for road trenching.[790] On 16 February at 10pm, a night patrol consisting of three officers and eighteen men left Bandon and travelled by lorry via Western Bridge to Kilgobbin Cross. There they came across a party trenching the road, and there was a brief exchange of fire but no causalities. From this point, the Essex advanced on foot bounding towards Crushnalanny Crossroads, 'the patrol mov[ing] in three parties, fifty yards apart, and, on reaching the crossroads, a rebel armed piquet was observed crouching behind a bank.'[791] A quick and one-sided fire fight resulted in the four IRA volunteers being killed. 'The surprise of the rebel piquet was due to the fact that the troops travelled on foot, and that their boots were wrapped up in sacking so as to deaden the sound of footsteps.'[792] The silent nature of the approach employed by the patrol also meant that when 'the rebels endeavoured to break away from one party they ran into another, which inflicted further causalities on them.'[793] A search of the bodies confirmed that the dead had been members of the IRA. This account shows that a mixture of aggression and stealth was employed by these platoons, which were designed to be flexible, independent, able to conduct offensive operations and showed a high degree of fighting confidence. This represented a considerable innovation in British military thinking in Ireland, and shows that the British Army was able to adapt its tactics to the locale, culture and specific kind of warfare it faced. A capacity for this kind of adaptability was something that Paddy Griffiths acknowledged about the British Army in 1918, when he noted: 'tactical innovation was a game that almost everyone was playing, even including the woolly old cavalry generals.'[794]

Charles Browne of the Macroom Company described the tactics of the new Essex flying column, 'operat[ing] with field kitchens and travell[ing] on foot, often crossing country, with one platoon of forty men mounted on cycles. These men acted as flankers, using parallel roads to the main body.'[795] The targeting and elimination of IRA active service units was not the only task of these columns, as a memorandum from HQ 16th Infantry Brigade explained: 'I want OC Flying Columns to bear in mind that one of the objects of the Flying Column is to get troops and police in touch with the people in a friendly way, so as to enlist the waverers on our side.'[796] In other words, they were also to engage in a rudimentary 'hearts and minds' operation.

One member of the IRA, Tim Herlihy of 1st Cork Brigade, particularly remembered the speed and silence of the new units, and described them as 'mobile [and] lightly equipped,' adding that 'they quickly and silently infiltrated our area,' often evading or immobilising the scouts deployed to detect them.[797] After the success of the Essex flying column, other units began to adopt the method. *The Hampshire Regimental Journal* noted that, 'on May 4th a mobile company consisting of a platoon from each company of the battalion, left Barracks for a week's tour of the surrounding country.'[798] This column killed one man who was attempting to escape. The Royal Field Artillery also began to use this strategy, their records revealing that a Lieutenant Waycott and seven men formed part of a flying column which spent seven days in the field in East Cork in June 1921.[799] The records of the 25th Battery of the RGA recorded that 'in May a dismounted "Flying Column" under Captain R.C. Lowndes, M.C. R.G.A., Lieut. R.M.H. Simonds, R.G.A., and B.S.M. West went out into the Kilworth mountains to look for rebels – but they meet with no success.'[800]

The capture of Sean Moylan provides another example of this new approach. This operation was organised by the Gloucestershire Regiment, and was intelligence-based, the army having received information locally that the IRA were staying in Knockavoreen, about one mile south-west of Kiskeam. The 'locality of the dug-out where four men lived had been roughly given, and lastly John Moylan had of late passed through Meelin supposedly for the Kiskeam and Rockchapel district.'[801] As the use of motor transport or bicycles might alert local volunteers to the possibility of a raid, it was

> ...decided to send one party by night on foot across country to some spot as near as possible, to lie up hidden all the next day, to push on again that night to form the furthermost cordon round the locality to be searched. Cyclists were then to be rushed up to close the cordon on the near side, which would, if possible, be the line of a road.[802]

The plan required a high degree of field craft, confidence and stealth. As was the case with most British operations in Cork, it was nocturnal. On 14 May the Gloucesters, five officers and 58 men, roughly two platoons, accompanied by four RIC men, began a night march to Boherbue in North Cork. They moved slowly, the prime consideration being to avoid all contact with locals. As a result, the seven-mile march took close to five hours.[803] They had selected a small wood as a resting spot and observation post, but arriving there found it unsuitable, many of the trees having being cut down. A hurried reconnaissance of the locality identified a large cowshed some 500 yards from the wood as a good alternative. Before dawn the column quickly secured the building and surrounding area, and set up a defensive perimeter around their temporary camp. The Gloucesters, showing the patience that was a hallmark of these small unit operations, had to wait over eighteen hours before they could begin their descent on Kiskeam. They spent the day in the shed but were discovered by a local farmer, who though initially held, was released, the officers being persuaded of his loyalty by the RIC. Nevertheless, it was only 'decided to release him under terrible threats.'[804]

The following day, Gloucester cycle patrols reconnoitred the area around Boherbue and Kiskeam and captured two IRA volunteers, Maurice Clancy, captain of the Derrygallon Company, and Pat Cronin of Ballyhoulihan. That night the phone lines were cut by the Newmarket detachment of the regiment to ensure that no information about the imminent raid could be passed on. At 11.45pm on Sunday, the Gloucesters broke camp and headed for Kiskeam and Moylan. Though locals rang cow horns and lit fires, the soldiers 'believed that the enemy was uncertain of the exact whereabouts and objectives of the party.'[805] With the cycle patrol in position to the east and south-east of the area, the patrol encircled the remaining area, dropping off a group of one officer and six men every 400 yards. Because of the darkness, the final cordon was tighter than planned, and while the cowbells were still being rung and signal fires lit, they were now well outside the tightening cordon. This may have given Sean Moylan and others a false sense of security.

The remaining two officers and eighteen men pressed forward along a sunken lane, with one of the officers and an RIC man leading. At this point they came under and returned fire, but there were no casualties on either side. Sean Moylan now ran into the piquet at O'Mahoney's farm, where he was fired on, but escaped. The first piquet dropped was also heard to fire shots. However, luckily for the army, due to the 'unintentional reduction of the area within the cordon, plenty of troops were available to carry out a thorough search.'[806] IRA papers and a revolver were found in a local farmhouse, while a large box found embedded in a ditch contained a Hotchkiss gun with ammunition and spare parts, a Mauser automatic, telephone equipment and many more IRA documents. Sean Moylan was captured nearby in possession of a revolver, a grenade, copies of *An t'Ólgach*, a typewriter and in his despatch case a bundle of letters for the OC 1st Southern Division. It could be argued that the loss of the Hotchkiss and the seizure of the documents were more serious than the capture of Moylan. All the men in the area were then rounded up and twelve were detained.

Not everyone was supportive of the new military flying columns; the county inspector of the West Riding in Cork believing their effect to be 'only transient'.[807] Showing that the example of a previous campaign can be a hindrance as well as a help, and demonstrating a questionable tactical appreciation of the situation, he advocated a return to the Boer War tactics of blockhouses. Lowe, a British officer who served in the flying columns, showed a greater appreciation of their effectiveness, and described how they had reduced their military equipment to the minimum required: 'The men wore short khaki trousers, and for equipment they carried rifles, bandoliers of ammunition, and haversacks.'[808] The soldiers needed to be incredibly fit and able to cover up to 25 miles a day, only returning to barracks to rest and refit. Still Lowe seems to have enjoyed the work, describing it as 'a thrilling and a fascinating occupation'.[809] The IRA considered that only significantly improved infantry training would ever enable it to cope with this threat, and as an internal IRA memo recorded, 'Our infantry training can never be adequate no matter what time we devote to it.'[810] A clear acknowledgement by the IRA that it would never be able to combat these proto British Special Forces in the open.

As Hopkinson has correctly pointed out, in the last months of the war British casualties were due mainly to roadside bombing and assassination.[811] In discussing 1921, Charles Townshend overestimated the IRA military capacity when he concluded that 'Irishmen ... turned out to be natural adepts at fire and movement, and the vital fusion of discipline and initiative which governed every guerrilla combat.'[812] The British flying columns have perhaps a greater claim to this accolade and in many ambushes, such as Clonbannin in March 1921, the IRA never pressed home their attack. As Sir Robert Thompson pointed out regarding the later campaign in Malaya, to be effective in counter-insurgency an army would 'need well trained elite units to operate like guerrillas.'[813] By the time of the Truce it was clear that the British Army had accepted that the flying column was to be the cornerstone of any future British military operations in Ireland, the army having discovered that 'the best way of harrying the rebels is by means of patrols in bicycles or foot that keep out in the country for several days at a time.'[814]

One of the most overlooked areas of the history of the War of Independence has been the tactical employment of air power by the British Army. Considerable academic attention has, of course, been paid to the deployment of air power in other British conflicts of the 1920s, notably in David Omissi's work which has shown its considerable value in Iraq and India.[815] An examination of the use of airpower in the War of Independence in Cork shows that it had the same tactical importance in Ireland.

The official debate on the employment of aircraft was opened by Macready in a letter to Winston Churchill on 18 August 1920 in which he detailed an incident concerning an undated ambush of a mail lorry. An RAF plane had flown over the site but was unable to intervene owing to the restrictions imposed on air operations by the British government. In this letter Macready explicitly requested that the 'Memorandum on the use of Aircraft in connection with riots' be modified, 'in order to admit of the use of machine guns and bombs from aeroplanes in such cases as that mentioned above, viz.; when the occupants of the aeroplanes can clearly distinguish a party carrying out an attack against members of the forces of the Crown.'[816]

He also pressed his case with the War Office in September 1920, pointing out that in Ireland special circumstances existed which merited an amendment of the existing rules. 'There are undoubtedly cases where fire from aeroplanes would materially assist the forces on the ground, and could be directed with little or no danger to harmless individuals.'[817] He outlined two possible scenarios where he believed that aerial action would be mutatis mutandis useful and justified.

> Mail cars, Lorries, Police and Military patrols, etc., are frequently held up by armed rebels, often in large numbers, on isolated roads. In such cases there is practically no fear of harmless civilians being in the vicinity and the open hostility of the assailants would, in the majority of cases, be perfectly obvious even to a man in an aeroplane.[818]

The second example was 'where civil disturbances occur in streets or in the vicinity of towns.'[819]

> It is inevitable that the crowd should include a considerable number of persons who have collected from mere curiosity. In such cases, it is admittedly impracticable for fire to be directed from the Air unless warning is first given as to the intention of opening fire.[820]

His suggestion for informing the people on the ground of any possible action was through the dropping of aerial leaflets. Macready also pointed out that the absence of hostile anti-aircraft guns would make matters easy for the RAF. Nevertheless, his request for the use of airpower in Ireland was strongly opposed by the chief of the air staff, Hugh Trenchard. Trenchard's biographer, Andrew Boyle, claimed that 'Trenchard was appalled ... [aeroplanes were] the worst possible weapon for such a purpose.'[821] This dispute reveals the doctrinal divisions amongst senior officers over the employment of aeroplanes in counter-insurgency, particularly in politically sensitive theatres. Trenchard, a former infantry officer and Boer War veteran, was very clear in a memorandum rebutting Macready's position. He pointed out that in his opinion it would not be easy for any pilot to distinguish forces on the ground and considered the distribution of pamphlets from the air to be too haphazard a means of warning anyone on the ground:

> To sum up, if offensive action is permitted, the innocent will suffer much more than they suffer when fire is opened on the ground. Accidents will happen in spite of all precautions. A runaway gun or a bomb which drops too late cannot be prevented, and therefore large numbers of innocent people will be killed, and this cannot be helped. A great popular outcry will be created against the unfortunate pilots who are involved in the action, from which it will be impossible to shield them. Further, a feeling of annoyance and exasperation at the reckless use of such a powerful arm, which once loosed in the air cannot be delicately controlled, will infallibly arise and engender great bitterness.[822]

Trenchard was also concerned that unarmed pilots and RAF personnel would become the victims of retaliation in Ireland, as had been the case in Iraq.[823] In an earlier letter to Winston Churchill, who was also Secretary of State for Air in October 1920, he cited different reasons for his opposition to the use of planes in Ireland, believing that the campaign was too difficult, with no clear tactical role for the RAF.[824] Trenchard was not alone in his opposition to the employment of aeroplanes in irregular campaigns; Lieutenant-General Deverall of the Indian Army opposed their use in the sub-continent, on the grounds that it was impossible to distinguish between combatants and non-combatants.[825] The history of the operations conducted in Waziristan produced by the General Staff of Indian Army headquarters disagreed with Deverall: 'It is impossible to overestimate the value of aircraft in tactical cooperation with other arms … [aeroplanes] employed in tactical cooperation did considerable damage and helped in no small measure towards the success of many of the actions.'[826] Trenchard's opposition was noted by David Omissi, who is one of the few historians to have at least recognised that armed operations were conducted by the RAF in Ireland.[827]

Trenchard also had support within the army. A memorandum drafted in Wilson's office, written by an unnamed staff Lieutenant-Colonel, stated: 'Mistakes are bound to happen and we have quite enough difficulties to contend with, without having an uninformed British press campaign or an organised Sinn Féin press against us.'[828]

There was a general feeling in London that any aerial action would only achieve negligible results, although it is entirely possible that this attitude may also have stemmed from a political desire within the army to limit the scope of the newly formed RAF. As a result of this debate, the War Office, perhaps primarily on the basis of Trenchard's views, refused Macready's request.

> It is considered that the difficulty of observation from aeroplanes, the uncertainty of communication with them from the ground, and the insufficient accuracy of fire from the air precludes the exercise of that delicate control which is necessary, and makes careful discrimination between friend and foe under all circumstances extremely difficult to ensure. With these views before them the Army Council do not consider that the possibility of effective intervention by aeroplanes outweighs the risks that must inevitably be involved.[829]

Macready remained undeterred and in a letter to the Secretary of State in March 1921 once again sought a change in the rules of engagement for aircraft. His central argument was that military conditions in Ireland had undergone a significant change, which in turn called for a change in policy. While the active-service platoons had been an organic development from army units in the frontline of the conflict in Cork, Macready's pursuit of airpower shows that even the senior generals in Ireland were capable of grasping and pursuing innovative solutions to the specific problems posed by the campaign. Macready argued:

> In the first place a stage has now been reached in which the rebels in the martial law area carry out operations on a larger scale than previously, and attacks by large commandos of armed men frequently resemble a minor military engagement as distinct from small ambushes formed by men who shot and ran away …[830]
>
> … When aeroplanes were first employed in this country, their moral effect was possibly in itself sufficient, there is every indication that such is no longer the case. The rebels are becoming adepts at concealment from aircraft, and several cases have been reported of aeroplanes having been fired at from the ground. The fact that the pilot is unable to reply to such fire will inevitably lead to the rebels discovering this fact, if they have not already done so, that the aeroplanes are unarmed. The consequence of this is obviously to discount to a large extent the value of aircraft.[831]

In this letter, in order to reassure the skeptics in London, Macready suggested several measures that might be used to control the operational activity of aircraft. He proposed that armed aircraft would only be employed in the martial law area, and within that, only in rural areas.[832]

Macready's continued push for air support was supported by the operational evidence coming from the North-West Frontier and Iraq concerning the suitability of airplanes as a resource in small unit warfare. During operations in Waziristan in 1920, 'Bristol fighters had provided remarkably effective close-support to the Derajat Column' causing heavy casualties to the Waziris.[833] Macready was also encouraged in his pursuit by the development of IRA flying columns, and a belief that the IRA were planning a rising. The army actually looked forward to the opportunity such a rising would give, allowing them at last to '[engage] them in considerable numbers … Such a chance must be seized with vigour.'[834] This memorandum tasked the 16th Infantry Brigade with the responsibility of defending the aerodrome at Fermoy, 'as aerodromes are being made a special target of the IRA,' an instruction that indicates that the RAF was indeed having a considerable impact on IRA activities.[835]

Perhaps as a result of the operational success of aeroplanes in India and Iraq, and because the government was desperate to force an end to the conflict in Ireland, Macready now finally began to find some support in London. A letter from the War Office to the Air Ministry in March 1921 encouraged a change of position:

> The situation in Ireland has also altered to a great extent as pointed out in General Macready's letter. It appears therefore, on the surface, an opportunity of using aeroplanes effectively against concentrations of rebels, provided the difficulties pointed out by the C.A.S. and entertained also by ourselves, if they can not altogether be ignored, can now be reduced considerably by the issuing of strict instructions whereby possible accidents can be avoided.[836]

This time Macready was successful, and authorisation was given for the use of aircraft in action in Ireland, with No. 2 Squadron in Fermoy receiving instructions for the commencement of these operations. But they were warned that 'there still remains a large portion of loyalists, women and children and non-combatants. The destruction of these or damage to their property would seriously embarrass the government and be a source of propaganda for the rebels.'[837] The new procedures for the conduct of air operations were reviewed and approved by David Lloyd George personally on 29 March 1921, as his handwritten initials on the instructions show.[838]

Nevertheless there remained the practical issue of implementing these guidelines and securing effective air-to-ground coordination in operations. By May 1921, armed aeroplanes were regularly called on by the British Army to take part in operations or respond to IRA activity. For example, the RAF received a request from Brigadier-General Higginson to conduct an armed reconnaissance of West Cork and to engage any rebels encountered during the flight.[839] Requests were also made by units in more immediate danger. A case in point is a request made on 2 July during an attack on Mallow RIC barracks that they be provided with armed aerial assistance to repel the assault.[840]

A special exercise was held in Kilworth on 27 May to further examine the tactical utility of aeroplanes in the Irish context. The outcome of the test was generally regarded as positive, and it was concluded that 'aeroplanes would prove of great use in operations against rebels, when the latter have been forced to "bolt" from their cover positions. The aeroplane can take offensive action.'[841] A report by the participating air crew, Flight Lieutenant Russell and Flying Officer Mackay, confirmed this view with the proviso that such flights would have to be at low levels to work effectively and identify IRA volunteers. They also noted that the British infantry, who wore khaki, were not so readily identifiable, making it difficult to determine the distance between the IRA and soldiers if action was to be taken.[842]

While Charles Townshend has suggested that no radio system existed for the aircraft in Ireland,[843] the RAF base in Fermoy could coordinate and communicate with planes through wireless.[844] At a meeting held in Victoria Barracks on 7 March 1921, in a discussion of how best to conduct the tactical employment of aeroplanes, the key difficulty noted by those present was that the army could not communicate directly with the fighters, the only means of communication with the aircraft being relaying messages by using the aerodrome at Fermoy as a relay station. A key decision taken at the meeting to improve tactical cooperation on the ground, was that a RAF Type XI wireless station should be based at Buttevant barracks allowing the army direct communication with any aircraft, and that in addition four mobile wireless ground stations would be secured from the depot at Woolwich to allow troops conducting drives and sweeps to communicate with participating aircraft.[845] This type of technology had been used by British forces since 1915.[846] No reason is given for the selection of Buttevant, but its central location may well have afforded the best signal coverage.

An examination of the operational work by RAF No 2 Squadron in April 1921 shows there were 41 mail flights (totalling 56 hours 30 minutes), 74 patrol, reconnaissance and escort flights (86 hours 50 minutes), and 23 flights classified as 'other' (20 hours 20 minutes).[847] This suggests that the bulk of RAF operations in Munster were in the active support of military operations. So while some historians have asserted that the use of planes for reconnaissance was rare, it actually seems to have been comparatively common.[848] Indeed at the aforementioned meeting held in Victoria Barracks on 7 March 1921 the army expressed its satisfaction with the reconnaissance and patrolling work provided by the RAF in support of the army.[849]

Armed RAF operations began in April 1921, 'the first time Lewis guns were carried by "A" Flight, No. 2 Squadron, for the purpose of escorting a troop train from WATERFORD to FERMOY.'[850] Two months later the carrying of guns had become standard operating procedure.[851] Bombing practices were also conducted in June and the operations report by the 11th (Irish) Wing recorded the use of Lewis guns in a round-up near Rathmore on the Cork-Kerry border.[852]

Some historians of counter-insurgency have failed to give full consideration to the role of the RAF in Ireland. Thomas Mockaitis for instance has claimed 'the British were willing to forego the military advantage of the aeroplane in order to preserve principle of minimum force.'[853] While he argues that the air-power in Malaya played a valuable role in transportation, reconnaissance and in the distribution of propaganda, he fails to see that the bulk of aerial support operations in Ireland were engaged in the same activities.[854] The advantages the aeroplane offered in Malaya were precisely the advantages it conferred in Ireland. Indeed, aerial escorts of troops in Ireland were considered by the RAF to have great tactical value and were regarded as 'the best means of preventing ambushes taking place on either roads or railway.'[855] The army agreed with this view, as the 6th Division History noted after one ambush the IRA retreated 'when they saw an aeroplane which happened to be passing along, and which they thought was about to attack them. It shows of what great use planes could be in all guerrilla operations.'[856]

IRA testimony also bears out the role of air power in preventing ambushes in Cork. As Richard Willis noted, he and other IRA volunteers were involved in preparing an ambush on the Fermoy-Ballyduff Road but were forced to abandon the position after the appearance of a British fighter.[857] Willis remembered how 'the aeroplane followed us up and we only lost it on getting into a wooded area in the mountain.' This account was supported by James Brennock and William Buckley, two other IRA volunteers who were present on that occasion.[858] IRA worries concerning air power extended beyond Cork, with one of the most iconic IRA commanders of the war, Michael Brennan of Clare, admitting that the 'addition of [more] aeroplanes and armoured vehicles would have made short work of us.'[859]

There existed a high degree of concern in the IRA about the use of air power, as a report in *an t-Ólgach* in May 1921 concerning a British drive in West Cork shows. It states that 'enemy aircraft were a factor which our troops had to give serious attention' going on to say that the retreat of the volunteers on the ground was greatly complicated by 'keeping in cover from the aircraft' before concluding that 'the most dangerous thing was being observed by his aircraft.'[860] The use of aircraft for intelligence gathering also worried the IRA: 'Positions can be located by aeroplane photography and air observation … [it is] by means of photographs from the air that positions are definitely located in the map.'[861] *An t-Ólgach* consequently urged IRA units to be more cautious and to ensure the highest standard of camouflage of all locations. These statements completely contradict Peter Hart's assertion that 'aircraft were a failure at reconnaissance – nothing to see.'[862] Even prior to the use of armed aircraft in attacks on IRA positions and columns, aeroplanes had a demonstrated impact on the tactical considerations of the IRA. Indeed the IRA were right to be worried, as T.R. Moreman's examination of British operations in the different context of the Indian North-West Frontier of India in the early 1920s noted, aerial photographs had become invaluable in the provision of tactical intelligence.[863] This view was supported by the Indian Army in their history of the Afghan War of 1919, when they recorded that aeroplanes 'proved [their] value ... in long-distance strategical reconnaissances.'[864]

Macready believed that airpower would be a decisive factor in any conflict that might develop after a breakdown of the Truce, and proposed 'therefore to give the Air Force a free hand with one restriction only viz:- that only competent pilots are employed on offensive action.'[865] He based his confidence in the success of this approach on the fact that 'troops and aeroplanes have now had considerable experience in working together in Ireland.'[866]

The Myth of Crossbarry

Myth plays a huge part in the historiography of key founding moments in the history of any nation. Of all the encounters during the War of Independence – those that have not only received the greatest popular and academic attention but have also been proportionately mythologised – Kilmichael and Crossbarry stand out. Nationalist history has always presented Crossbarry as a magnificent IRA victory against the odds, an opinion adopted uncritically by many academic studies. In his survey work, *The Irish War of Independence*, Michael Hopkinson described the encounter as 'the nearest approximation to a conventional battle in the whole War,' adding that 'with considerable justice, Crossbarry is regarded as a victory for the IRA.'[867]

Hopkinson tells us that the information which led to the operation was provided by an IRA officer who informed the British of the location of the IRA column, but fails to wonder how a prisoner captured a month prior to Crossbarry would know the location of the column at that point, an issue that historian William Kautt has raised, questioning how 'this individual would have had the necessary information about where the flying column would be in one month.'[868] Hopkinson also repeats wholesale the myth that, 'sensing there was no safe recourse, Barry decided that they would fight their way out. British casualties vastly exceeded those of the IRA, who made a long retreat successfully.'[869] Hopkinson is by no means alone here. Peter Hart is also drawn into the myth-making stating that the IRA, 'when caught at Dripsey, Clonmult, and Crossbarry ... fought against overwhelming odds.'[870]

All this stems from Tom Barry's assertion that at Crossbarry he faced 'four hundred troops [from] Cork, two hundred [from] Ballincollig, three hundred [from] Kinsale and three hundred and fifty [from] Bandon. Later one hundred and twenty Auxiliaries left Macroom.'[871] This is repeated by Meda Ryan in her book *Tom Barry: IRA Freedom Fighter.* 'On the morning of 19 March, 400 troops left Cork, 200 Ballincollig, 300 Kinsale, and 350 Bandon. Later Auxiliaries left Macroom, later, still more troops left Clonakilty.'[872] Few, if any, of the historians of Crossbarry, with the exception of Kautt, though many have accessed the Strickland and Percival papers in the Imperial War Museum, attempt to deal with their contradictory figures. As we will see, Barry's figures in *Guerrilla Days in Ireland* are inaccurate. In fact they are refuted by Tom Barry in his own report on Crossbarry, when he informed HQ Cork No. 3 Brigade that his ambush party encountered '[a] large raiding party of 150 returning from Ballymurphy [who] came on our rear and were engaged by No. 7 section.'[873] In his official report Barry makes no mention of any attempt to surround him, and it is also quite clear that the column was focused on the ambush rather than any defensive action against a large body of British troops. In fact, much of the detail of the report tallies with the British accounts of the operation and Liam Deasy's recollections. William Kautt asserts that 'Barry's decision to fight there was all the more remarkable, since he clearly believed he was outnumbered,'[874] but Barry did not believe he was being surrounded as his own report clearly shows. In fact, given the number of the Essex Regiment soldiers present, it was the British troops that were outnumbered by a margin of almost two to one.

As we examine the accounts of all participating sides, a very different picture emerges from the account in *Guerrilla Days in Ireland*. The action at Crossbarry was the largest set-piece engagement of the campaign in Cork. The official history of the 6th Division opens its account of Crossbarry thus:

> On March 19th, the biggest battle of the campaign, and one more nearly approaching to an action as fought in normal warfare, took place between Bandon and Cork. If the outcome had been completely successful, this action might quite easily have had decisive results as regards rebel activity in West Cork.[875]

British forces had indeed been given information from the IRA officer captured at the Upton Ambush that the headquarters and arms dump of the local flying column was located in the Crossbarry area, prompting the British Army to conduct search operations on 19 March 1921. As Percival told a class at Sandhurst 'This man hoping to save his life, one day, asked to see the Brigade IO at Cork and informed him [about] the headquarters of the 3rd Cork Brigade. The IRA were located in a group of farms in the Ballymurphy townland and there was a dug-out in the same locality.'[876]

The Crossbarry operation, organised in the brigade headquarters on 18 March 1921, was to be a joint operation involving the Essex and Hampshire Regiments, officers from both of which attended the meeting. The plan was to commence a cordon-and-search operation in the Ballymurphy area at 6am the following morning, the agreed goals being to locate the HQ and arms dump and to capture if possible Séan Hales and the flying column which the British forces assumed was under his command. The operation involved 81 officers and men from the

Hampshire Regiment under the command of Captain Atchison, and 60 officers and men from the Essex Regiment under the command of Major Halahan, although there is some slight confusion over the Essex figures, as Percival recalled that only 60 men from the Essex were detailed for the search.[877] What is true is that in no account, either in the British records or Tom Barry's official report, do they reach the levels claimed later by him in *Guerrilla Days in Ireland*.

The British problems began early the following morning, when the Hampshire Regiment failed to follow the route assigned to it so that it was out of position at the beginning of the operation, consequently playing only a minimal role in the ensuing encounter. The Essex Regiment operation went more smoothly leaving them at their assigned area at 6am, with their transport instructed to return later to collect the search party at daybreak, approximately 7.30am. However, the transport group disobeyed their orders. 'The lorry drivers, anxious to reach the rendezvous and to eat their breakfast there, started before the appointed time and ran into the deadly ambush.'[878] After scouting the area, but failing to see the ambush, Lieutenant Tower called the transport party into Crossbarry. It would turn out to be a fatal error for the dozen or so men with the lorries.

The firing alerted the search parties of the Essex Regiment to the ambush. According to Percival, 'a heavy burst of firing was heard from Crossbarry and we at once guessed that our own lorry convoy with the skeleton escort had been ambushed there.'[879] They immediately started south-west in an attempt to save the transport party. Various contemporary newspapers accounts described the ambush and the resulting fire fight, *The Times* reporting how 'the next instant a hail of bullets was rained upon them [the British] by ambushers, who were all under cover. Machine-guns, rifles, revolvers, and bombs were used against them, and in the early stage of the encounter the Crown forces suffered heavily.'[880] The *Irish Times* reported that the army ran into an ambush 'laid by nearly 500 men, and a battle ensued, which continued for several hours, resulting in heavy loss of life on both sides.'[881] The *Essex County Standard, West Suffolk Gazette and Eastern Counties' Advertiser* informed their readerships that

> The detachments having left their lorries, proceeded on foot in search of the criminals, and when they were some distance from the motors, the latter, which had been left in the charge of the Essex Regiment and the Royal Army Service Corps, were attacked by an overwhelming number of rebels who suddenly appeared on the scene. The detachment in charge of the transport put up a splendid fight against very heavy odds.[882]

A report in the *Liverpool Daily Post and Mercury* only mentions the destruction of three lorries, namely two three-ton vehicles and a Crossley tender.[883] This figure is supported by Liam Deasy[884] and is also the figure mentioned by Tom Barry in his report, when he wrote 'you will understand that we only had three lorries within our line of fire.' Barry could not destroy another six lorries as they were protected by British troops who had taken up a strong defensive position.[885] Meda Ryan is incorrect when she claims that sixteen British lorries were present, and is perhaps relying here too heavily on Barry's version of events in *Guerrilla Days*. It must be remembered that this work was written much later than the events it describes, and was perhaps an attempt to sustain the legend of the ambush rather than record accurately the events of the day.[886] According to newspaper reporting, British reinforcements arrived in the area far later than Tom Barry suggested.[887]

The Regimental Strengths of the Hampshire and Essex Regiment in Ireland, 1921[888]

Regiment	Officers	Ranks	Location
Hampshire	20	487	Cork
	9	124	Youghal
Essex	13	264	Kinsale
	7	161	Fort Charles
	I	28	Old Head of Kinsale
	6	82	Bandon
	4	60	Clonakilty
	I	28	Courtmacsherry
Essex totals	32	623	

In *Guerrilla Days in Ireland*, Tom Barry had claimed that over 650 members of the Essex Regiment were present, yet there were only 655 in Ireland; likewise, he claimed that 120 Auxiliaries came from Macroom, but they were in fact only 78 stationed there.[889] With regard to the Essex figures, when you factor in those assigned to regimental, escort or guard duties or the numbers resting, on leave or on sick parade, it is simply not possible for the figures at Crossbarry to reach those claimed by him in *Guerrilla Days in Ireland*.

Despite the various detailed accounts in the press of the day, the 'battle' merited only a single paragraph in the *Record of the Rebellion*:

> The rebel column attacked the transport and overcame the escort, doing considerable damage before the main body of the troops arrived. On the arrival of the troops the rebels stood to fight. A fierce fight ensued and finally the rebels withdrew. The Crown forces suffered sixteen casualties, killed or wounded, of whom the majority were the transport party. Of the rebels six were killed, six captured and about seven wounded.[890]

Interestingly, Percival's account of the casualty figures differed, giving the advantage to the IRA. According to him, British losses were 'one officer and nine men killed and two officers and five men wounded, while we had two lorries completely destroyed. The losses of the IRA were four killed and three prisoners, and a number of wounded whom they succeeded in getting away.'[891] Percival also noted the capture and destruction of the IRA's ammunition cart. This is a very important point because if the IRA had remained in control of the battlefield as claimed by Tom Barry, they would never have surrendered their ammunition. Barry in his report to IRA brigade headquarters does acknowledge that he quit the ambush under pressure and that the column was only 'pursued by 25 British troops'.[892]

This considerably less hyperbolic account of events is supported by the 2nd Battalion Notes in the *Hampshire Regimental Journal*, which confirms that only the Essex and Hampshire Regiments were involved in the operations on the day. It also confirms that the Hampshire Regiment was not involved in the fire fight at Crossbarry at all since 'the information on which we were acting gave the rebels' position as some miles north of what was actually the case, and before the Hampshires could come up with them they had fled.'[893] The journal notes that the rebels were chased through rough country for over ten and a half miles in conditions of driving rain. The only solace for the soldiers on the day was a ration of rum upon returning to Ballincollig. The notes also found time to poke fun at one of the officers:

> It is rumoured that during this chase a certain prominent last year's Army Cup finalist, who had been reading his 'little yellow book' before leaving barracks, decided to make use of his long range weapons and accordingly opened fire at 700 yards. The result of this enterprise is not definitely known but it is believed that certain rebels who had thought they were out of range had the shock of their lives.[894]

Percival was satisfied that in the British action on the day was successful: 'This was the last big ambush in that part of the country, and the moral effect of our sudden appearance on the enemy's flank made him very "chary" of again laying ambushes of the roads.'[895] This assessment was endorsed in one of the regimental histories that claimed that, 'the influence of this action upon the Sinn Féiners was such that they never again faced the Essex men in the open.'[896]

The troops from the Manchester Regiment that were sent to assist in the aftermath of Crossbarry comprised eight officers and 80 other ranks, led by Lieutenant. Colonel Evans.[897] However, part of the function of these reinforcements was not the pursuit of the flying column but the continuing search for the IRA headquarters dug-out, which the British were now convinced was in the Ballymurphy area.

In the end, when Crossbarry is analysed using all the remaining evidence from British and Irish sources and when compared to his original report, Tom Barry's account of the events in *Guerrilla Days in Ireland* is shown to be somewhat self-serving, and unreliable. The testimony of IRA veterans like Liam Deasy, the British Army records, contemporary newspapers reports and Barry's own report all can be seen broadly to agree on the events of the day and reveal that only approximately 70 British soldiers were in action against the flying column on the day, not the 1,200 claimed by Barry in his book. Moreover, the only British Army units in action during the event were the Essex and Hampshire Regiments, and not any of the other units that some writers and historians have claimed. The traditional and inflated account of Crossbarry is simply not supported by the complete body of evidence concerning the encounter. The primary goal for the British Army on the day was not to launch a massive action against a flying column, but to locate the IRA dumps in the area and seize the arms they contained. Contrary to popular belief, it was the IRA that quit the battlefield. In short, the myth that has developed around the 'battle' of Crossbarry, and the over-reliance on a deeply prejudiced source for the narrative thread of the event highlights the great dangers of this type of historical reconstruction. Despite its many glaring inaccuracies, the Crossbarry myth has been repeated without any degree of reflection or investigation by both local and academic historians. The danger of these uncritically reused 'false' histories has been their use by extremists to justify physical force republicanism. But when the full evidence concerning Crossbarry is considered, it is clear that it was no republican Thermopylae.

Crossbarry is a litmus test of historiography of the War of Independence, demonstrating the need for a corrective dose of revisionism, something that this book is attempting to do with regard to a reconsideration of British military attitudes and tactics.

'Framework Deployment'

The British Army intelligence-led ambushes and attacks placed the IRA under enormous pressure, as did the improvement in transportation and the use of air support. As James Brennock of the Rathcormac company recalled, 'the column was continually harassed by large forces of the enemy, in endeavours to round it up.'[898] Daniel Canty, the OC of Newcestown Company, confirmed that: 'during [May 1921], all IRA were mainly engaged in avoiding arrest.'[899] For others, the pressure had come even earlier. Philip Chambers, of the 3rd Battalion, 3rd IRA Brigade, remembered how, 'some time in February 1921, the column was temporarily disbanded, due as far as I know, to the heavy enemy pressure at that stage.'[900] Con Meaney of the 2nd Cork Brigade IRA remembered the disbandment of his column with the words: ''twas hard to keep a column together then.'[901] The success of British operations like Clonmult was clearly a factor in reducing IRA effectiveness. Michael Burke, a member of 1st Cork Brigade, IRA, explicitly acknowledged that 'the column in the 4th Bn. Area was finished after the fight at Clonmult.'[902]

Tactical flexibility is identified by Mockaitis as one of the key characteristics of British counter-insurgency, a thesis that holds true when tested against British operations in Cork city and county. The 6th Division, through its own collective efforts and the efforts of individual officers, continually refined its practices, abandoning ineffectual tactics and reinforcing and developing the areas which brought most success. The use of Q lorries, the creation of battalion scouts, the employment of airpower and the use of wireless telegraphs to improve unit co-ordination, all attest to a military that was prepared to adapt to the particular challenges presented by the IRA in the War of Independence.[903] In addition to the various tactical innovations, the assignment of specific units to particular geographic areas meant that 'individual units were in fact discovering what would in Malaya come to be called framework deployment.'[904]

Chapter Six

The End of the Guerrilla Campaign

Drives and sweeps are often seen by modern historians as a poor choice of tactics in Ireland. Thomas Mockaitis, the leading historian of British counter-insurgency, has noted that 'activity in Cork, where the worst fighting took place, reveals a constant pattern of futile large-scale operations and successful small ones.'[905] The principal reason for the dismissal of this tactic has been the belief that it caused the demor-alisation of soldiers, and was a drain on military resources that the end results never justified. However, this view was not held by many of the British officers of the period; a Major T.A. Lowe noted that the drives during the winter of 1920 were successful and were responsible for rounding up hundreds of rebels.[906] The key role of drives and sweeps was to target the static infrastructure of the IRA in the form of arms dumps, hidden vehicles and local IRA personnel, and as such a perfectly valid tactical choice.

Drives such as that at Nad in North Cork did indeed produce the desired results, as the following comment by the commander of the drive shows:

On arrival at Inchamay, the OC 17th Infantry Brigade troops, handed over to me the males of the village. He told me that they had been interrogated, and that they were apparently only yokels. I told my Brigade Intelligence Officer to look them over. He did not identify anyone, but not liking the look of four of them, he brought them to headquarters. Next morning, an agent, who chanced to be in barracks, identified all four as members of the Nad flying columns.[907]

Drives and sweeps were largely felt by the army to be a valuable weapon in their arsenal of operational methods. 'Large columns and small officer patrols scoured the country. Districts which had never set eyes on the British Army before became cen-tres of military activity.'[908] The value of this physical military presence should not be underestimated. As Marie Coleman and others have pointed out, 'the disappearance of the RIC from large sections of rural Ireland' hampered the campaign.[909] Military drives and sweeps were designed to counter this. Moreover, they were not wasteful, the vast majority of drives having a very definite objective, such as the location and destruction of an IRA headquarters.[910] Indeed, drives continued to be a key tactic until the end of the conflict, with several in West Cork and areas around Cork city during May and June 1921, as well as in other areas covered by the 6th Division such as Clare and Tipperary.[911] No plans to abandon this method of operation were ever considered. In fact, the Royal Artillery Mounted Rifles was created for the express purpose of investing more resources into this very activity; the conduct of drives and sweeps was to be its primary function.[912] It must also be remembered that the coordination and execution of drives and sweeps became more sophisticated as the conflict progressed, and as one British officer involved noted, this older tactic was actually allied with the newer one of active-service platoons, and that 'a number of military flying columns would be co-ordinated in their action.' Aircraft were also integrated into these operations with considerable success.[913]

One of the greatest difficulties in ensuring the success of drives was the maintenance of secrecy. The details of some were even reported in the local press, as when the *Cork Examiner* reported in relation to a drive in West Cork that 'the military expeditionary forces were … supplied with stretchers, and such like paraphernalia, indicating serious business afoot.'[914] Urban drives particularly were often conducted in full view of a frequently jaundiced public eye. On 26 November 1920 a large part of the city centre in Cork was closed off and civilians and houses searched, and as the army 'drove away through Patrick St. the two prisoners were loudly cheered by the people who has assembled to watch the operations of the military and the police.'[915]

An examination of the Nad drive (see map on page 14 of the picture section) shows how this tactic was employed in the field. The main objective of the drive was to unearth the headquarters of the 2nd Southern Division, IRA and if possible effect the capture of Liam Lynch. As in the later Clydagh Valley operations, positions were taken at 4am, and 5am saw the commencement, the troops in question being provided by both the 17th and Kerry Brigades. At 4am, the troops of the Kerry Brigade were to be in position along the black line.[916] While along the dotted line, in stationary positions, were soldiers from the 1st Battalion Royal Fusiliers, the 1st Battalion Machine Gun Corps, and the 1st Battalion the Gloucesters, supported by 'L' company, the Auxiliaries.

At 5am, the Machine Gunners began to search the houses and farms along the black line, while the other elements of the Kerry Brigade began advancing across country towards the second black line, searching as they went. After 8am, all the Kerry units were to move from the second line, covering the ground towards the dotted line, and driving all retreating or fleeing elements of the IRA into the path of the 17th Brigade troops. All went according to plan, but at one point there was a break in the right flank caused by the slowness of the Machine Gunners' advance.

The numbers netted were admittedly modest in this case. One local was shot for failing to halt, and while 80 men were captured and held by the troops, only

21 were detained further through problems with identification. Six motor cars and six bicycles were found, and one car which could not be moved was destroyed. The cars were found only by accident, when 'a sick man, whilst being escorted to the rear by a comrade actually fell on top of one of them.'[917] The technique of the troops involved was criticised by the colonel of the Kerry Brigade who was unhappy with some of the searches performed by his troops, stating that they were 'liable to bunch during the advance, and naturally take the lines of least resistance … [and] failing any excitement, the thickest and roughest portions of the hills are liable to be skirted and left alone.'[918] Nevertheless, despite seemingly poor results, overall the army was satisfied with these June drives, because 'no place, however remote, could be regarded as a safe retreat for the wanted men.'[919] Drives were considered an effective technique long after the Irish war, the British Army continuing to employ this tactic in Palestine, Burma, Indochina, Greece and Malaya.[920] Tim Jones describes how in the 1930s this tactic was still important: 'The Army's counter-guerrilla strategy was to encircle target areas, and its favoured tactics involved large numbers of troops undertaking "drives" towards stop-lines provided by their colleagues.'[921]

The largest drive in Cork was the Clydagh Valley operations on the Cork-Kerry border in early June 1921. This sweep is described in the *Record of the Rebellion* as one of the 'most extensive and elaborately organised operations' that took place in the 6th Division area.[922] The operations involved close to 2,000 men from the 17th Infantry Brigade, the Kerry Brigade and Auxiliaries, as well as RAF aircraft. The headquarters of the 6th Division believed that the valley was being used as a base of operations by the IRA for attacks in Cork and Kerry, and 'further information to the same effect was received from an informer, who was thought to be speaking the truth.'[923] However as was later acknowledged, 'the information on which the operation was based was evidently untrue.'[924]

The 17th Brigade provided 880 officers and men to operate in three columns, starting out from Ballymakeery, Gorteenakilla and Kilgarvan, while the Kerry Brigade deployed over 990 soldiers, using Lough Guitane, Gullan, Rathmore and Lackdotia House as their starting points. A party of Auxiliaries was also based in the Caherbarnagh Mountains to prevent any retreat in that direction. The operation began at 4am with the troops encircling the valley. 'The night approach marches and deployment were well carried out, in spite of the difficult country, and the fact that no previous reconnaissance had been possible.'[925]

At 5am the troops began to move into the valley. The Royal Fusiliers were able to capture a despatch rider with his documents and three other men. Over 100 men were rounded up, and one old man was hurt by a ricochet bullet, which had been fired to force others to halt. Three motor cars were found but as vital parts were missing, the army was unable to remove them from the site and so they were destroyed. 'Aeroplane[s] cooperated from 1000 hours onwards, and dropped messages at the Brigade Headquarters giving the position of the troops. If severe opposition had been met with, the aeroplanes would undoubtedly have been very useful.'[926] Although there was strict operational secrecy, once the presence of the troops was detected by locals, signal fires were lit on surrounding mountains and at one point a flare warning of the soldiers' approach was spotted.

In an effort to improve the tracking of IRA volunteers after ambushes and during round-ups, bloodhounds were introduced. Reports of the use of these dogs were dismissed by Sinn Féin as scaremongering; however they were used successfully in Cork, all the more so perhaps for being dismissed. Strickland retained a *Daily Mail* article in his private papers which noted that 'it appears that the deep bay of this specimen of propaganda at three o'clock in the morning in the Bantry district had a far greater effect on the members of the IRA than the circular on the subject by Sinn Féin headquarters. The subsequent running to ground of the brothers Dineen has increased this effect.'[927]

The evidence demonstrates that drives and sweeps played a key role in the reduction by the British Army of the IRA's operational capability, not only by the destruction of physical resources and the removal of safe areas for headquarters and training facilities, but by maintaining a psychological pressure on the IRA rank and file.

A Terrorist Strategy

During 1921 the British forces began to take control of the countryside through the continual patrolling of their own flying columns and aerial patrols. As Hart has noted of the IRA in Skibbereen, 'the battalion's men were not only not showing up for parades, many of the trainee column had deserted.'[928] This phenomenon was not restricted to Cork, as Michael Farry has noted with regard to Sligo, reminding us that 'by mid 1921, small groups of IRA were surviving on the run in County Sligo and were at best able to carry out small-scale actions without ever seriously challenging the British Forces,'[929] a fact Marie Coleman has also noted in the case of Longford where 'the North Longford flying column was under severe pressure from the enhanced strength and effectiveness of the Crown Forces.'[930] Suffering from a reduction in manpower due to internment, the IRA was forced to adopt a radical strategy – the killing of ex-servicemen and loyalists.

There has been considerable debate amongst Irish historians over the significance of these killings. Some have suggested that this was republican anti-Protestantism at work, while others have tied it more to the intelligence war particularly in Cork. John Borgonovo in his fascinating study, *Spies, Informers and the Anti Sinn Fein Study* concludes that assassinated ex-servicemen were not simply executed because of their status, rather that those killed were selected because of their involvement with British Forces.[931] This is true in many of the cases, but it still does not discount or exclude Jane Leonard's theory that they were selected as the softest targets in the British system – given that the IRA could no long access soldiers without considerable risk, these men were more vulnerable. So this type of IRA action can perhaps be more satisfactorily accounted for in a third way, namely as a means of continuing some form of military pressure on the British state by highlighting at an individual level its failure to stabilise the security situation in Cork city and county. In reaction to the British pressure from the ground and the air, and the deterioration of IRA resources, the IRA made a strategic choice to target individuals. This is confirmed in an IRA memo, when it noted that 'we can place against any military losses we may suffer the serious civil losses we can inflict.'[932]

During 1921 the persecution and murder of loyalists and Protestants in the south of Ireland increased significantly. 'The rebel offensive was directed entirely against them.'[933] This assessment by the British highlights what was one of their greatest difficulties entering into the summer of 1921 – the protection of individual civilians against IRA assassination. By mid 1921, 'The real problem which was becoming more and more urgent was that of the loyalists.'[934] This view was also supported by the RIC, who felt 'a new feature of the IRA campaign was the murder of respectable and loyal Protestant farmers, on the grounds that they were giving information to the military.'[935] This posed a huge challenge for the army in Cork, for as Mockaitis points out, 'if a government cannot provide security of life and property for those who support it, it cannot begin to win the hearts and minds campaign.'[936]

During 1921 the assassination of individual soldiers also became a dominant IRA tactic in Cork. At the end of April 1921 six British soldiers had been shot dead in the city and another four wounded. These soldiers were particularly vulnerable, being unarmed and outside of the barracks, and mostly in the company of local women.[937] As the *Cork Weekly News* reported, 'the unfortunate men were walking in more lonely spots on the outskirts of the city with girlfriends.'[938] Some soldiers were warned by locals of the intent of the IRA in the area and managed to escape the attacks.[939] An unarmed private from the East Lancashire Regiment, Private Fielding, was killed near Liscarroll in March.[940] The killing caused a great deal of anger in the East Lancashires, as their journal recorded: 'The murder of Pte. Fielding was one of the foulest crimes in the particularly foul record of the IRA, the poor lad was walking alone and was absolutely unarmed when he met his death.'[941] The RIC county inspector for the city noted the continuation of this new strategy in April.[942] In the *Irish Independent* of 16 May no fewer than three separate incidents were reported: the killing of Privates Hunter, Chalmers, and McMillan of the King's Own Scottish Borderers in Bantry, a sniper attack which resulted in the death of Private Sheppard of the Essex Regiment in Bandon and the killing of two gunners of the Royal Marine Artillery in East Ferry.

Serving soldiers were by no means the only target in this campaign. Three ex-servicemen, Daniel Hawkins, Edward Hawkins and John Sherlock working in Victoria Barracks were killed in May 1921. Once again the army adapted to IRA tactics and 'a scheme was instituted by which large numbers of selected men in plain clothes, armed with automatics patrolled the streets where soldiers were allowed to "walk out".'[943]

Allied to individual assassination was the campaign of road-trenching, the army noting that the two tactics were intertwined, forming a two-pronged tactic that involved 'hindering the movements of the Crown Forces and murdering any offic-ers or men whom they could attack without any danger to themselves.'[944] The trenching of roads did undeniably hinder British road transport but as most offen-sive operations in the summer of 1921 were conducted by active service platoons and mobile columns with air support, there was little slow-down in the pace of military activities. Just prior to this period, in the spring of 1921, the targeting of soldiers and policemen had fallen off considerably, with the county inspector in Cork city noting that 'no policeman has been fired at in Cork city for over two months.'[945] Hopkinson points out that as ambushes became more difficult in 1921, the IRA again refocused on smaller-scale activities.[946] And while individual attacks and killings had always been an important strand of IRA pressure, by 1921 'their scale of operations was always limited by the availability of weapons and ammuni-tion.'[947] So the IRA had indeed shifted their attention to softer targets than the army and the police in an effort to retain some pressure on the British Forces. Four Protestants were shot and killed in West Cork, and the county inspector of the West Riding noted that loyalists were either selling up and leaving or being burnt out.

As Mockaitis points out, 'terrorism is the final weapon in the insurgent arsenal,'[948] and as another theorist of counter-insurgency Dr Paul Melshen has also suggested, 'terrorism is a tactic, not a form of warfare. Terrorism is a psychological tactic.'[949] Soon officers such as Percival began to believe that the creation of protected areas for loyalists would be necessary to win the campaign.[950] As Strickland commented, 'while the army hunted the rebel bands, the rebels murdered the loyalists and burnt their homes.'[951] The British Army testified that a 'reign of terror [had] developed in West Cork,'[952] although a more palatable explanation from a nationalist perspec-tive for the shooting of ex-servicemen and loyalists was that they were providing damaging intelligence of a military nature to the Crown forces. An example of this was the shooting of two protestant farmers, Connell and Sweetman, who were both in their sixties, for allegedly reporting a local Sinn Féin councillor, Florence MacCarthy, for collecting money for an arms fund.[953] Even though official reprisals had ended on 6 June 1921, the loyalist community of West Cork continued to be targeted, with over fourteen Protestant-owned houses being destroyed by the IRA in June alone. As Hart has noted, 'Cork's Protestant minority increasingly came to be seen by the IRA, as the "enemy within".'[954] This has also been documented by Marie Coleman in Longford, when she writes 'the killing of Protestants increased towards the end of the war.'[955]

The pressure that these new IRA tactics placed on the British forces is clear from Strickland's reaction. He noted that loyalists could hardly be expected to rally to the government cause if it 'allows them to be killed or their homes burnt without admitting any responsibility toward them at all.'[956] As Laffan points out, of the more than 200 civilians killed by the IRA in 1920–21, 70 were Protestant, and that of the houses they destroyed, 85 per cent were Protestant-owned.[957] Just as the IRA flying columns were the product of British pressure in 1920, so the increase in British pressure on a wide variety of fronts in 1921 forced the IRA to remould its strategy into one that conformed to the definition of a terrorist rather than a guerrilla campaign. One only also has to look at Liam Lynch's reaction to the Special Powers Act, passed by an Irish state, when he issued orders to kill all civilian supporters of the Free State to see the direction a future IRA campaign could have taken.[958] If the IRA campaign had continued after July 1921, the improvised bomb and individual assassination would have become the tactics of choice.

The Military Realities of the Truce

The *Record of the Rebellion* begins its commentary on the period of the Truce with the statement that it was 'a strange commentary on the "war" conducted by the "Republican army" to say that the "army" itself never appeared until after the Truce was signed.'[959] When one considers the period from 11 July 1921 up to the final withdrawal of British forces, this period was in many ways the most testing for the army's patience and discipline in Cork. Tension between the army and the British Cabinet is equally in evidence in the military documents of this period.

The Truce did not get off to the best of starts, as the responsibilities and obligations were understood very differently by the army and the IRA. A statement from Parkgate, the British Army's headquarters in Ireland, identified the government obligations as: the cessation of all raids and searches; the restriction of military activity to the support of the police in their normal civil duties; the removal of curfew restrictions; the suspension of the dispatch of reinforcements from England; and that the policing of Dublin should be carried out by the DMP. But the *Irish Bulletin* attempted to add to the army's commitments, saying that there were to be no secret agents, no noting of descriptions or movements, no interference with the movements of Irish persons, military or civil, and no attempt to discover the haunts and habits of Irish officers and men. There was also to be no pursuit or observance of the IRA lines of communication.

The obligations of the IRA were detailed in the British statement: to cease all attacks on Crown forces and civilians; to prohibit use of arms; cease military manoeuvres of all kinds; to abstain from interference with public and private property; and to discountenance and prevent any action likely to cause disturbance of the peace which might necessitate military interference. These were repeated faithfully in the *Irish Bulletin* this time, with no attempt to extend the IRA's obligations.

Of course, some of the differences obviously involved public relations and the placation of the protagonists' respective constituencies. But there were some perhaps more vital differences. The army, for example, never agreed to curtail or cease its intelligence operations with regard to the IRA. If anything, these intensified during the Truce as intelligence officers sought to confirm the identities of IRA officers and of the various orders of battle, 'profit[ing] by the Truce to check their data about the rebel organisation and individuals.'[960] The IRA in turn felt it could continue military training and did so openly, even though the army interpreted this as breaching the ban on military manoeuvres. The Crown forces did not agree to restrict the importation of munitions, as they would have required ammunition for training purposes.

Perhaps the most interesting point to be taken from the above is the agreement by the IRA not to interfere with 'Government' property, a slip perhaps by Barton and Duggan, the IRA's negotiators, which could be seen to concede the legitimacy of that title in relation to Dublin Castle. On the other hand, perhaps this was nothing more than a practicality, using a term that could readily be understood by all involved.

On the very morning of the Truce in Cork, and not auguring well for the peace, four British soldiers were found blindfolded and dead on the outskirts of Cork city, in a field near St Finbarr's Cemetery.[961] They were two members of the South Staffordshire Regiment and two sappers of the Royal Engineers who had been kidnapped the night before near Gaol Cross. A Private Latter of the Machine Gun Corps was killed the same night by several armed men near Doneraile in North Cork, though he was unarmed at the time, as was Major G.B. O'Connor, a JP in the Douglas Petty Sessions who was abducted from his home and killed.[962] His body was found the following morning by his wife.[963] Major O'Connor had stood many years previously as a Unionist candidate in Dublin's College Green division, and was later involved in the Dominion Home Rule League.[964]

Shortly after the Truce, Strickland wrote to Macready to express his frustration at the state of affairs in Munster, saying it is 'beyond human endurance for some people to lie down and be kicked by murderers.'[965] He pointed out that the IRA was now able to practise open terrorism, and concluded, 'I think the whole situation is damnable.'[966]

A month later Strickland was clearly angered by the direction of events and wrote to General Macready that 'The so-called "Truce" is in reality not a truce at all. Apart from the actual murder of Crown Forces, the rebels have not complied with any of the terms of the agreement.'[967] He went on to point out that the IRA were displaying their arms openly, often in uniform, and were drilling and conducting tactical exercises, while the position of loyalists was becoming impossible, with many 'being bullied and molested, and in some cases ordered to leave the country.'[968] He stated very plainly that he believed the current situation to be untenable, arguing that both the IRA and Sinn Féin should honour the terms of the Truce, or that the army should recommence operations against them since 'either alternative is infinitely preferable to the present states of affairs.'[969]

Strickland himself was at the receiving end of complaints, as shown by a letter from Lieutenant-Colonel Savage, the acting colonel commandant of 17th Infantry Brigade. The primary purpose of the letter was to complain about the activities of a certain under-secretary in Dublin Castle, Alfred Cope. Cope had promised the army to make inquiries with members of the IRA regarding the fate of a kidnapped soldier,

Private Dawson of the Essex Regiment.[970] Cope's suggestion that Dawson give the IRA his parole in return for release was met with the following hostile comment:

> I take strong exception to insinuations of this nature, made by a civilian on a subject about which he is quite ignorant, it is obviously impossible for a soldier to give his parole when captured by rebels who are fighting against their King.[971]

Adding to Savage's outrage was an instruction by Cope that a stolen car which the Essex Regiment had confiscated from the IRA and returned to its owner, a Colonel Lucas of Ballinadree, be returned to the IRA. In his letter, Savage asked Strickland if anything could be done to 'restrain persons like Mr. Cope from preaching rebel doctrines in this Brigade Area.'[972] He also added that Cope was testing the patience of the Essex men, although in the event, the discipline of the army held and Cope remained unmolested.

The army did not consider the liaison arrangements with the IRA satisfactory and felt that there was little done to address their complaints. They felt that the Republican liaison officers were ineffective figureheads and that 'their personal qualifications were not as a rule, such as to appeal to the officers with whom they were supposed to have dealings.'[973] In particular, there was a struggle over the legal status of IRA volunteers. Under orders from General Macready, Strickland would not officially acknowledge any IRA rank, liaison officials being treated as the representatives of de Valera. In Macready's words,

> I passed word to the Divisional Generals that neither the IRA nor any military rank could be recognised by us, because if the peace negotiations broke down the Irish would at once argue that we had recognised their Army status and claim to be treated as belligerents.[974]

This presented Strickland with problems in his relationship with Tom Barry, who as the liaison officer for the martial law area was 'tenacious of his rank in the IRA' and 'finally behaved in such an overbearing and insulting manner that Strickland very properly refused to see him.'[975] This may have reflected some insecurity on the part of Barry and others when dealing with senior British officers. Indeed, Tom Barry, for his part, was not happy with the situation either, and instructions to IRA officers were printed in the *Cork Examiner* of 25 July 1921 ordering them to cease cooperation with the British military. Barry's reason was that the army had refused to cooperate with the liaison officers by refusing to treat them 'in the only capacity in which they can act, viz. as officers of the Irish Republican Army.'[976] There was to be no cooperation until 'the British Authorities deal with us in our proper status.'[977] Though nothing in the terms of the truce obliged the army to deal with the IRA in this fashion, it became an issue of fundamental importance to the IRA.

Another item of contention was the refusal of the army to accept any complaints on the official notepaper of the IRA. This dispute was also played out in public. The reaction of the chief liaison officer, Eamonn Duggan, to the dispute was published in the *Cork Examiner* of 26 July 1921, where he sought to reassure readers that the problem would not affect the Truce, while acknowledging that British officers were refusing to address members of the IRA by their military titles and to accept complaints on official paper. Duggan emphasised that liaison officers were continuing to accept complaints concerning RIC and army activities. Tom Barry was so irate that he went to Dublin, and wanted to travel on to London to see de Valera. Duggan brought Barry to see Macready, who upon seeing him remarked that now he 'quite sympathised with Strickland's difficulties'.[978] Macready in his autobiography, *Annals of an Active Life*, reported a conversation concerning Barry he overheard between the butler and an old pensioner who was the doorkeeper; 'Said the butler: "Well, Mr. Kennedy, you may have been here for twenty-six years, but you've never opened the door to a thing like that before!" And I don't suppose he ever had!'[979] This anecdote showed the class prism through which the senior British officers viewed the IRA commanders, so Barry got little sympathy from Macready. Later when as the result of a car accident Tom Barry was replaced, his replacement was recorded as being 'much to the relief of both sides'.[980]

However, apart from personal conflicts with senior British figures, Tom Barry undoubtedly had legitimate points to make. The *Cork Examiner* reported him as saying that 'breaches of the Truce by the British forces are becoming more numerous since the refusal of IRA liaison officers to deal with the British authorities in any way whatever except on the basis of their proper status as officers of the Irish Republican Army.'[981] In reports published in the paper he made several complaints about arms being openly carried by the RIC and the army in violation of the Truce,[982] and drew attention to the fact that armed British soldiers had been placed on sentry duty at various points on the Cork, Bandon, and South Coast Railway on 27 July.[983]

Barry presumably considered these to be provocative displays of force but that is perhaps open to question. After all, the RIC had retained the right to police, and the army retained the right to provide aid to the civil power. Another complaint related to British activity on 27 July when two lorries of soldiers stopped at Drinagh on the Rosscarbery-Clonakilty Road and allegedly searched several civilians, an event that would certainly have constituted interference with civilian movement and would have been a breach of the terms of the Truce. Barry also noted other more serious incidents, claiming that British soldiers had fired their weapons on several occasions, and that at 10.15am on 21 July an officer of the Essex Regiment fired a shot at Kinsale Junction.[984] He also claimed that British troops in lorries near Ardrow Hill, near Glenville, had fired shots four days later at a volunteer on a bicycle, and that Crown forces also opened fire in the Manch district near Dunmanway.[985]

Some of this alleged misconduct by Crown troops was a direct reaction to IRA misconduct. In one case, for example, Tom Barry complained that two lorries of soldiers travelling between Fermoy and Tallow, who, when confronted with the

IRA destruction of Lukey's bridge, simply broke the ditch and travelled round the bridge through the fields. Obviously, had the bridge been intact, the British would not have needed to divert around it! Another complaint related to the difficulties of receiving post in West Cork. This was primarily due to trenched roads, which was acknowledged by the *Cork Examiner,* mail delivery was impeded because 'owing to roads being impassable, conveyance by motor is impracticable.'[986] In a local effort to address this, young men from the area were filling in the trenches and the post was being delivered to Castletownbere by the Bantry Bay Steamship Co. There were other complaints about the treatment of prisoners. In Spike Island, Bere Island and Furious Pier internment camps the conditions were believed to be 'very bad, and in view of the truce, the least that maybe expected is that they should be treated decently or as prisoners of war.'[987]

The British Army had its own complaints to make, and in at least a few cases these were far more substantive than those of the IRA, even after the passing of the Treaty by the Dáil. Other British servicemen who were kidnapped were not as fortunate as Private Dawson mentioned above. On 26 April 1922, Lieutenants R.A. Harry of the Royal Warwickshire Regiment, R.A. Dove of the 2nd Hampshire, K.R. Henderson, of the 2nd Green Howards and Private J. Brooks of the Royal Army Service Corps left Victoria Barracks and were kidnapped near Macroom.[988] A particular concern for the British commanders was that two of the officers had been involved as intelligence officers in the conflict, and it was feared they would be shot immediately.[989] Significantly, Lieutenant Dove had been one of the officers involved in the destruction of an IRA flying column at Clonmult. The matter was immediately raised by General Strickland with liaison officers from the Provisional Government, and, in fact both Michael Collins' and Eamon de Valera's assistance was sought,[990] but the men were killed.

> Three battalions of the garrison were affected by this outrage, each of the missing officers belonging to a different unit, yet the self-restraint of their comrades was beyond all praise. The younger officers and men found it difficult to understand why they should be kept in the country for no obvious purpose, the butts of insolent natives, and powerless to react to recent outrage. Before the truce, nearly a year ago, when the 'war' was in progress, certain measures were taken if outrages occurred, thereby giving an outlet to the feelings of the troops, but under the conditions prevailing at the time of the Macroom murders they were, for political reasons, condemned to sit still and brood over the situation for the convenience of the very men who a few months before had been their bitterest enemies.[991]

Macready himself visited Macroom, and British military action against the Anti-Treaty faction holding Macroom Castle was seriously considered, with Macready noting that ordering such an attack, 'would have given me infinite satisfaction, and … General Strickland even greater satisfaction to carry out.'[992] Cork was not the only location where British soldiers were still being killed after the Truce; Gunner James Rolfe was shot dead on Bachelors Walk in Dublin in May 1922.[993] Despite the various kidnappings and other attacks the army felt that

> The invariable good humour, however, of the British soldier, added to a certain amount of amusement at the antics of the mock army opposed to him, served him in good stead, and although soldiers were kidnapped, arms stolen, etc., there was never any danger of relations becoming really strained.[994]

The army did not just sit idly by during this period, and careful plans were prepared for a resumption of hostilities. One of the aims was that the intelligence organisation 'be developed to the highest pitch of perfection to render potential operations in the future more effective'.[995] The Cork city intelligence model was applied to the organisation of intelligence in the neighbouring county of Limerick. The freer movement of British officers and men allowed intelligence officers to meet and compare notes and methods. An intelligence conference about the campaign was held in Chester in November 1921, and a similar conference for the intelligence officers of the Auxiliary companies took place at the divisional headquarters in Cork.[996] It was generally felt by the officers as they checked their existing information that the investigations that the Truce had made possible had demonstrated the quality of the information they were receiving, and shown much of their data to be accurate. In addition, 'the identification of individuals would in future have proved a far easier task, as most of the rebel leaders [now] showed themselves openly, and there was no difficulty in becoming acquainted with their appearance.'[997]

Apart from the improvement of the intelligence service during the post-Truce period, other improvements were also made such as the increase in wireless sets; by November 1921 every unit HQ and almost all detachments possessed a set.[998] This securing of the British lines of communication in the event of resumed hostilities would have practically eliminated all the intelligence the IRA had been receiving from the postal and telephone system, with its attendant consequences. Command and control issues were not forgotten in this improvement drive either, and by November, the scheme to form two additional brigades had been 'carried into effect'.[999]

'Close on my Trail'

The IRA was under great pressure from the British Army ambushes and drives during the summer of 1921, so much so that they began to utilise terrorist tactics rather than those of guerillas. Even such a change in operational style did not greatly improve matters, as they were still 'continuously harassed'[1000] and spent much time trying to avoid arrest,[1001] to the extent that some IRA columns were disbanded.[1002] There were difficulties in maintaining cohesion within the groups.[1003] Apart from the general harrying of IRA personnel, successful British operations such as Clonmult had a great impact on IRA operations, the latter effectively destroying any military capability of the local column.[1004]

The letters of Liam Lynch also confirmed that the British Army was on the cusp of success. One of the most committed IRA leaders, he significantly altered his view, writing to his brother Tom in July 1920 that 'John Bull should give in soon,' but admitting to his mother by July 1921 that before the Truce the 'enemy were continually dogging me and often close on my trail.'[1005] Even earlier than this, Liam de Roiste, in a section of his diary captured by the British, acknowledged that 'we cannot beat the English Forces in arms: this is accepted by even the most sanguine of volunteers.'[1006] The introduction of new British tactics into areas outside of Cork county was recognised as a severe setback by individuals like Michael Brennan who noted that the arrival of flying columns 'made things awkward and the uncertainty the practice caused meant that when moving at night, we always had to be ready for action.'[1007] Florence O'Donoghue, the IRA intelligence officer in Cork, also felt that this new tactic was the greatest threat the IRA had faced during the entire campaign, but felt that it received no support from the military establishment and that its 'true value was not appreciated by the higher military authorities.'[1008] Others, like Michael Coleman, the captain of the Barryroe Company, simply recorded this period as being one of considerable frustration with 'many failures and disappointments when we were out with the column. Ambushes which were prepared did not come off and barrack attacks petered out owing to mine failures.'[1009]

As mentioned previously, Mockaitis has identified the tactical flexibility of the British against the Irish insurgency to have been a defining characteristic during the War of Independence. This supposition is supported by the evidence of operations in the Cork area, specifically the tactics of the 6th Division with regard to the continual refining of strategy and the introduction of new tactics such as the use of scouts, RAF air power, wireless telegraphs and the Q lorry trap. The British Army's ability to win the tactical arms race against the IRA therefore shows that they were highly adaptable, contrary to much of the received wisdom to be found in many historical studies of the period.[1010] The British even utilised tactics that would be used fighting guerrillas during the Malayan Emergency, [1011] and in this they were anything but a static reactive force.

It can be argued that if any side was reactive, it was the IRA. Its flying columns were created not as part of any coherent military strategy on the part of the republican movement, but as a result of volunteers having to go on the run from internment. The burning of unionist households was also a direct response to official reprisals, rather than a proactive military strategy. The shift towards the end of the war to the use of roadside bombs and the individual targeting of servicemen and unionists was also reactionary, this time to the army's elimination of the IRA flying columns.

The idea that British pressure had an impact on IRA strategy is not new. Michael Laffan credits such British pressure with the development of the IRA flying column, as indeed do most historians of the conflict. The IRA also admitted this at the time, as IRA Organisation Memo No. 1 revealed: 'At the present time a large number of our men and officers are on the run in different parts of the country. The most effective way of utilising these officers and men would seem to be by organising them as a flying column.'[1012] The RIC in the summer of 1921 concurred with the idea that increased army activity and internment were causing a slump in IRA operations 'due to the fact that all local leaders have been either killed or captured.'[1013]

The army had every confidence that any resumption of hostilities would play into their hands, and that 'the experiences of the IRA, which had – on their own admission – become almost unbearable in the summer of 1921, would have been far worse in the winter of 1921–1922.'[1014] As Mockaitis has pointed out 'all of Britain's counter insurgency victories were won by regular army operating in platoon and sections.'[1015] Cork saw the employment of this technique in the creation of the active service platoons, and these undoubtedly had a detrimental impact on the IRA campaign. These tactics can be seen in other British campaigns of the inter-war years, being used by 2/9th Gurka Rifles during the Moplah rebellion, and in Burma in 1932.[1016]

Hardly surprisingly in the Irish context, weather was also a factor and despite the trenching of the roads, the army felt that the good weather of the late summer of 1921 would given them ample opportunity to conduct any operations they wished in the Irish countryside.[1017] The army clearly believed towards the end that it was gaining the upper hand in the rural guerrilla war and that 'a few more battles like those at Clonmult and Crossbarry would have gone a long way towards putting an end to flying columns.'[1018] This was also the opinion of the RIC, its Inspector General noting that 'there is no doubt, to judge from information, that the IRA were a bad way, and that several months of intensive action by the Crown Forces would have beaten them out of the field.'[1019] Townshend notes that adding to this pressure in the field the decision to send British Army reinforcements 'had, belatedly, made it clear to the rebels that the military balance had turned against the Republic.'[1020] Indeed, Henry Wilson's view of the campaign was long term, noting in a letter dated 18 September 1920 and addressed to the Secretary of State for War, 'I see no reason why, with patience and firmness, we may not wear the trouble down in the course of a few years.'[1021]

The British Army through the development of its own flying columns had undeniably found the perfect means to reduce the threat of IRA columns and it had improved its intelligence system. However, by the Truce it had not devised any defence against the threat of road-side bombs, a new strategy that evolved out of the deteriorating military position of the IRA in Cork and the reduced numbers at its disposal as a result of internment. Significantly, little discussion concerning this particular challenge can be found in the surviving British sources, and yet it was arguably the single greatest problem facing the army in Cork during the final months of the conflict. (The IED, the road-side bomb, today of course causes the greatest number of casualties to NATO forces in Afghanistan.)

Ireland has to be understood in the context of the other British conflicts running concurrently with the campaign in Ireland. In Mesopotamia from June to October 1920, for example over 416 British and Imperial personnel were killed in action, and over 1100 wounded.[1022] The international political context and not any given local IRA or indeed British military strategy was, in the end, perhaps what determined the outcome of the conflict most.[1023] Michael Laffan noted in *The Resurrection of Ireland* that, 'Lloyd George's government changed its policy more in response to international hostility, and to the shame and revulsion felt by the British public opinion, than as a consequence of military weakness or defeat.'[1024] Indeed, contrary to the popular idea of an Irish victory against British military might, such was the decline in IRA activity toward the summer of 1921 because of the effectiveness of the British campaign, that some British troops became fond of hill walking. One officer 'started taking the troops for walks in the country, whenever [they had] a day off', noting that his men preferred the countryside to the city.[1025]

Conclusions

'At the time of the Irish rebellion it [The York and Lancaster Regiment] went over to Ireland then came back to Pembroke Dock.'[1026] This extraordinary precis from a British regimental history shows how the conflict in Ireland was largely ignored and lost between the two world wars. The absence of significant British literature on the campaign has left the presentation and analysis predominantly to Irish veterans and historians. Some British historians like Charles Townshend were initially heavily influenced by the Irish material, as in *The Campaign in Ireland* (1975) when he stated that the 'republican guerrilla campaign proved too determined, too resilient, and too resourceful.'[1027] However by 1983, Townshend's view of the military situation in Ireland appeared to have altered significantly when he noted in his work *Political Violence in Ireland* that British 'military success did play a big part in bringing the Sinn Féin leaders into negotiations, and a bigger part in determining their outcome.'[1028] Townshend went even further in 1991, when in *Ireland: The 20th Century* he argued that the IRA was under 'intense pressure from the British Military'.[1029] He asserted that both Michael Collins and Richard Mulcahy feared that the IRA would disintegrate.[1030] However the dominant perspective remains that British military operations were ineffective and were poorly executed. Even Mockaitis, referring to the adoption of small-unit tactics, claimed that 'although they were discovered too late in the day to affect the outcome in Ireland, the methods developed to combat the IRA contributed to the eventual development of British counter-insurgency.'[1031] Stalemate is a word used by many of the historians of the conflict such as Nicolas Mansergh, who concluded that 'on the military side, the position of the British Army was variously reported as precarious and well-nigh desperate, in a position of stalemate.'[1032]

Much of the nationalist historiography has presented the War of Independence as a nationalist military victory, a triumph for political violence, guerrilla tactics and terrorism. Irish historians are not alone; Richard Popplewell has noted that 'all current work on counter-insurgency agrees that the first British counter-insurgency campaign of the twentieth century was fought in Ireland against the IRA,'[1033] and Popplewell believed that Britain failed. David Fitzpatrick is of the opinion that 'no victims of the Irish revolution suffered keener humiliation than the police and military forces of the Crown'[1034] due to the 'inadequacy of army response to Irish challenge – apparent at the time.'[1035] Therefore, in populist and academic Irish history, as well as in military history, the independence campaign has remained a war waged by the gallant volunteers of the IRA who forced the British government to negotiate and concede the Irish Free State.

However, as shown here, this interpretation cannot hold. The IRA in the summer of 1921 was under the severest pressure from the British Army. Over the previous two years, the British government and the army had developed a series of responses including internment, the employment of 'active-service' platoons, wireless telegraphy and air power. The introduction of these measures meant that the IRA had ceased to provide a significant military threat, and by 1921 their operations had been reduced to measures that constituted a terrorist rather than a military campaign. It must also be remembered that the British Army was on an active footing for only one year, from the summer of 1920.

The absence of a British perspective in much if not all of the history produced on the Irish War of Independence has left us with a distorted and fragmented view of the campaign. We have been largely dependent on the personal memoirs of the IRA servicemen for our information and theories. If the IRA did not carry the day during the war, they have certainly won the peace. This dependency now continues through the release of the papers in the Bureau of Military History, which, even though they have been of no small use in the creation of this work, give only one version of the conflict, a version that, like the published testimony of the IRA, has often been accepted by both professional and amateur historians in an uncritical and unquestioning manner. It has often been accepted as fact, with little attempt at corroboration.

While no equivalent of the Bureau of Military History exists in the United Kingdom, a different and richer fund of material exists on the campaign, much richer than has previously been thought. This material includes newly discovered personal testimonies, the regimental journals, local and regional British newspapers and RAF files. These sources offer key information on various events and personnel in the campaign in Cork, and throw new light on the relative strengths and weaknesses of the opposing sides.

Another disappointment with regard to the historiography of the campaign has been the fact that it has largely been under-researched from the British perspective. Effectively it was lost in the historiography of the First World War, a fact borne out by the approach of many regimental histories. On the few occasions when it has received the attention of historians, it has been used to repeat the general accusation levelled at the British military over the conduct of the First World War, that of incompetence and failure. The key allegation made by many historians was that the army was institutionally incapable of innovation and change, an allegation this study refutes. Archival material, particularly those sources detailing the experience of British servicemen, show a diversity of opinions, both official and unofficial, across a range of issues from the political justification of the war through the choice of tactics to views on the Irish and the IRA. What the material clearly suggests is the multiplicity of perspectives and the absence of any consensus on many vital issues. Some servicemen regarded the IRA as patriots; others could not see any real ideology behind Irish nationalism, consistently seeing the IRA as cowardly criminals and rebels against their lawful king.

The war in Ireland was a transitional campaign, and elements of older tactics remained, as British forces did use cavalry columns and infantry drives. However, new tactics emerged which predicted the future of British counter-insurgency and the campaign in Ireland was a clear step forward in British military thinking. New innovations, such as the use of active service platoons in Cork, show an understanding that the adoption of certain guerrilla tactics was often seen as the best way forward. These active service platoons were to have a major impact in Cork towards the end of the campaign and in many ways contributed to the reduction in IRA guerrilla activity as they spread uncertainty and fear in the IRA's ranks. The evidence of this innovation contradicts some of the IRA testimony. The key conclusion of this book is that it can clearly be evidenced that the British Army was effective in its operations in Cork, certainly far more effective than has previously been believed. During its nearly twelve months of active operations, it was able to end the threat of IRA flying columns and force the IRA to adopt the terrorist tactics of road-side bombing, kidnap and assassination.

The sophistication of the British approach in Cork can be seen in an examination of the legal conduct of the war, which clearly supports the views of the leading British historian on counter-insurgency, Thomas Mockaitis, that law and legality form a core element of the conduct of British counter-insurgency. As best as could be managed in trying circumstances, trials were held in public and reported in the newspapers. The normal rules of evidence applied, and cases had to be proved before sentence was passed. While many individuals were interned, many were also acquitted. The passing of the Restoration of Order in Ireland Act 1920 was in some ways an ancestor of the current British legislation passed for the war on terror. Martial law was not imposed as some republicans claimed as yet another attack on the people of Ireland. It was only applied in the counties with the highest rates of violence, and it was almost identical to the martial law imposed in the Rhineland during the same period, and during the Boer War. With regard to the application of the death penalty, no uniformity existed in British military circles in its application, and Macready faced considerable opposition from the Judge Advocate General when the execution of IRA prisoners was at issue.

One of the consistent themes in Irish nationalist history commenting on this period is the idea of the 'outrage'. This has largely relied on the accounts of contemporary journalism, especially the partisan *Irish Bulletin*. Military riots in Cork, Fermoy, Mallow, Cobh and other towns are held up as examples of occasions when the British government directed troops to sack settlements. The reality is different; most of the rioting and street fighting took place at weekends and was driven not by ideology but by drink and rivalries over local women. British officers from Strickland down to junior men, such as Dallas-Edge and Wimberley, far from being complicit, were active in the suppression of this activity and in its punishment, as evidenced by the jailing of many NCOs from the 17th Lancers. The complex problems facing troops seeking to restore law and order come across clearly when we see in Cork the RIC baton-charging British soldiers who were fighting with locals. Moreover, the emotive topic of 'reprisal' has to be seen in a new light, namely that while the provocation was nearly always the murder of a soldier, alcohol and local rivalries played perhaps the most significant part, with nearly all these 'reprisals' as mentioned taking place on weekends. Thus these 'reprisals' are closer to the street fights that constantly took place across Britain and Ireland than they are to any official reprisals that followed in 1921. Significant efforts were made by junior and senior officers to prevent, control, and end them. This was done for the preservation of both army discipline and to some extent for the preservation of peaceful local relations between army and citizenry. British soldiers were punished for taking part in such disturbances, which were finally brought to an end before the introduction of official reprisals under martial law. Reprisals must then be seen in the context of the British Isles as a whole; ex-servicemen in various British towns also conducted 'reprisals' when they felt aggrieved or threatened by the police, and indeed Irish ex-servicemen were not immune from this as the 'reprisal' in Cork and the death of Gunner Bourke show.

While some historians have suggested a great hatred for the Irish within the army, it is fair to say that the more consistent theme in the British military material was hostility to British politicians. There was a belief that they did not understand the nature and difficulty of the type of warfare the army was being asked to conduct and that the politicians were tarnishing the good name of the army in its involvement in Ireland. The military view of the campaign was actually quite complicated. As outlined, many men missed their families and were eager for an end to the conflict; indeed many officers refused to serve in Ireland. A hatred for the IRA and its actions is clear from some of the British material, but some writers found it possible to voice an understanding of the intent of the IRA and to accept their patriotism. There was considerable sympathy for both the loyalists and ordinary civilians, and arising from that a belief that the army must remain in Ireland until order and peace were restored. Most of the extant British documentation is less concerned with hatred for the IRA but rather more with poking fun at the IRA's perceived obsession with status and rank.

The military problem posed by the campaign in Ireland has often been underestimated. As Ian F.W. Beckett pointed out, the IRA 'was the true forerunner of modern revolutionary groups in terms of its politically inspired campaign against the British in Ireland in 1919–1921.'[1036] Mockaitis has stated that the successful tactics of the future, such as limited military action allied with broad social, economic and political reform were not employed in Ireland.[1037] Others have pointed out the success of such measures during the Malaya campaign, when participation in local elections, citizenship, and better access to government posts and other resources were offered to the ethnic Chinese community.[1038] This use of mixed tactics was not unknown to the British officers in Ireland: 'The first and most effective remedy to be sought by the Great Power is the removal of the main causes of grievance' was the opinion of a Major Dening, in the *Army Quarterly and Defence Journal* in 1927.[1039] But this was not an option open to the British in 1921 for the simple reason that most of these reforms had already been implemented. Nationalist control of local government had been established in 1898, the police force was largely Catholic and nationalist, and Home Rule had been on the statute books since 1914 and its implementation was expected at the end of the First World War. Catholics occupied the majority of the lower government posts in Ireland and their numbers in the more senior posts had been steadily rising. Ireland had experienced an economic boom during the First World War. It is difficult to see how a hearts and minds campaign similar to the one crafted in Malaya in the 1950s could have been constructed.

One of the key factors which characterised the operation in Cork was the successful application of technology to the tactical problems presented by the campaign. Road transportation was made more secure by greater vehicle numbers, the employment of armoured cars and the provision of various armouring systems. Aeroplanes were assigned as additional security for both road and rail transportation. In addition, aerial reconnaissance was employed to support localised military operations such as drives and military foot patrols. Aerial reconnaissance was also used as a strategic tool to target the IRA's physical infrastructure. They helped to prevent any terrorist 'spectaculars' such as the assassination of senior commanders by providing secure transport for them. Aeroplanes were employed to secure military communications through the creation of an airmail service and sensitive military communications previously vulnerable to IRA interception were secured through the development of a wireless telegraphy network. As well as counter-intelligence, basic intelligence was improved through the creation of a photographic bureau.

Neither can the British Army be accused of tactical stagnation in Cork. At a regimental level, officers were able to develop responses to the problems of convoy security and the protection of government property by the creation of 'Q lorries', which used deception to lure and attack IRA saboteurs. 'Active service' platoons were created by the Essex Regiment and spread to the various other units, and as we have seen played a considerable role in the elimination of the rural guerrilla war. This is now acknowledged by historians like William Kautt who changing his past views, writing that 'through trial and error, the British discovered that patrolling and escorting, cordon and search and checkpoints were effective means of dealing with many types of rebel activity.'[1040] The futility of any further rural guerrilla campaign has been documented by Joost Augusteijn in *From Public Defiance to Guerrilla Warfare* when he notes 'approaching the Truce most active areas were militarily unable to keep their large flying columns in the field. They were disbanded ... The fighting that flared up during 1921 made the position of most Flying Columns in the country untenable.'[1041] At a strategic level, other decisions taken up to and including Cabinet level also had a significant impact on the development of local military operations. It was the Cabinet which authorised the use of armed aeroplanes to support operations and this became a critical factor in ending the rural guerrilla war, for the simple reason that an IRA flying column in open countryside had no defence against aircraft.

Intelligence improved rapidly as the campaign progressed. Structural improvements were made, such as the appointment of brigade and battalion intelligence officers. More resources were assigned, technology improved and intelligence was focused on the production of tactically useful information. From 1921 on, ambushes such as those at Dripsey and Mourneabbey were thwarted by advance information, the capture of various IRA units, such as the active service unit at Rananisky House, and of individual commanders like Sean Moylan, and even the killing of IRA officers such as Walter Leo Murphy, were all based on intelligence provided by the public. By the Truce, the British Army knew the IRA order of battle in Cork – the structure of the Southern Division, the composition and location of its battalions and companies.

The British came late to the propaganda war, but they did come with a clear plan. They divided the local population and identified various segments within it, producing material that directly targeted the concerns of these groups, especially the farming community's economic fears with regard to trade and the preservation of private property. They appealed to the religious sensibilities of the more devout volunteers and they sought to undermine the authority of the IRA leadership by highlighting that the rules of war allowed the execution of volunteers. Pamphlets reinforced fears that in defeat the rank and file would be abandoned, and that aid from America was impossible. Other leaflets, such as the *An t-Óglach Lie System* sought to undermine the accounts of ambushes that were given to the volunteers. A special paper was also prepared for distribution in the United Kingdom to counter the work of the *Irish Bulletin*. This work in Britain was assisted by the various regimental journals.

Ireland was a significant campaign. It provided a template for future campaigns, and it was also different from other campaigns that the British Army waged during this period, notably those in Iraq and Waziristan. These were fought in a more traditional style and in a manner which can be seen to provide continuity with previous colonial operations, using large mobile columns, punitive measures against the local populations, blockhouses, local troops and levies. Imperial policing was often the term used to describe the British Army's role within the Empire; this description refers to the often considerable use of the military as a supplement to local police forces, under the term 'aid to the civil power'. One of the key texts produced on this was Major-General Gwynn's *Imperial Policing*, printed in 1930. This detailed several campaigns – Amritsar, the Molpah Rebellion, Egypt and Burma. However Ireland was notably absent from the list. Perhaps the concept of imperial policing was not something appropriate to discuss in the context of a home country.

Nevertheless, it is enlightening to examine the principles that Gwynn set out for the conduct of these campaigns and compare them to operations in Ireland.

Townshend made the argument that 'the British military and police authorities faced an armed conflict which was quite outside their experience.'[1042] This was of course true to a degree, as was pointed out in a British Army journal of the period: 'Guerrillas have in fact, today, a new weapon, political propaganda which draws blood upon the home front of the Great Power.'[1043] However, the British Army was not inexpert in small-unit warfare or in counter-terrorism, as Popplewell points out in his article 'Lacking Intelligence: Some Reflections on Recent Approaches to British Counter-Insurgency, 1900–1960'. Since 1907, the British had been dealing with a Bengalese terrorist movement which was only defeated in 1916.[1044] Service on the North-West Frontier saw the British and Indian armies engage in 52 separate operations between 1849 and 1914.[1045] As Ian Beckett noted, 'British expeditions on the North-West Frontier were cheerfully labelled "butcher and bolt" by the troops involved.'[1046] Indeed similar operations were also conducted on the North-East Frontier of India from 1917 to 1919 against the Kuki tribes by the Assam Rifles and the Burmese Military Police.[1047] While counter-insurgency did not appear on the Sandhurst syllabus until 1961, there was no lack of material for British officers to consult and consider, such as Francis Younghusband's *Indian Frontier Warfare*, W.C.G. Heneker's *Bush Warfare*, T. Miller Maguire's *Strategy and Tactics in Mountain Ranges* and Charles Callwell's *Small Wars: Their Principles and Practice*. Callwell has been described as the 'most significant early theorist of modern counterinsurgency'.[1048] All these works provided a good grounding for the type of warfare experienced in Cork.

It can be argued that the lessons of Ireland were not institutionalised in the British Army. The *Record of the Rebellion* remained unfinished and unpublished, and the campaign in Ireland was largely ignored by the regimental histories. Ireland was absent from key military texts on small warfare of the interwar years. The study of conventional war dominated military thinking and education, a problem which was pointed out by Gwynn: 'To minds framed to think in terms of the events of the Great War, the police duties of the Army, even when they take the form of small wars, may appear of insignificant importance.'[1049]

The army in Ireland did have its problems; in the beginning it did face issues with the quality of its manpower. It was, as Townshend characterised it, 'a raw and under-strength army which faced a complex and demanding security situation.'[1050] This was also attested to by a British commander in Ireland, Lieutenant-Colonel French of the Manchester Regiment, who wrote that the Manchesters as a battalion had been 'practically recreated immediately previous to its arrival in Ireland and it came to Cork untried and untrained.'[1051]

Significant problems remained for the British Army, principally the IRA's use of roadside bombs as its main new offensive tactic, allied with the targeting of isolated individuals, both soldiers and civilians. But given the degree of success with which the IRA tactics had been met in less than twelve months, it is safe to say that in time, these too would probably have been greatly reduced or eliminated, either through the elimination of IRA explosives stocks through British seizures or the expansion of internment. But British officers realised that any military victory would only represent a temporary solution, and this was understood all the way down the ranks, from Macready to young captains like Wimberley. However, the success of the British Army in Ireland was certainly acknowledged and understood by Michael Collins and the other Irish delegates to the Anglo-Irish talks of 1921, and this gave both strength and potency to David Lloyd George's threat to return to war.

One of the great failings of Irish academic historiography and of Irish popular history has been a narrow focus on the relationship between Ireland and Great Britain. All the actions of British governments tend to be viewed by many in Ireland as a personal offence, or as vindictive national persecution. Little consideration is paid to the broader strategic issues facing the British government, which might have restricted or facilitated them in considering political and military options in Ireland and no attention at all is given to the conduct of other powers in similar situations – a comparative study that awaits its historian. The tactics employed in Cork by the British Army were developed in the light of British experience in South Africa, the North-West Frontier and Iraq; they would influence the later campaigns in Palestine, Cyprus, Malaysia and Kenya. When compared to the international campaigns of the period, such as those of the Austrians in Bosnia, the United States in the Philippines, the Turks in Armenia, the Germans in Belgium and the Spanish in Morocco, British conduct can certainly be said to have adhered to the principles of minimum force.

As Keith Jeffery noted in *The British Army and the Crisis of Empire*, Henry Wilson as Chief of the Imperial General Staff 'faced greater military responsibilities than any of his predecessors.'[1052] His 'deep concern about the inadequacy of the number of troops available fell on deaf ears in a Cabinet more concerned with domestic political realities.'[1053] David Lloyd George and his Cabinet were coping with Labour success in local elections and public discontent over government spending and taxation. Indeed the British government was under such incredible strain, both externally and internally, that one historian, M.J. Daunton, suggested that the entire financial basis of the British state was under threat, and 'there was a real danger that the fiscal policy of the British State would no longer secure consent, but would become a fault line of conflict.'[1054] So as Jeffery pointed out, 'despite the army's manifold post-war burdens, Churchill, continually under pressure from both the Prime Minister and Chancellor, laboured to reduce military spending.'[1055]

The pressure was so great that even Lord Alfred Milner, one of the architects of Empire, actually recommended limited independence for Egypt in 1920. Despite all these problems, as Jeffery pointed out, the 1921 Treaty by securing both Partition and dominion status 'was regarded by many as a great triumph for the British Government.'[1056] As Townshend concluded, 'The essential fact about the Government's policy in 1919–21 is that it was not an attempt to re-conquer

Ireland.'[1057] This is the context in which British military action in Ireland must be understood. The use of military force from 1920 to 1921 was to compel the republican movement to accept measures as close to the previous constitutional settlement as possible. In the end, it was the effectiveness of British military action in Ireland that impelled Sinn Féin and the IRA to the negotiating table. The acceptance of the Anglo-Irish Treaty was forced on the IRA by the threat of complete defeat by the British Army.

'Guerrilla war in Cork in 1921 was not primarily an affair of ambushes and round-ups. It was terror and counter terror, murder after murder, death squad against death squad, fed by both sides' desire for revenge.'[1058] This is Hart's summary of the war in Cork. This does not represent the whole reality of the war. In the end, as Thomas Marks has pointed out, it is difficult 'to assess the state of insurgency from either side of the fence, when what we have is not science but art.'[1059] Insurgency is perhaps the most complex form of military conflict for a regular army. It is, as Mockaitis defined it, 'a hybrid form of conflict that combines subversion, guerrilla warfare, and terrorism.'[1060] If the campaign in Ireland is to be properly understood it must be remembered, as David Anderson and David Killingray explain, that 'Ireland marks the beginning of a new learning curve in the handling of insurgency.'[1061] If, as Charles Townshend correctly states, the IRA campaign was 'a remarkable pioneering endeavour',[1062] then perhaps the British Army's campaign in Ireland represents something similar.

Appendix One

Official Punishments Carried Out Under Martial Law, 1921

Houses Destroyed

Month	17th Brigade	18th Brigade	Kerry Brigade
January	9	4	6
February	0	12	0
March	7	0	0
April	12	14	8
May	25	15	19
June	2	7	0
Total	55	52	33

Property Destroyed

Month	17th Brigade	18th Brigade	Kerry Brigade
January	0	1	0
February	0	2	0
March	0	0	0
April	0	1	0
May	5	0	0
June	1	2	0
Total	6	6	0

Appendix Two

Restoration of Order in Ireland Act, 1920

Be it enacted by the King's most Excellent Majesty, by and with the advice and consent of the Lords Spiritual and Temporal, and Commons, in this present Parliament assembled, and by the authority of the same, as follows:

(1) Where it appears to his Majesty in Council that, owing to the existence of a state of disorder in Ireland, the ordinary law is inadequate for the prevention and punishment of crime or the maintenance of order, His Majesty in Council may issue regulations under the Defence of the Realm Consolidation Act, 1914 (hereinafter referred to as the principal Act) for securing the restoration and maintenance or order in Ireland, and as to the powers and duties for that purpose of the Lord Lieutenant and the Chief Secretary, and of members of His Majesty's forces and other persons acting on His Majesty's behalf, and in particular regulations for the special purposes hereinafter mentioned:

Provided that all regulations so made shall be laid before both Houses of Parliament as soon as may be after they are made, and, if an address presented to His Majesty by either House within the next fourteen days during the session of Parliament after such regulation is laid before it praying that the regulation may be annulled. His Majesty may annul the regulation and it shall thenceforth be void, without prejudice to validity of anything done thereunder, or to the power of making a new regulation; and the regulations shall not be deemed to be statutory rules within the meaning of section one of the Rules Publication Act, 1893.

(2) The provisions of the principal Act with the respect to the trial by courts-martial or courts of summary jurisdiction and punishment of persons committing offences against the Defence of the Realm Regulations, shall extend to the trial of persons alleged to have committed, and the punishment on conviction, of persons who have committed crimes in Ireland, whether before or after the passing of this

Act, including persons committed for trial or against whom indictments have been found, so, however, that

(a) any crime when so tried shall be punishable with the punishment assigned to the crime by statute or common law;

(b) a court martial when trying a person charged with a crime punishable by death shall include as a member of the court one person (who need not be an officer, or, if an officer, need not possess such qualification as is mentioned in subsection (3) of section forty-eight of the Army Act) nominated by the Lord Lieutenant or the Lord Chief Justice of England to be a person of legal knowledge and experience; and regulations under the principal act may be made accordingly.

(3) Regulations so made may also

(a) provide that a court of summary jurisdiction, when trying a person charged with a crime or with an offence against regulations or when hearing or determining any application with respect to a recognisance, shall except in the Dublin metropolitan police district, be constituted of two or more resident magistrates, and that a court of quarter sessions, when hearing or determining an appeal against a conviction of a court of summary jurisdiction for any such crime or offence, or against an order made on any such application, shall be constituted of the recorder or county court judge sitting alone.

(b) confer on a court-martial the powers and jurisdiction exercisable by justices or any other civil court for binding persons to keep the peace or be of good behavior, for entreating and enforcing recognisances, and for compelling persons to give evidence and to produce documents before the court;

(c) confer on persons authorised to summon witnesses before a court-martial the power of issuing warrants for compelling persons to attend as witnesses, and any warrant so issued shall have the like effect and be executed in the like manner as if issued by a justice or court of summary jurisdiction having jurisdiction in the place in which it is executed or sought to be executed;

(d) authorise the imposition by courts-martial of fines in addition to or in substitution for any other punishments for offences against the regulations, as well as for crimes and provide for the manner in which such fines are to be enforced;

(e) authorise the conveyance to and detention in any of His Majesty's prisons in any part of the United Kingdom of any persons upon whom a sentence of imprisonment has been passed in Ireland, whether before or after the passing of this act;

(f) provide for any of, the duties of a coroner and the coroner's jury being performed by a court of inquiry constituted under the Army Act instead of by a coroner and jury;

(g) provide that, where the court house or other building in which any court is usually held has been destroyed or rendered unfit or is otherwise unavailable for the purpose, the court may be held in such other court house or building as may be directed by the Lord Lieutenant;

(h) authorise the trial without jury of any action, counter claim, civil bill, issue, cause, or matter in the High Court or a county court in Ireland which, apart from this provision, would be triable with a jury;

(i) provide for the retention of sums payable to any local authority from the Local Taxation (Ireland) Account, or from any Parliamentary grant, or from any fund administered by any Government department or public body, where the local authority has in any respect refused or failed to perform its duties, or for the purpose of discharged amounts awarded against the local authority in respect of compensation for criminal injuries, or other liabilities of the local authority, and for the application of the sums so retained in or towards the purpose aforesaid.

(4) Any such regulations may apply either generally to the whole of Ireland or to any part thereof, and may be issued at any time, whether before or after the termination of the present war, and the principal Act shall continue in force so far as may be necessary for that purpose, and the regulations may contain such incidental, supplemental, and consequential provisions as may be necessary for the carrying out of the purposes of the Act, and shall have effect as if enacted in this Act.

(5) Section two of the Defence of the Realm (Amendment) Act, 1915, shall apply to proceedings before a court-martial in respect of a crime or an offence against the regulations, but, save as aforesaid, that Act shall not apply.

(6) In this act, unless the context otherwise requires-
The expression "crime" means any treason, treason felony, felony, misdemeanour, or other offence punishable, whether on indictment or on summary conviction, by imprisonment or by any greater punishment, other than offences against the Defence of the Realm Regulations:
The expression "person committed for trial" shall include a person who has entered into a recognisance conditioned to appear and plead an indictment or to take his trial upon any criminal charge, or who has been committed to prison there to await his trail for any crime.

2. This Act may be cited as the Restoration of Order in Ireland Act, 1920

Appendix Three

The Operational Procedures for Air Offensive Actions in Ireland, 1921

1. Offensive action is to be restricted to country areas away from Towns
2. Orders for the offensive use of Aircraft are to be accepted only from Superior Military Authorities, not below the rank of Colonel Commandant, and wherever possible definitely in writing.
3. Vague orders must not be accepted. To be accepted orders must accurately give an objective for the aerial operation, the extent of the offensive action required or any limit imposed on the nature of the action.
4. Offensive action is to be divided into two categories (1) Machine gun action (2) Bombing action.
5. The pilots concerned must use their discretion as to which type of action is to be employed to meet the requirement of individual cases of action.
6. Each Officer must be instructed that in no case may he take offensive action from the air until he is satisfied as far as is possible that the body of men he is attacking are actually hostilely engaged with the Forces of the Crown or beyond any doubt have been lately so engaged.
7. The greatest care must be exercised in dealing with besieged garrisons. Firing or bombing into streets or at loopholed houses of villages and towns is on no account to be undertaken.
8. It may be impossible for written orders to be issued, but the details mentioned in 3 are on all occasions to be obtained before machines are dispatched for action. When it is impossible to receive written orders in time for action, a written confirmation must be obtained as soon as possible.
9. Action where machine gun fire may be brought into effect will present itself in the form of assistance to isolated police barracks if attacked, dispersal of ambushes which have engaged convoys, parties of troops, dispersal of

ambushes which may have been definitely located by troops, if so ordered, the prevention of parties of rebels which may have been dislodged by our troops from escape, heading them back. Dropping bombs in open against small bodies will be ineffective and this mode of action should not be resorted to unless a favourable target presents itself, i.e., a party of not less than 30 men in close order.

10. Care must be taken that pilots fully understand their orders and appreciate their responsibility before going into action. Only reliable pilots are to be employed when action is taken. It is conceivable that the position may have considerably altered between the time orders have been issued and the time the aeroplane arrives on the scene of action, and unexpected local circumstances may render the precise execution of these orders unsuitable or impracticable, under such circumstances the pilot must assume the responsibility for judging whether offensive action should be employed, being guided by the above instructions, and be prepared to act accordingly. Should a pilot find it necessary to depart from the orders received he will take steps to notify the issuer.

12. Only when aerial action is called for will machines carry offensive armament.

13. In the event of a forced landing, every effort must be taken to destroy the armament of the machine if there is the slightest possibility of such armament falling into the hands of the enemy.[1063]

Appendix Four

Tom Barry's IRA Report on Crossbarry

Column Report NO: 5 Week Ending 19.5.21

To: C.O. 3rd Cork Brigade

From O.C. Flying Column

The Column mobilised on 14.3.21. It now consisted of 78 officers and men. It was my intention to force a battle of a larger scale than usual on the enemy. On the 15th. inst. I occupied a position at Balteenbrack between Dunmanway and Bandon, but the enemy did not travel.

On 17th. inst. I occupied a position about 16 miles eastward at Shipool on the main road between Bandon and Kinsale in anticipation of a convoy of 7 lorries, but again with no success.

I rested the column on the 18th., and on that night I moved to a position on one of the Main Roads between Cork and Bandon known as Crossbarry.

Whilst resting in billets within half a mile of the position our scouts informed me of enemy movements in the locality. I immediately moved 5 of the 7 sections into position.

The position was not an ideal one. It was extended for about 500 yards. To the east about 800 yards was Kinsale Junction. To the west Upton Station about two miles. The ground sloped gradually upward and the fields were small; the ditches affording good cover. There was a high-detached lane running out of the top of the hill from the position which would serve admirably for a retiring ground. Our front embraced two large protestant farmhouses and yards. Immediately on taking up positions the five sections commenced fortifying their positions by placing large boulders from an adjoining position on the ditch in front of them making loopholes. I next divided NO. 6 Section and placed half on them on either flank and to the rear about 150 yards. NO. 7 Section was placed in the centre and acted both as a reserve and guard against attack from the rear.

Incidentally we had a piper beyond one of the houses who played some martial airs as soon as the firing opened.

About 7 a.m. the enemy appeared in 9 lorries. When they had reached Section NO. 2, they must have observed one of our men's rifles which was not sufficiently hidden. The first lorry halted and we immediately fired. You will understand that we had only three lorries within our line and six lorries halted some distance back. After about 7 minutes we had killed or wounded most of the occupants of those three lorries.

I next brought a section back to where the other lorries had halted, but I found that the enemy had abandoned them and taken up positions about 800 yards away, leaving two dead in those lorries. Leaving that Section to hold the enemy in case they returned I went back to where the first three lorries were halted.

We relieved the enemy of their equipment and burned three of their lorries and damaged a fourth. It was my intention to try and flank a portion of the enemy who were isolated. Immediately the lorries burned the train arrived in Kinsale Junction and simultaneously fire opened in our rear. A large raiding party estimated at 150 retuning from Ballymurphy came on our rear and were engaged by NO. 7 Section. At the same time a party of 40 from the train at Kinsale Junction were engaged by NO. 5 Section.

I immediately strengthened NO. 7 section by 5 men and retired the remainder in sections to the top of the hill.

I next proceeded to relieve NO. 7 Section by brining fire from a section on the enemy's rear. The enemy immediately retired and NO. 7 Section was enabled to retire bringing two wounded with them. The enemy at this time was in a disordered condition.

The Column continued its retirement in good order. NO. 4 Section was now rearguard Section, but it was easy to hold the enemy in check. He sent a forward party of 25 to keep in touch and to help [sic] firing so as to guide the main body of the enemy after us.

That was how matters were four hours after the fight had started at 11 a.m. Three miles from the ambush position I ordered 6 men back to wait under cover for the enemy advance party. They did so and fired on them, killing one and wounding two. The remainder immediately ran back.

About 2 miles further on we again took up positions but the enemy never ventured near us. We held this position until darkness and then continued our retirement.

Our casualties were three dead and two wounded. We brought away our wounded. We lost no equipment or rifles.

We captured one Lewis gun with 8 drums, 12 rifles, 600 rounds .303, 3 revolvers, coats, bayonets, etc.

We burned 3 lorries and damaged the fourth.

The enemy casualties are unknown but we can account for at least 23 dead.

(Signed)

O.C. Flying Column

Appendix Five

The British Officers

Army Headquarters and Others

General Sir Cecil Fredrick Neville Macready, CMG, KCB

General Macready was commissioned into the Gordon Highlanders on 22 October 1881 as a lieutenant. He was promoted Captain on 4 March 1891 and Major on 14 December 1899. He made Brevet Lieutenant-Colonel on 29 November 1900 and Colonel on 29 November 1903. He was appointed Major-General on 31 October 1910, and served as a temporary Lieutenant-General from 13 September 1914 to 2 January 1916. He was made a Lieutenant-General on 3 June 1916 and appointed a full General 3 September 1918.

He took part in the Egyptian Expedition of 1882 and fought at the Battle of Tel-El-Kebir, for which he received the General Service Medal with clasp and the Bronze Star. He served as a Staff Lieutenant Military Police in Cairo from 1 July 1884 to 23 August 1885, during which time he temporarily served as the Assistant Provost Marshall. He also served as a Staff Captain in Egypt from 24 August 1885 until 4 September 1889. He served as an Adjutant to the Volunteers from 1 January 1894 to 31 December 1898.

During the Boer War he served in a number of positions. He was an Assistant Provost Marshall from 19 October 1901 to 23 December 1901. He served as a DAAG from 24 December 1901 to 8 October 1902. He served in the Cape Colony as AAG from 9 October 1902 to 22 March 1904 and as AQMG from 23 March 1904 to the end of October 1906. During the Boer War, he took part in operations in Natal in 1899, seeing action at Elandslaaste, Lombards Kop and in the Defence of Ladysmith, where he took part in the action of 6 January 1900. He also saw action at Laing's Nak on 6–9 June 1900. In late 1900 he served in operations in the Transvaal, east of Pretoria, including the actions at Belfast on 26/27 August and at Lydenbery on 5–8 September. From 1901 to 1902, he served on operations in the Transvaal and Cape Colony. He also served as Commandant of Haman's Kraal from 24 November to 12 December 1900, of Waterval North in December 1900 and of Pietpotgietersust from 13 October to 24 November 1901. He was mentioned twice in dispatches for his service in South Africa and awarded the QM with six clasps and the KM with two clasps.

From 1 March 1907 to 9 August 1909 he served as an AAG at Army Headquarters. He became the commander of the 2nd Brigade at Aldershot, and served there from 10 August 1909 until 31 May 1910. He was employed as Director of Personal Services at the War Office from 1 June 1910 to 4 August 1914. He was Adjutant General of the British Expeditionary Forces from 5 August 1914 to 21 February 1916, and from 22 February 1916 to 30 August 1918 he was Adjutant General for the British Army in France. He served as the Commissioner of the London Metropolitan Police from 31 August 1918 to 13 April 1920. He arrived in Ireland as General Officer Commanding, the British Army in Ireland on 14 April 1920.

Major-General Sir Hugh Sandhan Jeudwine KCB

General Jeudwine was commissioned into the Royal Artillery as a Lieutenant on 22 February 1882. He was promoted Captain on 1 January 1891, Major on 3 January 1900, Lieutenant-Colonel on 5 April 1909 and Colonel on 7 March 1912. He served as a temporary Brigadier-General from 4 January 1915 to 2 January 1916, and as a temporary Major-General from 3 January 1916 to 2 June 1916. He was appointed a Major-General on 3 June 1916.

Jeudwine served as an instructor at the School of Gunnery from 22 March 1894 to 12 December 1899. From 13 December 1899 to 24 September 1902 he was on special service in South Africa during the Boer War. He also served as a DAAG in South Africa from 6 December 1902 to 15 March 1903, and from 16 March to 29 May 1904 he held the post of DAQMG. He was Assistant Superintendent of Experiments at the School of Gunnery from 30 May to 21 October 1904. From 27 October 1904 to 31 December 1908 he was employed at Army Headquarters as a DAQMG and a General Staff Officer, Grade 2. He moved at that grade to the Staff College on 1 January 1912, was promoted while there to General Staff Officer, Grade 1. He left on 4 August 1914 to fill that grade with the 1st Army Corps of the British Expeditionary Force, and also served at that grade with the 1st Cavalry Division. On 4 January 1915 he was appointed as a temporary Brigadier-General on the General Staff of the 5th Army Corps. He became Brigade Commander of 41st Infantry Brigade of the British Expeditionary Force on 28 September 1915, and the commander of the 55th Division on 3 January 1916, a position he held until 14 March 1919, when he became a Divisional Commander with the British Army of the Rhine. From 17 August 1919 until 26 October 1919 he was Chief of Staff of the British Army of the Rhine. He became the commander of the 5th Division in Ireland on 27 October 1919.

Colonel John Edward Brind, CMG, DSO

Brind was commissioned into the Royal Artillery on 23 December 1897 as a 2nd Lieutenant and made Lieutenant on 23 December 1900. He was promoted Captain 11 April 1902 and served as an Adjutant from 1 February 1903 to 13 March 1906. He was a temporary Major from 5 August to 29 October 1914, and was appointed to the rank on 30 October 1914. He was made a temporary Lieutenant-Colonel on 6 February 1916, a Brevet Lieutenant-Colonel on 3 June 1916, Brevet Colonel on 1 January 1919 and appointed Colonel on 7 April 1920.

He fought in the Boer War, winning the QM and two clasps. He served as DAQMG for the 2nd Division of the British Expeditionary Force from 5 August 1914 to 13 July 1915. From 14 July 1915 to 5 February 1916 he served as a General Staff Officer, Grade 2 to the 10th Army Corps, British Expeditionary Force. He was promoted to a General Staff Officer Grade 1 and served in this capacity with the 56th Division and the 1st Army from 6 February 1916 to 26 November 1917. He was appointed to the General Staff of the 11th Army Corps as an acting Brigadier-General on 27 November 1917, and served with this Corps until 28 March 1919. On 1 March 1919 he was transferred to the General Staff of the Irish Command at the same rank.

During the First World War he was mentioned in dispatches eight times. He was awarded the 1914 Star, the BWM, the VM, the CMG and the DSO. He was also awarded the Legion of Honour 4th Class, the French War Cross, the Order of St Maurice and St Lazarus 4th Class and the Military Order of Avis (Grand Officer).

6th Division Headquarters

Major-General Sir Edward Peter Strickland KGB, CMG, DSO

General Strickland was commissioned as a 2nd Lieutenant in the Norfolk Regiment on 10 November 1888. He was promoted to Lieutenant on 29 April 1891 and to Captain on 21 October 1899. He was made a Brevet Major on 22 October 1899 and a Major on 8 September 1908. He was appointed as a Lieutenant-Colonel in the Manchester Regiment on 1 June 1914, and promoted to Brevet Colonel on 18 February 1915. During the First World War he was a temporary Brigadier-General from 4 January 1915 to 11 June 1916, and a temporary Major-General from 12 June 1916 to 31 December 1917. He was commissioned as a Major-General on 1 January 1918.

Strickland took part in the Burmese Expedition of 1887–89. He served with the Egyptian Army from 1 April 1896 to 31 March 1903, and during this period he served on the Expedition to Dongola 1896, the Nile Expedition of 1897 and the Nile Expedition of 1898, where he took part in the battles of Atbara and Khartoum. He also took part in operations on the White Nile against Ahmed Fedil's army for which he was awarded the DSO. He served with the West African Frontier Force from 3 February 1906 to 2 August 1913.

During the First World War he served as the Brigade Commander for the Jullunder Brigade and the 98th Infantry Brigade respectively from 4 January 1915 to 11 June 1916. He served as the commander of the 1st Division of the British Armies in France from 12 June 1916 to 12 March 1919; he then took part in the occupation of Germany as the commander of the Western Division of the British

Army of the Rhine from 13 March to 16 September 1919. It was from here he was sent to Ireland and took command of the 6th Division in Ireland on 8 November 1919, a position he held until 19 May 1922.

General Strickland was mentioned in dispatches twelve times, he held the Egyptian Medal with seven clasps, the Order of Leopold with Palm 3rd Class, the Belgian War Cross, the French War Cross, the 1914 Star with clasp, BWM, VM, CMG and the KGB. He was wounded twice in France.

Major-General Charles Guinard Blackadder, CB, DSO

General Blackadder was commissioned as a 2nd Lieutenant in the Leicestershire Regiment on 22 August 1888. He was promoted to Lieutenant on 21 March 1890 and Captain on 6 December 1895. He was made a Major on 10 September 1904, a Lieutenant-Colonel on 10 September 1912 and a Colonel of the Leicestershire Regiment on 18 February 1915. During the First World War he served as a temporary Brigadier-General from 8 January 1915 to 11 July 1916 and a temporary Major-General from 12 July 1916 to 31 December 1917. He was appointed a full Major-General on 1 January 1918.

Blackadder was employed with the West African Frontier Force from the 27 November 1897 to the 24 June 1899. He served as an Adjutant in the Volunteers from 1 August 1902 to 9 September 1904. He was the Brigade Commander of the Garhwa and 177th Infantry Brigades from 8 January 1915 to 25 June 1916 and was the commander of the 38th Division of the British Armies in France from 12 July 1916 to 8 June 1918. He was the commander of the Southern District of the Irish Command from 21 November 1918 to 7 February 1919; he left to become Commander, the Troops, Southampton.

Colonel Edward Henry Willis, CB, CMG (Royal Artillery)

Colonel Willis was commissioned into the Royal Artillery as a 2nd Lieutenant on 14 February 1890 and promoted to Lieutenant on 14 February 1893. He was made a Captain on 19 January 1900 and a Major on 3 April 1907. On 30 October 1914 he was appointed a Lieutenant-Colonel, a Brevet Colonel on 1 January 1916 and a full Colonel on 30 October 1918. During the First World War he was a temporary Brigadier-General from 30 January 1916 to 11 September 1919.

He served with the Colonial Forces in Queensland from 12 March 1891 to 11 March 1899. He was an acting Brigadier-General in the 12th Division and the 17th Army Corps, the British Armies in France from 30 January 1916 to 24 March 1919. He served in the same capacity in the 4th Army Corps, British Army of the Rhine from 25 March to 11 September 1919. He joined the 6th Division in Ireland on 17 March 1920.

Colonel Archibald Cameron, CB, CMG (Commander 16th Brigade)

Colonel Cameron was commissioned into the Royal Highlanders on 1 March 1892 as a 2nd Lieutenant, and promoted to Lieutenant on 3 August 1896. He was promoted Captain on 6 October 1899 and served as Adjutant of the Battalion from 21 April 1900 to 20 April 1904. He was promoted Major on 13 June 1908, Lieutenant-Colonel on 25 February 1915 and full Colonel on 25 February 1919.

He fought in the Boer War and was severely wounded at Magersfontien. He also took part in operations in the Orange Free State, including an action at Vet River. He was the Garrison Adjutant at Landbrand. He was mentioned in dispatches and won the King's and Queen's Medals. He served as ADC to the Governor and Commander in Chief of the Cape of Good Hope from 3 December 1904 to 31 December 1907 and held the post of Commander of the Company of Gentlemen Cadets at the Royal Military College from 1 February 1909 to 31 January 1913. He served as a General Staff Officer, Grade 2 at the Staff College from 16 May to 4 August 1914, and at the same grade with the 5th Division of the British Expeditionary Force from 5 August 1914 to 21 March 1915. He was promoted to a General Staff Officer, Grade 1, and remained with the 5th Division until 20 October 1915. He then served as an acting Brigadier-General on the General Staff of the 10th Army, the 4th Army and the 9th Army Corps, British Army of the Rhine, and with the Eastern Home Command, from 21 October 1915 to 17 April 1920. He arrived in Ireland on 18 April 1920 to take command of the 16th Infantry Brigade, 6th Division.

During the First World War he was wounded and was mentioned in dispatches seven times. He was awarded the 1914 Star, the BWM, the VM, the CB and the CMG. He was also awarded the French War Cross.

Colonel Harold Whitla Higginson, CB, DSO (Commander, 18th Infantry Brigade)

Colonel Higginson was commissioned into the Royal Dublin Fusiliers on 10 October 1894, and promoted to Lieutenant on 23 October 1896. He was promoted Captain on 16 December 1899, and served as the Adjutant of the Battalion from 26 May 1911 to 24 January 1913. He was promoted Major on 25 January 1913. He served as a temporary Lieutenant-Colonel from 25 June 1915 to 6 May 1916, from 7 May 1916 to 25 April 1918, he served as a temporary Brigadier-General, and as a temporary Major-General from 26 April 1918 to 17 March 1919. He was appointed a Brevet Lieutenant-Colonel on 3 July 1916, a Brevet Colonel on 1 January 1918 and made a full Colonel on 2 June 1919.

Colonel Higginson was employed with the West African Frontier Force from 27 November 1897 to 24 June 1899, where he served in operations on the Niger Expeditions to Capia and Argeyah. He fought in the Boer War, was mentioned in dispatches and awarded the QM with four clasps and the KM with two clasps. In 1903 he took part in operations in the interior of Aden. He served as an Adjutant to the Militia from 1 February 1904 to 31 January 1907. In 1908 he served in the Sudan, taking part in operations on the Blue Nile.

He served as Brigade Major to the War Infantry Brigade of the Southern Command from 1 May to 4 August 1914. From 5 August 1914 to 5 June 1915, he .

held the post of Brigade Major to the 143rd Infantry Brigade of the Central Force Home Defence. He was the Brigade Commander of the 53rd Infantry Brigade from 7 May 1916 to 25 April 1918. From 26 April 1918 to 17 March 1919 he served as the commander of the 12th Division. He came to Ireland on 1 November 1919 to take command of the 18th Infantry Brigade, 6th Division.

During the First World War he was mentioned in dispatches eight times. He was awarded the 1914–15 Star, the BWM, the VM, the CB and the DSO with Bar. He was also awarded the Legion of Honour, 4th Class, and the Order of Star of Romania 3rd Class.

Colonel Thomas Bruce, CMG, DSO (6th Division Staff)

Colonel Bruce was commissioned into the Royal Artillery on 13 February 1891 and promoted Lieutenant on 13 February 1894. He was promoted Captain on 13 February 1900, served as an Adjutant within the Royal Artillery from 29 April 1907 to 11 September 1908 and was promoted Major on 12 September 1908. He was appointed Brevet Lieutenant-Colonel on 18 February 1915, Lieutenant-Colonel on 1 April 1915, Brevet Colonel on 3 June 1918 and Colonel 1 April 1920. During the First World War he served as a temporary Brigadier-General from 18 June 1916 to 13 May 1919.

Bruce served in operations on the North-West Frontier from 1897 to 1898 with the Tirah Expeditionary Force, and saw action at Dargai and Sararn Sar. He was awarded the Afghan Medal with two clasps. He was an Adjutant in the Volunteers from 25 November 1899 to 31 October 1903. He served as an ADC to the GOC Thames District and the Commander of Eastern Command Coastal Defences from 14 November 1903 to 8 December 1906. He served as an acting Brigadier-General (Royal Artillery) with the 26th Division, Egyptian Expeditionary Force and British Salonika Force. He joined the 6th Division in Ireland on 8 May 1920 as AA & QMG.

During the First World War he was mentioned in dispatches six times. He was awarded the 1914 Star, the BWM, the VM, the CMG and the DSO. He was also awarded the Order of St Anne 3rd Class, with swords.

Colonel Cuthbert Henry Tindall Lucas, CMG, DSO (Commander, 17th Brigade)

Colonel Lucas was commissioned into the Royal Berkshire Regiment on 7 May 1898 as a 2nd Lieutenant and became a Lieutenant on 1 August 1900. He was promoted Captain on 1 April 1909. He was made a Brevet Major on 18 February 1915 and a Major on 1 September 1915. He became a Brevet Lieutenant-Colonel on 8 November 1915, a Brevet Colonel on 1 January 1919 and a Colonel on 30 October 1919. He was an acting Brigadier-General from 15 August 1915 to 14 October 1918 and an acting Major-General from 15 October 1918 to 17 March 1919.

He was employed with the West African Frontier Force from 12 December 1900 to 21 January 1901. He fought in the Boer War, serving in operations in the Orange

Free State from March to May 1900. From July to August 1900 he was in the Transvaal, east of Pretoria, seeing action at Zilikats Nek. He took part in operations in the Orange River Colony from May to July 1900. From November 1901 to May 1902 he served in the Cape Colony. For his services in South Africa he was awarded the QM with 3 clasps and the KM with 2 clasps. He served with the Egyptian Army from 5 April 1905 and 24 April 1909.

He was an Assistant Military Landing Officer for the British Expeditionary Force for the first two weeks of the First World War in August. He served as the Brigade Major to the 87th Infantry Brigade (Mediterranean Expeditionary Force) from 15 August 1915 to 6 December 1916, during which time he served at Gallipoli. He acted as Brigade Commander for the 214th and 87th Brigades from 11 December 1916 to 19 January 1918. He was Commander of the Machine Gun Training Centre from 2 February to 27 March 1918. From 30 March to 14 October 1918, Lucas served as a temporary Brigadier-General on the General Staff at GHQ. He commanded the 4th Division from 15 October 1918 to 17 March 1919. He was the Brigade Commander of the 2nd Brigade, Southern Division of the British Army of the Rhine from 18 March to 29 October 1919. He was made Brigade Commander of the 17th Infantry Brigade, 6th Division on 30 October 1919.

During the First World War he was mentioned in dispatches nine times. He was awarded the 1914 Star, the BWM and the VM. He was also awarded the Legion of Honour 4th Class and the French War Cross.

Colonel Hanway Robert Cumming DSO (Commander Kerry Brigade)

Colonel Cumming was commissioned into the Durham Light Infantry as a 2nd Lieutenant on 8 June 1889 and became a Lieutenant on 28 July 1891. He was promoted Captain on 24 November 1897, made Brevet Major on 29 November 1900 and promoted Major on 2 June 1909. He served as a temporary Lieutenant-Colonel from 24 August 1915 to 28 February 1916 and as a temporary Brigadier-General for various periods from 28 November 1916 to 26 April 1919. He was made a Brevet Colonel on 1 January 1919 and a Colonel on 7 June 1920.

He served as a Staff Captain during the Boer War from 28 June to 18 July 1900. He was DA & QMG and DAAG in Ceylon from 31 July 1903 to 19 January 1906. From 20 January 1906 to 30 July 1907 he served as a staff officer in the Welsh & Midland and Western Commands of Costal Defence Command and was the Commander of the Company of Gentlemen Cadets at the Royal Military College from 29 January 1909 to 28 January 1913. He saw service in India during 1914 and 1915 as a General Staff Officer, Grade 2. He served at the same grade in the 31st Division from 11 June 1915 to 23 August 1915; he was promoted to General Staff Officer, Grade 1 on 24 August 1915 and continued to serve with the 31st Division until 1 April 1916, when he was transferred to the 48th Division, where he served until 26 August 1916. From 28 November 1916 to 26 May 1917 he was Brigade Commander of the 91st Infantry Brigade. From 3 August 1917 to 1 February 1918 he served as the Commander of the Machine Gun Training Centre. He was the Brigade Commander of the 110th and the Durham Light Brigade from 16 March 1918 to 7 June 1920.

Lieutenant-Colonel Denis John Charles Kirwan Bernand, CMG, DSO

Bernand was commissioned as a 2nd Lieutenant into the Rifle Brigade on 22 October 1902 and promoted Lieutenant on 21 July 1906. He was an Adjutant in the Rifle Brigade from 17 July 1909 to 16 July 1912. He was made Captain on 25 May 1912, Brevet Major on 3 June 1916, Major on 22 October 1917 and Brevet Lieutenant-Colonel on 3 June 1917.

He was a Transport Officer with the British Expeditionary Force from 5 August 1914 to 1 December 1914. He served as a General Staff Officer Grade 3 with the 10th Division, Mediterranean Expeditionary Force from 10 February 1915 to 23 September 1915, was promoted to General Staff Officer, Grade 2 and remained with this division until 22 November 1915. He was transferred at the same grade to the GHQ of the Mediterranean Expeditionary Force, and served there from 23 November 1915 to 21 April 1916. He was promoted and served as the General Staff Officer, Grade 1 with the 1st Australian Division from 23 April 1916 to 19 December 1917. From 20 December 1917 to April 1920, he served at the same grade in GHQ France, the Inspectorate of Training, France, and the 1st Division, France. He joined the 6th Division, Irish Command on 6 April 1920.

Lieutenant-Colonel Pierse Joseph Mackesy, DSO (Royal Engineers)

Lieutenant-Colonel Mackesy was commissioned as a 2nd Lieutenant in the Royal Engineers on 23 August 1902. He was promoted to Lieutenant on 21 March 1905 and Captain on 23 August 1913. He was held the post of an Adjutant in the Royal Engineers from 15 January 1915 to 13 January 1916. He was an acting Brigade Major in the Territorial Force, Royal Engineers from 9 March to 19 May 1917. He was promoted Major on 23 August 1917 and made Brevet Lieutenant-Colonel on 11 November 1919.

He was employed on survey duty in the Gold Coast from 8 February 1911 to 11 January 1915. He served as a Brigade Major, Royal Engineers in the 8th Army Corps from 20 May 1917 to 29 March 1918. From 30 March 1918 to 18 July 1920 he served as a General Staff Officer, Grade 2 with the 6th Army Corps, the 2nd Division at GHQ, with the expedition to Murmansk and the British Military Mission to Southern Russia.

Major D.M. King

He served in Egypt with the Egyptian Expeditionary Force from December 1914 to May 1916, during which time he took part in the Gallipoli landings. He served from May 1916 to the end of the war in France and Belgium. He was mentioned in dispatches four times and awarded the 1914–1915 Star, the BWM, the VM, the DSO with Clasp and the MC.

Major T.R. Eastwood

He took part in operations in German Samoa in August 1914. From March 1914 to April 1916, he served in Egypt, during which time he took part in the landings at Gallipoli. From 12 April 1916 to 11 November 1918 he served in France and Belgium. He was mentioned in dispatches five times and was awarded the 1914–1915 Star, the BWM, the VM, the DSO and the MC.

Major J.M. Hulton

He served in the Boer War from 1901 to 1902, taking part in operations in the Transvaal, the Orange River Colony and the Zululand Frontier of Natal. He was awarded the QM with five clasps. He served in France and Belgium during the First World War. He was mentioned in dispatches three times and was awarded the 1914–1915 Star, the BWM, the VM, the CBE and the DSO. He was also awarded the Order of the Nile 3rd Class, the Order of the Crown of Italy 4th Class and the Order of the Rising Sun 4th Class.

The Essex Regiment

Lieutenant-Colonel Frederick William Moffitt, DSO

Lieutenant-Colonel Moffitt was commissioned into the Essex Regiment on 8 October 1890 as a 2nd Lieutenant. He was promoted Lieutenant on 20 February 1895, Captain on 11 May 1900, Brevet Major on 22 August 1902, Major on 4 May 1915, Brevet Lieutenant-Colonel on 1 June 1918 and Lieutenant-Colonel on 26 September 1919. He also served as a temporary Lieutenant-Colonel from 20 January 1915 to 7 December 1917.

Moffitt took part in the Tirah Expeditionary Force on the North-West Frontier of India in 1898. He fought in the Boer War from 1900 to 1902. In May 1900, during operations in the Orange Free State, he took part in actions at Vet River and Zand River. During operations in the Transvaal in the summer of 1900, he was involved in actions at Johannesburg, Pretoria and Diamond Hill. Autumn 1900 saw Moffitt involved in operations in the Transvaal, east of Pretoria, and he took part in the action at Belfast on 26/27 August. Later operations west of Pretoria saw him in action at Frederickstad and from April to May 1902 he was involved in operations in the Orange River Colony. He served as a Staff Captain in 5th Division, Irish Command from 16 January 1909 to 1 April 1912, and as a DAQMG from 2 April 1912 to 13 January 1913. From 20 January 1915 to 1 July 1916 he served as an AAG with Southern Command. He served as a General Staff Officer, Grade 1 with the Australian Training Centre in Salisbury from 2 July to 7 December 1917.

He was mentioned in dispatches in the Boer War twice, and was awarded the QM with five clasps and the KM with two clasps. He served in France and Belgium during the First World War, was wounded and mentioned in dispatches once. He was awarded the 1914 Star, BWM, the VM and the DSO.

Major H.R. Bowen

Bowen served in the Boer War from 1900 to 1902. In August 1900 he took part in operations in the Transvaal, east of Pretoria, seeing action at Belfast on 26/27 August. Later that year he saw action at Frederickstad from 17 to 25 October. From 30 November 1900 to 31 May 1902 he served in the Transvaal and Cape Colony. He was awarded the QM with three clasps and KM with two clasps.

During the First World War he saw action at Gallipoli from 25 April to 19 December 1915. He served in Egypt from 20 December 1915 to 18 March 1916, and with the Egyptian Expeditionary Force from 20 December 1916 to 16 August 1918. He was in command of the 1/5 Battalion of the Welch Regiment (Territorial Force) from 12 March 1917 to 30 July 1918. He was wounded twice. He was mentioned in dispatches four times, and awarded the 1914–1915 Star, the BWM, the VM and the DSO. He was also awarded the French War Cross.

Major A.C. Halahan

He served in South Africa from 1901 to 1902. He was employed on mounted infantry operations in the Orange River Colony from December 1901 to May 1902 and was awarded the QM with four clasps. He served in France and Belgium during the First World War and was the commander of the 1st Battalion Essex Regiment from 5 June 1916 to 24 April 1917. He was Commandant of the 29th Division training camp from 25 April to 13 July 1917 and from 14 July he was Commandant of the 14th Army Corps Musketry and Training Camp. He served in Italy from 18 November 1917 to 10 July 1918. He was mentioned in dispatches twice, was awarded the 1914 Star with clasp, the BWM and the VM.

Major R Neave

He served in South Africa from 1901 to 1902, taking part in operations in the Transvaal from May 1901 to May 1902. He was awarded the QM with four clasps. He served in France and Belgium during the First World War, but also took part in the Gallipoli landings from 25 April to 29 June 1915, serving as a Brigade Machine Gun Officer for the 88th Infantry Brigade. He was awarded the 1914–1915 Star, the BWM and the VM.

Major R.N. Thompson

He served in South Africa in 1902, taking part in operations in the Orange River Colony from January to May 1902. He was awarded the QM with three clasps. He served in France and Belgium during the First World War, employed as a Brigade Machine Gun Officer with the 12th Infantry Brigade until 9 January 1916. He held the command of the 2nd Battalion Essex Regiment for various periods: from 2 July to 6 November 1916; 9 December 1916 to 9 August 1917; and 24 October 1917 to 12 May 1918. He was mentioned in dispatches three times and was awarded the 1914–1915 Star, the BWM and the VM.

Captain A.E. Percival (Brevet Major)

Percival served in France and Belgium during the First World War. He held Battalion command for three periods, with the 7th Service Battalion Bedfordshire Regiment from 20 June 1917 to 4 July 1917, and again from 16 January to 25 May 1918. From 26 May to 11 November 1918 he was the Battalion Commander of the 2nd Battalion Bedfordshire Regiment. He served in Russia from 31 May to 8 October 1919, and was wounded there. He was mentioned in dispatches three times and was awarded the 1914–1915 Star, the BWM, the VM, the DSO with clasp and the MC. He was also awarded the French War Cross.

The East Kent Regiment (The Buffs)

Lieutenant-Colonel Robert McDouall, CB, CMG

Lieutenant-Colonel McDouall was commissioned into the East Kent Regiment as a 2nd Lieutenant on 9 January 1892. He was promoted Lieutenant on 4 October 1893 and Captain on 13 November 1899. He was a Battalion Adjutant from 1 October 1906 to 30 September 1909 and was promoted Major on 4 August 1910. He served as a temporary Lieutenant-Colonel from 15 December 1914 to 20 December 1914 and from 29 February 1915 to 1 June 1915. He was made a Brevet Lieutenant-Colonel on 3 June 1915. He served as a temporary Brigadier-General from 19 August 1916 to 30 June 1919 and was made a Lieutenant-Colonel on 27 April 1919.

McDouall took part in the operations in Chitral with the relief force in 1895, including actions at Panjkova River and Mamagai. He was employed with the South African Constabulary from 23 October 1900 to 22 October 1905. He took part in the relief of Kimberley and was involved in early 1900 in operations in the Orange Free State, including actions at Paardeberg, Poplar Grove and Dreifontein. In late 1900 he was involved in operations in the Transvaal, and from November 1900 until May 1902 he took part in operations in the Transvaal and Orange River Colony. He also served with the West African Frontier Force from 8 February 1911 to 29 October 1913.

He served as a General Staff Officer, Grade 2 and then Grade 1 with the British Expeditionary Force from 4 August 1914 to 28 July 1916. He served as a Brigade Commander for the 141st, 18th Reserve, Highland Reserve and 142nd Infantry Brigades from 19 August 1916 to 10 December 1918. From 11 December 1918 to 30 June 1919 he served as Base Commandant at Dunkirk.

His various decorations include the Afghan Medal with Clasp, the QM with 4 clasps and the KM with 2 clasps; he was also awarded the DSO during the Boer War. During the First World War he was awarded the 1914 Star, the BWM, the VM, the CB, the CMG and the CBE. He was also awarded the Legion of Honour 4th Class by the French. He was mentioned twice in dispatches during the Boer War and six times in dispatches during the First World War.

Major R. E. Power

He took part in operations in Chitral on the North-West Frontier of India, with the Relief Force in 1895, and saw action at Mamagai. He was awarded the Afghan Medal with clasp. He saw action again from 1897–1898, again on the frontier with the Malakand Field Force. He took part in operations in Bajaur and in the Mamuad Country, where he was wounded. He fought at Utman Khel and was involved in the attack on and capture of the Tanga Pass. He was involved in operations in the interior of Aden in 1904, and during 1905–1906 he saw service in West Africa (South Nigeria), and was involved in operations in the Kwale-Ishan District. During the First World War he served in France, commanding the 2/4 Battalion Yorkshire Light Infantry (Territorial Force) from 25 April to 10 December 1917. He also commanded the 1st Battalion of the East Kent Regiment from 11 December 1917.

He was wounded in France and mentioned in dispatches four times. He was awarded the 1914–1915 Star, the BWM, the VM and the DSO.

Major G. Lee

Major Lee served in South Africa from 1901 1902, taking part in operations in the Cape Colony, from July to November 1901. He was awarded the QM with two clasps. From 1903 to 1904 he served in Aden on operations in the interior, and from 1909 to 1910 he served in West Africa and saw action, being award a GSM with clasp.

During the First World War he served France and Belgium; he was mentioned in dispatches three times. He was awarded the 1914 Star, the BWM, the VM, DSO and the MC. He was also awarded the Legion of Honour 5th Class, the Order of Leopold 5th Class, and the Belgian War Cross.

Major L. W. Lucas

Lucas served in 1903 in operations in the interior of Aden. He served in France during the First World War. He was the Adjutant of the 1st Battalion, East Kent Regiment from 9 September 1914 to 31 August 1915 and the Commandant of No2 Army School from 1 September 1915 to 15 March 1916. He was in command of the 8th Battalion of the East Kent Regiment from 16 March 1916 to 26 January 1917.

During the First World War he was mentioned in dispatches three times. He was awarded the 1914 Star with clasp, the BWM, the VM, the DSO and the MC.

Major J Crookenden

Crookenden fought in the Boer War from 1901 to 1902, where he served mainly in the Transvaal. He was awarded the QM with five clasps. He served in France during the First World War, was mentioned in dispatches once and awarded the 1914–1915 Star, the BWM, the VM and the DSO. He was also awarded the Legion of Honour 5th Class.

The Royal Fusiliers

Lieutenant-Colonel Carlos Joseph Hickie CMG, DSO

Lieutenant-Colonel Hickie was commissioned into the Gloucestershire Regiment as a 2nd Lieutenant on 21 October 1893 and promoted Lieutenant on 12 January 1898. He became a Captain in the Yorkshire Light Infantry on 22 March 1902 and later a Major in the Royal Fusiliers. He was made a Brevet Lieutenant-Colonel in the Royal Fusiliers on 1 January 1917 and a Lieutenant-Colonel on 25 August 1920. He served as temporary Lieutenant-Colonel commanding the 14th (Service) Battalion of the Hampshire Regiment from 12 January to 29 August 1916. He served as a temporary Brigadier-General from 30 August 1916 to 12 April 1919, and then as a temporary Lieutenant-Colonel in the Royal Fusiliers from 14 April 1919 to 25 March 1920.

Hickie served in the Boer War from 1899 to 1902. He took part in the operations in Natal in 1899, seeing action at Reitfonten, where he was wounded, and at Lombard's Kop. He also took part in the Defence of Ladysmith. From March to June 1900 he again took part in operations in Natal. From November 1900 to May 1902 he served in the Transvaal and was awarded the QM with two clasps and the KM with two clasps. He then served as an Adjutant in the Territorial Force from 16 September 1908 to 15 September 1911.

From 1 April 1913 to 4 August 1914, he served as Brigade Major to the East Lancashire Infantry Brigade, Western Command and with the East Lancashire Infantry Brigade and the 126th Infantry Brigade in the Central Force Home Defence in Egypt and the Mediterranean from 5 August 1914 to 30 June 1915, where he was action at Gallipoli. Again serving as a Brigade Major, he served in France from 10 December 1915 to 11 January 1916 with the 10th Reserve Infantry Brigade of the New Armies. From 20 March 1917 to 12 April 1919 he served as the Brigade commander of the 224th and 7th Infantry Brigades.

He was wounded during the First World War and was mentioned in dispatches five times. He was awarded the 1914–1915 Star, the BWM, the VM, the CMG and the DSO. He was also awarded the Legion of Honour 5th Class.

Major S. Gubbins

He served in South Africa from 1900 to 1902, where he served in operations in the Transvaal, the Orange River Colony and the Cape Colony. In September and October 1901, he took part in operations on the Zululand frontier of Natal. He was awarded the QM with five clasps. During the First World War he served in France and Belgium; he was mentioned in dispatches once, and awarded the 1914–1915 Star, the BWM, the VM, the DSO and the OBE.

Major R.H. Pipon

He served in East Africa in operations in Somaliland from 1908 to 1910, for which he was awarded the GSM with clasp. During the First World War he served in

France and Belgium; he was mentioned in dispatches three times, was awarded the 1914 Star with clasp, the BWM, the VM, the DSO with clasp and the MC. He was also awarded the Legion of Honour 5th Class.

Major H.F. Whinney

During the First World War he served in France and Belgium. He was mentioned in dispatches five times. He was awarded the 1914 Star with clasp, the BWM, the VM, the DSO and the OBE, and was also awarded the Legion of Honour 5th Class.

The King's Liverpool Regiment

Lieutenant-Colonel Llewellyn Murray Jones, CMG

Lieutenant-Colonel Jones was commissioned into the King's Liverpool Regiment from the militia as a 2nd Lieutenant on 17 January 1891, and promoted to Lieutenant on 1 March 1893. He was a Battalion Adjutant from 20 March 1898 to 26 August 1902. He was made Captain on 5 February 1900 and Major on 18 September 1909. For various periods from 14 January 1916 to 31 July 1919 he served as a temporary Lieutenant-Colonel. He was made a Brevet Lieutenant-Colonel on 1 January 1918 and a Lieutenant-Colonel on 17 February 1920.

Jones served in the Boer War from 1899 to 1902. During operations in Natal in 1899, he took part in actions at Rietfontein, Lombard's Kop and the defence of Ladysmith. He took part in further operations in the Transvaal and Natal, seeing action again at Belfast in August 1900. He served as the Adjutant for the 1st Battalion also during this period and a Commandant of Waterval Onder from 17 November to 15 December 1900. He served as an Adjutant to the Volunteers from 9 March 1903 to 8 July 1906.

From 17 November 1913 to 17 November 1914 he was a staff captain in No4 District Western Command. He served as temporary DAAG Western Command from 18 November 1914 to 3 January 1916 and from 14 January to 14 February 1916 he was AA & QMG to the 2nd East African Division, East African Force. He was Base Commandant for East African Force from 27 May 1917 to 16 March 1918. While in Africa, he took part in operations in British, German and Portuguese Africa, in Nyasaland and in North Rhodesia. He again served as an AA & QMG for the Humber Garrison from 24 April to 25 July 1918, and for the 35th Division in France from 6 September 1918 to 30 June 1919. He was AAG for No.4 Area, France from 1 July 1919 to 31 July 1919.

He was mentioned three times in dispatches during the Boer War, and was awarded the QM with three clasps, the KM with two clasps and the DSO. During the First World War he was mentioned in dispatches twice, and awarded the BWM, the VM and the CMG. He was also awarded the French War Cross.

Major W.K. Pinwell (Brevet Lieutenant-Colonel)

Pinwell fought in the Boer War, and in 1899 he took part in operations in the Transvaal and saw action at Rietfontein, at Lombards Kop and the Defence of Ladysmith. While at Ladysmith he was involved in the sortie of 7 December 1899 and the action on 6 January 1900. In the spring and summer of 1900 he was again involved in operations in Natal, including the action at Laing's Nek on 6–9 June. He took part in operations in the Transvaal from July 1900 to May 1902, including an action at Belfast on 26/27 August 1900. He also served as a Commandant at Kaapsche Hoop in 1901. He was mentioned in dispatches once and awarded the QM with three clasps and the KM with two clasps.

He served in France and Belgium during the First World War. He was mentioned in dispatches three times. He was awarded the 1914–1915 Star, the BWM, the VM and the DSO.

Major D.R. O'Flynn

He served in Africa, France and Belgium during the First World War. He was awarded the 1914–1915 Star, the BWM and the VM.

Major V.C. Gauntlett

He served in France and Belgium during the First World War. He was wounded and awarded the 1914 Star with clasp, the BWM and the VM.

Major p. Hudson (Brevet Lieutenant-Colonel)

Hudson served in the Boer War from 1900 to 1902. From February to May 1900 he was in the Orange Free State, and saw action at Karee Siding, Vet River and Zand River. He took part in operations in the Transvaal during May and June 1900, seeing action near Johannesburg and Pretoria. Later in 1900, he saw action east of Pretoria at Belfast. From December 1901 to May 1902 he remained on active duty in the Transvaal, serving as an Assistant Provost Marshall and Assistant Press Censor from 14 December 1901 to 30 January 1902. He was awarded the QM with three clasps and the KM with two clasps.

He served in France and Belgium during the First World War and was wounded. He was mentioned in dispatches six times. He was awarded the 1914 Star, the BWM, the VM, the CMG and the DSO. He was also awarded the Belgian War Cross, the Order of Leopold 4th Class and the Order of Merit (Agriculture) 4th Class.

Major R.C.R. Jones

Major Jones served in South Africa from 1899 to 1902. In 1899 he took part in operations in Natal, including the actions at Dietfontein and Lombards Kop. He took part in the Defence of Ladysmith, including the sortie on 7 December 1899 and the action of 6 January 1900. From March to June 1900 he continued to serve in Natal, seeing action again at Laing's Nek on 6–9 June. He then served in the Transvaal from July 1900 to May 1902, and saw action at Belfast on 26/27 August 1900. He was awarded the QM with three clasps and the KM with two clasps.

During the First World War he served in France and Belgium until 10 May 1916; from 24 September 1916 to 31 October 1918 he served with the Egyptian Expeditionary Force. He was Adjutant to the 4th Battalion Liverpool Regiment until 10 May 1916. He was mentioned in dispatches once, and awarded the 1914–1915 Star, the BWM and the DSO.

The East Lancashire Regiment

Lieutenant-Colonel William Henry Traill, CMG, DSO
Lieutenant-Colonel Traill was commissioned into the East Lancashire Regiment as a 2nd Lieutenant on 17 December 1892, and promoted to Lieutenant on 10 October 1895. He was promoted Captain on 11 September 1901 and Major on 10 September 1914. He served as a temporary Lieutenant-Colonel from 4 August 1914 to 30 June 1915 and from 17 November 1916 to 29 March 1919. He was acting Lieutenant-Colonel for 53 Battalion the Manchesters from 1 April to 10 November 1919. He was Brevet Lieutenant-Colonel on 1 January 1918 and Lieutenant-Colonel on 13 April 1920.

He took part in the Tirah Expeditionary Force on the North-West Frontier of India from 1897 to 1898, receiving the Afghan Medal with clasp. He served as a Brigade Major in India from 18 February 1908 to 16 February 1912. He was General Staff Officer, Grade 2 in Southern Coastal Defence Command from November 1913 to 4 August 1914. From 5 August 1914 to 30 June 1915 he served as a General Staff Officer, Grade 1 in the Portsmouth Garrison. He served as a General Staff Officer, Grade 2 from 1 July 1915 to 16 November 1916 with the 33rd Division, New Armies, 2nd Army Corps, British Expeditionary Force, and the 16th Division. From 17 November 1918 to 29 March 1919 he served as a General Staff Officer, Grade 1 with the 3rd Division.

During the First World War he was mentioned in dispatches five times and awarded the 1914–1915 Star, the BWM, the VM, the CMG and the DSO. He was also awarded the Legion of Honour 5th Class.

Major F.H. Edwards
Edwards served in South Africa from 1899 to 1902. From March 1900 to January 1901 he served in operations in the Cape Colony, and he served in the Transvaal from October 1901 to May 1902. He also served as Commandant of Victoria West from 22 June to 10 July 1901. He was awarded the QM with three clasps and the KM with two clasps. During the First World War he served in France and Belgium; he was mentioned in dispatches five times and awarded the 1914 Star, the BWM, the VM, the DSO and the MC.

Major G.E.M. Hill

Hill served in South Africa from 1899 to 1902. In 1899, he took part in operations in the Cape Colony. From February to May 1900, he served in the Orange Free State, seeing action at Poplar Grove, Driefontien, Vet River and at Zand River. The summer of 1900 saw him involved in operations in the Transvaal, seeing action near Johannesburg, Pretoria and Diamond Hill. Later in the year he took part in operations east of Pretoria, including an action at Reit Vlei. He took part in operations in the Cape Colony again from November to February 1901. He also served in the Orange River Colony from April to December 1901 and from March 1901 to May 1902. He also served as an Adjutant to the Mounted Infantry from February to May 1902. He was mentioned in dispatches once and awarded the QM with four clasps and the KM with two clasps.

During the First World War he served in France and Belgium, he was mentioned in dispatches once. He was awarded in 1914 Star with clasp, the BWM, the VM the DSO.

Major A.A. Sharland

He served in France and Belgium during the First World War. From 18 April to 3 October 1917 he commanded the 2nd Battalion East Lancashire Regiment. He was mentioned in dispatches once and was awarded the BWM, the VM and the DSO.

The South Staffordshire Regiment

Lieutenant-Colonel A.H.C. James

James served in South Africa from 1899 to 1902. In the summer of 1900 he took part in operations in the Orange Free State, and from May to November 1900 in operations in the Orange River Colony, including the action at Wittebergen from 1–29 July. He continued to take part in operations in the Orange River Colony from November 1900 to March 1902. During this time, he also took part in operations in the Transvaal in July 1901. He served as the Adjutant for the 1st Battalion South Staffordshire Regiment from 14 August 1901, and was attached to the Army Service Corps from 25 January to 16 April 1900. He was mentioned in dispatches twice and awarded the QM with three clasps and the KM with two clasps.

During the First World War he served in France and Belgium, where he was wounded. He was mentioned in dispatches four times. He was awarded the 1914 Star with clasp, the BWM, the VM, the MVO and the DSO. He was also awarded the Legion of Honour 4th Class.

Lieutenant-Colonel Stephen Seymour Butler, CMG, DSO

Lieutenant-Colonel Butler was commissioned from the Militia into the Royal

Warwickshire Regiment as a 2nd Lieutenant on 20 May 1899, and was promoted Lieutenant on 1 April 1900. He was made Captain on 18 January 1908, and on 20 May 1908 he transferred to the South Staffordshire Regiment at that rank. He was promoted Major on 12 August 1915. He served as temporary Lieutenant-Colonel from 14 January to 17 March 1918, and a temporary Colonel from 18 March 1918 to 18 March 1919. He was made Brevet Lieutenant-Colonel on 3 June 1918. He again served as a temporary Lieutenant-Colonel from 12 June 1919 to 30 August 1920.

He served with the King's African Rifles from 21 August 1905 to 4 April 1908, where he saw action in Nandi and in East Africa. He served with the Egyptian Army from 22 April 1909 to 17 May 1915, seeing action in the Sudan in 1910, during operations in Southern Kordofan. He was employed as a General Staff Officer, Grade 3 and then Grade 2 with the ANZAC Army Corps, Mediterranean Expeditionary Force, from 18 May to 19 December 1915, where he took part in the Gallipoli landings. He then served with the ANZAC Army Corps in France from 25 March 1916 to 13 January 1918. He served as a General Staff Officer, Grade 1 from 14 January 1918 to 30 August 1920 with the British 5th Army at GHQ in France and also with British Forces in Constantinople.

During the First World War he was mentioned in dispatches five times; he was awarded the 1914–1915 Star, the BWM, the VM, the CMG and the DSO. He was also awarded the French War Cross and the Order of the Sacred Treasure 3rd Class.

Major S. C. Welchman

He served in West Africa in 1898, seeing action at Borgn, and was awarded the GSM and clasp. He served in South Africa from 1900 to 1901, taking part in operations in the Orange River Colony from May to November 1900, and was involved in the action at Wittebergen from 1–29 July. From November 1900 to March 1901 he took part in operations in the Transvaal and later in the Cape Colony from March to August 1901. He was mentioned in dispatches once and was awarded the QM with three clasps. During the First World War he served in France and Belgium. He was wounded once and awarded the 1914 Star, the BWM, the VM and the OBE.

Major W.J.J. Collas

He served in France and Belgium during the First World War and held two battalion commands; from 21 January 1917 to 8 April 1918 he commanded the 2/1 Battalion London Regiment and from 9 April to 10 June he commanded the 2nd Battalion South Staffordshire Regiment. He served on staff for the reminder of the war. He was mentioned in dispatches twice and was awarded the BWM, the VM and the DSO.

Major M.B. Savage

He served in France and Belgium during the First World War, both on staff and in the trenches, and was wounded. He was mentioned in dispatches five times and was awarded the 1914 Star, the BWM, the VM, the CBE and the DSO.

Captain F.P. Duck

He served in South Africa in 1902, taking part in operations in the Transvaal and the Cape Colony. He was awarded the QM with three clasps. During the First World War he served in France and Belgium, in Egypt and with the Egyptian Expeditionary Force, seeing action at Gallipoli. He also served in British, German and Portuguese East Africa and Northern Rhodesia. He was mentioned in dispatches once and awarded the 1914–1915 Star, the BWM, the VM and the DSO.

The Queen's Own Cameron Highlanders

Lieutenant-Colonel George Cecil Minett Sorel-Cameron

Lieutenant-Colonel Sorel-Cameron was commissioned into the Camerons on 5 April 1893 and promoted Lieutenant on 7 December 1895. He was made Captain on 21 May 1899, and Major on 7 September 1910. He served as a temporary Lieutenant-Colonel to the 6th Battalion from 6–30 September 1914 and again from 17 January to 1 June 1919. He was made Lieutenant-Colonel on 2 June 1919. He served with the Egyptian Army from 7 December 1899 to 26 December 1906. He took part in the Nile Expedition of 1898 and fought at the Battles of Atbara and Khartoum. He was awarded the Egyptian Medal with two clasps. He served in France during the First World War and was awarded the 1914 Star, the BWM and the VM.

Major J. G. Ramsay

Ramsay served in the Boer War from 1901 to 1902. From September 1901 to 31 May 1902 he served in the Transvaal. He also took part in operations in the Cape Colony in May 1902. For his service in South Africa he was awarded the QM with five clasps.

During the First World War he served for three periods on staff in France and Belgium: from 24 January to 26 April 1915; from 7–22 January 1916; and from 14 April 1917 to 11 November 1918. He was in Gallipoli from 16 July 1915 to 9 January 1916. From 10 January to 18 March 1916 he served in Egypt, then served with the Egyptian Expeditionary Force until he was wounded on 6 June 1916. He was mentioned in dispatches three times and was awarded the 1914–1915 Star, the BWM, the VM, the DSO and the OBE. He was also awarded the Belgian War Cross.

Major W.M. Stewart

Major Stewart served in the 1898 Nile Expedition and fought at the Battle of Atbara. He was awarded the Egyptian Medal with clasp. He then served in the Boer War. From February to May 1900 he took part in operations in the Orange Free State, and fought at the actions at Vet River and Zand River. During the summer of 1900 he served in operations in the Transvaal and saw action near Pretoria and

Johannesburg. From May to November 1900 he was in the Orange River Colony, seeing combat at Wittebergen and Ladybrand. He returned to the Transvaal on two more occasions, from January to August 1901 and February 1902 to May 1902. From 30 November 1900 to January 1901 he was in the Orange River Colony and in May 1902 he was in the Cape Colony. He was slightly wounded twice during the war. He was mentioned in dispatches once and was awarded the QM with three clasps and the KM with two clasps.

During the First World War he served in France and Belgium. He was on staff for two periods, 20 September 1914 to 6 April 1915 and 11 February 1917 to 11 November 1918. He was wounded and mentioned in dispatches four times. He was awarded the 1914 Star with clasp, the BWM, the VM, the DSO and the CMG.

Captain D. Cameron (Brevet Major)

He fought in France and Belgium during the First World War. He served on staff for various periods: 14 August to 25 October 1914; 28 April to 25 November 1915; 11 January to 25 August 1917; and 1 May to 11 November 1918. He was wounded once and mentioned in dispatches twice. He was awarded the 1914 Star with clasp, the BWM, the VM and the MC.

Captain I.C. Cameron

Captain Cameron began his service during the First World War in France and Belgium. From 12 December 1915 to 11 November 1918 he served in Greek Macedonia, Serbia, Bulgaria, European Turkey and the islands of the Aegean Sea. He served in Russia in 1919. He was mentioned in dispatches once and was awarded the 1914–1915 Star, the BWM and the VM.

Captain A.L. Collier

He served in France and Belgium at the beginning of the First World War, spending a period on staff from 29 January to 29 November 1915. From 30 November 1915 to 11 November 1918 he served in Greek Macedonia, Serbia, Bulgaria, European Turkey and the islands of the Aegean Sea. He served in Russia in 1919. He was mentioned in dispatches twice and was awarded the 1914–1915 Star, the BWM, the VM and the MC. He was also awarded the Order of the White Eagle with swords 5th Class.

Captain R. Letters

Letters served in the Boer War from 1899 to 1902 with the 1st Battalion Argyll and Sutherland Highlanders. He took part in the advance on Kimberley and saw action at Modder River and at Magersfontein, where he was wounded. In early 1900 he served in operations in the Orange Free State, including action at Paardeberg on 17–26 February. He also saw action at Poplar Grove and Dreifontein. In late 1900 he was involved in operations in the Transvaal, east of Pretoria, seeing action at Zilikats Nek, and he served in the Orange River Colony. From 30 November 1900 to May 1902 he served in the Transvaal. He was awarded the QM with four clasps and the KM with two clasps. During the First World War he served in France and Belgium. He was mentioned in dispatches twice and awarded the 1914–1915 Star, the BWM, the VM and the MC.

Captain D. N. Wimberley

He served in France and Belgium during the First World War, first with the Camerons and from January 1916 as a temporary Major in the Machine Gun Corps. He was wounded and awarded the 1914–1915 Star, the BWM, the VM and the MC.

The Hampshire Regiment

Lieutenant-Colonel C. N. French

He served in the Boer War from 1900 to 1902. From February to May 1900 he took part in operations in the Orange Free State, seeing action at Paardeberg and he was seriously wounded at Karee Siding. He took part in operation in the Transvaal from September 1901 to April 1902.

During the Boer War he was awarded the QM with three clasps and the KM with two clasps. He was mentioned in dispatches once during the First World War and was awarded the BWM and the CMG. He was also awarded the Belgian Order of the Crown 4th Class, the Legion of Honour 4th Class, the Order of St Maurice and St Lazarus 4th Class and the Order of St Stanislas 2nd Class.

Major R. S. Allen (Brevet Lieutenant-Colonel)

Major Allen fought in the Boer War from 1899 to 1902. From May to June 1900 he was involved in operations in the Transvaal. From July to November 1900 he was involved in operations east of Pretoria. From November 1901 to May 1902 he remained on active duty in the Transvaal. For his South African service he was awarded the QM with one clasp and the KM with two clasps.

During the First World War he served in France and Belgium. He was mentioned in dispatches four times and was awarded 1914–1915 Star, the BWM, the VM and the DSO.

Major L. C. Morley (Brevet Lieutenant-Colonel)

Morley served in East Africa from 1902 to 1904, where he took part in operations in Somaliland. He commanded the 11th Somali Camel Corps from 21 January 1904 to 24 February 1904. He was also involved in Directorate of Supply and Transport in Somaliland from November 1902 to May 1904. He was awarded a GSM and clasp.

During the First World War he served in France and Belgium. He was mentioned in dispatches once and was awarded for 1914–1915 Star, the BWM, the VM, the OBE and the CBE.

Major W.H. Middleton

He served in South Africa in 1902, taking part in operations in the Transvaal and Orange River Colony. He was awarded the QM with two clasps. In 1903 and 1904 he served in East Africa, where he took part in operations in Somaliland and saw action at Jidballi, winning the Service Medal with two clasps.

During the First World War he served in France, Belgium and Italy. He was mentioned in dispatches four times and was awarded the 1914–1915 Star, the BWM, the VM and the DSO. He was also awarded the Italian Silver Medal for Military Valour.

The Manchester Regiment

Lieutenant-Colonel E Vaughn

He served in Boer War from 1899 to 1902, taking part in operations in the Transvaal in 1900. During October 1900 he served as Commandant at Badfontien. He also served as Adjutant to the 2nd Johannesburg Mounted Rifles during 1901. He was mentioned in dispatches twice and awarded the QM with five clasps and the KM with two clasps. He served in France during the First World War and was mentioned in dispatches three times. He was awarded the 1914–1915 Star, the BWM, the VM, the CMG and the DSO. He was also awarded the Legion of Honour 5th Class and the Belgian War Cross.

Major F.H. Dorling

He served in South Africa from 1900 to 1902. From April to May 1900 he took part in operations in the Orange Free State. Later that year he saw action in the Transvaal east of Pretoria, and he was also engaged in operations in Orange River Colony, including the actions at Wittebergen from 1–29 July. In April 1900 he also took part in an operation in the Cape Colony. From November 1900 to May 1902 he was involved in operations in the Orange River Colony. He was awarded the QM with three clasps and the KM with two clasps.

During the First World War he served in France and Belgium, with periods on staff from August to November 1914 and July 1916 to July 1918. He was mentioned in dispatches five times and awarded the 1914 Star with clasp, the BWM, the VM and the DSO.

Major W.K. Evans

Evans served in South Africa from 1900 to 1902. During 1900 he was involved in operations in the Orange Free State and the Orange River Colony. He served with the mounted infantry. He was awarded the QM with three clasps and the KM with two clasps. He served in France and Belgium during the First World War. From 30 October 1914 to 1 August 1915 he was the Adjutant to 2nd Battalion Manchester Regiment. He was Battalion commander of the 11th Service Battalion Cheshire Regiment from 13 July 1916 to 24 September 1917. He also served on staff. He was mentioned in dispatches eight times and was awarded the 1914 Star, the BWM, the VM, the CMG and the DSO with clasp.

Major J.A. Dearden

He served in South Africa in 1902, taking part in operations in the Transvaal, the Orange River Colony and the Cape Colony. He was awarded the QM with three clasps. During the First World War he served in Egypt until 2 May 1915, and then at Gallipoli from May to July 1915. He also served as the Adjutant to 1/9 Battalion Manchester Regiment (Territorial Force).

Major A.G. Foord

Foord served in South Africa from 1899 to 1902. From 1899 to 1900 he was involved in operations in the Cape Colony south of the Orange River, and from July 1901 to May 1902 he served in the Transvaal. He was awarded the QM with three clasps and the KM with two clasps. During the First World War he served in France and Belgium. He served as the Brigade Major for the 173rd Infantry Brigade from 25 January to 12 May 1917. He served as the Battalion commander for the 2/6 London Regiment (Territorial Force) from 15 May to 20 September 1917. He was mentioned in dispatches once and was awarded the 1914 Star with clasp, the BWM, the VM and the DSO.

Major A.E. O'Meara

O'Meara served in South Africa from 1900 to 1902, taking part in operations in Transvaal, the Orange River Colony, and the Cape Colony. He was awarded the QM with three clasps. During the First World War he served in Togoland from 7–26 August 1914, and in Kamerun and Nigeria from 27 August 1914 to 13 June 1915. He served in Mesopotamia from 24 March 1916 to 10 April 1918, and with the Egyptian Expeditionary Force from 23 April to 31 October 1918. He served as a Staff Captain to the 8th Infantry Brigade from 29 June to 11 November 1916. He was awarded the BWM and the VM.

Major C.C. Stapleton

He served with the mounted infantry in South Africa during the Boer War. From 1901 to 1902 he took part in operations in the Transvaal and Cape Colony. He served in France and Belgium during the First World War. He was mentioned in dispatches once and awarded the 1914 Star with clasp, the BWM and the VM.

The 17th Lancers

Lieutenant-Colonel Bertie Drew Fisher

Lieutenant-Colonel Fisher was commissioned into the 17th Lancers as a 2nd Lieutenant on 25 May 1900. He promoted to Lieutenant on 29 July 1901. He served as Battalion Adjutant from 1 November 1904 to 31 October 1907. He was promoted Captain on 7 September 1905 and Major on 7 January 1914. He served as a temporary Lieutenant-Colonel to the Leicestershire Yeomanry from 7 July to 27 August 1915. He was made Brevet Lieutenant-Colonel on 3 June 1916. He served as a temporary Lieutenant-Colonel to the 1st Battalion Lincoln Regiment from 24 January to 11 April 1918. He was made Lieutenant-Colonel of the 17th/21st Lancers on 24 February 1919 and Colonel on 31 June 1920.

He fought in the Boer War, serving in operations in the Transvaal, east of Pretoria, from July to November 1900. From May to November 1900 he also took part in Operations in the Orange River Colony, where he saw action at Caledon River on 27/29 November. He took part in operations in the Cape Colony and the Orange River Colony from November 1900 to May 1902. He was awarded the QM with the KM with two clasps.

He served as a General Staff Officer, Grade 3 at the War Office from 13 October 1913 to 4 August 1914. He remained at the War Office from 5 August to 15 September 1914 as a temporary General Staff Officer, Grade 2. From 20 September 1914 to 3 April 1915 he served as a Brigade Major in France and with the Home Forces. He served as a General Staff Officer, Grade 2 and then Grade 1 in France from 4 April 1915 to 17 January 1918. He also served as a temporary Brigadier-General from 12 April 1918 to 17 March 1919.

During the First World War he was mentioned in dispatches five times. He was awarded the 1914 Star, the BWM, the CMG and the DSO with clasp. He was also awarded the Legion of Honour 4th Class.

Major E. Sopper

During the First World War he served in France and Belgium at the beginning of the war. He served at Gallipoli from 14 August to 31 October 1915. From 7 November 1915 to 7 May 1916 he served in Greek Macedonia, Serbia, Bulgaria, European Turkey and the islands of the Aegean Sea. He served with Egyptian Expeditionary Force from 4 June 1916 to 19 April 1918, and again in France and Belgium from 8 June to 11 November 1918.

He served as the Adjutant of South Worcestershire Hussars Yeomanry (Territorial Force) from 22 October to 6 November 1915, and as Adjutant of a Composite Yeomanry Regiment from 7 November 1915 to 17 February 1916. He also served as a General Staff Officer, Grade 3 for the 26th Division from 18 February to 27 December 1916. He was mentioned in dispatches once and awarded the 1914–1915 Star, the BWM, the VM, the DSO and the MC.

Major T.P. Melvill

During the First World War he served in France and Belgium. He was mentioned in dispatches twice and awarded the 1914 Star, the DSO and the French War Cross.

Major D.H. Talbot

He served in South Africa from 1901 to 1902, where he took part in operations in the Cape Colony from December 1901 to May 1902. He was awarded the QM with three clasps.

During the First World War he began his service in France and Belgium. He served in Egypt from January to March 1916, served in France and Belgium from March 1916 to February 1917, and from November 1917 to November 1918 in Italy. He served as Adjutant of the Lancashire Hussars Yeomanry in January 1916, and afterwards spent time on staff. He was mentioned in dispatches twice and was awarded the BWM, the VM, the DSO, the MC and the Italian War Cross.

The Gloucestershire Regiment

Lieutenant-Colonel Francis Courtenay Nisbet

Nisbet was commissioned into the Gloucestershire Regiment on 29 March 1890, and was promoted to Lieutenant on 21 October 1891 and Captain on 24 February 1900. He was promoted Major in 1913. He served as temporary Lieutenant-Colonel in the Gloucestershire Regiment from 12 June 1915 to 16 March 1916, and in the same rank with a Service Battalion of the Duke of Cornwall's Light Infantry from 19 May to 30 November 1916. He was promoted Brevet Lieutenant-Colonel on 1 January 1917 and Brevet Colonel on 3 June 1919. He served as a temporary Brigadier-General from 22 March 1918 to 3 October 1919, serving firstly as the commander of the 84th Infantry Brigade of the British Salonika Force and then as commander of the 83rd Infantry Brigade of the British Army of the Black Sea.

He fought in the Boer War from 1899 to 1901, serving on staff and operations. In Natal in 1899 he took part in actions at Rietfontein and Lombards Kop. He served in the Transvaal in the summer of 1900, and later that year in the Cape Colony, south of Orange River. He was awarded the QM with three clasps. He fought in the First World War, seeing action in France and Eastern Europe. He was mentioned in dispatches five times and awarded the DSO.

Lieutenant-Colonel Joseph Robert Wethered

Wethered was commissioned into the Gloucestershire Regiment on 19 July 1893, and promoted Lieutenant on 8 February 1897. He served as an Adjutant from 12 July 1902 to 11 July 1905. He made Captain on 12 July 1902 and Major on 11 May 1915. He held the rank of temporary Lieutenant-Colonel from 27 July 1917 to 16 February 1920. He was made Brevet Lieutenant-Colonel on 1 January 1918.

He fought in the Boer War from 1900 to 1902, taking part in the Relief of Kimberley. He took part in operations in the Orange Free State, including those at Paardeburg and in the actions at Poplar Grove and Dreifontein. In 1900 and 1901 he served in with the Mounted Infantry in operations in the Orange River Colony, and also in the Cape Colony. He was awarded the QM with four clasps and the KM with two clasps. He served as a Brigade Major with the Black Watch in 1913 and in the same capacity from 30 May to 29 September 1913 with the 14th Infantry Brigade, Irish Command, in both Ireland and France. From 29 September 1914 to 21 April 1916 he served as a Brigade Major with the Special Reserve Infantry Brigade, Harwich Detachment and the 62nd Infantry Brigade, British Expeditionary Force. He was promoted to a General Staff Officer, Grade 2 and served at this rank with the 15th and 17th Army Corps in France. On 27 July 1917 he was promoted to General Staff Officer, Grade 1 and served for the rest of the war in this capacity with the 57th Division, and after the war with the Forth Garrison until 16 February 1920. He was mentioned in dispatches six times and was awarded the 1914 Star, the BWM, the CMG and the DSO.

Major Alfred Hutton Radice

Radice was commissioned into the Gloucestershire Regiment on 21 October 1893 and promoted Lieutenant on 26 May 1897. He made Captain on 2 June 1903. He served as Adjutant with the regiment from October 1911 to October 1914. He held the rank of temporary Major from 6–31 August 1915 and was promoted to Major in the regiment on 1 September 1915. From 21 June 1916 to 23 October 1919 he served as a temporary Lieutenant-Colonel with the 14th Battalion of the Gloucesters and the 14th Battalion of the South Wales Borderers. During the First World War he also served as the Commander of the Gentleman Cadets at the Royal Military College.

He fought in the Boer War from 1899 to 1900, serving on operations in Natal, the Transvaal, and the Orange River Colony, and was in action at Rietfontein and Lombard's Kop. He was awarded the QM with three clasps. In the First World War he served in France and Belgium and in Italy, was mentioned in dispatches three times and was awarded the 1914 Star, the BWM, the DSO and the Italian War Cross.

Major Julian Fane

Fane was commissioned from the Militia into the Gloucestershire Regiment on 4 May 1898, was promoted Lieutenant on 24 February 1900 and Captain 25 July 1906. He was given the rank of Major on 1 September 1915 and served as a temporary Lieutenant-Colonel from 1 September 1915 until 13 November 1919, commanding the 9th Battalion, Gloucestershire Regiment, the 4th Battalion, the Shropshire Light Infantry and the 8th Battalion Gloucestershire Regiment.

Fane fought in the Boer War from 1900 to 1902, taking part in the Relief of Kimberley, and in operations in the Orange Free State in 1900, seeing action at Paardeberg, Poplar Grove, and Dreifontein, and also serving in the Orange River Colony and in the Cape Colony, both north and south of the Orange River. 1901 saw Fane serve in the Transvaal, and again in the Orange River Colony and the Cape Colony, while 1902 saw a return to operations in the Transvaal. He was awarded the QM with four clasps and the KM with two clasps. He served with the West African Field Force from 7 October 1905 to 6 April 1910, taking part in operations in the Kwale-Ighan District and serving on the Bende-Onitgha Expedition. Fane was awarded a (?) medal with clasp. During the First World War he served in France and Belgium, was mentioned dispatches three times and was awarded the VM, the BWM and the DSO.

Major Alexander William Pagan

Pagan was commissioned into the Gloucestershire Regiment on 11 February 1899, promoted Lieutenant on 24 February 1900 and made Captain on 29 September 1906. He served as an Adjutant from 12 July 1908 to 11 July 1911, as an Adjutant to the Special Reserve from 16 November 1911 to 2 January 1915 and was appointed Major on 1 September 1915. He served as a temporary Lieutenant-Colonel with the Gloucesters from 1 September 1915 to 27 March 1918, and was made a Brevet Lieutenant-Colonel on 1 January 1917. Pagan also served as the commander of the 184th Infantry Brigade from 28 March to 16 October 1918.

Pagan fought in the Boer War from 1900 to 1902. He took part in the Relief of Kimberley, and in operations in the Orange Free State, seeing action at Dreifontein and Poplar Grove. Later in 1900 he took part in operations in both the Orange River Colony and the Cape Colony, and in 1901 in operations in the Transvaal and again in the Orange River Colony. He was awarded the QM with four clasps and the KM with two clasps. He served in France and Belgium during the First World War, was mentioned in dispatches four times and awarded the BWM, the DSO and the Order of Leopold 4th Class.

Major William Percy Stilles Foord

Foord served in the Militia prior to being commissioned as a 2nd Lieutenant in the Gloucester Regiment on 21 February 1903, promoted Lieutenant on 24 January 1906 and Captain on 22 January 1912. He was appointed a temporary Major in the 14th Battalion of the Gloucestershire Regiment from 15 July to 21 August 1916, and a temporary Lieutenant-Colonel from 22 August 1916 to 23 February 1918. He was appointed a Major on 3 May 1917 and a Brevet Lieutenant-Colonel on 3 June 1918. From 24 February to 24 April 1918 he was a temporary Lieutenant-Colonel of the 19th Battalion, Northumberland Fusiliers. From 25 April 1918 to 14 April 1919 he served as Brigade commander of the 32nd Infantry Brigade in France, and then returning to the rank of temporary Lieutenant-Colonel with the 51st and 53rd Battalions of the Northumberland Fusiliers from 16 April 1919 to 21 March 1920.

He served in the Boer War from 1901 to 1902 on operations in the Transvaal and in the Orange River Colony. He served in France in the First World War and was mentioned in dispatches four times, awarded the DSO twice, and the French War Cross.

Major John Lennoy Frobes Tweedle

Tweedle was commissioned into the Gloucestershire Regiment on 4 April 1900, promoted Lieutenant on 2 June 1903 and Captain on 14 January 1911. He was promoted Major on 1 September 1915, and from 20 July 1916 to 26 June 1919 he served as a temporary Lieutenant-Colonel with the 12th Battalion, Lancashire Fusiliers and with the Gloucestershire Regiment.

Tweedle fought in the Boer War in 1901 and was awarded the KM with two clasps. He served with the Egyptian Army from 25 December 1909 to 16 May 1915. He also served in France and Belgium during the First World War, was mentioned in dispatches twice, and awarded the DSO twice, and the Order of the White Eagle 4th Class with swords.

Captain Montague Walter Halford

Halford was commissioned into the Gloucestershire Regiment on 5 October 1910, promoted Lieutenant on 6 March 1912. He served as a temporary Captain from 15 November 1914 to 10 May 1915, and was appointed to the rank on 11 May 1915. He served as a temporary Major with the Gloucesters from 5 September to 8 October 1916, 25 June to 13 November 1917 and April 1918, and with the 1/5th Devonshire Regiment from 4 May to 9 November 1919. Halford was an acting Lieutenant-Colonel with the Cheshire Regiment from 14 November to 27 December 1917, with the Bedfordshire Regiment from 1 May to 19 June 1918 and with the Devonshire Regiment from 5 July 1918 to 3 May 1919.

He fought in France and Belgium during the First World War and was awarded the 1914 Star and MC.

Captain Lucien Austin Lachlan

Lachlan was commissioned into the Gloucestershire Regiment on 20 September 1911, promoted Lieutenant on 6 July 1912, served as a temporary Captain from 20 September to 13 October 1915 and was appointed Captain on 14 October 1915. He served as an Adjutant with the Special Reserve from 7 April 1917 to 29 April 1918, as a Staff Captain at the Prees Heath Reserve Centre from 23 September 1918 to 13 May 1919 and with the Midland Reserve Brigade Forces in Great Britain in May 1919.

During the First World War, he fought in France and Belgium and was wounded.

Captain Robert Spurrell Dacres Stuart

Stuart joined the Gloucestershire Regiment as a Captain from the Territorial Army on 23 March 1917. He fought in France and Belgium during the First World War and was wounded twice.

Captain Donald Duncan

Duncan was commissioned from the Reserve into the Gloucestershire Regiment on 27 May 1911, promoted Lieutenant on 29 May 1912. He served as a temporary Captain from 17 May to 7 September 1915, and was appointed to the rank on 8 September 1915. Duncan served as a Staff Captain with the 3rd Infantry Brigade from 24 June 1916 to 6 March 1919, as DAAG & QMG with the 37th Division, and later as DAAG, Shorncliffe Area, Eastern Command from 7 March 1919 to 25 March 1920. He was made a Brevet Major on 3 June 1919.

Duncan fought in France and Belgium during the First World War, was mentioned in dispatches three times and was awarded the 1914 Star, the DSO and MC.

Captain Robert Michael Grazebrook

Grazebrook was commissioned into the Gloucestershire Regiment on 5 February 1913, promoted Lieutenant on 24 October 1914, and served as temporary Captain from 5 February 1915 to 16 August 1919, during which time he served as a GSO Grade 3 at the School of Instructors at Berkhamstead.

Grazebrook fought in France and Belgium during the First World War, was wounded twice, and mentioned in dispatches once. He was awarded the 1914 Star and the MC.

The King's Own Scottish Borderers

Lieutenant-Colonel H.D.N. Maclean

Maclean served on the Tirah Expeditionary Force on the North-West Frontier from 1897 to 1898. He fought in the Boer War from 1899 to 1902. In 1900 he took part in operations in the Orange Free State, seeing action at Paardeberg, Poplar Grove, Karee Siding, Vet River and Zand River.

In the summer of 1900 he served in the Transvaal, taking part in actions at Johannesburg and Pretoria. He again took part in operations in the Transvaal in 1901 and 1902. He was mentioned in dispatches once, was awarded the QM with three clasps, the KM with two clasps and the DSO. He served in France and Belgium during the First World War.

Major Edward Nicholson Broadbent

Broadbent was commissioned into the KOSB on 28 September 1895, promoted Lieutenant 26 October 1897 and Captain 18 May 1901. He was promoted Major on 1 September 1914 and Brevet Lieutenant-Colonel on 3 January 1915. Broadbent served as a temporary Lieutenant-Colonel from 1 December 1915 until 1 May 1919 in the role of Assistant Quartermaster General with the British Army in Egypt and the Egyptian Expeditionary Force, and as a temporary Brigadier-General in the role of Commander, Kantara Area, Egyptian Expeditionary Force from 6 May to 18 July 1919.

Broadbent served on the North-West Frontier of India from 1897 to 1898 with both the Tochi Field Force and the Tirah Expeditionary Force. He was awarded the (?) Medal with clasp. From 1900 to 1902 he fought in the Boer War. In 1900 he served in the Orange Free State, seeing action at Paardeberg, at Poplar Grove and Karee Siding. He took part in operations in the Transvaal from 1900 to 1902. He was awarded the QM with three clasps and the KM with two clasps. From 19 October 1905 to 18 May

1911 he was employed with the Egyptian Army and served as Commandant of the Camel Corps School from 19 May 1911 to 26 September 1914.

During the First World War he served in the Middle East, was mentioned in dispatches four times, was awarded the CBE, the CMG, and the DSO and was also awarded the Legion of Honour 4th Class, the Order of the Sacred Treasure 3rd Class and the Order of the White Eagle 4th Class.

Major John Charles Walter Connell

Connell was commissioned from the Militia into the KOSB on 15 May 1897, was promoted Lieutenant on 1 January 1898 and Captain 9 October 1901. Connell was an Adjutant for the Volunteers from 28 October 1903 to 28 January 1905, for the Territorial Force from 3 July 1907 to 31 March 1908 and for the Officer Training Corps from 1 April 1908 to 31 March 1911 and again from 8 July 1913 to 4 September 1914. He served as a temporary Major with the KOSB from 11 September to 10 December 1914, appointed Major on 11 December 1914. From 11–27 October 1915 he was a temporary Lieutenant-Colonel with the 7th Battalion, KOSB and again a temporary Lieutenant-Colonel from 7 November 1918 until 25 September 1919 with the Young Soldiers Battalion, the Durham Light Infantry and the 1/5th Battalion, KOSB.

Connell served on the North-West Frontier of India in 1897 and 1898, taking part in the Tirah Expeditionary Force, being awarded the (?) Medal with clasp. During 1902 he served in South Africa on operations in the Transvaal, and was awarded the QM with clasp. During the First World War he served in France and Belgium, was mentioned in dispatches twice and was awarded the 1914 Star and DSO.

Major Charles Fraser Kennedy

Kennedy was commissioned from the Militia into the KOSB on 11 January 1899, promoted Lieutenant on 24 June 1900 and Captain on 3 July 1907. He served as an Adjutant from 25 July 1905 to 24 July 1908. He served as an ADC to a Divisional Commander in India from 15 October 1911 to 14 July 1913, and as ADC to GOC Ireland from 24 March to 12 July 1915. He was appointed Major on 1 September 1915. From 3 September to 16 November 1915 he served as a Brigade Major with the 65th Division in Britain. In late 1916, Kennedy worked as an intelligence officer in Gibraltar.

Kennedy fought in the Boer War with the mounted infantry. In 1900 he took part in operations in the Orange Free State, the Transvaal, the Orange River Colony and the Cape Colony, seeing action at Paardeberg, Poplar Grove, Houtnek (Thoba Mountain), Zand River, Johannesburg, Pretoria, Diamond Hill, Wittebergen and Bothaville. From 1901 to 1902 he served in the Transvaal and the Orange River Colony. He was mentioned in dispatches once and was awarded the QM with four clasps and the KM with two clasps. During the First World War he fought in France and Belgium, was wounded and awarded the 1914 Star.

Captain Cecil Tidswell Furber

Furder was commissioned into the KOSB from the Militia on 20 May 1905, promoted Lieutenant 3 July 1907 and made Captain on 19 February 1914. He served as an Adjutant in the Regiment from 25 July 1911 to 14 May 1914. He served as an Adjutant with the Indian Volunteers from 15 May 1914 to 2 June 1915 and as a Brigade Major with the Indian Army from 5 June 1915 to 12 December 1916. He was an acting Major with the KOSB from 17 February to 7 August 1917. From 8 August 1917 to 10 August 1920 he served as a temporary Lieutenant-Colonel with KOSB, with the 12th Battalion, Highland Light Infantry, the 21st Battalion, the Hampshire Regiment and the 29th Battalion the King's Liverpool Regiment. He was made Brevet Major on 3 June 1919.

Furder served in the Boer War with the Militia, employed with the mounted infantry, and from 1901 to 1902 he took part in operations in the Cape Colony, the Orange River Colony and the Transvaal. He was awarded the QM with three clasps. During the First World War he served in Belgium and France, was mentioned in dispatches three times and awarded the DSO with clasp.

Notes

1　Charles Townshend, *Easter 1916: The Irish Rebellion* (London, 2006), p.352
2　*Sean Moylan in His Own Words* (Cork, 2004), p.195
3　Mike Cronin and John M. Regan, (eds.) 'Introduction' in *Ireland: The Politics of Independence 1922–1949* (London, 2002), p.7
4　Sean Moylan, *Sean Moylan in His Own Words*, p.ii
5　Ibid, p.vi
6　Senia Paseta, 'Ireland's Lost Home Rule Generation: The Decline of Constitutional Nationalism in Ireland 1916–1930', in Mike Cronin and John Regan (eds.) *Ireland: The Politics of Independence 1922–49.* (London, 2000), pp 13–14
7　*Easter 1916: The Irish Rebellion*, pp 13–14
8　Tim Sheehan, *Execute Hostage Compton-Smith* (Cork, 1993), p.62
9　Ibid
10　Ibid, p.70
11　Liam Deasy, *Towards Ireland Free* (Cork, 1973), pp 314–315
12　Brian Murphy, *The Origin and Organisation of British Propaganda in Ireland 1920* (Cork, 2006), p.76
13　Ibid, p.79
14　See Hart's work on Cork, namely of course, his monograph, *The IRA and Its Enemies: Violence and Community in Cork, 1916–1923* (Oxford, 1998)
15　J.J. Lee, *The Modernisation of Irish Society 1848–1918* (Dublin, 1973), p.4
16　Tom Garvin, *Nationalist Revolutionaries in Ireland 1858–1928* (Oxford, 1987), p.1
17　*Easter 1916: The Irish Rebellion*, p.353
18　Ibid, p.354
19　Joost Augusteijn, *The Irish Revolution 1913–1923*, Marie Coleman, *County Longford and the Irish Revolution* (Dublin, 2002); Peter Hart, *The IRA and its Enemies* (Oxford, 1998); Michael Farry, *The Aftermath of Revolution: Sligo 1921–1923* (Dublin, 2000)
20　Charles Townshend, 'Historiography: Telling the Irish Revolution', *The Irish Revolution 1913–1923* (London, 2002), p.8
21　*County Longford and the Irish Revolution*, p.130; *The IRA and its Enemies*, pp 88–89
22　Tom Bowden, 'The Irish Underground and the War of Independence', *Journal of Contemporary History*, Vol. 8, No. 2, April (1973), p.21
23　Ibid
24　Ibid
25　William H. Kautt, *The Anglo-Irish War, 1916–1921* (Connecticut, 1999), p.107
26　Ibid, p.113
27　Paul McMahon, *British Spies and Irish Rebels: British Intelligence and Ireland*

1916–1945 (London, 2008), pp 165–166

28 Ibid, p.42
29 Michael Hopkinson, *The Irish War of Independence* (Dublin, 2002), p.114
30 Diarmaid Ferriter, *The Transformation of Ireland* (London, 2005), p.236
31 Richard English, *Irish Freedom: The History of Nationalism in Ireland* (London, 2006), p.288; David Fitzpatrick, *Politics and Irish Life* (Dublin, 1977), p.187
32 Charles Townshend, *The British Campaign in Ireland, 1919–1921, The Development of Political and Military Policies* (Oxford, 1975), p.52. He also makes this point again in p.88
33 *The British Campaign in Ireland 1919–1921*, p.145
34 Ibid, p.202
35 LHCMA, Brigadier Frederick Clarke Papers, GB 99 KCLMA Clarke
36 IWM, Captain R.D. Jeune Papers, 72/172/1
37 Ibid
38 IWM, Brigadier F.H. Vinden Papers, 96/36/1
39 NAUK, WO 141/94, *Record of the Rebellion*, Vol. I., p.54
40 IWM, Sir Peter Strickland Papers, P363, 6th Division History, pp 128–129
41 *Dáil Debates*, Vol. 3, 22 December, 1921, Debate on the Treaty. (http://historical-debates.oireachtas.ie/en.toc.dail.html)
42 Ibid
43 Ibid
44 Gary Sheffield, *Forgotten Victory: The First World War, Myths, and Realities* (London, 2002) p.xix
45 Ibid, p.3
46 *The Great War*, broadcast in 1964 and 1965 on BBC TV
47 David Stevenson, *1914–1918, The History of the First World War* (London, 2004), p.593
48 IWM, C. Cordner Papers, 86/86/1
49 *Wellington Journal and Shrewsbury News*, 20 September 1919
50 W.J.P. Aggett, *The Bloody Eleventh: History of the Devonshire Regiment, Volume III 1915–1969* (Exeter, 1995), p.201
51 IWM, Lieutenant-Colonel Hughes-Hallett Papers, 86/13/1 (Memoir)
52 *Wellington Journal and Shrewsbury News* 20 September 1920
53 Ibid, 16 September 1919
54 There are conflicting newspaper accounts in *II* 29 July 1920, and *CE* 29 July 1920. The *II* declared that there would be no inquest and the *CE* stated that a decision had been made by the coroner to hold one
55 *II* 30 August 1920
56 *CE* 29 June 1920
57 Ibid
58 Ibid
59 IWM, Lieutenant-Colonel Hughes-Hallett Papers, 86/13/1
60 *CE* 11 November 1919
61 *CC* 11 November 1919
62 *CWN* 15 November 1919
63 Jon Lawrence, 'Forging a Peaceable Kingdom: War, Violence and Fear of Brutalisation in Post First World War Britain' *The Journal of Modern History*, Vol. 75, No.3, September 2003, pp 557–589
64 *TS* 23 July 1919
65 Ibid
66 Clive Emsley, *The Great British Bobby: A History of British Policing from the 18th Century to the Present* (London, 2009), p.191

67 *TS* 22 July 1919
68 Ibid
69 Ibid
70 Keith Jeffery, *The British Army and the Crisis of Empire, 1918–22* (Manchester, 1984), p.15
71 Charles Carrington, *Soldier from the War Returning* (Yorkshire, 2006), p.244
72 Ibid, p.254
73 NAUK, WO 141/94, *Record of the Rebellion*, Vol. 1, p.15
74 Ibid
75 *CE* 19 July 1920; *II* 19 July 1920
76 *II*, 20 July 1920
77 *TS*, 19 July 1920
78 BIM, CO 904/112, RIC County Inspector's Report, East Riding and City, July 1920
79 A captain of the Irish Guards, a company sergeant major of the Royal Engineers, two sergeants of the Royal Field Artillery, two sergeants of the Lenister Regiment, two sergeants and seven corporals of the Royal Munster Fusiliers
80 *CWN*, 24 July 1920
81 David Fitzpatrick, Militarism in Ireland, 1900–22', Thomas Bartlett and Keith Jeffery (eds.), *A Military History of Ireland* (Oxford, 1996.), p.397
82 *II*, 20 July 1920; *CE*, 20 July 1920
83 *II*, 20 July 1920
84 CCA, Terence MacSwiney Papers, PR4/4/67, MacSwiney to the head of ex-servicemen in Cork, dated 17or 19 July 1920
85 BIM, CO 904/112, RIC Inspector General's Report, July 1920
86 *CC*, 21 July 1920
87 Ibid
88 *CE*, 23 June 1917
89 *CE*, 28 September 1917
90 BIM, CO 904/103, RIC County Inspector's Report, East Riding and City, July 1917
91 Resolution of the Annual Synod of the Diocese of Cork, in *CE*, 10 July 1917
92 *CE*, 4 September 1917
93 *CE*, 19 March 1918
94 BIM, CO 904/157, Intelligence Officer's Report, September 1917; CO 904/105, RIC County Inspector's Report, East Riding and City, March, 1918; CO 904/103, RIC County Inspector's Report, East Riding and City, July 1917
95 IMA, BMH, Leo Buckley, WS 1714
96 Ibid
97 IWM, Major-General H.H. Tudor Papers, Misc 175 -2655, Joy Cave, *A Gallant Gunner General*, unpublished biography of H.H. Tudor
98 General Neville Macready, *Annals of An Active Life* (1925), p.441
99 Parliamentary Debates, Commons, HC, 126, 1920, p.314
100 BIM, CO 904/157, Intelligence Officer's Report, March 1918
101 LHCMA, Major-General Charles Howard Foulkes Papers, GB 99, KCLMA, Foulkes 7/34, Sinn Féin War on Women
102 Ibid
103 *CE* 9 May 1921
104 *CWN* 1 January 1921
105 *CE* 9 September 1919
106 IWM, Lieutenant-Colonel Hughes-Hallett Papers, 86/13/1 (Memoir)
107 BMH, IMA, WS 1003, Patrick Ahern

108 *CE* 9 September 1919
109 NLI, Flower Papers, Ms 13,017, 9 September 1919
110 *ATO*, 15 December 1919
111 *II* 29 June 1920
112 *CE* 29 June 1920
113 NAUK, WO 141/43, This is confirmed by a note dated 3 July 1920 from Lieutenant T.H. Keble to Lieutenant-Colonel McDouall of the Buffs
114 NAUK, WO 141/43, Lieutenant-Colonel MacKensie, commanding the 2nd Brigade, RFA to Brigadier-General Willis, Royal Artillery
115 Ibid
116 NAUK, WO 141/43, Bartlett Witness Statement
117 NAUK, WO 141/43, Stewart Witness Statement
118 *II* 29 July 1920
119 *CE* 29 July 1920
120 Ibid. Father McSwiney had that very morning formed part of the funeral procession for Sgt. Mulhern, RIC
121 *CE* 28 August 1920
122 *II* 30 August 1920
123 IMA, BMH, WS 1424, Michael Burke
124 NLI, Florence O'Donoghue Papers, Walter Callan RM, Cobh to a John McMahon, quoted in a letter dated 24 September 1920, from the Adjutant-General, IRA to Florence O'Donoghue
125 Ibid
126 Ibid
127 *CE* 29 September 1920
128 *TS* 29 September 1920
129 *II* 30 September 1920
130 *CE* 30 September 1920
131 *II* 11 November 1919
132 *CE* 10 November 1919
133 *CE* 10 November 1919; *II* 11 November 1919
134 *II* 11 November 1919
135 *II* 11 November 1919
136 *CWN* 15 November 1919
137 *CC* 11 November 1919
138 Ibid
139 *CWN* 15 November 1919
140 Ibid
141 *CC* 11 November 1919
142 *CE* 12 November 1919
143 *CE* 20 July 1920
144 *II* 20 July 1920
145 For example, Timothy Cooney, shot in the thigh, Mary Donovan, shot in the thigh, Denis McCarthy, shot in the groin, Denis Callanan, shot in the hand, Mr Malone, shot in both legs, Eily Ahern, shot in the leg, John Collins, shot in the leg, John McCarthy, shot in the leg. *II* 20 July 1920
146 Ibid
147 *Irish War of Independence*, p.81
148 J. Bowyer-Bell, *The Secret Army: The IRA 1916–1979* (Dublin, 1979), p.21
149 John Borgonovo, *Informers, intelligence and the Anti-Sinn Féin Society: the Anglo-Irish Conflict in Cork City, 1920–1921*, MA thesis, UCC (1997), p.16
150 NAUK, WO 141/46, Macready to Wilson, 23 October 1920

151 NAM, Lieutenant-Colonel Fitzgerald Papers, 7912–76 (Memoir)

152 IWM, Lieutenant-Colonel Hughes-Hallett Papers, 86/13/1 (Memoir)

153 *CC* 12 September 1919

154 The East Kent Regiment

155 NAUK, WO 141/43, Dennis Witness Statement

156 NAUK, WO 141/43, Captain Dallas-Edge to Lieutenant-Colonel MacKenzie, Commander of the 2nd Brigade RFA, 28 June 1920

157 NAUK, WO 141/43, Strickland to Macready, 8 July 1920

158 Ibid

159 The file name is WO 141/43

160 RSM means the Regimental Sergeant Major. This is the most senior non-commissioned officer in a regiment

161 William Sheehan, *British Voices from the Irish War of Independence* (Cork, 2005), p.172

162 Ibid

163 Ibid

164 *CE* 28 August 1920

165 *II* 30 August 1920

166 NAUK, WO 32/9537, Wilson to Secretary of State for War, 18 September 1920

167 NAUK, WO 141/46, Macready to Wilson, 23 October 1920

168 Parliamentary Debates, Commons, HC, 134, 1920, 9 November 1920

169 IWM, Sir Peter Strickland Papers, P363, Strickland Diary, 11 November 1919

170 *CC* 11 November 1919

171 *CWN* 15 November 1919

172 *CE* 14 November 1919

173 BIM, CO 904/109, RIC County Inspector's Report, November 1919

174 *CC* 13 November 1919

175 *CWN* 15 November 1919

176 *CE* 14 November 1919

177 NAUK, WO 35/88 Brigadier-General Willis RA to Strickland, 9 November 1919

178 *CE* 10 September 1919

179 Ibid

180 *Ibid; CE* 28 August 1920

181 George Walker was in fact a Liverpudlian, employed by the War Office, and had served twenty-one years in the British Army, he had fought in the Boer War, and in the First World War. He was wounded twice during the First World War, and was crippled as a result of these wounds, and needed a stick to walk. He was shot for not raising his hands promptly enough in response to a command from the patrol

182 NLI, Florence O'Donoghue papers, MS 10,556 (2), Unsigned letter to Lord Bentinck, 30 May 1921

183 IMA, BMH, WS 1424, Michael Burke

184 NLI, Florence O'Donoghue Papers, Ms 10,556(2), Malcolm Moloney affidavit

185 Ibid

186 NAUK, WO 141/94, *Record of the Rebellion*, Vol. 1, p.22

187 Ibid, p.62

188 *Annals of an Active Life*, Vol. II, p.495

189 NAUK, WO 141/94, *Record of the Rebellion*, Vol. 1, p.22

190 *Annals of an Active Life*, Vol. II, p.500

191 Ibid, p.509

192 *CE* 23 May 1921

193 NLI, Florence O'Donoghue Papers, MS 31,201, Operations Memorandum issued by Chief of Staff, 2nd Cork Brigade, 30 October 1920

194 *CE* 20 July 1920
195 W.J.P. Aggett, *The Bloody Eleventh*, p.201
196 BMH, IMA, Joseph Ahern, WS 1,367
197 'Some Reflections', *The Army Quarterly and Defence Journal*, p.54
198 T.R. Moreman, 'Small Wars and Imperial Policing: The British Army and the Theory and Practice of Colonial Warfare in the British Empire, 1919–1939, *The Journal of Strategic Studies*, 1997, part. 4, p.107
199 NAUK, WO 32/9572, Macready to Wilson, 23 May 1921
200 IWM, Sir Hugh Jeudwine Papers, 72/82/8, Jeudwine to Macready, 9 December 1920
201 NAUK, WO 32/9572, Macready to Wilson, 23 May 1921
202 NAUK, WO 141/46, Wilson to Churchill, 23 October 1920
203 Ibid
204 Nigel Hamilton, *The Full Monty – Montgomery of Al Alamein, 1887 -1942* (London, 2001), p.135
205 Ibid, p.135
206 IWM, H.L. Adams Papers, 83/50/1
207 LHCMA, Brig-General Philip Cadoux-Hudson Papers, GB 99 KCLMA, Cadoux-Hudson, Cadoux-Hudson to his Mother, 24 April 1921
208 LHCMA, Brig-General Philip Cadoux-Hudson Papers, GB 99 KCLMA, Cadoux-Hudson, Cadoux-Hudson to his Mother, 24 November 1920
209 *Annals of an Active Life*, Vol. II, p.53
210 Ibid, p.544
211 *Imperial Policing*, p.100
212 IWM, Sir Peter Strickland Papers, P363, 6th Division History, p.81
213 'Some Reflections', *The Army Quarterly and Defence Journal*, pp 53–54
214 *LG* September 1921, p.3
215 IWM, Sir Peter Strickland Papers, P363, Mock Version of An T Oglac [sic], The Offical Organ of the I RAN AWAY
216 Ibid
217 IWM, Lieutenant-General A.E. Percival Papers
218 *HRJ* 29 February 1921, p.22
219 *ATO* 30 November 1918
220 BMH, IMA, Thomas Barry, WS 430
221 BMH, IMA, Denis Collins, WS 827
222 Ibid
223 Ibid
224 This refers to the American Civil War
225 NAUK, WO 141/94, *Record of the Rebellion*, Vol.1, p.57
226 *The Dragon*, January, 1921, p.4
227 *British Voices*, p.173
228 NLI, Florence O'Donoghue Papers, MS 31,223, Captured Letter from Montgomery
229 IMA, BMH, WS 1254, Michael Coleman
230 Ibid
231 UCDA, O'Malley Notebooks, Mick Murphy, P176/11
232 IMA, BMH, WS 1707, Patrick Collins
233 Ibid
234 UCDA, O'Malley Notebooks, P176/11, Mick Murphy
235 David Fitzpatrick, *Politics and Irish Life*, p.31
236 IMA, BMH, WS 827, Denis Collins
237 *County Longford and the Irish Revolution*, p.120

238 Borgonovo, MA thesis, UCC, p.111
239 David Fitzpatrick, 'Militarism in Ireland, 1900–1922, in *A Military History of Ireland*, p.401
240 NAUK, WO 141/94, *Record of the Rebellion*, Vol.1, p.53
241 IWM, Sir Peter Strickland Papers, P363, *Land of the Free*
242 IWM, Sir Peter Strickland Papers, P363, Strickland Diary, 17 May 1922
243 Ibid
244 *British Voices*, p.192
245 LHCMA, Lieutenant Evelyn Lindsay-Young Papers, GB99 KCLMA Lindsay-Young.
246 LHCMA, Brig-General Frederick Clarke Papers, GB99 KCLMA Clarke
247 *ERG* January 1923, p.23
248 *LG* March 1922, p.68
249 Ibid
250 Ibid
251 LHCMA, Clarke Papers, GB99 KCLMA Clarke
252 Ibid
253 IWM, Lieutenant-General A.E. Percival Papers
254 Ibid
255 NLI, Florence O'Donoghue Papers, Ms 10,556 (2)
256 IWM, Sir Peter Strickland Papers, P363, Strickland Diary, 30 December 1919
257 *The IRA and Its Enemies*, p.82
258 NLI, G.K. Cockerill Papers, MS 10,606, 'Appreciation of the Situation in Ireland', May 1921
259 NAUK, WO 141/94, *Record of the Rebellion*, Vol. II, p.37
260 *HRJ* January, 1921, p.6
261 LHCMA, Brig-General Philip Cadoux-Hudson Papers, GB99 KCLMA Cadoux-Hudson, Cadoux-Hudson to his Mother, 7 August 1921
262 Ibid, Cadoux-Hudson to his Mother, 1 November, 1921
263 NAUK, CO 904/168 Dublin Castle Press Statement
264 NLI, Florence O'Donoghue Papers, Ms 31,223 (4)
265 IWM, Strickland Papers, P363, *Sinn Fein and the Irish Volunteers*, p.2
266 *The Bloody Eleventh*, p.202
267 SOGM, RM Grazebrook Diary, 31 March 1921
268 IWM, C. Cordner Papers, MS. 86/86/1
269 NLI, G.K. Cockerill Papers, MS 10, 606 (1)
270 H. C. Wylly, *History of the Manchester Regiment*, Vol. II, 1883–1925 (London, 1925), p.211
271 NAUK, CO 904/168, Dublin Castle Press Statement
272 *CE* 2 October 1920
273 Ibid
274 *HRJ* March, 1921, p.39
275 *HRJ* April, 1921, p.60
276 IWM, Sir John French Papers, JDPF 8, French to Bonar-Law, 13 September 1919
277 *HRJ* April 1920, pp 65–66
278 *Annals of Active Life*, p.39
279 IWM, Sir John French Papers, JDPF 8, Macready to Wilson, 19 February 1921
280 *LG* December 1920, p.27
281 *HRJ* April 1920, p.65
282 *HRJ* December 1920, p.233
283 *The 79th News* April 1921, p.142
284 *HRJ* April 1920, p.65

285 Ibid

286 Ibid

287 *MRG* January 1921, p.24

288 *MRG* April 1921, p.68

289 *HRJ* August, 1920, p.152

290 Ibid

291 *The 79th News* January 1921, p.22

292 Ibid

293 *LG* September, 1921, p.3

294 J.G. Fuller, *Troop Morale and Popular Culture in the British and Dominion Armies, 1914–1918* (Oxford, 1990), p.147

295 Ibid

296 Alan Wykes, *The Royal Hampshire Regiment* (London, 1968)

297 John Downham, *The East Lancashire Regiment* (London, 2000)

298 Gregory Blaxland, *The Queen's Own Buffs, The Royal Kent Regiment* (Kent, 1974)

299 Michael Barthop, *The Northamptonshire Regiment* (London, 1974)

300 Michael Langely, *The Loyal Regiment* (London, 1974) p.79

301 Michael Glover, *That Astonishing Infantry, Three Hundred Years of the History of the Royal Welch Fusiliers (23rd Regiment of Foot) 1689–1989* (London, 1989) p.180

302 Ibid

303 Ibid

304 *History of the Manchester Regiment*, p.205–206

305 Geoffrey Powell, *The History of the Green Howards: Three Hundred Years of Service* (London, 1992), p.171

306 J.M. Cowper, *The King's Own: The Story of a Royal Regiment, Vol. III. 1914 to 1950* (Aldershot, 1957), p.253

307 Ibid

308 David Scott Daniell, *Regimental History of the Royal Hampshire Regiment,* Vol. 3 (Aldershot, 1985)

309 *History of the ManchesterRegiment*, p.207

310 C.T. Atkinson, *The South Wales Borderers, 24th Foot, 1689–1937* (Cambridge, 1937), p.453

311 *Green Howards*, p.171

312 Ibid

313 Ibid

314 NLI, G.K. Cockerill Papers

315 Daniell, *Hampshire Regiment*, p.9

316 David Fitzpatrick, *Politics and Irish Life 1913 to 1921: Provincial Experience of War and Revolution* (Dublin, 1977), p.27

317 *The IRA and its Enemies*, p.93

318 NAUK, WO 141/94, *Record of the Rebellion,* Vol. IV, Part II, p.139

319 Ibid

320 Ibid

321 Ibid

322 David A. Percox, 'British Counter-Insurgency in Kenya 1952–56: Extension of Internal Security or Prelude to Decolonisation, *Small War and Insurgencies,* Vol. 9, No. 3 (Winter 1998), p.53

323 NAUK, WO 141/94, *Record of the Rebellion,* Vol. IV, Part II, p.139

324 NAUK, WO 141/94, *Record of the Rebellion,* Vol. IV, Part II, p.140

325 Ibid

326 NAUK, WO 141/94, *Record of the Rebellion,* Vol. IV, Part II, p.144

327 Paul McMahon, *British Spies and Irish Rebels: British Intelligence and Ireland,*

1916–1945 (Suffolk, 2008), p48 Peter Hart, *British Intelligence in Ireland, 1920–1921* (Cork, 2002)

328 SOGM, RM Grazebrook Diary, 7 April 1921

329 IWM, Sir Peter Strickland Papers, P363, 6th Division History, p.21

330 NAUK, WO 141/94, *Record of the Rebellion*, Vol. IV, Part II, p.144

331 NAUK, WO 141/94, *Record of the Rebellion*, Vol. II, p.7

332 NLI, Florence O'Donoghue Papers, MS 31, 205, Tom Barry, OC Flying Column to the OC 3rd Cork Brigade, 7 February 1921

333 UCDA, O'Malley Notebooks, P176/111, Jack Buttimer

334 NLI, Florence O'Donoghue Papers, MS 31,208, Publicity Memorandum No. 1, IRA GHQ

335 Ibid

336 *TS* 10 September 1919

337 IMA, BMH, WS 1003, Patrick Ahern

338 IMA, BMH, WS 978, Leo O'Callaghan

339 IMA, BMH, WS 1538, John Barrett

340 BIM, CO 904/108, RIC County Inspector's Report, East Riding and City, April 1919

341 BIM, CO 904/109, RIC County Inspector's Report, East Riding and City, June 1919

342 NAUK, WO 141/94, *Record of the Rebellion*, Vol. II, p.7

343 *British Intelligence in Ireland 1920–1921*, pp 9–10

344 IWM, Sir John French Papers, JDPF 8, Sir John French to Winston Churchill, 10 April 1919

345 IWM, Sir Peter Strickland Papers, P363, Strickland to Macready, 13 May 1920

346 NAUK, WO 141/94, *Record of the Rebellion*, Vol. II, p.4

347 IWM, Sir Peter Strickland Papers, P363, Strickland Diary, 7 April 1920

348 IMA, BMH, WS 879, Charles Browne

349 NAUK, WO 141/94, *Record of the Rebellion*, Vol. IV, Part II, p.165

350 IMA, BMH, WS 1009, William Buckley

351 Tameside Archives, Manchester Regiments Archives, Captain Thomspon Papers, MR 1/16/18, Lieutenant-Colonel Dorling to Secretary of State for War, 24 November, 1920

352 Tameside Archives, Manchester Regiments Archives, Manchester Regiment Digest of Service, 22 November, 1920

353 NAUK, WO 141/94, *Record of the Rebellion*, Vol. IV, Part II, p.165

354 Siobhan Lankford, *The Hope and Sadness* (Cork, 1980), p.183

355 UCDA, O'Malley Notebooks, P176/112, Martin Corry

356 Sir Kenneth Strong, *Intelligence at the Top* (London, 1968), p.1

357 IMA, BMH, WS 1695, Maurice Brew

358 BIM, CO 904/115, RIC County Inspector's Report, East Riding and City, May 1921

359 *CE* 9 May 1921

360 NLI, Florence O'Donoghue Papers, Ms 31,207 (2), Memorandum from HQ 1st Cork Brigade, 24 September, 1921

361 IWM, Captain R.D. Jeune Papers, 76/172/1

362 IMA, BMH, WS 978, Leo O'Callaghan

363 SOGM, RM Grazebrook Diary, 19 April 1921

364 The I.R.A men killed were Lt. Ned Waters, and Volunteers Kiely, Herlihy, and Twomey

365 *British Spies and Irish Rebels*, p.45

366 BIM, CO 904/109, RIC Inspector General's Report, October 1919

367 BIM, CO 904/113, RIC County Inspector's Report, October 1920
368 *Liverpool Daily Post and Mercury* 21 February 1921
369 *ATO* 17 June 1921
370 CCA, Seamus Fitzgerald Papers, PR 6/32, Thomas Cotter to Seamus Fitzgerald, 1938
371 *Intelligence at the Top*, p.1
372 NAUK, WO 141/94, *Record of the Rebellion*, Vol. II, p.25
373 UCDA, Mulcahy Papers, P7/A/38, OC Flying Column to HQ Cork No. 3 Brigade, 6 April 1921
374 NLI, Florence O'Donoghue Papers, MS 31,443, Lecture on Military Intelligence
375 NAUK, WO 141/94, *Record of the Rebellion*, Vol. II, p.20
376 *Imperial Policing*, p.9
377 NLI, Florence O'Donoghue Papers, MS 31,443, Lecture on Military Intelligence
378 Sir Robert Thompson, 'Regular Armies and Insurgency', in *Regular Armies and Insurgency* (ed.) Ronald Haycock (London, 1979), p.14
379 Ibid, p.16
380 NAUK, WO 141/94, *Record of the Rebellion*, Vol. IV, Part II, p.144
381 IWM, Sir Peter Strickland Papers, P363, 6th Division History, p.22
382 *British Intelligence in Ireland, 1920–1921*, p.12
383 IWM, Sir Peter Strickland Papers, P363, 6th Division History, p.22
384 Ibid, p.39
385 NAUK, WO 141/94, *Record of the Rebellion*, Vol. II, pp 9–12
386 Ibid, p.11
387 Ibid, p.13
388 IWM, Sir Peter Strickland Papers, P363, 6th Division History, pp 66–67
389 Ibid, p.26
390 IWM, Lt Col J.B. Jarvis Papers, 98/11/1, Black List No. 2
391 Ibid
392 Ibid
393 Ibid
394 IWM, Sir Peter Strickland Papers, P363, 6th Division History, p.77
395 NAUK, WO 141/94, *Record of the Rebellion*, Vol. II., p.24
396 Ibid, p.30
397 *British Intelligence in Ireland, 1920–1921*, pp 11–12
398 NAUK, WO 141/94, *Record of the Rebellion*, Vol. II., p.24
399 *CC* 13 September 1919
400 The documents being searched for included any material defined as seditious literature, *the Irish Bulletin, An t-Oglach*, any Cumann na mBan literature, any Fianna literature, Ard Feis reports, Ard Chomhairle reports, Comhairle Ceanntar reports, any IRB, IRA, Citizen Army documents, any drill books, relevant correspondence, or propaganda
401 NAUK, WO 141/94, *Record of the Rebellion*, Vol. II., p.24
402 SOGM, RM Grazebrook Diary 11 March 1921
403 LHCMA, Lieutenant-Colonel Evelyn Lindsay-Young Papers, GB 99 KCLMA Lindsay-Young
404 LHCMA, Major-General Charles Howard Foulkes Papers, GB99 KCLMA Foulkes, 7/21, Captain Boddington, Ruse and Interrogations, in a Synopsis of Eleven Lectures, from Intelligence Conference, held in Chester, October, 1921
405 Ibid
406 LHCMA, Lieutenant-Colonel Evelyn Lindsay-Young Papers, GB99 KCLMA Lindsay-Young
407 Ibid. Crofter being a vernacular word in Scotland for small-holder

408 IMA, BMH, WS 827, Denis Collins
409 NAUK, WO 141/94, *Record of the Rebellion*, Vol. II, p.26
410 NLI, Florence O'Donoghue Papers, MS 31,228, Captain Kelly to Lieutenant H.H. Davis, 13 April 1921, Michael Collins to Florence O'Donoghue, 5 April 1921
411 Dan Harvey and Gerry White, *The Barracks: A History of Victoria/Collins Barracks, Cork* (Cork, 1997), p.64 A full list of those captured in the raid in given on the page
412 Borgonvo, MA thesis, p.5
413 BIM, CO 904/114, RIC County Inspectors Report's, February, March, April, 1921, East Riding and City
414 BIM, CO 904/114, RIC County Inspector's Report, February 1921, East Riding and City
415 *The IRA and its Enemies*, p.312
416 NAUK, WO 141/94, *Record of the Rebellion*, Vol. II., p.12
417 Ibid
418 IWM, Sir Peter Strickland Papers, P363, 6th Division History, Appendix VI, p.1
419 Ibid, p.2
420 Ibid
421 Ibid
422 LHCMA, Brig-General Philip Cadoux-Hudson Papers, GB 99 KCLMA Cadoux-Hudson, Cadoux-Hudson to his mother, 5 April, 1921
423 IWM, Sir Peter Strickland Papers, P363, 6th Division History, Appendix VI, p.5
424 Ibid
425 Ibid, pp 5–6
426 NLI, Florence O'Donoghue Papers, MS 21,223, Engineering Circular No. 8, April 1921
427 BIM, CO 904/114, RIC County Inspector's Report, East Riding and City, December 1920
428 NLI, Florence O'Donoghue Papers, Ms 31,443
429 NLI, Florence O'Donoghue Papers, MS 31,207, 1st Cork Brigade Report, 15 November, 1921
430 NLI, Florence O'Donoghue Papers, MS 31,230 (1), Communication Intercept
431 Ibid
432 IMA, BMH, MS 1133, Anne Barrett
433 NAUK, AIR 5/772, Wireless Communication in Ireland, 1 April 1921
434 IWM, Sir Peter Strickland Papers, P363, Strickland Diary, 7 April 1920
435 UCDA, Mulcahy Papers, P7/A/33, Communications Intercept, December 1921
436 NAUK, AIR 5/772, Major Dickenson to Units of 16th infantry Brigade, 14 March 1921
437 IWM, Sir Peter Strickland Papers, P363, 6th Division History, Appendix VI, p.6
438 NAUK, WO 141/94, *Record of the Rebellion*, Vol. I, p.43
439 *CWN* 12 February 1921
440 NAUK, WO 141/94, *Record of the Rebellion*, Vol. VI, Part 2, p.174
441 Ibid
442 *CWN* 12 February 1921
443 All were tried by court-martial in Victoria Barracks, eleven were found guilty and sentenced to terms ranging from ten to fifteen years. However two of the men and a woman were found not guilty
444 *HRJ* March 1921, p.37
445 *CWN* 12 February 1921
446 NAUK, WO 141/94, *Record of the Rebellion*, Vol. VI, Part 2, p.174
447 NAUK, WO 141/94, *Record of the Rebellion*, Vol. IV, Part II, p.170

448 Ibid, p.171
449 Ibid
450 Ibid
451 *II* 11 March 1921; *IT* 21 March 1921 The arms found were 21 Webley revolvers, and 1,600 rounds for these, 11 bombs, 11 German automatic pistols, and 2,000 rifle rounds
452 NAUK, WO 35/88, Operational Report, 18 February 1921, Major Halahan to HQ 17th Infantry Brigade
453 *CWN* 26 March 1921
454 *The British Campaign in Ireland 1919–1921*, p.171
455 Ibid, p.195
456 NAUK, AIR 5/214, Flying Operations Report, 11th (Irish) Wing, May 1921
457 *ATO* 17 June 1921
458 NLI, Florence O'Donoghue Papers, MS 31,223 (3), Colonel Cameron, Commanding Officer, 16th Infantry Brigade, to his various battalion commanders, 17 June 1921
459 The fact that Captain Vining and the other British officers had been provided with information from locals has been supported by several members of the 3rd Battalion, 1st Cork Brigade, IRA, see WS 810 in the BMH, IMA.
460 IWM, Sir Peter Strickland Papers, P363, 6th Division History, p.124
461 Ibid
462 *HRJ* July 1921, p.110
463 NLI, Florence O'Donoghue Papers, MS 31,443, Lecture on Military Intelligence
464 UCDA, Mulcahy Papers, P7/A/46, Weekly Memorandum No. 10, 23 January 1921
465 *The IRA and its Enemies*, p.312
466 Thomas Mockaitis, *British Counter-Insurgency, 1919–60* (London, 1990), p.75
467 *British Spies and Irish Rebels*, p.45
468 NAUK, WO 141/94, *Record of the Rebellion*, Vol. III, p.10
469 *CE* 7 October 1918. The following areas were listed as falling within the SMA, Bandon, Bantry, Ballyvourney, Ballineen, Ballydehob, Clonakilty, Carrigadrohid, Drimoleague, Dunmanway, Enniskeane, Glengarriff, Goleen, Inchigeela, Kilbrittain, Macroom, Millstreet, Rosscarbery, Schull, Skibbereen, and Timpleague
470 *CE* 12 February 1919
471 *CE* 14 February 1919
472 *CC* 11 September 1919
473 NAUK, WO 141/94, *Record of the Rebellion*, Vol. III, Law, p.10
474 Ibid
475 NAUK, WO 141/94, *Record of the Rebellion*, Vol. III, Law, p.11
476 IWM, Sir John French Papers, 75/46/9, JDPF 8/1A, State of Ireland Report, January 1918
477 BIM, CO 904/105, RIC County Inspector's Report, June 1918
478 BIM, CO 904/105, RIC County Inspector's Report, July 1918
479 *The British Campaign in Ireland 1919–1921*, p.12
480 BIM, CO 904/108, RIC County Inspector's Report, West Riding, January 1919
481 Ibid, RIC Inspector General's Report, January 1919
482 IWM, Sir John French Papers, JDPF 8, Undated Memorandum by Col Brind, attached to a letter from Lieutenant-General Shaw to Field Marshall French, 1 May 1919
483 Michael Laffan, *The Resurrection of Ireland, The Sinn Féin Party, 1916 to 1923* (Cambridge, 1999), p.269
484 BIM, CO 904/169, Petition from Bantry Branch of Cork County and City Traders Association

485 Ibid
486 Ibid
487 Ibid
488 Ibid
489 Ibid
490 *CE* 17 August 1920
491 IWM, Sir John French Papers, JDPF 8, French to the Chief Secretary, 18 February, 1920
492 Ibid
493 Keith Surridge, 'Rebellion, Martial Law, and British Civil-Military Relations: The War in Cape Colony, 1899–1902,' *Small Wars and Insurgencies*, Vol. 8, Autumn 1997, pp 35–60
494 *CC* 11 September 1919
495 NAUK, WO 141/94, *Record of the Rebellion*, Vol. III, Law, p.8
496 Ibid, p.10
497 Ibid, p.8
498 LHCMA, Lieutenant-Colonel Evelyn Lindsay-Young Papers, GB99 KCLMA Lindsay-Young
499 *CE* 6 February 1920
500 *CE* 3 July 1920
501 NAUK, WO 141/94, *Record of the Rebellion*, Vol. III, Law, p.1
502 *The British Campaign in Ireland 1919–1921*, p.31
503 NAUK, WO 141/94, *Record of the Rebellion*, Vol. III, Law, p.13
504 *CE* 9 September 1920
505 NAUK, WO 141/94, *Record of Rebellion*, Vol. III, Law, p.13
506 Ibid, p.14
507 Ibid
508 Ibid
509 Ibid, p.3
510 IWM, Major-General Hawes Papers, 87/41/2 Detailed accounts and analysis of the occupation of the Rhineland are contained in Brigadier-General Edmonds, *The Occupation of the Rhineland, 1918–1929* (1987), and in Ernest Fraenkel's *Military Occupation and the Rule of Law: Occupational Government in the Rhineland, 1918–1923* (1944)
511 Ibid
512 Ibid
513 Ibid
514 Ibid
515 Sheila Lawlor, *Britain and Ireland, 1914–1923*, p.69
516 *British Counter-Insurgency 1919–60*, p.65
517 *II* 20 July 1920
518 *II* 22 July 1920
519 *CE* 7 August 1920
520 *IT* 2 August 1920 noted that curfew patrol were the subject of rifle fire and bomb attack. As did the *CE* of the same date although it blamed the military for both the rifle and bomb attacks
521 *CE* 2 August 1920
522 *CE* 13 September 1920
523 *CE* 15 November 1920
524 NAUK, WO 141/94, *Record of the Rebellion*, Vol. III, Law, p.6
525 *CE* 8 November 1920
526 *HRJ* March 1921, p.39

527 Ibid

528 *CE* 13 December 1920

529 *CE* 29 November 1920

530 *CE* 13 December 1920

531 *CE* 1 December 1920

532 NAUK, WO 141/94, *Record of Rebellion,* Vol. III, Law, p.3

533 *CE* 1 January 1921

534 *II* 4 January 1921 Col. Moore had been a Gaelic Leaguer, a military adviser to the early Volunteer movement, but had supported Redmond in 1914

535 *Manchester Guardian* 4 February 1921

536 *TS* 9 February 1921

537 *Manchester Guardian* 11 February 1921

538 Tameside Archive, Manchester Regiments Archives, Manchester Regiment Digest of Service, 27 January 1921

539 *The IRA and Its Enemies,* p.73

540 IWM, Sir Peter Strickland Papers, P363, Strickland Diary, 14 February 1920

541 *The Resurrection of Ireland,* p.296

542 *Irish War of Independence,* p.94

543 IWM, Field Marshal Henry Wilson Papers, Macready to Wilson, 19 February 1920

544 *The British Campaign in Ireland 1919–1921,* p.147

545 IWM, Field Marshal Henry Wilson Papers, Macready to Wilson, 19 February 1920

546 Sir Robert Thompson, 'Regular Armies and Insurgency' in *Regular Armies and Insurgency,* p.14

547 Major B.C Dening, 'Modern Problems of Guerrilla Warfare', *The Army Quarterly and Defence Journal,* 13 January (1927), p.352

548 Tameside Archives, Manchester Regiment Archives, Manchester Regiment Catalogue of Civil Arrests

549 NAUK, WO 141/94, *Record of the Rebellion,* Vol. III, Law, p.4

550 NAUK, WO 141/94, *Record of the Rebellion,* Vol. III, Law, p.4

551 For an example of the application of the principle of collective punishment outside of Ireland, read *Operations in Waziristan, 1919–20,* a history produced by the General Staff Headquarters, India (1923). On p.142, it notes the destruction of an entire village to force the submission of a local tribe. This principle was still in evidence in the 1950s, when the Kikuyu tribe were subjected to a punitive tax to pay for the cost of combating the Mau Mau insurgency. (See David A. Percox, 'British Counter-Insurgency in Kenya', *Small Wars and Insurgencies,* Vol. 9, No. 3 (Winter 1998), p.58

552 *CE* 27 September 1920

553 Ibid

554 *CE* 11 October 1920

555 *CE* 11 October 1920

556 *The British Army and the Crisis of Empire,* p.86

557 Ibid

558 *IT* 4 January 1921

559 Michael Hopkinson, 'Negotiation: The Anglo-Irish War and the Revolution' in *The Irish Revolution, 1913–1923,* Joost Augusteijn (ed.) (London, 2002)

560 *TS* 3 January 1921, recorded the following names and addresses of those punished by official reprisal, John O'Shea, Paul McCarthy, and Edmond Carey of Midleton, Samuel Cotter, and a M Donovan of Ballyadam, and Michael Durgan and a M Aherne of Knockgriffin

561 *TS* 3 January 1921

562 *II* 3 January 1921

563 *TS* 3 January 1921
564 IMA, BMH, WS 1367, Joseph Ahern
565 *TS* 3 January 1921
566 *HRJ* June 1921, p.93
567 Ibid
568 *HRJ* February 1921, p.22
569 *CE* 9 May 1921
570 NLI, Florence O'Donoghue Papers, Ms 10915, Sean O'Donoghue
571 *HRJ* February 1921, p.23
572 *County Longford and the Irish Revolution*, p.130
573 *The IRA and its Enemies*, p.80
574 *British Counter-Insurgency 1919–60*, p.66
575 NLI, Florence O'Donoghue Papers, MS 31,223 (3), Colonel Cameron to his Unit Commanders, 17 June 1921
576 NAUK, WO 141/46, Sir Henry Wilson to Winston Churchill, 23 October 1920
577 *Manchester Guardian* 4 February 1921
578 IWM, Sir Peter Strickland Papers, P363, Lindsay Notes
579 Ibid
580 NAUK, WO 141/48, Sir Felix Cassel to Sir George Macdonogh, 12 January 1921
581 Ibid, General Sir Neville Macready to Winston Churchill, 9 January 1921
582 Ibid, Minute from DPS to Sir George Macdonogh, 16 January 1921
583 Ibid
584 NAUK, WO 141/48, Sir Felix Cassel to General Sir Neville Macready, 15 February 1921
585 Ibid
586 Ibid, Sir Felix Cassel to Sir Laming Worthington Evans, transmitted through the office of Sir George Macdonogh, 21 February 1921
587 Ibid, General Macready to Sir Laming Worthington Evans, 18 February 1921
588 Ibid, Sir Felix Cassel to Sir Laming Worthington Evans, transmitted through the office of Sir George Macdonogh, 21 February 1921
589 *II* 25 February 1921
590 NAUK, WO 141/94, *Record of the Rebellion*, Vol. III, Law, p.4
591 Those executed were, John Allen of Tipperary, and Thomas O'Brien, Daniel O'Callaghan, Patrick O'Mahony, Timothy McCarthy, and John Lyons of Cork, *Freemans Journal*, 1 March 1921
592 *CE* 29 April, 1921. The men involved Maurice Moore and Patrick O'Sullivan of Cobh, and Patrick Ronayne and Thomas Mulcahy of Burnfort.
593 *CE* 3 May 1921
594 *CE* 16 May 1921; *II* 17 May 1921
595 IWM, Sir Peter Strickland Papers, P363, Sir Henry Wilson to British Commanders in Ireland, 1 December 1920
596 IMA, BMH, MS 1003, Patrick Ahern
597 IMA, BMH, MS 810, Dick Cotter
598 Richard English, *Irish Freedom: The History of Nationalism in Ireland* (London, 2006). p.287 *County Longford and the Irish Revolution*, p.153
599 *The Resurrection of Ireland*, p.277
600 NAUK, WO 141/94, *Record of the Rebellion*, Vol. III, Law, p.12
601 LHCMA, Major-General Charles Howard Foulkes Papers, GB 99 KCLMA Foulkes, 7/2, Production of the Weekly Intelligence Summary
602 Ibid
603 NAUK, WO 141/94, *Record of the Rebellion*, Vol. II, p.14
604 Ibid

605 LHCMA, Major-General Charles Howard Foulkes Papers, GB99 KCLMA
     Foulkes, 7/1, Secrets of Crewe House
606 Ibid, Note on Publicity Duties
607 Ibid
608 LHCMA, Major-General Charles Howard Foulkes Papers, GB 99 KCLMA
     Foulkes, 7/1, Report, 16 June 1921
609 LHCMA, Major-General Charles Howard Foulkes Papers, GB 99 KCLMA
     Foulkes, 7/4, Some Special Points as regards Propaganda in Ireland
610 Ibid
611 Ibid
612 Ibid
613 Senia Paseta, "'Ireland" Last Home Rule Generations: The Decline of
     Constitutional Nationalism in Ireland, 1916–30', in *Ireland: The Politics of
     Independence, 1922–49*, Mike Cronin and John Regan (eds.) (London, 2002)
614 Ibid
615 LHCMA, Major-General Charles Howard Foulkes Papers, GB99 KCLMA
     Foulkes, 7/11, Foulkes to GHQ, 16 May 1921
616 Ibid. The Kenyan Colonial Government had a similar view of the social origins
     of the Mau Mau, and called them in a report from the Internal Security Working
     Committee, "'[C]orner boys … [who] have little to lose by the disruption to
     society.' See David A. Percox, 'British Counter-Insurgency in Kenya,' *Small Wars
     and Insurgencies*, Vol. 9, No. 3 (Winter 1998), p.57
617 LHCMA, Major-General Charles Howard Foulkes Papers, GB99 KCLMA
     Foulkes, 7/1, Foulkes to Col. Walker, 29 April 1921
618 Ibid, Unaddressed Letter, 1 July 1921
619 Ibid, Note on Propaganda, Undated
620 LHCMA, Major-General Charles Howard Foulkes Papers, GB99 KCLMA
     Foulkes, 7/25, *To the Irish Republican Army*
621 Ibid, *U.S. and Ireland*
622 Ibid, *Irishmen*
623 Ibid, *The Farmer's Peril*
624 BIM, CO 904/115, RIC County Inspector's Report, May 1921
625 J.J. Lee, *The Modernisation of Irish Society, 1848–1918* (Dublin, 1973), p.11 Senia
     Paseta, 'Ireland's Last Home Rule Generation', in *Ireland: The Politic of Independence*,
     p.21
626 UCDA, Mulcahy Papers, P7/A/37, 5 Battalion to OC Cork No. 1 Brigade, 29
     October 1921
627 LHCMA, Major-General Charles Howard Foulkes Papers, GB99 KCLMA
     Foulkes, 7/25, *To the Irish Republican Army*
628 NAUK, AIR 5/776, *To Members of the IRA*
629 LHCMA, Major-General Charles Howard Foulkes Papers, GB99 KCLMA
     Foulkes, 7/25, *The An T'Olgac* [sic] *Lie System*
630 NAUK, WO 32/9536, Proclamation No. 1
631 *LG* September 1921, p.13
632 *HRJ* April 1921, p.60
633 *British Spies and Irish Rebels*, p.47
634 *British Counter-Insurgency 1919–60*, p.69
635 NAUK, WO 141/94, *Record of the Rebellion*, Vol. III, Law, p.11
636 *British Counter-Insurgency 1919–60*, p.65
637 BIM, CO 904/107, RIC Inspector General's Report, October 1918
638 *CWN* 18 January 1919
639 BIM, CO 904/108, RIC County Inspector's Report, West Riding, Cork, April 1919

640 NAUK, WO 141/94, *Record of the Rebellion,* Vol. IV, Part II, p.143
641 *The British Campaign in Ireland 1919–1921*, p.44
642 *IT* 10 September 1919
643 See Chapter One for full discussion
644 Private Newman had joined the Army at 18, and had served in the British Army of the Rhine, he had lost a brother in combat in the First World War. *CC* 5 March 1920
645 This regiment is also known as the Sherwood Foresters
646 *CC* 5 March 1920
647 *CC* 1 March 1920
648 *CC* 5 March 1920
649 *CC* 3 March 1920
650 Ibid
651 Ibid
652 *British Voices*, p.173–174
653 *CE* 7 June 1920
654 *IT* 7 June 1920
655 IMA, BMH, WS 1367, Joseph Ahern
656 IWM, Sir Peter Strickland Papers, P363, Strickland Diary, 6 June 1920
657 *IT & II* 29 September 1920
658 *II* 26 August 1920
659 *IT* 28 August 1920
660 *British Voices*, p.174
661 NAUK, WO 141/94, *Record of the Rebellion,* Vol. IV, Part II, p.154
662 Ibid
663 *CE* 11 October 1920
664 Ibid
665 NAUK, WO 141/94, *Record of the Rebellion,* Vol. IV, Part II, p.164
666 Ibid
667 *CE* 23 October, 1920 Lieutenant Alfred Dickenson, a Catholic officer, was killed, as was a Private Reid, and a Sergeant Bennett of the RASC, Corporal Woodford, Corporal Decker, and Privates Dowse and Walding were wounded
668 *II* 23 October 1920
669 *CE* 23 October 1920
670 *II* 23 October 1920
671 NAUK, WO 141/94, *Record of the Rebellion,* Vol. IV, Part II, p.172
672 *IT* 31 January 1921
673 NAUK, WO 141/94, *Record of the Rebellion,* Vol. IV, Part II, p.173
674 IWM, Sir Peter Strickland Papers, P363, 6th Division History, p.74
675 IWM, Sir Peter Strickland Papers, P363, 6th Division History, pp 80–81
676 NAUK, WO 141/94, *Record of the Rebellion,* Vol. IV, Part II, p.176
677 IWM, Sir Peter Strickland Papers, P363, *The Irish Republican Army*
678 UCDA, Mulcahy Papers, P7/A/38, HQ Cork No. 2 Brigade to Chief of Staff IRA, 4 March 1921
679 *The Hope and the Sadness*, p.191
680 *Gloucestershire Chronicle* 19 February 1920
681 IWM, Sir Peter Strickland Papers, P363, *The Irish Republican Army*
682 *Liverpool Daily Post and Mercury* 16 February 1921
683 NAUK, WO 141/94, *Record of the Rebellion,* Vol. IV, Part II, p.160 and p.167
684 Ibid, p.161
685 Ibid, p.159 Lt. Hotblack, the officer in charge of this unit was later killed in action at Crossbarry

686 Ibid, p.164

687 Ibid, p.179

688 Ibid

689 The details were provided by Anne Barrett, a supervising telephonist in Mallow, who listened in on an Army conversation about the Colonel's movements

690 NAUK, WO 141/94, *Record of the Rebellion*, Vol. IV, Part II, p.180

691 *II* 7 March 1921

692 UCDA, Mulcahy Papers, P7/A/38, Report on the Rathcoole Ambush, 17 June 1921

693 *LG* September 1921, p.5 The Latin phrase means 'a soldier amongst soldiers'

694 NAUK, WO 141/94, *Record of Rebellion*, Vol. IV, Part II, p.189

695 IWM, Sir Peter Strickland Papers, P363, 6th Division History, p.84

696 IMA, BMH, WS 1523, Daniel Cashman, Ws 1523

697 NAUK, WO 35/88, Operational Report by Brigadier-General H.W. Higginson, to HQ 6th Division, 22 February, 1921

698 Ibid, Operational Report by Lt. Colonel French of the Hampshire Regiment to Brigadier-General H.W. Higginson, 21 February 1921

699 *ATO* 8 April 1921

700 NAUK, WO 35/88, Operational Report by Lieutenant Koe of the Hampshire Regiment to Lt. Colonel French, 20 February, 1920

701 *HRJ* March 1921, p.37

702 Daniell, *Hampshire Regiment*, p.11

703 NAUK, WO 35/88 Operational Report by Lieutenant Koe of the Hampshire Regiment to Lt. Colonel French, 20 February, 1920

704 Ibid, Operational Report by Lieutenant-Colonel French, of the Hampshire Regiment to Brigadier-General H.W. Higginson, 21 February 1921

705 Lieutenant-General Sir Alymer Haldane, *The Insurrection in Mesopotamia, 1920* (London, 2005), p.341 (This is a reprint of a 1922 publication)

706 BIM, CO 904/114, RIC County Inspector's Report, Mallow, January 1921

707 *CE* 3 May 1921

708 BIM, CO 904/157, Intelligence Officer's Report, April 1918

709 BIM, CO 904/108, RIC County Inspector's Report, East Riding and City, April 1919

710 Ibid, RIC County Inspector's Report, East Riding and City, May 1919

711 BIM, CO 904/111, RIC County Inspector's Report, West Riding, February 1920

712 IMA, BMH, WS 1714, Leo Buckley

713 *CWN* 3 May 1919

714 The others who were injured were Mrs McMahon, Cissie Moore, Diarmuid Twomey and Timothy Hegarty

715 *CWN* 3 May 1919

716 *CWN* 10 May 1919

717 *CWN* 27 November 1920

718 UCDA, O'Malley Notebooks, P176/111, Mick Murphy

719 *CE* 9 October 1920

720 UCDA, O'Malley Notebooks, P176/111, Mick Murphy

721 *CE* 9 October 1920

722 Ibid

723 Ibid

724 Ibid

725 *CE* 9 October 1920

726 UCDA, O'Malley Notebooks, P176/111, Mick Murphy

727 Ibid

728 Denis Buckley sustained wounds to his right hip and shoulder, while the calves of Thomas Madden's legs were sliced by shrapnel, and Katie Fitzgerald suffered leg and hip wounds. *CE*, 9 October 1920

729 *CE* 1 July 1920

730 IWM, Sir Peter Strickland Papers, P363, Strickland Diary, 30 June 1920

731 *CE* 13 April 1921

732 *CE* 23 May 1921

733 *CE* 13 April 1921

734 *CE* 2 April 1921

735 Ibid

736 *ATO* 22 April 1921

737 Reports on robberies of this kind are contained in the County Inspector's Report, East Riding and City, October 1920, CO 904/113, and County Inspector's Report, East Riding and City, December 1920, CO 904/114

738 IMA, BMH, WS 1318, Denis Murphy

739 IMA, BMH, WS 1523, Daniel Cashman

740 UCDA, Mulcahy Papers, P7/A/17, HQ Cork No. 2 Brigade to Chief of Staff, IRA, 3 March 1921

741 *CE* 1 June 1921

742 *Hampshire Telegraph and Post* 17 June 1921

743 NLI, G.K. Cockerill Papers, MS 10606, Note of Hampshire bombing

744 IWM, Vice Admiral H.T. Baille-Groham Papers, P366, Unpublished Manuscript, *Flashlights on the Past.*

745 BIM, CO 904/168, Press Release

746 *CE* 2 June 1921

747 *Hampshire Telegraph and Post* 17 June 1921

748 NLI, G.K. Cockerill Papers, MS 10606, Note of Hampshire bombing

749 Ibid

750 LHCMA, Brig-General Philip Cadoux-Hudson Papers, GB99 KCLMA Cadoux-Hudson, Cadoux-Hudsonto his Mother, 6 June 1921

751 Daniell, *Hampshire Regiment*, p.11

752 *CE* 2 June 1921

753 NAUK, WO 141/94, *Record of the Rebellion*, Vol. 1, p.43

754 UCDA, Mulcahy Papers, P7/A/50, Engineering Circular No. 14, 28 June 1921, Engineering Circular No. 15, Undated, Engineering Circular, No. 16, Undated, Engineering Circular No. 17, 11 July 1921

755 NAUK, WO 141/94, *Record of the Rebellion*, Vol. IV, Part II, p.154

756 Sergeant Jackson of the MGC and Driver Cowman of the ASC were killed in the attack, while Corporal Grattage, and Privates Chapman, King, and Lavellie were wounded. This concern of the protection of the lines of communication was not confined to Ireland, it was also a concern for Egypt. See *Imperial Policing*, pp.74–79

757 NAUK, WO 32/9541, Memorandum by Secretary of State War to Cabinet, 7 December 1920

758 Ibid

759 IMA, BMH, WS 1367, Joseph Ahern

760 UCDA, Mulcahy Papers, P7/A/38, Report by OC Flying Column, Cork No. 3 Brigade, 6 March 1921

761 *CE* 9 November 1920

762 BIM, CO 904/114, RIC County Inspector's Report, West Riding, April, 1921

763 SOGM, RM Grazebrook Diary, 19 April 1921

764 LHCMA, Brig-General Frederick Clarke Papers, GB99 KCLMA Clarke

765 Ian F.W. Beckett, *Modern Insurgencies and Counter Insurgencies: Guerrillas and their*

Opponents since 1750 (2001)

766 *CWN* 1 January 1921

767 IWM, Sir Peter Strickland Papers, P363, 6th Division History, p.70

768 IMA, BMH, WS 1270, James Cashman

769 *Sean Moylan in his Own Words*, pp 88–89. An additional factor affecting Moylan's decision was that amongst the hostages was a personal friend and prominent IRA supporter, Denis Curtin.

770 *County Longford and the Irish Revolution*, p.130

771 *Liverpool Daily Post and Mercury*, 17 February 1921

772 NAUK, WO 151/54, Hook was recommended by Gen. Macready for an OBE for developing this approach, in a Recommendation for Honours Form, signed by the General, 25 August 1921

773 Ibid, Recommendation for Honours Form, 25 August 1921

774 *CE* 7 September 1920

775 IWM, Sir Peter Strickland Papers, P363, 6th Division History, p.51

776 SOGM, RM Grazebrook Diary, 16 April 1921

777 Ibid

778 SOGM, RM Grazebrook Diary, 19 April 1921

779 See Charles Townshend, 'The Irish Railway Strike of 1920: Industrial Action and Civil Resistance in the Struggle for Independence', *Irish Historical Studies*, Vol. XXI, 1977/78, for a detailed analysis of this strike and its impact of the War of Independence

780 NAUK, WO 141/94, *Record of the Rebellion*, Vol. IV, Part II, p.176

781 Ibid

782 UCDA, Mulcahy Papers, P7/A/17, HQ Cork No. 3 Brigade to the Chief of Staff, 3 March 1921

783 Charles Townshend, 'The Irish Insurgency 1919–21' in *Regular Armies and Insurgency* (ed.) Ronald Haycock (London, 1979)

784 SOGM, RM Grazebrook Diary, 27 March 1921

785 Tom Barry, *Guerrilla Days in Ireland* (Tralee, 1962), p.122 (First published in 1949)

786 UCDA, O'Malley Notebooks, P176–111, Jack Buttimer

787 *CE* 7 May 1921

788 Tim Jones, 'The British Army and Counter-Guerrilla Warfare in Transition, 1944–1952', *Small War and Insurgencies*, Vol. 7, No. 3 (Winter 1996), p.266 He is supported in this assessment by David A. Percox, in 'British Counter-Insurgency in Kenya', *Small War and Insurgencies*, Vol. 9, No. 3 (Winter 1998), p.48

789 NAUK, WO 141/94, *Record of the Rebellion*, Vol. IV Part II, p.177 For Percival's experiences in more open warfare than the First World War, see Clifford Kinvig, *Churchill's Crusade: The British Invasion of Russia* (2006), pp 241–243

790 SOGM, RM Grazebrook Diary, 12 April 1921

791 NAUK, WO 141/94, *Record of the Rebellion*, Vol. IV Part II, p.177

792 Ibid

793 Ibid

794 Paddy Griffith, *Battle Tactics of the Western Front: The British Army's Art of Attack, 1916–18* (1994), p.193

795 IMA, BMH, WS 873, Charles Browne

796 NLI, Florence O'Donoghue Papers, MS 31,223 (3), A captured memorandum from H.Q. 16th Infantry Brigade, 17 June 1921

797 IMA, BMH, WS 810, Tim Herlihy

798 *HRJ* June 1921, p.93

799 RAM, Historical Sheet, 21st Battery, RFA

800 RAM, Digest of Service, 25th Battery RGA

801 NAUK, WO 141/94, *Record of the Rebellion*, Vol. IV Part II, p.191
802 Ibid
803 Ibid
804 Ibid
805 Ibid
806 Ibid
807 BIM, CO 904/115, RIC County Inspector's Report, West Riding, May 1921
808 Major, T.A. Lowe, 'Some Reflections,' *The Army Quarterly and Defence Journal*, 5 October 1922, p.55
809 Ibid
810 UCDA, Mulcahy Papers, P7/A/50, Report on Enemy Flying Columns, June 1921
811 *Irish War of Independence*, pp 95–96
812 *The British Campaign in Ireland 1919–1921*, p.61
813 Sir Robert Thompson, 'Regular Armies and Insurgency' in Haycock, Ronald, *Regular Armies and Insurgency* (1979), p.13
814 NAUK, AIR 5/789, Memorandum from Major Dickenson, the Brigade Major of the 16th Infantry Brigade to OC Troops in the Brigade, 18 August 1921
815 David Omissi, *Air Power and Colonial Control: The Royal Air Force, 1919–39* (Manchester, 1990).
816 NAUK, WO 141/44, General Macready to Secretary of State for War, 18 August 1920
817 Ibid, General Macready to Secretary of State for War, 30 September 1920
818 Ibid
819 Ibid
820
821 Andrew Boyle, *Trenchard, Man of Vision* (London, 1962), pp 370–371
822 NAUK, WO 141/44, Trenchard Memorandum, 9 October 1920
823 In one case, in Iraq, two downed pilots were captured, their ears were cut off as trophies, and their teeth sold in local markets. See Mark Jacobson, 'Only by the Sword: British Counter-Insurgency in Iraq, 1920, *Small Wars and Insurgencies*, Vol. 2, No. 2 (August 1991), pp 323–363
824 NAUK, AIR 8/22, Trenchard to Secretary of State Air, dated 4 October 1920
825 *British Counter-Insurgency 1919–60*, p.29
826 General Staff, Indian Army Headquarters, *Operations in Waziristan* (1923), p.156
827 *Air Power and Colonial Control: The Royal Air Force 1919–1939*, p.43
828 NAUK, WO 141/44, CIGS Office Memorandum, 14 October 1920
829 Ibid, War Office to Macready, 29 October 1920
830 NAUK, WO 141/45, General Macready to Secretary of State for War, 12 March 1921
831 Ibid
832 Ibid
833 T. R. Moreman, *The Army in India and the Development of Frontier Warfare – 1849–1947* (1998), p.131
834 NAUK, AIR 5/776, Memorandum by Lt. Colonel Hutchison, General Staff, 6th Division, to Brigade Commanders, 20 March 1921
835 Ibid
836 NAUK, WO 141/45, War Office to Air Ministry, 19 March 1921
837 NAUK, WO 141/45, Instructions to No 2 Squadron, Fermoy, March 1921
838 See Appendix Four for the Operational Procedures imposed
839 NAUK, AIR 5/775, Note from Brigadier-General H. W. Higginson, 15 May 1921
840 NAUK, AIR 5/766, Note to Squadron Leader No. 2 Squadron, from HQ 16th Infantry Brigade, 2 July 1921

841 Ibid, Memorandum by Colonel Bernard, General Staff, 6th Division circulated to the Brigade Commanders, 13 June 1921

842 Ibid, Report by Flight Lieutenant Russell and Flying Officer Mackay, 30 May 1921

843 *The British Campaign in Ireland 1919–1921*, p.171

844 NAUK, AIR 5/775, Note from HQ 6th Division to Commanders, 16th, 17th, 18th and Kerry Brigades, 18 April 1921

845 NAUK, AIR 5/776, Notes on the Tactical Employment of Aeroplanes based on a meeting in Victoria Barracks held 7 March 1921

846 Nick Lloyd, *Loos 1915* (London, 2006), p.87

847 NAUK, AIR 5/214, War Diary, No. 2 Squadron, April 1921

848 *Irish War of Independence*, p.113

849 NAUK, AIR 5/776, Notes on the Tactical Employment of Aeroplanes based on a meeting in Victoria Barracks held 7 March 1921

850 NAUK, AIR 5/214 Flying Operations carried out by the 11th (Irish) Wing, April 1921

851 Ibid, Flying Operations carried out by the 11th (Irish) Wing, April 1921

852 Ibid

853 *British Counter-Insurgency 1919–60*, p.35

854 *British Counter-Insurgency 1919–60*, p.36

855 NAUK, AIR 5/214, Flying Operations carried out by 11th (Irish) Wing, April 1921

856 NAUK, WO 141/94, *Record of the Rebellion*, Vol. IV., p.208

857 IMA, BMH, WS 808, Richard Willis

858 IMA, BMH, WS 1113, James Brennock, and WS 1009, William Buckley

859 Michael Brennan, *The War in Clare 1911–1921* (Dublin, 1980), p.94

860 *ATO* 1 May 1921

861 *ATO* 6 May 1921

862 *The IRA and its Enemies*, p.94

863 *The Army in India*, p.131

864 General Staff Headquarters, Indian Army, *The Afghan War 1919: The Official Account* (India, 1926), p.133

865 NAUK, WO 141/95, Macready to the Secretary of State for War, 18 November 1921

866 Ibid

867 *Irish War of Independence*, p.111

868 William H. Kautt, *Arms and Armour: The Irish Rebellion 1919–1921* (Dublin, 2010), p.141

869 *Irish War of Independence*, p.111

870 *The IRA and its Enemies*, p.261

871 *Guerrilla Days in Ireland*, p.124

872 Meda Ryan, *Tom Barry: IRA Freedom Fighter* (Cork, 2003), p.133

873 UCDA, Mulcahy Papers, P7/A/38, Column No. 5 Report, 19 March 1921, OC Flying Column to HQ Cork No. 3 Brigade

874 *Arms and Armour*, p.141

875 IWM, Sir Peter Strickland Papers, P363, 6th Division History, p.92

876 IWM, Lieutenant-General A.E. Percival Papers, 4/1 Sandhurst Lectures

877 Ibid

878 John Williams Burrows, *Essex Units in the Great War 1914–1919* (1923), p.275

879 IWM, Lieutenant-General A.E. Percival Papers, 4/1 Sandhurst Lectures

880 *TS* 21 March 1921

881 *IT* 21 March 1921

882 *Essex County Standard, West Suffolk Gazette, and Eastern Counties Advertiser* 26 March 1921

883 *Liverpool Daily Post and Mercury* 21 March 1921

884 *Towards Ireland Free*, p.238

885 UCDA, Mulcahy Papers, P7/A/38, Column No. 5 Report, 19 March 1921, OC Flying Column to HQ Cork No. 3 Brigade

886 *Tom Barry: IRA Freedom Fighter*, p.139

887 *Towards Ireland Free*, p.238

888 NAUK, WO 35/179, Based on a Report sent to GHQ giving the various unit strengths and details of the senior officer 23 July, 1921

889 Ibid

890 NAUK, WO 141/94, *Record of Rebellion*, Vol. I, p.37

891 IWM, Lieutenant-General A.E. Percival Papers, 4/1 Sandhurst Lectures

892 UCDA, Mulcahy Papers, P7/A/38, Column No. 5 Report, 19 March 1921, OC Flying Column to HQ Cork No. 3 Brigade

893 *HRJ* April 1921, p.55

894 Ibid

895 IWM, Lieutenant-General A.E. Percival Papers, 4/1 Sandhurst Lectures

896 *Essex Units in the Great War 1914–1919*, p.275

897 Tameside Archives, Manchester Regiment Archives, Manchester Regiment Digest of Service, 20 March 1921

898 IMA, BMH, WS 1113, James Brennock

899 IMA, BMH, WS 1619, Daniel Canty

900 IMA, BMH, WS 736, Philip Cambers

901 UCDA, O'Malley Notebooks, P176/112, Con Meaney

902 UCDA, O'Malley Notebooks, P176/108, Mick Burke

903 This capacity for British Army Corps and Divisions has been also evidenced by the work of Tim Tavers, particularly in, *How the War was Won: Factors which led to Victory in World War One* (2005). In it he wrote, 'corps and divisions in the mid to late 1918, all essentially produced their own ideas and tactics.'

904 *British Counter-Insurgency 1919–60*, p.75

905 *British Counter-Insurgency 1919–60*, p.149

906 Lowe, T.A. Brevet Major, 'Some reflections of a junior commander upon the campaign in Ireland, 1920 and 1921', *The Army Quarterly and Defence Journal*, 5 October 1922, p.53

907 NAUK, WO 141/94, *Record of Rebellion* Vol. IV, Part II, p.197

908 Ibid, p.194

909 *County Longford and the Irish Revolution*, p.119 For an assessment of the ancestry of these tactics, read Virgina Crossman, 'The Army and Law and Order in the Nineteenth Century', in *A Military History of Ireland*, Thomas Bartlett and Keith Jeffery (eds.) (Cambridge, 1996), p.336

910 NAUK, WO 141/94, *Record of Rebellion* Vol. IV, Part II, p.187

911 Ibid, p.195

912 Ibid, p.197

913 Major, T.A. Lowe, 'Some Reflections', *The Army Quarterly and Defence Journal*, 5 October 1922, p.57

914 *CE* 9 November 1920

915 *CE* 27 November 1920

916 These troops were, the 1st Batt. Royal Fusiliers, the 1st Batt. Gloucestershire Regiment, the 1st Batt. Machine Gun Corps, with 'L' Company, the Auxiliaries

917 NAUK, WO 141/94, *Record of the Rebellion*, Vol. IV Part II, p.197

918 Ibid

919 Ibid, p.194

920 *British Counter-Insurgency 1919–60*, p.162 Its early success in Malaya in breaking up the Malayan Races Liberation Army is noted in Karl Hack's, 'British Counter-Insurgency in Malaya in the Era of Decolonisation: The Example of Malaya, *Intelligence and National Security*, Vol. 14, No. 2 (Summer 1999), pp 124–155

921 Tim Jones, 'The British Army and Counter-Guerrilla Warfare', *Small Wars and Insurgencies*, Vol. 7 No. 3 (Winter 1996), p.266

922 NAUK, WO 141/94, *Record of the Rebellion*, Vol. IV Part II, p.195

923 Ibid

924 Ibid

925 Ibid

926 NAUK, WO 141/94, *Record of the Rebellion*, Vol. IV Part II, p.196

927 IWM, Sir Peter Strickland Papers, P363, Undated *Daily Mail* Article

928 *The IRA and its Enemies*, p.261

929 Michael Farry, *The Aftermath of Revolution: Sligo 1921–23* (Dublin, 2000), p.17

930 *County Longford and the Irish Revolution*, p.154

931 John Borgonovo, *Spies, Informers, and the 'Anti Sinn Fein Society': The Intelligence War in Cork City 1920–1921*, see Chapter Four: Trends and Explanations, pp.66–104

932 UCDA, Mulcahy Papers, P7/A/42, IRA Memorandum, 'Offensive against Internal Morale of the Enemy'

933 NAUK, WO 141/94, *Record of the Rebellion*, Vol. IV, Part II, p.135

934 Ibid, p.194

935 BIM, CO 904/114, RIC County Inspectors Report, West Riding, February 1921

936 *British Counter-Insurgency 1919–60*, p.67

937 *II* 1 March 1921, *TS* 2 March 1921. The soldiers killed were, Pte. Wise RASC, Lance Cpl. Hodnett, RASC, Pte. Gill, 2nd Bn. Hampshires, Signaller Bowden, RE, Lance Cpl. Beattie, 2nd Bn. Hampshires, Bandsman Whitear, 2nd Bn. Hampshires. The soldiers wounded were Pte. Price, 2nd Bn. South Staffordshires, Pte. Bettesworth, 2nd Bn. South Staffordshires, Pte. Rollason, 2nd Bn. South Staffordshires, Pte. Hill, 2nd Bn. South Staffordshires

938 *CWN* 26 March 1921

939 BIM, CO 904/114, RIC County Inspector's Report, West Riding, March 1921

940 Ibid, RIC Inspector General's Report, April 1921

941 *LG* September 1921, p.3

942 BIM, CO 904/114, RIC County Inspector's Report, East Riding and City, April 1921

943 NAUK, WO 141/94, *Record of the Rebellion*, Vol. IV, Part II, p.179

944 Ibid, p.186

945 BIM, RIC County Inspector's Report, East Riding and City, March 1921

946 *Irish War of Independence*, p.73

947 Ian F. W. Beckett, *Modern Insurgencies* (2001), p.17

948 *British Counter-Insurgency 1919–60*, p.4

949 Dr. Paul Melshen, 'Mapping out a Counterinsurgency Campaign Plan: Critical Considerations in Counterinsurgency Campaigning', in *Small Wars and Insurgencies*, Vol. 18, No. 4, pp 665–698

950 *British Counter-Insurgency 1919–60*, p.67 This is also supported by Tim Jones in 'The British Army and Counter-Guerrilla Warfare,' *Small Wars and Insurgencies*, Vol. 7, No. 3 (Winter 1998), p.266 On this page he notes that the idea of population concentration first considered in Ireland, was applied in Burma.

951 Ibid

952 NAUK, WO 141/94, *Record of Rebellion*, Vol. IV, Part II, p.204

953 *CWN* 26 February 1921

954 *The IRA and its Enemies*, p.83
955 *County Longford and the Irish Revolution*, p.155
956 IWM, Sir Peter Strickland Papers, P363, Undated memorandum, 'Safeguarding Irish people who have given assistance to the British Forces'
957 *The Resurrection of Ireland*, p.294
958 John M. Regan, *The Irish Counter-Revolution, 1921–1936* (Dublin, 2006), p.114
959 NAUK, WO 141/94, *Record of the Rebellion*, Vol. IV, Part II, p.206
960 Ibid, p.207
961 *II* 12 July 1921
962 *CE* 12 July 1921
963 *II* 12 July 1921
964 Ibid
965 IWM, Sir Peter Strickland Papers, P363, General Strickland to General Macready, 24 July 1921
966 Ibid
967 IWM, Sir Peter Strickland Papers, P363, Strickland to Macready, 22 August 1921
968 Ibid
969 Ibid
970 Dawson was kidnapped by the IRA in West Cork on 7 September 1921, but escaped on 10 September
971 IWM, Sir Peter Strickland Papers, P363, Lieutenant-Colonel Savage to Strickland, 15 September 1921
972 Ibid
973 NAUK, WO 141/94, *Record of the Rebellion*, Vol. IV, Part II, p.206
974 *Annals of an Active Life*, Vol. II, p.581
975 Ibid, p.582
976 *CE* 25 July 1921
977 Ibid
978 *Annals of an Active Life*, p.582
979 Ibid. Macready also felt compel to reflect on Barry's career in the British Army, noting he had served in the Artillery in the First World War, but though promoted to Bombardier, was later reduced in rank for misconduct
980 NAUK, WO 141/94, *Record of the Rebellion*, Vol. IV, Part II, p.206
981 *CE* 28 July 1921
982 *CE* 25 July and 28 July 1921
983 *CE* 28 July 1921
984 Ibid
985 *CE* 4 August 1921
986 *CE* 5 August 1921
987 *CE* 21 July 1921
988 *CE* 24 May 1922 It should be noted that Lieutenant. K.R. Henderson of the 2nd Green Howards was a holder of the Military Cross for bravery
989 *Annals of an Active Life*, Vol. II, p.636
990 Ibid
991 Ibid, p.637
992 Ibid, p.636
993 *CE* 15 May 1922
994 NAUK, WO 141/94, *Record of the Rebellion*, Vol. IV, Part II, p.206
995 Ibid
996 Ibid, p.207
997 Ibid
998 Ibid, p.206

999 Ibid

1000 IMA, BMH, WS 1113, James Brennock

1001 IMA, BMH, WS 1619, Daniel Canty

1002 IMA, BMH, WS 736, Philip Cambers

1003 UCDA, O'Malley Notebooks, P176/112, Con Meaney

1004 UCDA, O'Malley Notebooks, P176/108, Mick Burke

1005 NLI, Liam Lynch Papers, MS 36,251, Lynch to his brother Tom, 3 July 1920 and to his mother, 22 July 1921

1006 NLI, G.K. Corkerill Papers, Ms 10, 606

1007 *The War in Clare*, p.40

1008 *The British Campaign in Ireland 1919–1921*, p.177

1009 IMA, BMH, WS 1254, Michael Coleman

1010 This capacity for British Army Corps and Divisions has been also evidenced by the work of Tim Tavers, particularly in, *How the War was Won: Factors which led to Victory in World War One* (2005). In it he wrote, 'corps and divisions in the mid to late 1918, all essentially produced their own ideas and tactics.'

1011 *British Counter-Insurgency 1919–60*, p.75

1012 *The Resurrection of Ireland*, p.275 IWM, Sir Peter Strickland Papers, P363, *The Irish Republican Army*

1013 BIM, CO 904/115, RIC Inspector General's Report, June 1921

1014 NAUK, WO 141/94, *Record of the Rebellion*, Vol. IV, Part II, p.206

1015 *British Counter-Insurgency 1919–60*, p.146

1016 Ibid, p.156

1017 NAUK, WO 141/94, *Record of Rebellion*, Vol. IV, Part II, p.186

1018 Ibid

1019 BIM, CO 904/115, RIC Inspector General's Report, July, 1921

1020 *The British Campaign in Ireland 1919–1921*, p.195

1021 NAUK, WO 32/9537, Wilson to Secretary of State War, 18 September 1920

1022 TS 23 October 1920

1023 For a detailed analysis of the pressures the British Government faced from the Commonwealth over Ireland, see Deirdre MacMahon's 'Ireland and the Empire-Commonwealth, 1900–1948,' in *The Oxford History of the British Empire Vol. 4*, edited by Judith M. Brown and W.M. Roger Louis, pp 138–162

1024 *The Resurrection of Ireland* (1999), p.294

1025 LHCMA, Brig-General Philip Cadoux-Hudson Papers, GB99 KCLMA Cadoux-Hudson, Letter from Cadoux-Hudson to his Mother, 16 May 1921

1026 Donald Creighton-Williamson, *The York and Lancaster Regiment* (London, 1968), p.108

1027 *The British Campaign in Ireland 1919–1921*, p.202

1028 Charles Townshend, *Political Violence in Ireland* (1983), p.359

1029 Charles Townshend, *Ireland: The 20th Century* (1991), p.101

1030 *Ireland: The 20th Century*, p.103

1031 *British Counter-Insurgency 1919–60*, p.12

1032 Nicolas Mansergh, *The Unresolved Question* (1991), p.160

1033 Richard Popplewell, 'Lacking Intelligence: Some Reflections of Recent Approaches to British Counter-Insurgency, 1900–1960', *Intelligence and National Security*, Vol. 10, No.2 (April 1995), p.339

1034 *Politics and Irish Life*, p.3

1035 Ibid, p.28

1036 *Modern Insurgencies and Counter Insurgencies: Guerrillas and their opponents since the 1750s*, p.16

1037 *British Counter Insurgency 1919–60*, p.63

1038 Karl Hack, 'British Intelligence and Counter-Insurgency in the Era of Decolonisation: the Example of Malaya, *Intelligence and National Security*, Vol. 14, No. 2 (Summer 1999) pp 124–155

1039 Major B. C. Dening, 'Modern Problems of Guerrilla Warfare', *The Army Quarterly and Defence Journal*, 12 January 1927, p.356

1040 *Arms and Armour*, p.228

1041 *From Public Defiance to Guerrilla Warfare*, p.184 and p.138

1042 Charles Townshend, 'The Irish Insurgency 1918–1921' in Ronald Haycock (ed.) *Regular Armies and Insurgencies* (London, 1979), p.32

1043 Dening, 'Modern Problems of Guerrilla Warfare', *The Army Quarterly and Defence Journal*, 12 January 1927, p.349

1044 Popplewell, 'Lacking Intelligence', *Small Wars and Insurgencies*, April 1995, p.340

1045 *Modern Insurgencies*, p.31

1046 Ibid, p.42

1047 Ibid, p.121

1048 T. R. Moreman, ''Small Wars' and 'Imperial Policing': The British Army and the Theory and Practise of Colonial Warfare in the British Empire, 1919–1932', *The Journal of Strategic Studies*, 1997, Part 4, p.110

1049 *Modern Insurgencies*, p.125

1050 Townshend, 'Irish Insurgency' in Haycock (ed.) *Regular Armies* (1979,) p.39

1051 NLI, Florence O'Donoghue Papers, MS 31,223 (4), A farewell letter by Lieutenant-Colonel French to the Manchester Regiment

1052 *The British Army and the Crisis of Empire*, p.13

1053 Ibid, p.16

1054 Daunton, M.J. 'How to pay for the War: State, Society, and Taxation in Britain, 1917–24', *The English Historical Review*, Vol. CXI, No. 443, September 1996, p.915

1055 *The British Army and the Crisis of Empire*, p.20

1056 *The British Army and the Crisis of Empire*, p.92

1057 *Political Violence in Ireland*, p.344

1058 *The IRA and its Enemies*, p.96

1059 Thomas Marks, Evaluating Insurgent/Counterinsurgent Performance', *Small Wars and Insurgencies*, Vol. 11 No. 3 (Winter 2000), p.22

1060 *British Counter-Insurgency 1919–60*, p.3

1061 David Anderson, and David Killingray, 'Introduction' in David Anderson and David Killingray, *Policing and Decolonization: Politics, Nationalism, and the Police, 1917–1965* (1992), p.3

1062 Charles Townshend, 'The Irish Republican Army and the Development of Guerrilla Warfare, 1916–1921,' *English Historical Review*, Vol. 94, No. 371 (April 1979), p.345

1063 Instructions to No 2 Squadron, Fermoy, March 1921, WO 141/45, the original copy incorrectly numbers the points in the document, and the number 11 is absent

Bibliography

Primary Sources

The National Archives, Kew

Admiralty
ADM 1/8574/329

Air Ministry
AIR 5/214
AIR 5/772
AIR 5/776
AIR 5/771
AIR 5/773
AIR 5/777
AIR 5/779
AIR 5/785
AIR 5/806
AIR 8/22
AIR 10/1196

Colonial Office
RIC Inspector General and County Inspector's Monthly Reports
RIC Illegal Drilling Reports
RIC Breaches of the Truce Reports
RIC Weekly Summaries 1920/21

British Cabinet Office
Weekly Surveys of the State of Ireland
Miscellaneous Cabinet Papers

Home Office
HO 144/10308
HO 348/19

War Office
WO 32/9572
WO 32/9536
WO 32/9537
WO 32/9541
WO 33/890
WO 035/88
WO 35/179
WO 141/43
WO 141/44
WO 141/45
WO 141/46
WO 141/48
WO 141/54
WO 141/94
Files on Sinn Féin Activists
Military Courts of Inquiry Reports
Registers of Military Prisoners and Internees
Register and Prosecution Records of Civilians tried by Courts-Martial
Registers of Courts of Inquiry in lieu of Inquests

Imperial War Museum
H.L. Adams Papers
Vice-Admiral H.T. Ballie-Grohman Papers
Captain C.W. Battine Papers
Commander J.E.P. Brass Papers
Captain C.A. Brett Papers
Lieutenant-Colonel E.J.A.H. Brugh Papers
Lieutenant C. Carter Papers
C. Cordner Papers
J.M. Cordy Papers
Brigadier-General E. Craig-Brown Papers
Lieutenant p.Creek Papers
Commander De L'Faunce Papers
Major E.S. Ettlinger Papers
Brigadier-General J.V. Faviell Papers
Field Marshall Sir John French Papers
Lieutenant-Colonel J.M. Galloway Papers
Brigadier-General A.C. Gore Papers

A. Griffin Papers
Lieutenant-Colonel Hughes-Hallett Papers
Lieutenant G. Hodgkinson Papers
Lieutenant-Colonel J.B. Jarvis Papers
Lieutenant-General Sir Hugh Jeudwine Papers
Captain R.D. Jeune Papers
Field Marshall Montgomery Papers
Flight Lieutenant F.C. Penny Papers
Lieutenant-General A. E. Percival Papers
C. Plumb Papers
Brigadier-General E.M. Ransford Papers
Lieutenant-General Sir Peter Strickland Papers
Private Swindlehurst Diaries
Brigadier-General H.G.N. Watson Papers
Brigadier-General J.S. Wilkinson Papers
Major-General Sir Douglas Wimberley Papers
Brigadier-General Vinden Papers

Liddell-Hart Centre for Military Archives, King's College London
Brigadier-General Philip Cadoux-Hudson Papers
Brigadier-General Frederick Clarke Papers
Major-General Charles Howard Foulkes Papers
Lieutenant-Colonel Evelyn Lindsay-Young Papers
Colonel Rory MacLeod Papers
Brigadier-General Charles Sherman Papers

British Regimental Papers
King's (Liverpool) Regiment Collection, Regional History Department, National
    Museums and Galleries on Merseyside
1st Battalion Digest of Service, 1919–1921

Manchester Regiment Archives, Tameside Local Studies Library
Lt. Col Dorling Papers
1st Battalion Record of Service, 1919–1921
Digest of Service 1919–1921
Records of Arrests in Ireland 1921

Queen's Lancashire Regiment Museum
2nd Battalion Loyal (North Lancashire), CO's Diary, 1921.
2nd Battalion Loyal (North Lancashire) Digest of Service 1919 – 1921.
2nd Battalion East Lancashire Digest of Service 1919 – 1921.

Royal Artillery Museum
Records of the 1st Regiment, Royal Artillery Mounted Rifles
Digest of Service, 25th Battery, RGA
Digest of Service, 26th Battery RGA
Digest of Service, 51st Battery RGA (later the 27th Battery, RGA)
Digest of Service, 21st Battery RFA
Digest of Service, 53rd Battery RFA
Digest of Service, 87th Battery RFA

Soldiers of Gloucestershire Museum
R.M. Grazebrook Diary, 1920–1922
Regimental Records, Twentieth Century, Vol. I, 1900–39

Irish Archives

Cork City and County Archives
Seamus Fitzgerald Papers
MacSwiney Papers

Irish Military Archives
Witness Statements

National Library of Ireland
Cockerill Papers
Flower Papers
Lynch Papers
Moore Papers
O'Donoghue Papers

UCD Archives
Mulcahy Papers
The O'Malley Notebooks
Newspapers and Periodicals

Aldershot Gazette and Military News
An t-Ólgach
Cork Constitution
Cork County Eagle
Cork Examiner
Cork Free Press
Cork Weekly Examiner
Cork Weekly News
Essex County Standard, West Suffolk Gazette & Eastern Counties Advertiser

Essex Regiment Gazette

Gloucestershire Chronicle

Hampshire Regimental Journal

Irish Times

Lilywhite's Gazette (Journal of the East Lancashire Regiment)

Liverpool Post and Mercury

Machine Gunner

Manchester Guardian Weekly

Manchester Regimental Gazette

Morning Post

Mildenhall Post and Advertiser

The 79th News (Journal of the Cameron Highlanders Regiment)

Staffordshire Weekly Sentinel

Southern Star

The Times

Wellington Journal and Shrewsbury News

Secondary Sources

Aggett, W.J.P., *The Bloody Eleventh: A History of the Devonshire Regiment, Vol. II, 1815–1914* (Exeter, 1994)

Anon, *The Burning of Cork* (Cork, 1978)

Amery, L.S., *My Political Life Vol. II, War and Peace 1914–1929* (London, 1953)

Andrew, Christopher, *Secret Service: The Making of the British Intelligence Community* (London, 1985)

Atkinson, C.T., *The South Wales Borderers, 24th Foot, 1689–1937* (Cambridge, 1937)

Augusteijn, Joost, (ed.) *The Irish Revolution, 1912–1923* (London, 2002)

Augusteijn, Joost, *From Public Defiance to Guerrilla Warfare: The Experience of Ordinary Volunteers in the Irish War of Independence, 1916–1921* (Dublin, 1996)

Augusteijn, Joost 'The Operations of the South Tipperary I.R.A., 1916–1921', *Tipperary Historical Journal*, 1996

Baker, A.J., *The West Yorkshire Regiment* (London, 1974)

Barry, Tom, *Guerrilla Days in Ireland* (Tralee, 1962)

Barthop, Michael, *The Northamptonshire Regiment* (London, 1974)

Beecher, Sean, *The Story of Cork* (Cork, 1971)

Bennett, R., *The Black and Tans* (London, 1970)

Blaxland, G., *The Queen's Own Buffs: The Royal Kent Regiment* (Kent, 1974)

Botman, Selma, *Egypt from Independence to Revolution, 1919–1952* (Syracuse, 1991)

Borgonovo, John, *Informers, Intelligence and the Anti-Sinn Féin Society: the Anglo-Irish Conflict in Cork City, 1920–1921*, MA thesis, UCC (1997)

Bowyer Bell, J., *The Secret Army: The I.R.A. 1916–1979* (Dublin, 1979)

Boyce, George G., 'Ireland and British Politics, 1900–1939', (ed.) Chris Wrigley, *A Companion to Early Twentieth Century Britain* (London, 2003)

Boyle, Andrew, *Trenchard, Man of Vision* (London, 1962)

Breen, Dan, *My Fight for Irish Freedom* (Tralee, 1964)

Brennan, Michael, *The War in Clare, 1911–1921* (Dublin, 1980)

Brown, Judith M., and Louis, W.M. Rodger *The Oxford History of the British Empire: The Twentieth Century* (Oxford, 2001)

Burke-Gaffney, J.J., *The Story of the King's Regiment, 1914–1948* (Liverpool, 1954)

Burrows, John William, *Essex Units in the War, 1914–1919* (Southend on Sea, 1923)

Callanan, Frank, *T.M. Healy* (Cork, 1996)

Campbell, Colm, *Emergency Law in Ireland, 1918–1925* (Oxford, 1994)

Carrington, Charles, *Soldier from the War Returning* (Yorkshire, 2006),

Clarke, Peter, *Hope and Glory, Britain 1900–1990* (London, 1996)

Coleman, Marie, *County Longford and the Irish Revolution, 1910–1923* (Dublin, 2003)

Coogan, Oliver, *Politics and War in Meath, 1913–1923* (Dublin, 1983)

Cowper, J.M., *The King's Own: The Story of a Royal Regiment, Vol. III. 1914 to 1950* (Aldershot, 1957

Creighton-Williamson, Donald, *The York and Lancaster Regiment* (London, 1968)

Daniell, D.S., *Cap of Honour, The Story of the Gloucestershire Regiment 1694–1950* (London, 1951)

Daunton, M.J., 'How to pay for the War: State, Society and Taxation in Britain, 1917–24', *English Historical Review*, Vol. CXI, No 443, September 1996

Deasy, Liam, *Towards Ireland Free: The West Cork Brigade in the War of Independence, 1917–21* (Cork, 1973)

Dockrill, Michael and French, David, (eds.) *Strategy and Intelligence: British Policy and Intelligence during the First World War* (London, 1996)

Downham, John, *The East Lancashire Regiment, 1855–1958* (London, 2000)

Edmonds, James, *The Occupation of the Rhineland 1918–1929* (London, 1987)

Emsley, Clive *The Great British Bobby: A History of Policing: A History of British Policing from the 18th Century to the Present* (London, 2009)

Feeney, P.J., *Glory O, Glory O, Ye Bold Fenian Men: A History of the Sixth Battalion, Cork First Brigade 1913–1921* (Dripsey, 1996)

Ferrar, M.L., *Officers of the Green Howards 1688–1931* (Belfast, 1931)

Ferriter, Dairmaid, *The Transformation of Ireland* (London, 2005)

Figgis, D., *Recollections of the Irish War* (London, 1927)

Fitzpatrick, David, *Politics and Irish Life 1913 to 1921: Provincial Experience of War and Revolution* (Cork, 1977)

Foster, R.F., *Modern Ireland, 1600–1972* (London, 1989)

Fuller, J.G., *Troop Morale and Popular Culture in the British and Dominion Armies, 1914–1918* (Oxford, 1990)

Franklyn, Arthur Johnson, *Defence by Committee: The British Committee of Imperial Defence, 1885–1959* (Oxford, 1960)

French, David, 'The British Armed Forces, 1900–1939', (ed.) Chris Wrigley, *A Companion to Early Twentieth Century Britain* (London, 2003)

Garvin, Tom, *The Evolution of Irish Nationalist Politics* (Dublin, 1981)

Garvin, Tom, *Nationalist Revolutionaries in Ireland, 1858–1928* (Oxford, 1987)

Bibliography

General Staff Headquarters, Indian Army, *The Third Afghan War, 1919* (India, 1926)

General Staff Headquarters, Indian Army, *Operations in Waziristan, 1919–20* (India, 1923)

Glover, Michael, *That Astonishing Infantry: Three Hundred Years of the Royal Welch Fusiliers* (London, 1989)

Godley, Sir Alexander. *Life of an Irish Soldier* (London, 1939)

Griffith, Paddy, *Battle Tactics of the Western Front: The British Army's Art of Attack, 1916–18* (London, 1994)

Grigg, John, *Lloyd George: War Leader* (London, 2002)

Gwynn, Charles, *Imperial Policing* (London, 1934)

Hack, Karl, 'British Intelligence and Counter-Insurgency in the Era of Decolonisation: The Example of Malaya', *Intelligence and National Security*, Vol. 14, No2, 1999

Haldane, Alymar, *The Insurrection in Mesopotamia, 1920* (London, 2005)

Hamilton, Nigel, *The Full Monty: Montgomery of El Alamein, 1887–1942* (London, 2001)

Hart, Peter, *The IRA and It's Enemies, Violence and Community in Cork, 1916 to 1923* (Oxford, 1999)

Hart, Peter, 'Class, Community and the Irish Republican Army in Cork, 1917–23' in p.O'Flanagan and P. Buttimer (eds.) *Cork History and Society* (Dublin, 1993)

Hart, Peter, 'The Geography of Revolution in Ireland, 1917–1923', *Past and Present*, Number 155, May 1997

Hart, Peter, 'Operations Aboard, The I.R.A. in Britain, 1919–1923', *English Historical Review*, Vol. CXV, February 2000

Harvey, Dan, and White, Gerry, *The Barracks, A History of Victoria/Collins Barracks, Cork* (Cork, 1997)

Herlihy, Jim, *The Royal Irish Constabulary* (Dublin, 1997)

Holt, E., *Protest in Arms, The Irish Troubles 1916–1923* (London, 1960)

Hopkinson, Michael, (ed.) *The Last Days of Dublin Castle: The Diaries of Mark Sturgis* (Dublin, 1999)

Hopkinson, Michael, *The Irish War of Independence* (Dublin, 2002)

Horne, Edward, *A Job Well Done: A History of the Palestine Police, 1920–1948* (Sussex, 2003)

Inoue, Keiko, 'Propaganda of Dáil Eireann, 1919–21', in Joost Augusteijn (ed.) *The Irish Revolution 1919–23* (Dublin, 2002)

Jacobsen, Mark, 'Only by the Sword': British Counter-Insurgency in Iraq, 1920', *Small War and Insurgencies*, Vol. 2, No. 2, 1991

Kautt, William H., *The Anglo-Irish War, 1916–1921* (Connecticut, 1999)

Jeffery, Keith, *The British Army and the Crisis of Empire, 1918–22* (Manchester, 1984)

Jeffery, Keith, (ed.) *The Military Correspondence of Sir Henry Wilson 1918–1922* (London, 1985)

Jeffery, Keith, *Field Marshal Sir Henry Wilson: A Political Soldier* (Oxford, 2006)

Jenkins, Roy, *Churchill* (London, 2001)

Kedourie, Elie, 'Great Britain, the Other Powers and the Middle East before and after World War 1', (ed.) Uriel Dunn, *The Great Powers in the Middle East, 1919–1939* (New York, 1988)

Kemp, P.K., *The Middlesex Regiment 1919 to 1952* (Aldershot, 1956)

Kinsella, Anthony, 'The British Military Evacuation', *The Irish Sword,* Winter 1997,Vol. XX, No82

Kinvig, Clifford, *Churchill's Crusade: The British Invasion of Russia, 1918–1920* (London, 2006)

Kitchen, Martin, 'The Empire, 1900–1939', (ed.) Chris Wrigley, *A Companion to Early Twentieth Century Britain* (London, 2003)

Jablonsky, David, 'Churchill's Initial Experience with the Conduct of Small Wars: India and the Sudan, 1897–98', *Small Wars and Insurgences,*Vol. 11, No1, 2000

Jones, Tim, 'The British Army, and Counter-Guerrilla Warfare in Transition, 1944–1952', *Small War and Insurgencies,*Vol. 7, No. 3, 1996

Kitson, Frank, *Low Intensity Operations, Subversion, Insurgency and Peace-Keeping* (London, 1971)

Knight, C.R.B., *Historical Records of the Buffs (Royal East Kent Regiment), 3rd Foot, 1919–1948* (London, 1951)

Kudaisya, Gyanesh, 'In Aid of Civil Power': The Colonial Army in Northern India, c. 1919–42', *The Journal of Imperial and Commonwealth History,*Vol. 32, No. 1, 2004

Laffen, Michael, *The Partition of Ireland, 1911–1925* (Dublin, 1983)

Laffen, Michael, *The Resurrection of Ireland, The Sinn Féin Party, 1916 to 1923* (Cambridge, 1999)

Langley, Michael, *The Loyal Regiment* (London, 1976)

Lankford, Siobhan, *The Hope and the Sadness* (Cork, 1980)

Lawlor, Sheila, *Britain and Ireland, 1914 to 23* (Dublin, 1983)

Lawrence, Jon, 'Forging a Peaceable Kingdom: War, Violence, and Fear of Brutalisation in Post-First World War Britain', *The Journal of Modern History,*Vol. 75, No.3, 2003

Leader, Stephen, 'British Intelligence in the Twentieth Century', *Intelligence and National Security,*Vol. 17, No1, 2002

Lee, J.J., *The Modernisation of Irish Society, 1848–1918* (Dublin, 1973)

Lee, J.J., *Ireland, 1912–1985, Politics and Society* (Cambridge, 1989)

Lewis, George Cornwall, *Local Disturbances in Ireland* (Cork, 1977)

Lloyd, Nick, *Loos 1915* (London, 2006)

Lowe, T.A., 'Some Reflections of a Junior Commander upon 'The Campaign' in Ireland 1919–1921', *Army Quarterly* (October) 1922

Lowe, W.J., 'The War against the R.I.C., 1919–1921', *Eire-Ireland,* XXXVIII, Fall/Winter 2002

Luvass, Jay, *The Education of an Army: British Military Thought 1815–1940* (London, 1965)

MacMahon, Paul, *British Spies and Irish Rebels: British Intelligence and Ireland 1916–45* (Suffolk, 2008)

Macready, Neville, *Annals of an Active Life* (New York, 1926)

Marks, Thomas, 'Evaluating Insurgent/Counter Insurgent Performance', *Small Wars and Insurgencies,*Vol. 11, No3, 2000

Marks, Thomas, 'Urban Insurgency', *Small Wars and Insurgences,*Vol. 14, No. 3, 2003

Maume, Patrick, *The Long Gestation: Irish National Life, 1891–1916* (Dublin, 1999)

McDonnell, K., *There is a Bridge in Bandon. A Personal Account of the Irish War of Independence* (Cork, 1972)

Mansergh, Nicholas, *The Irish Question, 1840–1921* (London, 1965)

Mansergh, Nicholas, *The Unresolved Question: The Anglo-Irish Settlement* (Yale, 1991)

Meron, Gil, 'Strong Powers in Small Wars: The Unnoticed Foundations of Success', *Small Wars and Insurgences*, Vol. 9, No2, 1998

Mockaitis, Thomas R., *British Counter-Insurgency, 1919–1960* (London, 1990)

Mockaitis, Thomas R., 'The Origins of British Counter-Insurgency', *Small Wars and Insurgencies*, Part 1, 1990

Moreman, T.R., *The Army in India and the Development of Frontier Warfare, 1849–1947* (London, 1998)

Moreman, T.R., "Small War' and 'Imperial Policing': The British Army and the Theory and Practice of Colonial Warfare in the British Empire, 1919–1939', *The Journal of Strategic Studies*, Vol. 19, Part 4, 1997

Mullaly, B.R., *The South Lancashire Regiment, the Prince of Wales Volunteers* (Bristol, 1955)

Murphy, John F., 'Michael Collins and the Craft of Intelligence', *International Journal of Intelligence and Counterintelligence*, Vol. 17, No. 2, 2004

O'Connor, Emmet, *A Labour History of Ireland, 1824–1960* (Dublin, 1992)

O'Day, Alan, *Irish Home Rule* (Dublin, 1998)

O'Dwyer, Kate, 'The Third Tipperary Brigade: It's Guerrilla Campaign (1919–1921)', *Tipperary Historical Journal*, 1997

O'Halpin, Eunan, *The Decline of the Union: British Government in Ireland 1892 to 1920* (Dublin, 1987)

O'Halpin, Eunan, 'H.E. Duke and the Irish Administration', *Irish Historical Studies*, Vol. XXII, 1980–81

Omissi, David, *Air Power and Colonial Control: The Royal Air Force, 1919–39* (Manchester, 1990)

Pakenham, F. *Peace by Ordeal* (London, 1972)

Paseta, Senia, 'Ireland's Lost Home Rule Generation: The Decline of Constitutional Nationalism in Ireland 1916–1930', in Mike Cronin and John Regan, (eds.) *Ireland: The Politics of Independence 1922–49* (London, 2000)

Percox, David A., 'British Counter-Insurgency in Kenya, 1952–56: Extension of Internal Security Policy or Prelude to Decolonization?', *Small Wars and Insurgencies*, Vol. 9, No3, 1998

Powell, Geoffrey Powell, *The History of the Green Howards: Three Hundred Years of Service* (London, 1992)

Power, Bill, *Mitchelstown through the Ages* (Fermoy, 1987)

Popplewell, Richard, *Intelligence and Imperial Defence: British Intelligence and the Defence of the Indian Empire 1904–1924* (London, 1995)

Popplewell, Richard, 'Lacking Intelligence: Some Reflections on Recent Approaches to British Counter-Insurgency, 1900–1960', *Intelligence and National Security*, Vol 17, No1, 2002

Schmidl, Erwin, A., 'The Evolution of Peace Operations from the Nineteenth Century', *Small Wars and Insurgencies*, Vol. 10, No2, 1999

Selth, Andew, 'Ireland and Insurgency: The Lessons of History', *Small Wars and Insurgencies*, Vol. 2, No. 2, 1991

Sheffield, Gary, *Forgotten Victory: The First World War – Myths and Realities* (London, 2002)

Sheehan, Tim, *Execute Compton-Smith* (Cork, 1993)

Sheehan, William, *British Voices from the Irish War of Independence* (Cork, 2005)

Sheffy, Yigal, *British Military Intelligence in the Palestine Campaign 1914–1918* (London, 1998)

Sheffy, Yigal, 'British Intelligence and the Middle East, 1900–1918, How Much Do We Know', *Intelligence and National Security*, Vol. 17, No1, 2002

Surridge, Keith, 'Rebellion, Martial Law and British Civil-Military Relations: The War in Cape Colony, 1899–1902', *Small Wars and Insurgencies*, Vol. 8, No2, 1997

Stevenson, David, *1914–1918: The History of the First World War* (London, 2004)

Strachan, Hew, *The Politics of the British Army* (Oxford, 1997)

Street, C.J.C., *The Administration of Ireland 1920* (London, 1921)

Strong, Kenneth, *Intelligence at the Top: The Recollections of an Intelligence Officer* (London, 1968)

Tavers, Tim, *How the War was Won: Factors that Led to Victory in World War One* (Yorkshire, 2005)

Thornton, Rod, 'The British Army and the Origins of its Minimum Force Philosophy', *Small Wars and Insurgencies*, Vol. 15, No. 1, 2004

Townshend, Charles, *The British Campaign in Ireland 1919–1921* (Oxford, 1975)

Townshend, Charles, *Ireland, The Twentieth Century* (London, 1999)

Townshend, Charles, *Political Violence in Ireland: Government and Resistance since 1848* (Oxford, 1983)

Townshend, Charles, 'The Irish Railway Strike of 1920: Industrial Action and Civil Resistance in the Struggle for Independence', *Irish Historical Studies*, Vol. XXI, 1977/8

Townshend, Charles, 'The Irish Republican Army and the development of Guerrilla Warfare, 1916–1921,' *English Historical Review*, Vol. 94, No. 371 (April 1979)

War Office, *Manual of Military Law*. HMSO, 1914

Wilkinson, Paul, 'The Role of the Military in Combatting Terrorism in a Democratic Society', *Terrorism and Political Violence*, Vol. 8, No. 3, 1996

Williams, D., (ed.) *The Irish Struggle 1916–1926* (London, 1966)

Wimberley, Douglas, 'Military Prize Essay, 1933', *The Army Quarterly*, June, 1933

Woollcombe, Robert, *All the Blue Bonnets: The History of the King's Own Scottish Borderers* (London, 1980)

Wykes, Alan, *The Royal Hampshire Regiment* (London, 1968)

Wylly, H.C., *History of the Manchester Regiment*, vol. II, 1883–1925 (London, 1925)

Index